Praise for *50 Years of the Indian Emergency*

'This timely volume presents a probing and kaleidoscopic reassessment of the origins, course and consequences of the Emergency from a range of vantage points: political and social, economic and international, literary and theoretical. In so doing, the book prompts us to reconsider the multiple dimensions and layers of a compacted historical period and the many frameworks that continue to influence our understanding of it. The editors' masterly Introduction is itself worth the price of admission.'

Srinath Raghavan, author of *Indira Gandhi and the Years that Transformed India*

'Fifty years after India's first experiment with dictatorship, this remarkable book explores not only the multiple facets of the Emergency but also the resistance it generated. The lessons the contributors draw from this short but intense episode of authoritarianism remain relevant for today's India. A very well researched and in-depth analysis of a key moment of India's history.'

Christophe Jaffrelot, CERI-CNRS Senior Research Fellow, Sciences Po, Paris

---

'This is the single most valuable, engaging, thoughtful and wide-ranging volume available on the Emergency. Its stellar cast of contributors have engaged with the subject personally or as scholars. They are all in top form, producing essays that deepen our historical, moral and political assessment of the Emergency.'

Pratap Bhanu Mehta, Princeton University

'. . . some of our best minds come together to put together an arresting tableau of troubled memories, and curious associations and conflicted lessons learnt. . . .'

Harish Khare, former press advisor to Manmohan Singh and former editor of *The Tribune*

50 YEARS *of the* Indian Emergency

LANDMARKS

The series commemorates and celebrates texts, events and personalities that have shaped societies, cultures and communities in India. The volumes bring together personal narratives and scholarly explorations as they reconsider and reread histories and cultures.

50 YEARS *of the* Indian Emergency

Lessons for Democracy

Edited by
Peter Ronald deSouza
Harsh Sethi

Orient BlackSwan

50 YEARS OF THE INDIAN EMERGENCY: LESSONS FOR DEMOCRACY

ORIENT BLACKSWAN PRIVATE LIMITED

Registered Office
3-6-752 Himayatnagar, Hyderabad 500 029, Telangana, India
Email: centraloffice@orientblackswan.com

Other Offices
Bengaluru, Chennai, Guwahati, Hyderabad,
Kolkata, Mumbai, New Delhi, Noida, Patna

First published 2025

ISBN 978 93 6973 340 8

Typeset in Minion Pro 11/13.2 *by*
K. Divya, Hyderabad 500 060

Printed in India at
Akash Press, Delhi

041015

Published by
Orient Blackswan Private Limited
3-6-752, Himayatnagar
Hyderabad 500 029, Telangana, India
Email: info@orientblackswan.com

To the victims of tyranny

Contents

Introduction
Revisiting the Emergency

Peter Ronald deSouza *and* Harsh Sethi

The iconic cartoon of Abu Abraham of the Emergency proclamation[1]

Revisiting the Emergency on its fiftieth anniversary serves a dual purpose. It is sufficiently distant in time from the original event and, because we know much more about the subsequent travails of democracy in India, revisiting it in 2025 allows us to more dispassionately examine the factors that made it happen and draw lessons from it. The Emergency has rightly been described as a 'dark period' in Indian democracy when constitutional protections were suspended – especially the writ of '*habeas corpus*' – constitutional amendments were introduced to give

---

[1] We are thankful to Janaki and Ayisha Abraham for permission to use the cartoon.

First published in *The Indian Express*, 10 December 1975. Reprinted with the permission of The Indian Express (P) Limited © 1975.

more power to the executive, thousands of citizens were jailed only on the basis of executive orders (and sometimes not even that), media was censored, homes were demolished by bulldozers (happening again today) and compulsory sterilisations were implemented. Fear gripped the land. Democracy in India was battered by the arrogance of unfettered power. The story of Prabir Purkayastha being picked up from the JNU campus because the police thought he was D. P. Tripathi, a case of mistaken identity, and jailed anyway because he was a member of the communist student's organisation SFI, is one example of the tyranny that had descended on India. Tyranny comes from both directions, from the state and from the mob. Both were active in the years of the Emergency. Prabir spent a year in jail, an institution that acquired a demonic status both as an existential threat and as an institution of incarceration (Purkayastha 2023). Jail became the symbol of the Emergency.[2] (See chapters by Gyan Prakash and Mahmood Farooqui in the volume.)

Before we begin our exploration of how the Emergency came about, and what happened there, we need to place it in its historical context. This emphasis on historical context is important because we believe it will introduce our evaluation to factors and perspectives that may be relevant and have possibly been overlooked or ignored. Because the Emergency was so brutal, in terms of the suspension of civil liberties and democratic rights, there is the risk of treating it in isolation from the context in which it occurred. Context gives the assessment an analytical ballast. It complicates the evaluation by introducing multiple narratives not all of which are aligned. But context, especially in the India of 1975 which was a young postcolonial country embarking on a bold

---

[2] *Prison Diaries*, the film made by Uma Chakravarthy, based on prison diaries, tells the story of Snehalata Reddy who was tortured and humiliated in jail and who died a few months after her release. It is a grim tale of the state's impunity. It is a forerunner of the later incarceration, under the current regime (2014–2025), of both Fr Stan Swamy and Professor G. N. Saibaba. The parallels are not incidental. The Emergency jail diaries of Ramchandra Singh and Jayaprakash Narayan find echoes in the post-Emergency diaries of Kobad Ghandy and Arun Ferreira.

experiment of building a plural, inclusive, egalitarian, democracy, requires us to see the Emergency as an event defined, constrained and challenged by the material, cultural and political conditions in which it occurred.

Contextualising the Emergency

We focus here on four dimensions of the context. The first is that the India of 1975 was a young constitutional democracy. A mere twenty-five years had elapsed since the constitutional architecture was instituted in India. We had to learn about the workings of the federal structure, about the deliberate dispersal of power among units along with the principle of shared governance. We had to acquire the competencies, both legal and cultural (this implies developing a mindset), that are required to manage the institutions of governance, specifically the deliberative, oversight, regulatory, administrative and penalty-imposing institutions. This required knowledge and familiarity with the rules and regulations of these institutions (North 1991) as well as the accompanying conventions and the institutional culture that makes them effective (Nehru 1988). In the first twenty-five years, that is, till 1975, this constitutional architecture was young and evolving, producing regular face-offs between the fence and the field. It was very fragile.

The second dimension concerns the material poverty of the economy in 1975. In addition to the stresses it faced after the tragedy of the Partition, India in the 1960s was challenged by a severe food crisis. It was dependent on food aid from the USA under the PL 480 programme, a crisis situation that sadly came to be described as living from 'ship to mouth'. Added to the food crisis were the two failed monsoons in the early 1970s, the inflationary pressures exacerbated by a five-fold increase in petroleum prices imposed by OPEC, the burden of hosting ten million refugees from East Pakistan, the imposition of sanctions after India tested a 'peaceful' nuclear device in 1974, and a debilitating railway strike. (See the chapter by Errol D'Souza.) The Indian economy was in a vulnerable state. India was susceptible to external pressures. Its foreign reserves had become perilously low, impelling a loan from the IMF that was accompanied by stiff conditionalities. It must be recognised that in 1975, India was nowhere as economically strong, and capable of autonomous decision making as it is today in 2025.

The third dimension is the intensification of the politics of demand. General elections to parliament and state assemblies not only gave voice to the electorate, but also produced group and identity politics of caste, community, language and region within an expanding and competitive party system. Top-down politics increasingly met a noisy bottom-up politics. There was a proliferation of regional parties, an increase in the number of political leaders at all levels and, significantly, an expansion in the number of non-party political formations, all of which impacted the political discourse. These found new ways to put political pressure on the system, pushing it into zones of conflict and competition where, sometimes, the opportunity for accommodation and compromise was unavailable. The run up to the Emergency was one such period wherein all political parties upped the ante, stretching the system to its limits (Kothari 1971; Sheth 2019).

The fourth dimension is the ideological contest that dominates all postcolonial polities. Key to this ideological debate is the different ways being considered to transcend the experience of colonialism and to build an independent nation. This contest draws from, and is dependent on, the prevailing global ideas on the way forward. The idea of India was, therefore, an intensely contested idea in the decades prior to the Emergency (Khilnani 1999).

India embarked on its journey as a postcolonial constitutional democracy by initiating four political processes simultaneously. It sought to strengthen its identity as an inclusive and secular nation, especially after the trauma of the Partition and the rejection of Jinnah's two-nation theory. Secular nationalism was an important aspiration. After considerable debate India chose to privilege public investment in development projects such as dams, agricultural universities, management institutes, cooperatives, etc., since these were believed to be better suited to address the curse of pervasive poverty. Nehru referred to these development projects as the 'temples of modern India'. State investment in 'development', a core policy goal, sought to establish a robust state structure that could handle these stresses of expanding demands. State-building was a primary concern to protect the state from the threatening pulls and pressures, even as India was committed to deepening its democracy by bringing in more voices, and the participation of hitherto excluded and suppressed groups, into the political realm. Democracy was the platform on which the future was to be built. More democracy, not less, was the commitment (deSouza et al. 2022). These four processes – secular nationalism, economic development, state-building, and an expanding democracy – were an ambitious exercise underway simultaneously. Sometimes the four processes functioned in tandem, and sometimes they were in opposition to each other, forcing the political executive to negotiate the difficult trade-offs between them.

Even before accounts of what transpired during the Emergency became available in the public domain through commission and committee reports, academic studies, memoirs, jail biographies, pamphlets, interviews, commentaries, etc.,[3] there were five main

---

[3] A great deal has been written about the Indian Emergency of 1975. There have been commission and committee reports that have reviewed cases of police torture, encounter killings, illegal arrests, forced sterilisation (Vicziany 1982) and summary demolition of houses, providing us with the factual details of Emergency's atrocities (The Shah Commission). Bookshelves are filled with engrossing Emergency biographies which recount the experiences of those arrested as well as those who managed to evade arrest. There are jail diaries that complement these reminiscences which tell us about the atmosphere of fear that prevailed and the yearning for freedom that consumed those who were incarcerated (Narayan 1979; Advani 1978; Nayar 2013; Singh 2018; Reddy 1977; Malkani 2021). Memoirs written by those who had a ringside view of the Emergency as it unfolded, give us insights into the discussions that took place (Dhar 2021; Kapoor 2015; Dayal and Bose 2018). There is even a diary of the meetings in the Prime Minister's Office during that period (Tandon 2002 & 2006). Protest pamphlets which were in circulation are available on the internet (PEN 1988). Scholarly books have been published that have looked at specific aspects of the Emergency such as the sterilisation excesses, or the coercive laws, or the media under censorship (Tarlo 2003; Williams 2014; Singh 2007;

frameworks available on how to read India's post-independence democratic journey. India was an outlier among postcolonial societies. Belying conventional wisdom, and the pronouncements of doomsday theorists, India, with a population that was poor, largely illiterate, diverse, divided by caste and ethnicity, and economically fragile, had survived as a democracy. We were, in fact, chugging along rather well – a bit like the Kalka–Shimla train that goes through 103 tunnels and winding hillsides as it climbs to its destination, sometimes with an additional engine at the back.

Five Frameworks to Explain the Emergency

The first comes from the debates of the 1960s within modernisation theories where Huntington contested the dominant proposition of the theorists that 'economic change and development' were the key 'factors responsible for the creation of stable democratic systems', and argued, in contrast, that it was 'political order' that was the first necessity. He stated this succinctly when he wrote that it is 'not the form of government but the degree of government' – implying thereby that 'political order depends in part on the relation between the development of political institutions and the mobilisation of new social forces into politics' (Huntington 2006, 3). In short, for Huntington, the goal of establishing political order in new postcolonial societies precedes the goal of encouraging

---

Verghese 2010; Singh 1980). There are also big-picture accounts of the period (Prakash 2019; Jaffrelot and Anil 2021a). These have been accompanied by a plethora of articles in journals discussing a range of issues such as the legal challenges to the Emergency (Noorani 1978; Tummala 1996; Shankar 2018), the weakening of key political institutions (Morris-Jones 1975), the enfeebled party system (Palmer 1976), and the Caesarist turn (Dasgupta 1976). Reading them, one gets a fuller picture of what has unanimously been regarded as a dark period of Indian democracy (Puri 1995). There is even an essay on cartoons that satirised the Emergency (Majumdar 2018). In addition, if one is still hungry for more, as I certainly am, there are biographies of Mrs Gandhi which provide a different lens to look at the Emergency (Jayakar 1995; Sehgal 2015; Malhotra 1991; K. B. 1985; Frank 2002), interviews (Fallaci – in Sri Kantha 2014) and commentaries (Mehta 1977 & 1980).

competitive democratic politics. For Huntington, political disorder is the result of a mismatch between the 'rapid growth of new groups in politics coupled with the slow development of political institutions' (4). This is an argument further developed by Francis Fukuyama (2006) and Fareed Zakaria to whom Huntington was a mentor. Zakaria advocated a minimum per capita income of between $3500 to $6000 for states to be able to transition successfully to democracies (Kagan 2003). Seen from within the Huntington framework, the Emergency – which was preceded by a growing political unrest leading to the removal of an elected government in Gujarat, an intensifying student movement in Bihar, an all-India twenty-one-day railway strike, and a trend of opposition protests that was spreading across the country leading chief ministers to worry about their inability to control the emerging disorder – was an illustration of this mismatch and tension between a contested politics and the ability of the institutions to manage it. There was a growing institutional overload. The Emergency was hence an attempt to impose order on what Mrs Gandhi and many others regarded as an increasing political anarchy. Vinoba Bhave's idea of *Anushashan* can perhaps be read as an allied concept, reminding us that, as much as governments, citizens too need to be disciplined to ensure a stable and peaceful society. (See the chapter by Tridip Suhrud.) In this reading, the Emergency was a significant moment that reaffirmed the thesis on the primacy of 'political order'.

The second framework from which to view the Emergency is the Marxist one. Here the Emergency is not distinctive but just another episode in the unfolding logic of capital in India, an attempt by the ruling class to safeguard their interests. Ranajit Guha states this position rather forcefully. 'The suppression of Indian democracy is not the work of an individual suddenly gone mad. It is the realization by the ruling classes, acting through their government of the day, of the full potential of the violence of a state which they had themselves conceived and set up as hostile to democracy' (Guha 2002, 584). This position sees governments as mere instruments of class rule. Constitutional provisions and enshrined liberties, such as fundamental rights, are understood as mere illusions helping conceal the reality of class rule. To state it in stark terms, when class interests are threatened by a popular uprising, the coercive power of the state will manifest itself (Prasad 1996). This is a point made again by Andre Gunder Frank.

> The suggestion is that the actions of the Government of India represents essentially the political-economic needs and interests of big industrial capital in what is primarily an inter-class struggle and that Indira Gandhi's intra-class conflict with her rivals turns on the secondary question of who will execute essentially the same capitalist policy and how. Any government of capitalist India that emerges from the present political crises will necessarily (have to) pursue the same political-economic policy for the foreseeable future of the permanent Emergency. (Gunder Frank 1977, 467)

The Marxist framework does not see this as a 'distinctively' dark period since the darkness (of capitalist exploitation) had been in place from before the coming of Independence, in fact from the time of colonial rule. Guha held that even Nehru earlier had presided over the 'perversion of Indian democracy' (for instance, in supporting restrictions on free speech, using repressive measures in controlling the unrest in Kashmir or the North East) that was 'done at the behest of the ruling classes' (Guha 2002, 580).

The third framework sees the imposition of the Emergency as a logical outcome of independent India retaining in the Constitution the coercive provisions of the colonial rule. These sections in the Constitution, articles 352 to 359, 'deal with the extraordinary powers of the executive during a grave emergency whereby the security of India or any part of the territory thereof (is) threatened, whether by war or external aggression or internal disturbance' (Koppell 1966). Having these powers in the Constitution gave a regime facing internal political opposition, as Mrs Gandhi's was in 1975, a constitutional instrument to save itself by declaring an emergency using the pretext of a national crises perceived to be threatening to the existence of the state. What was to be considered as a situation of national crises was, however, left to the discretion of the Executive. These Emergency provisions, although they had been considered necessary by members debating the draft of the Constitution in the Constituent Assembly, were for a colonial context, but were retained because the young nation had just witnessed a traumatic partition and wanted to protect the nascent state from such events in the future.[4] It was believed that these provisions would provide that safeguard. There was an extended discussion of this provision when it was introduced by Dr Ambedkar in the Assembly where some members raised the risk of its misuse and others of its necessity. Here is an excerpt from the intervention of Alladi Krishnaswamy Iyer in the debate:

> In this connection, I will remind the House of a famous saying that "a war cannot be fought on principles of the Magna Carta". Freedom of speech, right of assembly and other rights have to be secured in times of peace but if only the State exists and if the security of the State is guaranteed. Otherwise, all these rights cannot exist. We are envisaging a situation threatened by war, in a country with multitudinous people, with possibly divided loyalties, though technically they may be citizens of India. . . . Freedom of speech may be used for the purpose of endangering the State and resulting in crippling all the resources of the country. If only we realize that the country must exist, that the nation must exist, that the State must exist, if liberty and other things are to be guaranteed, there can be no possible objection to this article. (Constituent Assembly Debates, 20 August 1949, Part II)

Having preventive detention and Emergency provisions on the statute book strengthened the temptation for a regime that perceived itself, and the state, as under siege, to make use of these 'extraordinary' provisions and still claim 'constitutional' legitimacy for its actions. Because it was in the Constitution, it was available for the regime's purposes. This is the argument of the fourth framework with which to understand the Emergency. S. S. Ray, an expert on the Constitution, and Mrs Gandhi's close adviser, made the case for the use of the provision when she was initially disqualified by the Allahabad High Court for electoral malpractice, and subsequently given permission by the vacation bench of the Supreme Court to continue as prime minister but with weakened authority. She felt humiliated and diminished.

---

[4] Constituent Assembly Debates, 20 August 1949, Part II.

After initially considering resignation (Jayakar 1995, 271), she was persuaded by Ray and Sanjay Gandhi to declare an Internal Emergency. She did. She had evidently been convinced by her advisers that her remaining in office and imposing an Emergency was needed to safeguard the 'unity and integrity' of the country. (See the chapter by Ujjwal K. Singh and Anupama Roy and the one by R. Sudarshan.)

The fourth framework is the one most discussed in the academic literature. It regards the Emergency period, from 25 June 1975 to 21 March 1977, as a dark period because the writ protections of the Constitution were unavailable, democracy was suspended, thousands were arrested and thrown into jail and censorship was imposed, and because atrocities such as sterilisation, demolition of houses, encounter killings and torture took place, unfettered by the altered legal and constitutional orders. (See the chapters by Deepak Sanan and Pamela Philipose). The rule of law had morphed into rule by law. (See the chapter by Kalpana Kannabiran.) Mrs Gandhi had turned into a constitutional dictator (Dasgupta 1978; Lijphart 1978). Crucial to this framework was the debate on whether the writ of *Habeas Corpus* could be suspended and whether the basic structure of the Constitution was being undermined by the Emergency provisions. (See the chapter by R. Sudarshan.) The judgments by the various High Courts on the availability of *Habeas Corpus* and the subsequent, infamous, judgment of the Supreme Court, in what has come to be known as the '*ADM Jabalpur* case', where *Habeas Corpus* was declared as unavailable thereby overriding the positions of the various High Courts that it was available, constitute the core of this fourth framework. The *ADM Jabalpur* judgment was described by 'M. C. Chagla as "the worst in the history of the Supreme Court." Mr V. M. Tarkunde, a former Judge of the Bombay High Court and a leading member of the Supreme Court Bar, characterised it as "Judicial Suicide"' (Noorani 1978, 408). Debates around the centrality of civil liberties and democratic rights, and the hitherto unimagined possibility of the emergence of an autocrat through legal processes, and how all these would impact the democratic system, make up the bulk of the discussions in the fourth framework. It also looks at the excesses and atrocities that took place and asks: why do civil servants and judges so easily collude with tyranny? This remains one of the questions that are not fully answered even today, and is as relevant in 2025 as it was in 1975.

In contrast to this perspective which discusses the loss of civil liberties and the damage to the democratic system, is a position that views the imposition of the Emergency as beneficial especially for those who are oppressed by the practices of 'normalcy' of the political order, a 'normalcy' whose loss is being decried. For communities such as the Dalits and Adivasis, the 'normal' was oppressive. They saw the Twenty-Point Programme of the Emergency as a way to actually increase their freedom.[5] In the situation of so-called 'normalcy', Dalits suffer discrimination, humiliation, labour bondage and livelihood insecurity, all conditions that the Emergency regime sought to eliminate. So, if there was a loss of negative liberty for some during the Emergency, a diminished normal, there was also a gain of both positive and negative liberty for others, especially the Dalits who voted for Mrs Gandhi in the 1977 elections in Maharashtra, Andhra Pradesh and Karnataka. (See the chapter by Gopal Guru.) The contradictory and mixed experience of the Emergency in part helps explain

[5] In a detailed analysis of the Twenty-Point Programme, Jaffrelot and Anil (2021a, 18–28, Chapter 2) describe the programme as a mishmash of a range of populist measures, indifferently and unevenly implemented and 'lacking in originality'. 'They spanned a spectrum which at one end contemplated actually existing socialism for the benefit of the many, and on the other defended the corporate interests of the few.' These ranged from implementing land reforms and pushing land redistribution, housing the landless, declaring debt bondage illegal, announcing a moratorium on debt repayment of the rural poor, controlling the prices of essential commodities by expanding public distribution of foodgrains and acting against hoarders and smugglers, cracking down on tax evasion and so on (all designed to appeal to the poor), while also cracking down on trade unions and collective bargaining, imposing a wage freeze, reducing the bonus, among others, to appease the corporate class. Overall, they argue, Mrs Gandhi met with considerable success in pursuing her corporatist policies while her redistribution ambitions produced mixed results.

why groupings as far apart as the CPI and dominant sections of monopoly capital welcomed the declaration of the Emergency, at least in the earlier phase. The CPI argued that 'harsh measures' were necessary to consolidate the socialistic gains and the progressive measures initiated by Indira Gandhi. Her defiance of the US, and the strategic partnership with the Soviet Union, served as additional ideological justification for it. They were also in agreement with the crackdown on the RSS and Jan Sangh, seen by them as reactionary and communal forces threatening India's secular fabric. At the other end of the spectrum, the capitalist class welcomed the call to discipline and order, in particular the curb on militant trade union activity and civil disobedience, both of which were seen as disrupting economic activity. To argue, as many have done, that the Emergency produced universal revulsion, is to claim too much.

The fifth framework looks at the inner world of leaders (K. B. 1985; Puri 1995; Kaviraj 1986; Steinberg 2005). This is a framework which remains underdeveloped because the prevailing orthodoxies of the discipline have moved away from studying psychological and subjective factors in the world of political leaders, choosing instead to emphasise aspects of political economy and material conditions. The subjective world of leaders is important in explaining their key political decisions. This fifth framework is today making a comeback in democratic studies especially after the elections in India, Argentina, Türkiye, the Philippines, Israel and, most recently, the USA. The re-election of Donald Trump to the presidency of the United States has compelled scholars of democracy to look at how he tapped into the pervasive resentment of the citizens, dominated the symbolic universe with his appeal to young males, constructed a media image that found resonance among the voters, and transgressed many of the red lines thought inviolable by legal scholars of democracy. Much emphasis is being placed on his maverick personality. The coming to power of such leaders who receive the trust of the voters requires us to look at leaders differently. An examination of their narcissism, their self-belief (Trump will fix things), their non-consultative nature, and their decisiveness, may better explain their political support. Mrs Gandhi's decision to impose the Emergency can be seen through the literature on narcissism (Hermann et al. 2018). She believed that she alone was able to protect the nation against the anarchy that was threatening India. (See the chapter by Peter R. deSouza.) For Mrs Gandhi, no one else from her cabinet, not even seniors such as Jagjivan Ram and Y. B. Chavan, could protect and defend the nation against the gathering hostile forces and storm. Only she could do it. She had both the agenda and the capability. The Emergency was a necessary albeit unfortunate option in this postcolonial journey (Morris-Jones 1975).

Lessons for Democracy

The overwhelming lesson that we learn from studying the Emergency, in all five frameworks, is the failure of institutions. We had wanted to use a less dramatic term than 'failure', to describe the situation, such as 'infirmity', 'deficiency', or 'weakness', but the need to be true to the evidence compelled us to stay with 'failure'. The institutions that were chosen by the Constituent Assembly to safeguard our democracy from tyranny unfortunately failed us during the Emergency. This is true of the 'deliberative' institutions (the cabinet, parliament and state assemblies) as well as the 'oversight' institutions (the courts, CAG, CVC and media), as also the 'penalty imposing' institutions (the courts, police and jails). The Shah Commission report details this failure. The most disappointing of these institutions was the Supreme Court. The *ADM Jabalpur* judgement is a reminder of the highest court's potential for failure. It was only the dissenting Judge H. R. Khanna who demonstrated that it was possible to work for an institution, defending its independence in the face of an authoritarian Executive. Justice Khanna showed that the principles of 'separation of power' and 'checks and balances' need not be vacuous. He had the spine to uphold them. What makes for an independent judiciary? This is an urgent issue since it is at the centre of many of the challenges confronting democracies today in 2025 – in many democracies across the world such as Poland, Israel, India and the USA. When the Emergency was imposed, however, all institutions, for some reason, succumbed to the Executive, contributing to its transition from one that was constrained by these institutions to one that was unconstrained. A supreme authority emerged in the political realm – an Executive largely unbound. The parliament, for example, without much demur passed the 39th and 42nd Constitutional Amendments that Mrs Gandhi had wanted, giving herself extraordinary powers. (See the chapter by Ujjwal Kumar Singh and Anupama Roy, and also the one by R. Sudarshan.)

The failure of institutions is a fact. What is required, not just for India but also for other democracies, is an explanation for why this happened. Why did they crumble, even though they were not expected to, when faced with a demanding and fierce authority? Three possible explanations can be forwarded. The first is fear. Officials who hold important offices of the state, offices that can halt the movement towards tyranny, imagine that if they express their opposition to decisions of the Executive, they will face retribution. They hence choose the prudential route over the confrontational path. This fear of retribution grips the officialdom in a democracy when faced with an ascendent autocrat. This fear makes the institutions that are tasked with providing 'checks and balances' become weak, much weaker than the political and legal theory of institutions makes an allowance for. Aspiring tyrants therefore cause officials to look over their shoulders rather than at constitutional principles, and rules and regulations from which they draw their authority, while making decisions.

The second explanation is collusion. Officials collude in the arbitrary decisions of the authoritarian leader because they believe they can gain benefits, such as career advancement and plum postings, from such collusion. When this happens in the case of members of the judiciary, we must accept that we have lost an important, perhaps the key, bulwark against authoritarianism. The sad justification by Justice P. N. Bhagwati for his collusion in the *ADM Jabalpur* case shows this weakness to seduction by power. Is such collusion a unique instance, or is it perhaps intrinsic to the system of the modern state? We term it 'intrinsic' because such collusion takes place, fairly regularly, in all democracies. One does not need to look very hard to find such collusion. The challenge is how to fix it, if it is fixable at all. Justice P. N. Bhagwati who was a member of the notorious *ADM Jabalpur* bench of the Supreme Court wrote an obsequious letter to Mrs Gandhi when she returned to power in 1980 where he described her as the 'symbol of the hopes and aspirations of the poor' and praised her for her 'iron will and firm determination, uncanny insight and dynamic vision, great administrative capacity and vast experience'. For a sitting judge of the Supreme Court to write to a prime minister such a fawning letter is embarrassing.

> Thirty year later he regretted his being part of the majority vote on ADM Jabalpur. "I was wrong. The majority judgment was not the correct judgment . . . I would agree with what Justice Khanna did. I am sorry" (for the judgment) he told *The Indian Express* in 2011. Bhagwati added: "Initially, I did not favour the majority view. But ultimately, I do not know why I was persuaded to agree with them. I was a novice at that time, a young judge . . . I was handling this type of litigation for the first time. But it was an act of weakness on my part."[6] (*The Indian Express* 2011)

This is a pathetic admission coming from a former Chief Justice of India!

The third level of institutional failure is the delegation of authority – to implement the orders of the Emergency – to levels where it should not have been delegated, that is, to the jailors, constables and the petty officials, who are the face of the state for most common citizens. These are officials who do not necessarily carry with them the normative notion of limits, of the 'red lines' of a constitutional culture that should not be crossed. On the contrary, threats and the display of coercion are an essential aspect of their sense of office. In Indian colloquial usage, we refer to it as '*dandagiri*' and '*dadagiri*'. While higher levels of authority may have often crossed the 'red lines' specified by conventions and rules, their excesses can be called out by later Commissions, and they can be punished. An example would be the arrest of Prabir Purkayastha by DSP P. S. Bhinder, and keeping him in jail even though Bhinder knew that it was a case of mistaken identity; or Navin Chawla preparing lists of political opponents who were

---

[6] Fifty-plus years later there will be a debate whether his sycophancy has been exceeded by Mark Rutte, Secretary General of NATO, who referred to Trump as 'daddy' (Glasser 2025).

to be arrested. It is the jailor and the constable, however, who shaped the coercive dimension of the Emergency through torture and encounter killings. (See the detailing of these atrocities in the book by John Dayal and Ajoy Bose [2018].) This happened across the nation. It is the failure of the 'delegation function' that we are drawing attention to here, since it is at this level of official authority that the higher levels of tyrannical authority get a materiality. The excesses of sterilisation, demolition of houses, torture, encounter deaths, harassment, denial of the rights to assemble and protest, etc., can be located first at these levels. The responsibility for tyranny must hence also be placed here, in addition to locating it at the higher levels and certainly at the door of the prime minister. We flag it here because it is here where safeguards have to be considered, to eliminate both collusion and the tendency towards tyranny by the officials of the state. How does one protect democracy from the dangers of 'anticipatory obedience'? To an ordinary citizen, it is the '*thanedar*' who is feared even in normal times.

Beyond fear, self-interest and collusion, there were also individuals in the administration who, while disagreeing with many of the decisions taken, chose not to resign or openly dissent. Possibly, they felt that as insiders they might be in a position to help contain and dilute at least some of the excesses of the period. This is the classic challenge of 'now is not the time' that individuals in positions of authority face when their institutions are descending into tyranny. Universities across the Western world are plagued with this dilemma. The counter to this indecision is the other question, which must also be faced: 'if not now, when?'

During the Emergency, there were individuals who, in addition to recording the excesses, helped individuals evade arrest, provided information to regime opponents, and attempted to block/slow down proposals that they perceived as harmful. This conflicting tendency – to stay 'safe' and 'subvert from within' – sometimes successfully, more often not – is evident in the memoirs and reminiscences of several senior figures such as B. K. Nehru, P. N. Dhar and P. N. Haksar, to name a few. But whether these accounts are self-serving efforts to 'recover and restore' a tainted reputation or a post-facto attempt to set the record straight, remains unclear.

Without greater access to classified files, inter-departmental memos, and other records, it remains difficult to construct a fuller picture of what may have happened behind closed doors. Nevertheless, it is important that greater attention be focused on the 'intent and rationale' of key actors – politicians and officials – to better understand how decisions/choices are made in trying circumstances. While scholars have talked of agency to decipher the decisions of leaders, there is an inadequate probing of the minds and intentions of key decision makers.

It is often inadequately appreciated that no state is a monolith: the ideological orientation and practice of its functionaries are uneven across space, time and levels of responsibility. The culture of 'immunity' created by the Emergency left a degree of leeway to its functionaries to interpret both the 'desires' of the leaders and the 'need of the times'. So, while the culture of immunity, coupled with the compulsions to please the bosses, gave an impetus to a decentralised reign of terror against regime opponents, alongside the settling of personal scores, the uneven reach of the state also enabled an albeit small section of state functionaries, politicians and bureaucrats, to push progressive, pro-people measures promoted under the Twenty-Point Programme. So, debt relief, land redistribution, freeing of bonded labour, construction of grain banks and so on, got a boost, as did penal action against smugglers and hoarders or tax evaders. All this complicates the dominant narrative of the Emergency as democracy derailed.

Another theme that has gained relevance is the personality of the preeminent leader. The Emergency has highlighted the fact that we need to construct a psychological profile of the leader, map her inner world, to understand how she related to peers, and subordinates, within political institutions such as the Cabinet, parliament, political parties, judiciary, bureaucracy and the President of the Republic. This knowledge is useful since it gives us insights into how important decisions were made that had a wide impact on the polity. We need to construct the decision frame of the leader looking at both the inner elements of personality and subjectivity as well as the external elements that provided context to the decision. In normal times this is uneventful. It is significant, however, in extraordinary times such as an Emergency.

Understanding the personality of the leader helps us understand why institutions wilt under the leader's glare. Psychological studies also help us understand two additional aspects of Emergency-like situations: (1) the narcissism of the leader who believes that she is indispensable to the health of the nation and to its future success; and (2) the sycophancy of the officialdom that emerges as a result of a narcissistic leader's decisions, thereby weakening the functioning of democratic institutions. In the process, they get converted from institutions that serve the public, to institutions that serve the leader. A good example of this is the morphing of the rule of law into the rule by law. This is happening again in India and the USA today. In political commentary, *ADM Jabalpur* has become a metaphor. (See the chapter by Peter R. deSouza.)

Yet another theme that emerges from a study of the Emergency is the relationship between democracy and economic growth. The first year of the Emergency showed that the regime was able to stabilise an economy that was in a downward spiral. Some have attributed these favourable economic outcomes not to the authoritarian state but to a good monsoon. This relationship needs to be further probed in the case of India. In the early years of a polity emerging from colonialism, the question to be asked is: Is authoritarianism or democracy better for economic growth? The comparative study of 135 countries, over a forty-year period (1950–90), by Adam Prezworski et al. (2000), focusses on two questions: Is economic development conducive to political democracy? Does democracy foster or hinder material welfare? How did the economy fare during the Emergency is an issue that needs to be revisited. (See the chapter by Errol D'Souza.)

Amidst the grim accounts of what transpired during the Emergency are also uplifting accounts of the spirit of resistance to tyranny. The diaries of many of those incarcerated by the Emergency give us glimpses into the human spirit's eternal desire for freedom and its willingness to resist tyranny. You see these in the poems written during the Emergency. (See the chapter by Rukmini Bhaya Nair.) You see it in the strategies adopted by the media to bypass the censor. (See the chapter by Pamela Philipose.) You see it in the intimate letters exchanged between Madhu and Pramila Dandavate who were incarcerated in different prisons across the country. (See chapter by Gyan Prakash.) And you see it in the student protests that marked the politics of resistance to tyranny in the university. (See the chapter by Ravi Palat.)

While the dominant narrative of many of the studies of the Emergency is concerned with the dark period, there is a parallel narrative of hope and defiance. This is perhaps a pointer to a core dimension of the human condition – the spirit of longing for freedom. Sadly, tyranny reappears frequently in human societies. We see this in the genocide in Gaza.[7] But there is also the challenge to it, in poetry. The last post on social media by the Palestinian poet Hiba Abu Nada, hours before she was killed by an Israeli bomb – which celebrated those who have died resisting tyranny and ended with the defiant 'In Heaven, the new Gaza is free of siege' – bears testimony to this.[8]

Perhaps the hopeful lessons of the Emergency – hopeful even though there has been so much pain and suffering – is that resistance and protest will always accompany tyranny. Netanyahu has been alerted. History will not give him a free pass.

Then and Now: Continuities and Departures

More than five decades have passed since India experienced an Emergency, a first in its history. Arguing that there were serious internal disturbances, Mrs Gandhi, paradoxically, used specific constitutional provisions to suspend core provisions of the Constitution that protected fundamental rights and freedoms. Yet, despite numerous accounts of this period, a feeling persists that the Emergency has been overly mythologised. While broad-brush assessments of the Emergency, as a dictatorship, by its detractors, and as an unfortunate but necessary step to save the Republic and to safeguard progressive policies, by its apologists, exist, few have dealt with the complexity of the phenomenon. Why is this so?

---

7 https://www.icc-cpi.int/news/situation-state-palestine-icc-pre-trial-chamber-i-rejects-state-israels-challenges. (accessed 24 November 2024)

8 https://lithub.com/a-palestinian-meditation-in-a-time-of-annihilation/#:~:text=Hiba%20Abu%20Nada%20wrote%20her,to%20or%20martyr%20for%20liberation. (accessed 10 November 2023)

In part, this may be because of the 'unsettling nature' of what went on in those twenty-one months – so much so that 'politicians and political parties have been equally keen to deny their reality and suppress their memory' (Tarlo 2003, 2). Few today remember that when Indira Gandhi won the elections and returned as prime minister in 1980, she not only withdrew all cases against her in courts, but also ordered the destruction of all copies of the Shah Commission Report the government could lay its hands on. This is indicative of the enormous political effort that has gone into wiping out the Emergency as a 'live memory'.

Take for instance what at first sight would appear as straightforward cases of egregious human rights abuse – forced sterilisation and slum demolition drives carried out under the aegis of Sanjay Gandhi's Five-Point Programme. It was the widespread anger against the excesses which reportedly led to the decimation of the Congress Party in the North Indian states in 1977. However, a study of the subaltern responses – that is, of the victims of the two programmes – by Emma Tarlo, presents a more complex picture than conventionally assumed.

Tarlo's study, carried out twenty-five years after the Emergency in the trans-Yamuna Welcome Colony where many of the 'victims' were resettled, reminds us that even the most stark expression of the 'tyranny of the Emergency', were read through the experiences of people caught up in the moment. Those targeted in the slum clearance and sterilisation drives, and whose lives were profoundly disturbed, have more mixed memories than we imagine (Tarlo 2003, 16). Over 700,000 people were displaced to the margins of the city, and 161,000 were sterilised in Delhi alone. Her interviews show that alongside the residual anger, many of them, far from being resentful, remember Indira Gandhi, and even Sanjay Gandhi, as great leaders: '"Indira Gandhi? She was the best. If only there were others as good as her." Hindu sweeper' (Tarlo 2003, 206). '"She was a great leader. Her aim was to narrow the gap between the rich and the poor. It was she who gave us our plots". Muslim factory worker' (206). 'The image of Indira Gandhi emerged consistently untainted by the Emergency' (206).

Tarlo argues that such responses cannot be explained merely by referring to the time lag. For many of them, neither slum clearance nor birth control drives were anything new. In another study, Jaffrelot points out that 'over a million sterilisations took place every year in the late sixties, going up to 3.1 million in 1972–73, tellingly more than the 2.6 million figure for the first year of the Emergency' (Jaffrelot and Anil 2021a, 451). What was different was the 'scale of activities as also the speed of execution'. It may be pointed out that both these programmes continued under subsequent governments, the main difference being that now the pressure was placed on women, for men had become more defiant during the Emergency.

Looking at those targeted as only victims without agency, also ignores the fact that many of them participated in these campaigns for the incentives offered. There is no getting away from the compulsion/coercion dimension. But it cannot also be denied that many discovered ways of simultaneously benefiting from the programme. It is important to note that by the 1990s female sterilisation became the most popular form of birth control – especially across South India. The story of the slum clearance drive, spearheaded by Jagmohan during the Emergency, is similar, both pre- and post-dating the Emergency. For the average citizen little changed. Similar complexities need to be factored in when examining other examples of excesses under the Emergency regime, be it the anti-begging drive as part of urban beautification, or the steady dismantling of workers' unions to diminish their bargaining power and alter the balance between labour and capital.

This is not to suggest that what happened under the Emergency was not exceptional, or that the 'horrors and excesses' can be wished away. Nor that the overthrow of the Emergency changed little. One must not underplay the importance of the abrogation, by the Janata regime, of some of the worst changes in the Constitution imposed during the Emergency – such as reinstating fundamental rights and freedoms, a noticeable reduction in the climate of fear, and making the declaration of 'internal emergency' far more difficult. Yet, many of the restrictive, preventive detention laws were retained in the statutes, enabling subsequent regimes to reintroduce them, albeit in different forms.

The Emergency in our view remains a complex story of continuities and departures. Many of the initiatives credited to the

Emergency have long antecedents in the policies and practices of earlier regimes. Equally, despite criticism and protest, many made their way back into our politics and governance. In myriad ways, the experience of 1975–77 has left an indelible mark on our polity, as also our shared notions of what constitutes democratic politics governing the relations between the state and the citizen.

Finally, some pointers to our future as a democratic, secular Republic. The Emergency phase was marked by constitutional authoritarianism; a cult of the leader; the centralisation of power; a diminution in the autonomy of constitutional and regulatory institutions; a disciplining of the media; depoliticisation, if not criminalisation of politics, leading to the growth of a non-ideological and transactional political culture; heightened demands for conformity and stamping out of dissident activity; the enmeshing of the government with corporate capital; increasing recourse to repressive, preventive detention laws, etc., to list a few. Many of these tendencies are apparent today. In this sense, 2025 represents a continuity.

There are new elements like the growth of social media or the increasing reliance on digital technologies that need to be considered. The introduction of a unique identity system – Aadhaar – based on biometric features and linked to multiple databases creates a new challenge. Even as it improves efficiency and convenience, it can easily become a tool for surveillance and exclusion, enabling state intrusion into hitherto private domains. Equally important is the greater emphasis on homogenisation and a specific understanding of nationalism, often veering into ethnic majoritarianism. All these raise the apprehension of a fundamental redefinition of our Republic.

The idea of the Emergency could, possibly, be challenged because it represented a sharp rupture in the hitherto accepted modes of political and civic behaviour. The efforts of Nehru and his colleagues, despite limitations and contradictions, to cultivate a culture more helpful to a young democratic Republic, did retain some vitality among significant sections of the elite, including opposition politicians and activists. The Emergency damaged, if not broke, this compact. And once the initial 'shock and awe' of the dramatic promulgation began to fade, and the early gains – a stabilisation of the economy and decline in civic unrest – started tapering off, unease and resentment against capricious decisions and excesses began to grow. So, when an opportunity presented itself in 1977, the citizen voter chose to discipline the regime seen as responsible for the excesses and taking citizens for granted, above all in regions affected most by the Emergency. The choices made by the Emergency regime cast a long shadow over our political culture, leaders, activists and citizens. In many ways, much of what we witness in subsequent years under both Congress and non-Congress regimes, both at the Union and state levels, is a reflection of those years. It appears that as a country and people we have jettisoned the optimism about 'building a new and better society'. Unsurprisingly, the distortions of the present do not seem to disturb us enough to actively resist the enfeebling of our democracy.

Clearly, for many of the reasons listed earlier – a continuity of policies/programmes as also political culture under the successor Janata regime – the Indira Gandhi-led Congress was able to convincingly win back power in 1980. One clear lesson that both she and the opposition politicians seem to have learnt is to pursue their programmes and consolidate power by using the less blunt measures in their repertoire. The political class has realised the importance of a democratic, participatory form, to diminish resistance to its policies and programmes. Incremental changes in laws, procedures and institutions can as easily serve the purpose, more so if presented as a part of a larger project of nationalist consolidation and regeneration. To both understand and creatively respond to these shifts is the new challenge before democratic politics. Indira Gandhi's choice, as indeed that of some close advisors, to privilege a consolidation of order over respect for fundamental freedoms and human rights, a view which continues to enjoy resonance, may have ensured the survival of the state, but it severely damaged the project of building a constitutional, democratic Republic. We have still to overcome the shadows of our past.

References

Advani, L. K. 1978. *A Prisoner's Scrap-Book*. New Delhi: Ocean Books Pvt Ltd.

Dasgupta, J. 1976. A Season of Caesars: Emergency Regimes and Development Politics in Asia. *Asian Survey* 18.4: 315–49.

Dayal, John and Ajoy Bose. 2018. *For Reasons of State: Delhi under Emergency*. New Delhi: Penguin Viking.

deSouza, P. R., et al. 2022. 'Introduction'. In *Companion to Indian Democracy: Resilience, Fragility, Ambivalence*. New Delhi: Routledge.

Dhar, P. N. 2021. *Indira Gandhi, the "Emergency" and Indian Democracy*. New Delhi: Oxford UP.

Frank, Katherine. 2002. *Indira: The Life of Indira Nehru Gandhi*. Boston: Houghton Mifflin Harcourt.

Fukuyama, F. 2006. Foreword. In *Political Order in Changing Societies* by S. Huntington. New Haven: Yale UP.

Glasser, S. 2025. A Week for the Ages in the Annals of Trump Suck-Uppery. *The New Yorker*, 26 June.

Government of India. 1978. *Shah Commission Reports*.

Guha, Ranajit. 2002. Indian Democracy: Long Dead, Now Buried. In *The Small Voice of History*. Ranikhet: Permanent Black. 578–80.

Gunder Frank, Andre. 1977. Emergence of Permanent Emergency in India. *Economic and Political Weekly* 12.11: 463–75.

Hermann, A. D., Amy B. Burnell and Joshua D Foster. ed. 2018. *Handbook of Trait Narcissism*. London: Springer.

Huntington, Samuel P. 2006. *Political Order in Changing Societies*. New Haven: Yale UP.

Jaffrelot, C and Pratinav Anil. 2021a. *India's First Dictatorship, The Emergency 1975–77*. New Delhi: HarperCollins.

———. 2021b. Interpreting the Emergency. *Heidelberg Papers in South Asian and Comparative Politics* 79 (New Series).

Jayakar, P. 1995. *Indira Gandhi – A Biography*. New Delhi: Penguin.

K. B. 1985. Indira Gandhi: An Attempt at an Appraisal. *Economic and Political Weekly* 20.12: 496–503.

Kagan, R. 2003. The Ungreat Washed. *The New Republic*, 7 July.

Kapoor, Coomi. 2015. *The Emergency: A Personal History*. New Delhi: Penguin Random House.

Kaviraj, S. 1986. Indira Gandhi and Indian Politics. *Economic and Political Weekly* 21.38/39: 1697–708.

Khilnani, S. 1999. *The Idea of India*. New York: Farrar, Straus and Giroux.

Koppell, G. O. 1966. The Emergency, Courts and Indian Judiciary. *Journal of the Indian Law Institute* 8.3: 287–37.

Kothari, Rajni. 1970. *Politics in India*. Hyderabad: Orient Longman.

Lijphart, A. 1978. Emergency Powers and Emergency Regimes: A Commentary. *Asian Survey* 18.4: 401–07.

Majumdar, N. 2018. Indira Gandhi's Emergency Era through Cartoons. *The Print*, 25 June.

Malhotra, Inder. 1991. *Indira Gandhi: A Personal and Political Biography*. Boston: Northeastern UP.

Malkani, K. R. 2021. *The Midnight Knock*. New Delhi: Prabhat Prakashan.

Morris-Jones, W. H. 1975. Whose Emergency – India's or Indira's? *The World Today* 31.11: 451–61.

Mehta, Ved. 1977. The New India of Indira Gandhi. *The New Yorker*, 14 Feb: 56–101.

———. 1980. Indian Politics: A Family Affair. *The New Yorker*, 17 March: 98–157.

Narayan, Jayaprakash (Amritlal B Shah). 1979. *Prison Diary*. Washington: University of Washington Press.

Nayar, K. 2013. *Emergency Retold*. New Delhi: Konark publishers.

Nehru, Jawaharlal. 1988. *Letters to Chief Ministers, 1947–1964*. New Delhi: Oxford UP.

Noorani, A. G. 1978. The Judiciary and the Bar in India during the Emergency. *Verfassung und Recht in Übersee/Law and Politics in Africa, Asia, and Latin America* 11.4: 403–10.

North, Douglass C. 1990. *Institutions, Institutional Change, and Economic Performance*. Cambridge: Cambridge UP.

Palmer, N. D. 1976. Democracy in Eclipse. *Asian Survey* 16.2: 95–110.

PEN. 1988. *The PEN in Revolt: Underground Literature Published During the Emergency*. Souvenir, Press Institute of India.

Prakash, G. 2019. *Emergency Chronicles: Indira Gandhi and Democracy's Turning Point*. Princeton: Princeton UP.

Prasad, V. 1996. Emergency Assessments. *Social Scientist* 24.9/10: 36–68.

Prezworski, A. et al. 2000. *Democracy and Development: Political Institutions and Well Being in the World 1950–1990*. Cambridge: Cambridge UP.

Puri, Balraj. 1995. A fuller View of the Emergency. *Economic and Political Weekly* 30.28: 1736–44.

Purkayastha, P. 2023. *Keeping up the Good Fight: From the Emergency to the Present Day*. New Delhi: LeftWord Books.

Reddy, Snehalata. 1977. *A Prison Diary*. Human Rights Committee, Karnataka State.

Sehgal, N. 2015. *Indira Gandhi: Tryst with Power*. New Delhi: Penguin.

Shankar, S. 2018. The State of Emergency in India: Böckenförde's Model in a Sub-National Context. *German Law Journal* 19: 197–218.

Sheth, D. L. 2018. *At Home with Democracy: A Theory of Indian Politics*, with an Introduction by Peter Ronald deSouza. New Delhi: Palgrave Macmillan.

Singh, Indu B. 1980. The Indian Mass Media System: Before, During and After the National Emergency. *Canadian Journal of Communication* 7.2: 38–49.

Singh, Ramachandra. 2018. *13 Years: A Naxalite's Prison Diary*. New Delhi: Navayana.

Singh, Ujjwal K. 2007. *The State, Democracy and Anti-Terror Laws in India*. New Delhi: Sage.

Sri Kantha, Sachi. 2014. Indira Gandhi: Interviewed by Oriana Fallaci – Parts 1 and 2, *Ilnkai Tamil Sangam*, 24 Dec 24. https://sangam.org/indira-gandhi-interviewed-oriana-fallaci-part-2/ (accessed 13 July 2025)

Steinberg, B. S. 2005. Indira Gandhi: The Relationship between Personality Profile and Leadership Style. *Political Psychology* 26.5: 755–89.

Tandon, B. N. 2002. *PMO Diary I: Prelude to the Emergency*. New Delhi: Konark.

———. 2006. *PMO Diary II: The Emergency*. New Delhi: Konark.

Tarlo, Emma. 2003. *Unsettling Memories: Narratives of India's Emergency*. New Delhi: Permanent Black.

Tarlo, Emma. 1995. From Victim to Agent: Memories of Emergency from a Resettlement Colony in Delhi. *Economic and Political Weekly* 30.46: 2921–28.

The Indian Express. 2011. A Chief Justice of India Says, 'I am sorry', but 30 Years Too Late. 16 September.

Tummala, Krishna K. 1996. The Indian Union and Emergency Powers. *International Political Science Review* 17: 373–84.

Vicziany, M. 1982. Coercion in a Soft State: The Family-Planning Program of India: Part 1: The Myth of Voluntarism. *Pacific Affairs* (Autumn) 55.3: 373–402.

———. 1982–83. Coercion in a Soft-State: The Family-Planning Program of India: Part 2: The Sources of Coercion. *Pacific Affairs* (Winter) 55.4: 557–92.

Verghese, B. G. 2010. *First Draft: Witness to the Making of Modern India*. Chennai: Tranquebar.

Williams, R. J. 2014. Storming the Citadels of Poverty: Family Planning under the Emergency in India, 1975–1977. *The Journal of Asian Studies* 73.2: 471–92.

1

MISA and the Emergency: Laws, Lives and Afterlives

Ujjwal Kumar Singh *and* Anupama Roy

On 25 September 1975, amidst calls for strike in Jawaharlal Nehru University (JNU) to resist the Emergency, a young Prabir Purkayastha was 'kidnapped' by the Delhi Police from the University campus in what was a case of mistaken identity. Later a warrant was issued against Purkayastha on 30 September to make his detention *lawful* under the Maintenance of Internal Security Act (MISA 1975). The following grounds for his arrest were stated – he was a 'staunch Student Federation of India follower' who had stopped students from attending classes and used his 'political image' to persuade others to join his fold in opposing the Emergency. A list of JNU teachers and students who were to be similarly 'lifted' was given to the SP (North) by DIG Bhinder, who had led the police team that forcibly picked up Purkayastha (Prakash 2019; Purkayastha 2023).

MISA, under which Purkayastha and thousands of others were detained during the Emergency, was not an ordinary law. It was the extraordinariness inherent in MISA as a preventive detention law that made arbitrary arrest and detention possible. In a reply in the Lok Sabha to questions concerning 'release of persons detained during the Emergency', Charan Singh, the minister for home affairs, informed the House that 29,795 persons had been detained under section 16A of MISA.[1] Enacted in 1971 during the war with Pakistan, MISA was amended following the declaration of a national Emergency in June 1975. Under constitutionally sanctioned condition of suspension of the rights to freedom, life and liberty under the Emergency, and the

[1] Oral answers, Lok Sabha, 15 June 1977

'strengthening' of the Defence of India and Internal Security Act 1971 that provided special measures of arrest and detention to ensure 'public safety', 'defence of India and civil defence' to cover 'internal security', MISA became the most formidable preventive detention law in independent India. The enforcement of MISA produced power effects for the state that exceeded the exceptional provisions in the law, making it a *sine qua non* for the Emergency.

Proclaimed by the President on 25 June 1975 under Article 352 of the Constitution of India on the grounds that the 'security of India' was threatened by 'internal disturbance',[2] the Emergency was structured around two *deferrals*: the deferral of constitutional protections of fundamental rights, especially the right to life and liberty, and their redressal through writ petitions; and deferral of politics through the extension of the tenure of Parliament beyond its normal life of five years. Both the deferrals conjoined to suspend the constitutional order, paving the grounds for an exacerbated preventive detention regime which became constitutive of the order of the Emergency. While the Emergency enabled the concentration of powers in the executive, MISA ensured that there was no opposition to rule by the executive, facilitating the detention of parliamentary and non-parliamentary opposition without trial.

Yet, this was not the first time that an extraordinary law giving powers of preventive detention to the executive was legislated in India, nor would it be the last. Manifesting a consensus across political parties on the need for 'extraordinary laws' that give exceptional powers to the executive, an enduring string of extraordinary laws exist in India at the central and state levels, some of which, like the Defence of India Acts and Rules, have sustained from colonial times. From the Preventive Detention Act (PDA) 1950, enacted immediately after independence, through MISA 1971, and the Public Security Act (PSA) 1978, to the National Security Act (NSA) 1980, enacted three years after MISA was repealed, a preventive detention system (PDS) has existed 'parallel' to and 'in aid of' the 'ordinary' criminal justice system

[2] Notification no. II/16013/1/75-S&P (D-II), Gazette of India, Extraordinary, 26 June 1975, Part II, s 3, sub-s(i) at 1349.

(CJS). While the CJS is premised on social defence as its objective, due process as its strategy, and the pre-eminence of courts that are legalistic and pro-accused in their disposition, the PDS aims at repressing political opposition, thrives on minimal due process, denies the right to legal representation, and gives pre-eminence to executive decision-making and 'satisfaction' in the initiation and affirmation of extraordinary proceedings (Baxi 1982).

The parallel systems of PDS and CJS are intersected and exacerbated by a series of substantive extraordinary laws (EoL) like the Terrorist and Disruptive Activities (Prevention) Act (TADA 1984, 1987, now expired), Prevention of Terrorism Act (POTA 2002, repealed in 2004), Unlawful Activities Prevention Act (UAPA 1967, 2004, 2008, 2019) and the Armed Forces Special Powers Act (AFSPA 1958) – enacted to address terrorist and disruptive activities. Although they are not preventive detention laws, through stringent conditions of bail, inversion of burden of proof, exceptions in investigation and trial procedures, and diminution of evidentiary thresholds, they effectively function as detention laws, sharing with them the imperatives of an exponential expansion of state power, its concentration in the executive, and prolonged periods of detention without trial.

The unfettered accumulation of executive powers over matters of national security unleashes laws and policies based on 'ordered liberty' to protect and promote what is presented as national interest (Shulman 1999–2000, 289–300). Extraordinary laws represent *raison d'état* of the national security state – justifying the acquisition and exercise of unrestricted powers – as 'supreme necessity' not addressed by ordinary law. In October 2023, a seventy-three-year-old Purkayastha was detained yet again, this time under the UAPA, for 'unlawful activities', and 'raising funds for terrorist acts'. In May 2024, the Supreme Court declared the arrest of Purkayastha 'illegal'. As a person put under arrest, he possessed the 'fundamental and a statutory right' to be informed of the grounds of his arrest in writing, and given a lawyer of his choice – protections guaranteed to persons against arrest and detention under Article 22(1) of the Constitution – with the exception of those arrested under preventive detention laws. As a preventive detention law, MISA was constitutive of a legal regime of suspended rights under a constitutional emergency that institutionalised state impunity. MISA was survived by laws which sustained the logic of aggrandisement inherent in the modern state – in the diminution of the 'rule of law'– and consequently, mistrust of the justness of law by the people.

The 'Successful Rebel': Preventive Detention and Emergency Constitutionalism

Members of the first Law Commission of India, who framed the Indian Penal Code 1860, considered 'offences against the state' an especially 'heinous and formidable' category of crimes that required 'strong and sharp' measures. The reasons were explained in a note appended to the draft Code of 1837. Unlike the 'murderer' who is 'in greater danger after his victim is dispatched' or the 'thief' who is brought under the punitive control of the state after committing a theft, the 'rebel', if successful, 'is out of danger as soon as he has subverted the Government'. Such crimes, the argument went, were *peculiar* since their *successful* execution had the consequence of *securing* the criminal from punishment. The 'impotence' of the penal law 'against a successful rebel' produced the *necessity* of making laws *strong and sharp* 'against the first beginnings of rebellion, against treasonable designs which have been carried no further than plots and preparations'.[3] Those framing the Code worked with the objective of buttressing the state against the *successful rebel* through firm and effective 'protections'.

It is important to remember that constitutions are often framed under conditions of transition from war and uncertainty/insecurity to democracy. While constitutions envisage democratic futures with stable peace, they are fraught with anxieties over instability. Emergencies are made part of constitutional designs prescribing legal and institutional responses to prevent and mount over those crises that would make a constitutional order unstable. In inscribing these responses within the constitutional text the distinction between the state/political regime and a constitutional order that is expected to constrain arbitrary power, becomes blurred. It is the executive that declares the existence of a state of

[3] Appendix, Note C in Macaulay et al. (1888, 117).

emergency and prescribes responses that suspend the rule of law to substitute it with the 'constitutional' order of emergency. As an unforeseen and sudden situation requiring immediate action, an emergency assumes two things: the presence of an authority that decides on the existence of an exceptional situation; and the notion of a 'normal' situation, which needs to be restored. Carl Schmitt's works – generally seen as having produced a 'jurisprudence of crisis' – tell us that it is in the emergency/exception that the political is fully manifested, not only because it requires the assertion and affirmation of sovereign authority, but also because it assumes the existence of fundamental and intense antagonism of the nature of 'existential negation' between political entities, which compels/precipitates such assertion (Gross 2000a).

The justification of states of exception derives, however, from an understanding of the relationship between exception and norm in terms of a 'dichotomised-dialectic' or 'normalcy-rule, emergency-exception' paradigm (Gross 2000b). Histories of states are replete with episodes of both the 'dichotomised-dialectical' and 'authoritarian dictatorship' models of variable intensity and duration. These have resulted in a gradual 'piling up' of extraordinary measures that endure as 'crisis states', through the existence of a 'great number of parallel or simultaneous emergency rules' which accumulate as 'interlocking systems' of extraordinary and ordinary rules. While looking at extraordinary regimes of preventive detention, we use 'interlocking' as a lens to identify zones of permeability across legal regimes that prepare the ground for the permanence of the temporary.

Preventive detention in colonial India was interlaced with the logic of colonial rule in which law was an *accessory* to imperial domination. In the wake of Partition, the central government promulgated the Public Safety Ordinance 1948, providing for preventive detention. A number of Acts dealing with 'public security', 'maintenance of public order', 'public safety' and 'maintenance of essential supplies and services' were passed by state governments – for example, the West Bengal Security Bill 1947, empowering the government to detain anyone without trial. Deliberations in the Fundamental Rights Subcommittee, and debates in the Constituent Assembly (CA) in November 1948 on the draft Constitution, focussed on the 'basic predicament' of the degree to which the rights to life and personal liberty could be curtailed to secure 'governmental stability and peace' (Austin (1966) 2010). The CA agreed to limit rights by attaching conditions/provisos allowing their suspension in specific circumstances of emergency. On the question whether the legislature could empower the executive to detain a person without trial, the Assembly committed itself to due process only in the procedural sense. Govind Ballabh Pant contended that substantial due process would limit legislative powers and the country's future would be determined by the fiats of the judiciary (Austin (1966) 2010; Hallie 2016).

Preventive detention figures as an exception to 'protection against arrest and detention' guaranteed by Article 22(1) of the Constitution. In an exception to the ordinary criminal procedure, Article 22(2) allows the Parliament to empower the executive to detain a person without trial for a specified period. It is significant that Article 22, which was included in the Constitution as a 'compensation' for the abandonment of 'due process', was opposed by critics. Introducing the provision in the CA, Dr Ambedkar argued that rights against arrest constituted 'safeguards' against arbitrary inroads by the state into personal liberties, which could be withdrawn in situations of emergency, especially those involving 'tampering either with public order . . . or with the Defence Services'. In such conditions, the 'exigency of the liberty of the individual' could not be placed above the 'interests of the State' (Dr Ambedkar, CAD, 15 September 1949, 1497–1949; 16 September 1949, 1558, 1563).

The CA stressed the need for 'a strong Central government' to address the crises confronting the Indian state at the time of independence – Partition and communal violence, rehabilitation of refugees, economic problems and the food crisis, integration of provinces into the Indian territory – and the humongous responsibility of governing a large and diverse country. Brajeshwar Prasad cautioned against being suspicious of the state, which comprised individuals 'incapable of doing any wrong to the people'. As an 'embattled entity pitted against unscrupulous forces', it required discretionary powers to 'prevent the political reactionaries from gaining political power and ascendancy' (Prasad, CAD, 4 November 1948–8 January 1949; cited in Shankar 2009, 64). Some members, averse to the incorporation of emergency powers, argued that the Constitution was being made for 'normal' times, and the Partition should not be used to 'soft pedal' the freedom and personal liberty of the individual through 'extraordinary' procedures (K. T. Shah, CAD, 4 November 1948–8 January 1949, cited in Shankar 2009). The emergency powers provisions were criticised in the CA for 'their severe abridgement of civil liberties' and 'strong centralising tendency' (Iyer 2000, 83). H. V. Kamath saw in them the possibility of the end of democracy in India 'in the form of a Hitler-like take over by the Union Government'. K. M. Munshi, however, differed: 'The country is on the brink of a precipice . . . and extraordinary powers may be needed by the Union' (Austin (1966) 2010, 216). Arguing that the Constitution had sought to strike a 'balance', Dr Ambedkar reminded those who were critical of the strong centre: 'however much you may deny powers to the centre, it is difficult to prevent the centre from becoming strong. Conditions in modern world are such that centralization of powers is inevitable' (Dr Ambedkar, 4 November 1948, CAD, Vol. VII, 34–35).

The PDA, the first preventive detention law of the Indian Republic, was passed within a month of the enforcement of the Constitution, necessitated, as explained by Home Minister Vallabhbhai Patel, by 'labour trouble' and the Telangana movement (Bhagwat 1978). The enactment of MISA 1971, DIA 1962, PSA 1978, and the NSA 1980, sustained the tendency towards consolidating the security architecture of the state.

MISA and the Emergency: The Life of a Preventive Detention Law

Articles 20, 21 and 22 of the Indian Constitution protect personal life and liberties by limiting the power of the executive over arbitrary arrests and detentions. These protections, however, do not limit the powers of the legislature to make laws that could constrain civil liberties. Article 21 guarantees the fundamental right to life and liberty to all persons and simultaneously subjects the right to procedures established by law. Article 22 provides for protection against arrest and detention, laying down the rights that a person continues to possess upon arrest, including the right(s) to be informed of the grounds for arrest, to consult and be defended by a legal practitioner of his/her choice, to be produced before a magistrate within a stipulated time, and the right not to be detained in custody beyond the period of twenty-four hours without the authority of a magistrate. These rights, however, do not apply to enemy aliens and persons arrested or detained under a preventive detention law. While making these exceptions, Article 22 assures persons arrested under preventive detention laws, certain fundamental rights relating to the maximum period of detention, the provision of an Advisory Board consisting of persons qualified to be or who have been or are judges of a High Court to report on the sufficiency of the grounds for detention, the right to be informed of those grounds unless it is in the public interest not to, and the opportunity to make a representation against the detention order. While compensating for the withdrawal of an undiluted right to be informed of the grounds of arrest and of legal defence, ordinarily available to persons under arrest, these rights do not mitigate the conditions that the preventive detention system thrives on, that is, 'jurisprudence of suspicion' and minimal due process.

The PDA 1950 was enacted under the provisions of Article 22 and continued to be in force until 1969. For a year, until MISA was enacted in 1971, there was no central preventive detention law. The PDA allowed Central and State governments to detain a person if satisfied that it was necessary to do so for preventing the person from acting 'in a manner prejudicial to the defence of India', 'security of the State', 'maintenance of public order' or the 'maintenance of supplies and services essential to the country' (PDA 1950). In *A. K. Gopalan vs. the State of Madras* (1950) the Supreme Court upheld PDA's constitutionality arguing that detention being *preventive* and on the *discretion* of the Executive, the absence of satisfactory legal evidence and a judicial trial may not be construed as violation of principles of natural justice (AIR 1979, A 1950 SC 27). Agreeing that political freedoms guaranteed under Article 19 were fundamental, the court argued that they were not absolute. The validity of the law could be tested not against the right but against the restrictions (A. K. Gopalan, AIR 1979, A 1951 SC 27). The court took the view that the fundamental freedoms under Article 19 were available only to free citizens and not to those under preventive detention. Similarly, the expression, 'procedure established by law' in Article 21 was construed differently from 'due process of law' – a view which was reversed in the Maneka Gandhi case in which the Supreme Court held that the 'procedure established by law must also be just, fair and reasonable' (AIR 1978 SC 507).

MISA's life was contemporaneous with two emergencies which provided the context for its enactment and enforcement. Its enactment in July 1971 coincided with the declaration of an Emergency in December 1971 in the context of India's war with Pakistan. MISA 1971 gave broad application to provisions of Article 22 pertaining to the disclosure of the grounds of detention and opportunities to make representation against the order as well as Article 22(6) that permitted the detaining authority to conceal facts in the public interest (MISA, 1971, section 8). MISA assumed a more daunting avatar with the declaration of Emergency on 25 June 1975 under Articles 352(1) and 359(1) of the Constitution. Under the provisions of Article 352(1), before the 44th Constitutional Amendment Act (1978) replaced 'internal disturbance' with 'armed rebellion', a proclamation of emergency could be made if the President was satisfied that a grave emergency existed whereby the security of India or a part of it was threatened by a war or external aggression or internal disturbance.

Provisions of Article 359 came into effect with the declaration of emergency, empowering the President to *suspend* the right to move a court for the enforcement of fundamental rights and all proceedings pending in any court for their enforcement for the duration of the Emergency. In July 1975, immediately after the Emergency was declared, the 38th Constitutional Amendment Act made the adverse effects of the emergency on fundamental rights definitive, by inserting Clause 1(a) to Article 359 which stated that while the proclamation of emergency was in operation, 'nothing in Part III [Fundamental Rights] of the Constitution would restrict the power of the state . . . to make any law or take an executive action'. The Amendment also added clauses (4) and (5) to Article 352, stating that neither the Supreme Court nor any other court would have jurisdiction to entertain any question concerning the validity of a declaration of Emergency by the President. This insertion was removed later by the Janata government through the 44th Amendment, which also affirmed the deferral of political freedoms and other rights in Part III, while making an exception for Articles 20 and 21. This meant that all fundamental rights except those that gave protection in respect of conviction for offences and the right to life and liberty, would remain suspended during an emergency.

MISA was amended in June 1975 to insert Section 16-A under which provisions pertaining to disclosure of the grounds of detention, and the procedure of reference to the Advisory Board ceased to apply to detentions after the proclamation of Emergency on 25 June 1975. Another insertion – Section 18 – lay down that detainees would have no claims to personal liberty under natural law or common law. MISA was subsequently placed in the 9th Schedule of the Constitution, removed from the purview of judicial scrutiny by the Constitution (39th Amendment) Act, 1975. On 28 April 1976, the Supreme Court upheld the validity of MISA as amended (*ADM Jabalpur vs Shivakant Shukla* 1976 AIR 1207). It also held that no person could move a writ petition under Article 226 before a High Court for *habeas corpus* or challenge the legality of a detention order, removing the possibility of writs of *habeas corpus* under Article 226 which had hitherto remained effective despite the Proclamation of Emergency.

Lives under MISA

Behind the veneer of legality assumed by preventive laws are narratives of 'lawful' measures deployed to keep a person in a 'maze of arrests and rearrests' and 'ritual chants' of 'security of state' and 'public order' (Balagopal 1988, 102–04). Behind the 'mask of legality' (Rudra 1973) are stories of detention – of indiscriminate arrests, torture, and overcrowded prisons – under MISA *before* and *during* the Emergency. Figures of detention under MISA during the Emergency vary. The numbers reported by the home minister cited at the beginning of the chapter, are different from the Home Ministry statistics published by Amnesty

International which suggests that 36,039 political prisoners were held under MISA, apart from those detained under other laws such as the DIR and COFEPOSA during the Emergency (Amnesty International 1979). The data in Table 1 below, based on the state-wise figures of MISA detainees in the Shah Commission Report under the heads, 'political parties', 'banned organisations' and 'anti-socials, criminals, and others', places the number at 34,564.

Table 1: Detainees Under MISA[4]

State	Total number of MISA detainees	Members of political parties detained under MISA	Members of banned organisations detained under MISA	Anti-socials, criminals, others, detained under MISA
Andhra Pradesh	1135	210	512	413
Assam	533	203	143	187
Bihar	2360	530	269	1561
Gujarat	1762	404	135	1223
Haryana	200	172	24	4
Himachal Pradesh	34	17	8	9
Karnataka	487	156	165	156
Kerala	790	221	476	93
Madhya Pradesh	5620	1807	1593	2220
Maharashtra	5473	780	1717	2976
Manipur	231	14	2	127
Meghalaya	39	2	14	23
Nagaland	92	9	Nil	86
Orissa	408	141	112	155
Punjab	440	33	16	57
Rajasthan	542	213	154	175
Sikkim	4			
Tamil Nadu	1027	570	139	318

[4] The table has been drawn from data given in the Shah Commission Report (1978), Chapter XIX: 'Arrests and Detentions During the Emergency' (pp. 1–152).

State	Total number of MISA detainees	Members of political parties detained under MISA	Members of banned organisations detained under MISA	Anti-socials, criminals, others, detained under MISA
Tripura	77	18	9	50
Uttar Pradesh	6956	785	637	5534
West Bengal	4992	41	186	84
Andaman and Nicobar Islands	41	Nil	28	13
Arunachal Pradesh	Nil			
Chandigarh	27	15	6	6
Dadra and Nagar Haveli	Nil			
Delhi	1012	180	146	538
Goa	113	9	9	95
Lakshadweep	Nil			
Mizoram	70	12	Nil	58
Pondicherry	54	37	2	12
Total	**34564**	**6579**	**6502**	**16173**

Interestingly, the number of detainees under the head 'anti-social' was high in all states, leading the Shah Commission to conclude that 'quite often the distinction between public order and law and order was completely forgotten' and the police used MISA indiscriminately to 'avoid recourse to normal laws, which required detailed investigation and prosecution'. In Nagaland, however, the figures of those arrested 'for reasons of the security of state' were located under the category of 'anti-socials, criminals and others' (Shah Commission 1978, 58). Many arrests were made under the DIRs (Table 2) which along with MISA was the primary law for detaining political opponents, especially Naxalites/members of CPI(ML). Home Ministry sources cited by Amnesty International place the figure of political prisoners arrested under the DIRs at 77,297 (Amnesty International 1979) – a majority of whom were arrested before the Emergency. The DIRs lapsed in September 1977, six months after the revocation of the Emergency.

Table 2: Detainees and Prison Accommodation[5]

States	Authorised accommodation as on 25.6.75	Number of prisoners as on 25.6.75	Number of prisoners detained/arrested during the Emergency under different laws
Andhra Pradesh	5912	5885	MISA 1135 DIR 451 COFEPOSA 45
Assam	4930	7909	MISA 558 DIR 1933 COFEPOSA 53
Bihar	21140	38407	MISA NA DIR NA COFEPOSA NA
Gujarat	4972	3636	MISA 1762 DIR 2643 COFEPOSA 279
Haryana	2794	3003	MISA 200 DIR 1079 COFEPOSA 2 EC Act cum DIR 99 EC Act 869 151 CrPC 592
Himachal Pradesh	561	264	MISA 34 DIR 251 Various economic offences 403 Persons arrested u/s 151 of CrPC & other preventive detention laws 62
Karnataka	7311	5217	MISA 487 DIR 4015 COFEPOSA 119 CrPC 1232 Karnataka Police Act 1562
Kerala	5213	3478	MISA 790 DIR 6894 COFEPOSA 96

[5] Table based on Shah Commission Report. *Shah Commission of Inquiry, Third and Final Report*, Delhi, 1978.

States	Authorised accommodation as on 25.6.75	Number of prisoners as on 25.6.75	Number of prisoners detained/arrested during the Emergency under different laws
Madhya Pradesh	12388	16166	MISA (excluding 74 absconders) 5620 DIR 2521 COFEPOSA 11151 CrPC 26904
Maharashtra	14801	19786	MISA 5473 DIR 490 COFEPOSA 9799
Manipur	350	318	MISA 143 DIR 228 COFEPOSA 13
Meghalaya	335	521	MISA 39 DIR 20 COFEPOSA 6
Nagaland	700	450	MISA 92 DIR 4 (later all detainees transferred outside the state)
Orissa	6668	10222	MISA 408 DIR 3 COFEPOSA 762
Punjab	6746	7312	MISA 440 DIR 2423 COFEPOSA 73 U/Ss 107 & 151 of CrPC 3784 Economic offenders (U/Ss 7 of the EC Act & 114 of the DIR) 714 U/S 188 IPC 596 Others 25
Rajasthan	7515	6158	MISA 952 DIR 1360 COFEPOSA 23 151 CrPC 2600
Sikkim	30	99	MISA 4 (later sent to West Bengal)
Tamil Nadu	1459	4455	Not Available

States	Authorised accommodation as on 25.6.75	Number of prisoners as on 25.6.75	Number of prisoners detained/arrested during the Emergency under different laws
Tripura	519	730	MISA 77 DIR 99 (later 8 detained under MISA) CFE & PS Act 25
Uttar Pradesh	35339	33058	MISA 7185 DIR 24761 COFEPOSA 126
West Bengal	20237	25599	MISA 5320 DIR 80 COFEPOSA 2545
Andaman & Nicobar Islands	105	119	MISA 41 (including 2 detained twice and one detained at Madras) DIR 89
Arunachal Pradesh	No jails	No jails	No jails
Chandigarh	110	98	MISA 27 DIR 74 COFEPOSA 1
Dadar & Nagar Haveli	20	nil	MISA nil DIR 3 COFEPOSA 2
Delhi	1273	2669	MISA 1012 (DIR and COFEPOSA arrests also made but information not available)
Goa, Daman & Diu	445	147	MISA 113 COFEPOSA 68
Lakshadweep	Not Available	Not Available	No arrests during the Emergency
Mizoram	192	381	MISA 70 DIR 136
Pondicherry	2085	156	MISA 54 DIR 54 COFEPOSA 7

It must be remembered that prison population during the Emergency included those detained under MISA 16-A after the proclamation of the Emergency and those, largely Naxalite prisoners, who were detained before it. Andhra Pradesh, Bihar and West Bengal had large numbers of Naxalite prisoners some of whom had been in detention since 1971 under MISA or DIR. Of the total arrested, almost 18,000 had not been charged in court (AI Report, 1973, 73–74). Ramchandra Singh, a Naxalite, spent thirteen years in jail after his arrest in September 1970. His diary, smuggled out of prison by friends and published later, details the lives of prisoners in a 'larger jail called Emergency'. The trauma of prison life is interspersed with accounts of resistance. Singh writes about the conditions in Fategarh Central Jail where the number of prisoners rose to almost three thousand as MISA was invoked and political prisoners were 'thrown into the barracks':

> Security was tightened and jail employees were instructed to be more vigilant. But Superintendent G L Gupta's dictatorial attitude could not subdue these prisoners of state. The new arrivals shouted ear splitting slogans of "Bhujia ya tarkari hai, ya baillon ki hariyari hai?" (Is this food for humans or fodder for cattle?) And, "Gupta teri tanashahi, nahi chalegi, nahi chalegi" (Gupta you're a crook, your tyranny won't be brooked), directed at the mismanagement and adulterated food.
>
> . . . Despite Gupta's display of muscle power through a hundred baton-wielding nambardars and warders who followed him around, the deadlock could be resolved only through negotiation between the two groups. The inmates now realised that their bada sahib was not invincible after all. (Singh 2018)

Overcrowding in jails, reflected in the figures in Table 2, was only one of the factors which conditioned the treatment of detainees. Even in those states where guest houses were requisitioned for the purpose of detaining political prisoners, it was only a select few who benefitted depending on the classification and rules of detention. Prison memoirs and records show that 'isolation' and 'separation' of political prisoners was used punitively. A letter dated 7 August 1975, written by Members of Parliament Samar

Mukherjee, Somnath Chatterjee and Salil Ganguli to the home minister referred to the detention of Jyotirmoy Basu in Hissar jail in Haryana. The letter stated that Basu was being kept in an isolated cell with no windows. Two thick blankets on the courtyard gate obstructed further visibility, and a brick and mud mortar buffer wall was erected to reinforce his isolation, in violation of rules governing detention conditions of MISA detainees under the 'Haryana (Conditions of Detention) Order 1971', whereby a detainee was to be kept in wards with other convicts and allowed to work (Sharma 1977, 42–44).

Special arrangements were made for the detention of Jayaprakash Narayan first at a guest house at Sohna in Haryana and later at the Postgraduate Institute of Medical Research and Education at Chandigarh, because of his poor health, where he was kept in what Narayan called a 'painful' state of isolation. On 28 August 1976, he wrote,

> . . . during the 130 odd days of detention, I remained completely isolated. . . . The total isolation was very painful to me. . . . The loneliness caused a kind of mental torture. I urged the authorities to allow one of the many thousands arrested with me to stay with me. . . . In 1943 when I was a prisoner in connection with the 1942 movement I was kept alone and separately in Lahore. When I asked for a companion in detention the foreign government ultimately acceded to my request and allowed Ram Manohar Lohia, my colleague to meet me for an hour daily.[6]

There were numerous protests inside prisons. Political prisoners in Hazaribagh jail petitioned the superintendent pressing for the redressal of their grievances and subsequently resorted to a hunger strike. Detainees in Gujarat clashed with the jail staff in April 1976 demanding that they should not be locked up at night. In Thane District Prison, political prisoners resorted to a token hunger strike at least six times to press for their demand that they be shifted to jails near their home. In Moradabad District Jail, a few political prisoners were put in fetters and solitary confinement when

[6] 'A Letter to Friends', 28 August 1976 (in Bhargava 1977, 8–9).

they threatened to go on a hunger strike. Similarly, in Varanasi Central Jail, thirty-three detainees were put in fetters and solitary confinement when they refused food and raised slogans against the PM and the CM. In Assam, the Chief Secretary instructed that 'hunger strike in jail should be severely dealt with under the law . . . Discipline must be enforced' (Shah Commission 1978, 56).

When the Janata Party formed the government after the Emergency on the plank of restoration of civil liberties, a large number of MISA detainees were released. The government professed a 'new approach' towards Naxalites for bringing them into the 'national democratic mainstream'.[7] Accordingly, Naxalite detainees against whom no case was pending were to be released, against whom charges had been framed legal proceedings were to be expedited, and those convicted were to serve their sentence. On 15 June 1977, G. M. Banatwalla raised a question in the Lok Sabha regarding the release of MISA detainees and government policies towards RSS detainees whose release was pursued 'vigorously', and a different approach towards Naxalite prisoners. The Home Minister Charan Singh responded that of the 29,795 persons detained under section 16-A of MISA, 6,244 persons under MISA's 'normal' provisions, and 6,010 already in detention when MISA was applied in June 1975, only 1,796 persons remained in detention as of June 1977. Fifty-nine detainees had died in prison and during parole. The government, he argued, was not discriminating against the Naxalite prisoners, who in his 'definition' were 'demarcated' from 'other criminals' – not having committed 'any crime for their own personal interest . . . although they were mistaken in choosing the method that they chose in achieving their ends'.[8] In the years that followed, different state governments announced 'honours' and 'facilities' for Emergency/MISA detainees, emulating the recognition given to freedom fighters. The Samajwadi Party offered them cards identifying them as MISA/DIR detainees with pension and free treatment – the amount was subsequently hiked by the Yogi government

---

[7] Government Order dated 5 May 1977 to the state governments regarding the release of Naxalite prisoners, p. 16.

[8] Ibid., p. 24.

in 2018. The Rajasthan government under Vasundhara Raje Scindia declared those detained in Rajasthan 'Loktantra Senani' (democracy fighters) entitled to pension and medical allowance. Notably, these announcements were invariably made close to state assembly or parliamentary elections.

Conclusion: The Spectre of MISA

In 1977 MISA was repealed by the Janata Party government which won a massive electoral victory in the face of raging anti–Indira Gandhi sentiments. In December 1977, reflecting the 'dependence' of all political regimes on law as a political tool, the Janata Party government tried, unsuccessfully, to make MISA part of the ordinary law by bringing an amendment to the Criminal Procedure Code (CrPC). The 'Emergency' as an event and MISA as its legal embodiment may no longer be seen as an aberration. While MISA and POTA have been repealed and TADA was allowed to lapse, detention regimes have become normalised through a perpetuation of extraordinary laws that are substantive/punitive laws but enable long-term detention of persons without trial. Preventive detention laws – for example, Punjab Security of State Act (1953), Jammu and Kashmir PSA (1978), Andhra Pradesh Public Security Act (1992) and Karnataka Public Safety (Measures) Enforcement Act (2017) – which allow state governments to detain persons to prevent them from causing harm to the security of the state and public order; NSA (1989) which allows central and state governments to detain persons to prevent them from acting in a manner prejudicial to the security of India; and special laws such as Gujarat Control of Terrorism and Organised Crime Act (GUJCTOC 2003), and Maharashtra Control of Organised Crime Act (MCOCA 1999) on which POTA was modelled, continue.

TADA and POTA brought with them a jurisprudence of exception: as extraordinary measures in response to what are presented as extraordinary events/situations, they brought exceptional provisions pertaining to arrest, detention, investigation, evidence, trial and punishment. While setting up parallel/exceptional systems, EoLs also interlock with, and share provisions with, ordinary laws, leading to a general 'tightening up' throughout statutory law (Hillyard 1993, 263). The 'strengthening' of UAPA in 2004 through the incorporation of provisions of POTA, which was repealed in the same year, is a manifestation of this process. While extraordinary laws are assumed to be temporary, the accommodation of extraordinary provisions in permanent laws gives exceptional provisions an afterlife, without the requirement of periodic parliamentary scrutiny for extension.

As the primary law to address crimes of 'terror' and 'unlawful activities', the UAPA was 'strengthened' incrementally to enhance executive control over constitutional freedoms. Following the terror attacks of November 2008 in Mumbai, Section 43D(5) was added to UAPA, making bail exceedingly difficult to secure. An amendment in the UAPA in 2019, empowered the federal government to designate *individuals* as terrorists *even if they had not been convicted of a crime.* The process of normalisation was deepened with the enactment of the National Investigating Agency Act (NIA) 2008, which provides for the setting up of the NIA to investigate terror-related offences and try them in special courts. An amendment in 2012 in the UAPA permitted the NIA to attach 'properties acquired through proceeds of terrorism'. The UAPA has subsequently assumed a dual character: of enabling *detention* by facilitating long-term imprisonment without trial, prioritising the role of the political executive in determining that a crime has been committed under its exceptional provisions, and as a *substantive* law with exceptional procedures of investigation and trial, facilitating punitive procedures and enhanced punishment.

On 1 July 2024, the three law codes that hitherto constituted the legal system in India – the Indian Penal Code (1860), the Criminal Procedure Code, and the Indian Evidence Act – were replaced by the Bharatiya Nyaya Sanhita (BNS), Bharatiya Nagarik Suraksha Sanhita (BNSS) and Bharatiya Sakshya Sanhita (BSS). The new legal codes were introduced and endorsed by the BJP/NDA for decolonising Indian penal codes by placing justice rather than punishment at its core. The BNS retains provisions that reflect the 'logic of rule' associated with the colonial and postcolonial states as 'modern' forms of power. While sedition is no longer an enumerated offence (against the state), a cluster of 'new' offences which closely resemble it persist in Cl.150 of the

BNS (PRS 2023a), enhancing its purview and making it more dangerous.[9] In a continuation of the reasons of state associated with the national security state, the BNS includes 'terrorism' – hitherto part of the jurisprudence of exception – as an offence in the ordinary legal code. The BNS defines terrorism as an act that intends to (i) threaten the unity, integrity, and security of the country; (ii) intimidate the general public; or (iii) disturb public order. Terrorist acts include: (i) using firearms, bombs, or hazardous substances to cause death, danger to life, or spread fear; (ii) destroying property or disrupting essential services (PRS 2023b)[10] – a broad definition that has the potential of bringing a range of acts into its ambit. The new categories of offences in the BNS, including 'terrorism' and 'organised crime', already part of UAPA, MCOCA and GUJCTOC, produce a grid where the ordinary and the extraordinary interlock to 'tighten' ordinary laws generally and the policing function of the state specifically.

The alignment of extraordinary laws with regime sustenance is evident in the manner in laws like the UAPA replicate Emergency-like conditions without a formal proclamation of Emergency. The weaponisation of UAPA against activists, journalists, students and academics has exacerbated and the judiciary has until recently[11] adhered to the stringent bail conditions under section 43D(5) of UAPA. Data shows that the conviction rate in UAPA cases is low and the trial period is long, making the process a punishment for

---

9 https://p39ablog.com/2023/09/criminal-law-bills-2023-decoded-8-sedition-recast-implications-of-clause-150-of-the-bns-2023/ accessed on 11 March 2024.

10 https://prsindia.org/billtrack/prs-products/prs-bill-summary-4278, accessed 11 March 2024

11 In *Union of India v. K. A. Najeeb* (2021), the Court held that prolonged incarceration is a violation of the right to life. In other cases it emphasised the need to 'separate' evidence from what the NIA presents as inference (High Court judgment in the *State of NCT of Delhi v. Devangana Kalita 2021*) and to analyse evidence rather than apply the prima facie true test (*Vernon Gonsalves v. State of Maharashtra 2023*).

large numbers of people arrested merely for criticising government policies.

The death of G. N. Saibaba on 12 October 2024, who was acquitted by the Bombay High Court in March 2024, is a reminder of how the UAPA is a law designed to make the 'process' a punishment. Arrested under the UAPA with five others for alleged Maoist links, Saibaba – a professor in a Delhi University college – lost his job after arrest, and spent ten years in prison as an 'undertrial' before the Bombay High Court acquitted him on the grounds that there was no evidence against him. Wheelchair-bound with 90 per cent disability, Saibaba's health deteriorated in prison. In his prison memoir, titled *Why Do You Fear My Way So Much?*, Saibaba wrote about the 'excruciating relentless pain' he suffered in prison, as 'one after the other, my organs started bursting':

> My vocal chords acquired lesions making my voice a thin and inaudible squeak. My heart broke with hypertrophic cardiomyopathy. My brain has started having blackouts with a condition called syncope. My kidneys are silted with pebbles; my gallbladder gathered stones and pancreas grew a tail of pain called pancreatitis. Nerve lines in my left shoulder broke under the conditions of my arrest, known as brachial plexopathy. More and more organs of silence replaced the original. I have been living with explosive and shooting pain day in and day out. *I am living on the margins of life.* (Saibaba, cited in Sebastian 2024)

Saibaba was not the first or the only one to have perished to a regime of extraordinary laws. In July 2021, Stan Swamy, a Jesuit priest and an octogenarian Adivasi rights activist, suffering from Parkinson's disease, died nine months after being arrested under the UAPA by the NIA. Swamy was one of the sixteen persons arrested by the NIA for 'instigating caste violence' between Maratha and Dalit groups in Bhima Koregaon in 2018. Indeed, Umar Khalid and Safoora Zargar's detention since 2020 in a 'conspiracy' case involving riots in Northeast Delhi in the context of the sit-ins against the Citizenship Amendment Act 2019, with successive unsuccessful bail hearings, is a poignant reminder of how state practices of ruling are imbricated in producing precarious lives of indefinite detention. The spectre of dead MISA lingers on.

References

Amnesty International. 1973. *Annual Report on India, 1972–73.* London: Amnesty International.

Austin, Granville. (1966) 2010 Fifteenth Impression. *The Indian Constitution: Cornerstone of a nation.* Oxford: Clarendon Press.

Balagopal, K. 1988. We Shall Have Our Own Mandelas: Birth of the 'Political Prisoner'. *Economic and Political Weekly* 23.40: 2039–43.

Baxi, Upendra. 1982. *Crisis of the Indian Legal System.* Delhi: Vikas.

Bhagwat, Niloufer. 1978. Institutionalising Detention Without Trial. *Economic and Political Weekly* 13.11: 510–13.

Bhargava, G. S., ed. 1977. *J.P.'s Jail Life (A Collection of Personal Letters),* 1977. New Delhi: Arnold Heinemann.

Gross, Oren. 2000a. The Normless and Exceptionless Exception: Carl Schmitt's Theory of Emergency Powers and the "Norm-Exception" Dichotomy. *Cardozo Law Review* 21.

———. 2020b. Emergency Challenges. In *Constitutionalism Under Extreme Conditions: Law, Emergency, Exception,* ed. Richard Albert and Yaniv Roznai. Cham: Springer.

Hallie, Ludsin. 2016. *Preventive Detention and the Democratic State.* Delhi: Cambridge UP.

Hillyard, Paddy. 1993. *Suspect Community: People's Experience of the Prevention of Terrorism Acts in Britain.* London: Pluto Press.

Iyer, Venkat. 2000. *States of Democracy: The Indian Experience.* New Delhi: Butterworths.

Macaulay, T. B., J. M. Macleod, G. W. Anderson, and F. Millet. 1888. *Indian Penal Code as Originally Framed in 1837 and the First and Second Reports Thereon* by C. H. Cameron and D. Eliot. Madras: Higginbotham and Co.

Prakash, Gyan. 2019. *Emergency Chronicles: Indira Gandhi and Democracy's Turning Point.* Princeton & Oxford: Princeton UP.

Purkayastha, Prabir. 2023. *Keeping up the Good Fight: From the Emergency to the Present Day*. New Delhi: LeftWord Books.

Rudra, Ashok. 1973. The Politics of Legal Defence. *Frontier* 6.13, 7 July.

Sebastian, Manu. 2024. Professor G. N. Saibaba's Death is a Wake-up Call to Prevent Abuse of UAPA against Dissenters. https://www.livelaw.in/articles/professor-gn-saibabas-death-is-a-wake-up-call-to-prevent-abuse-of-uapa-against-dissenters-272292 (accessed 13 October 2024).

Shah Commission. 1978. *Shah Commission of Inquiry Third and Final Report*. Delhi.

Shankar, Shylashri. 2009. *Scaling Justice: The Supreme Court, Social Rights and Civil Liberties in India*. Delhi: Oxford UP.

Sharma, Dhirendra, ed. 1977. *The Janata (People's) Struggle*. New Delhi: Philosophy and Social Action Publication.

Shulman, Mark R. 1999–2000. The Progressive Era Origins of the National Security Act. *Dickinson Law Review* 104.2: 289–300.

Singh, Ramchandra. 2018. 'A larger jail called Emergency': A Naxalite's Diary on What Went on Inside Prisons at the Time. *Scroll.in*, 28 May. https://scroll.in/article/880259/a-larger-jail-called-emergency-a-naxalites-diary-on-what-went-on-inside-prisons-at-the-time (accessed 2 July 2025)

2

Aftermath of the Internal Emergency (25 June 1975–21 March 1977): The More Things Change, the More They Remain the Same

R. Sudarshan

India was under a state of Internal Emergency from 25 June 1975 till it was formally revoked on 21 March 1977. This was the only instance of an Emergency proclamation due to 'internal disturbance'. The two occasions when an Emergency was proclaimed earlier, on 26 October 1962 and 3 December 1971, were both on grounds of war. Soon after Prime Minister Indira Gandhi announced on 28 January 1977 that a General Election to the Lok Sabha would be held in March 1977, political prisoners were released from detention and censorship of the press was lifted.

On 12 June 1975, Justice Jagmohanlal Sinha of the Allahabad High Court delivered a historic verdict in the case of *Raj Narain v. Indira Gandhi*, which convicted the Prime Minister of electoral malpractice and struck down her election from Rae Bareli, with the consequence of banning her from contesting elections for six years. On appeal, the Supreme Court Vacation Judge, Justice V. R. Krishna Iyer, gave the Prime Minister only partial relief. He ruled that she could continue as the Prime Minister and attend Parliament but could not vote until the Supreme Court finally decided her appeal challenging the High Court's judgment.

Acting on her own (reportedly urged by Sanjay Gandhi, her second son, and his loyalist, Bansi Lal, then Chief Minister of Haryana), and without consulting the Council of Ministers (Cabinet), Indira Gandhi wrote to President Fakhruddin Ali Ahmed recommending that he declare a state of Internal

Emergency. The President signed the Proclamation stating: 'In exercise of the powers conferred by clause (1) of Article 352 of the Constitution, I, Fakhruddin Ali Ahmed, President of India, by this Proclamation, declare that a grave emergency exists whereby the security of India is threatened by internal disturbances'. On 27 June 1975, the President enforced Article 359 (1) of the Indian Constitution, as per which the right to approach courts under Article 14, Article 21 and Article 22 was suspended for the period of the national Emergency for all Indian citizens and foreigners. On 30 June 1975, the Maintenance of Internal Security Act 1971 (MISA) was amended through a presidential ordinance. After the Amendment, persons arrested under that Act did not need to be told why they were detained. The authority executing the arrest was only required to declare that it was necessary for the effective execution of the Emergency. The government had to review the detention only four months after the arrest.

According to the Shah Commission of Inquiry (28 March 1977–6 August 1978), which investigated the 'excesses' during the Emergency period, 110,806 persons were arrested, many tortured and detained without trial, causing their families untold suffering. Central and state government employees, numbering 25,962, were prematurely retired. Among the shacks of slum dwellers nationwide, 150,105 in Delhi alone were destroyed by bulldozers. There were 26,24,755 sterilisation operations reported in 1975–76. Under Sanjay Gandhi's Five-Point Programme, initiated in September 1976, compulsory sterilisation increased to 89,32,209 in 1976–77 (Sezhiyan 2010).

Even before the Emergency, the Defence of India Rules (DIR) and MISA had given the government extensive powers of arrest. Under the former, individuals had to be brought to court and charged, and could be released on bail. Under the latter, through an ordinance promulgated by the President on 29 June 1975, grounds no longer needed to be given to anyone, even the judiciary, for a person's detention. To this was added on 17 October 1975 the prohibition of bail for 'detenus' and the power to rearrest those whose detention orders had expired or been revoked. When MISA was first placed before the Parliament in

1971 the government had promised that the law would not be used against political opponents.

High Court Responses to Executive Actions under the Emergency

Many persons detained under MISA and the DIRs approached the courts for redress. On 25 July 1975, Kuldip Nayar of *The Indian Express* was arrested and detained under MISA. His wife filed a *habeas corpus* petition in the Delhi High Court. V. M. Tarkunde (Senior Advocate and Secretary, Citizens for Democracy) represented her.

The Delhi High Court accepted the plea and quashed the detention order on 14 September 1975. Justice S. Rangarajan delivered the judgement with the concurrence of his colleague Justice R. N. Aggarwal. They observed that

> there has been no suspension of the writ of Habeas Corpus (Article 226) in India. Personal liberty is sought to be regulated by law . . . the judicial power and self-restraint are but two sides of the same coin; in fact, they mutually support, do not destroy, each other. But if self-abnegation is allowed to masquerade as self-restraint, that may also amount to allowing self-restraint to destroy the judicial power. . . . We have endeavoured to indicate the availability of judicial review and also to indicate at least, broadly, at the same time, the limits subject to which it would be available at some length on account of this question being so important. What we have been at pains to explain is that the rule of law will not permit arbitrary executive action. (Delhi High Court 1975)

Interestingly, the government released Kuldip Nayar, hoping to prevent the High Court from delivering the judgement it had reserved. Having refused to provide the grounds for his detention, the government amended MISA to forbid the disclosure of such material. The government swiftly acted against these judges. Justice Rangarajan was immediately transferred to the Gauhati High Court. Justice R. N. Aggarwal, who was an Additional Judge, did not get confirmed as a permanent judge, and was reverted to his position four years previously as a Sessions Judge. The Shah

Commission concluded that this was a case of abuse of power and misuse of authority by the Prime Minister.

In another case, the Bombay High Court countered the government's actions under its emergency powers.[1] N. P. Nathwani, a former judge of the Bombay High Court, formed the Committee of Lawyers for Civil Liberties and convened a private meeting to be held at the Jinnah Hall on 18 October 1975 to discuss 'Civil Liberties and the Rule of Law under the Constitution'. However, the Commissioner of Police refused permission for that meeting. The government passed a Special Order under the Defence of India and Internal Security of India Rules, banning the holding of any public meeting where the Emergency was to be discussed or even referred to except after prior permission from the authorities. Nathwani and the office bearers of the Committee formally filed a writ petition in the Bombay High Court under Article 226 of the Constitution. The court declared that the petitioners have a right to hold the meeting of lawyers, restricted to invitees and to discuss matters regarding civil liberties and the rule of law. The orders refusing permission were also quashed. Justice V. D. Tulzapurkar wrote,

> Even during the Emergencies that are currently in operation, it is legitimate for any citizen to say that the proclamations of Emergency, which are legislative acts on the part of the President are unjustified or unwarranted; it is legitimate for any citizen to say that these Emergencies are being kept alive for suppressing democratic dissent and criticism and that these should be ended; it is legitimate for any citizen to say that the Presidential Order dated 27 June 1975, which in its blank form purports to take away the remedy by way of *habeas corpus* to challenge his detention even if it is made mala fide be revoked; and it is further legitimate for any citizen to say that parliament should meet to disapprove the Proclamation and the Presidential Order dated 27 June 1975.

---

[1] *N. P. Nathwani v. Commissioner of Police* (1976) 78 *Bombay Law Reporter* 1.

Unfortunately, when the Maharashtra government appealed, the Supreme Court stayed the High Court's operative order and the judgment.

In another case involving censorship of the press, the Bombay High Court ruled that the fundamental right to freedom of speech and expression mentioned in Article 19 (1) (a) of the Constitution is not a right created or conferred for the first time in the laws of India by the Article. It is a right under the Common Law of England which has been recognised and enforced by the courts in India before the Constitution came into force, and it has been continued in force by the Constitution.[2] Yet again, the Supreme Court stayed this judgement and its order.

The Gujarat High Court passed a similar order against a notice to the editor and printer of a journal that had published Justice Chagla's speech at a conference to show cause why copies of the journal and the press itself should not be forfeited. The judgement stated,

> The guidelines issued by the Chief Censor take a further stride and place a blanket ban on the publication of news, views, criticism and comments, however peaceful and orderly they may be if they are distasteful to the party in power.... Whether we are passing through an emergency or living in normal times, whether the uncommon situation in the country requires placing of restraint on the freedom of people, the guidelines issued by the Chief Censor and quoted above can never be upheld.[3]

In another case, Justice U. R. Lalit of the Nagpur Bench of the Bombay High Court released three boys, aged about 15, who had been arrested for possessing leaflets condemning the Emergency, declaring that the leaflets were not seditious.[4] This judgement served as a precedent for many magistrate courts across India to release persons detained in similar cases. The consequence for Justice U. R. Lalit, an additional judge, was that he did not get appointed to permanent vacancy (defying precedent) despite

---

[2] *Binod Rao v. M. R. Masani*, 78 (1975) *Bombay Law Reporter* 125.

[3] *Chunilal Vaidya v. HJ D'Penha* S.C.A.No. 141 of 1976.

[4] *Sunil W. Sarodi v. State of Maharashtra* Cr. A. No. 298 of 1975.

recommendations supporting his appointment from the Chief Justices of the Bombay High Court, the Chief Justice of India, the Governor and Chief Minister of Maharashtra, and the Law Minister in the Union Cabinet. The Prime Minister vetoed his appointment and he ceased to be a judge from 17 January 1976.

Other High Court judges were likewise penalised by the union government for defying orders justified by the Emergency Proclamation. Other judges who passed orders in similar *habeas corpus* cases met a similar fate. During the Emergency, Justices D. M. Chandrashekar and M. Sadananda Swamy quashed the detention of leaders of various political parties, including BJP leaders A. B. Vajpayee and L. K. Advani. Justice Swamy was transferred to the Gauhati High Court, and Justice Chandrashekar, who headed the Bench, was transferred to the Allahabad High Court. Twenty-one High Court judges were shifted during the Emergency for delivering judgements that defied the Executive.

A few High Courts had held that the Emergency Proclamation suspended the right to approach the judiciary to enforce the right to life and liberty under Article 21 of the Constitution. But this view was rejected by the nine High Courts of Delhi, Karnataka, Bombay (Nagpur Bench), Allahabad, Madras, Rajasthan, Madhya Pradesh, Andhra Pradesh and Punjab and Haryana. These courts had ruled that despite the Presidential Order, it was open to the detainees to challenge their detention on the ground that it is ultra vires, for example, by showing that the order, on the face of it, was passed by an authority not empowered to pass it or it is not in the exercise of the power delegated to the authority or that the power has been exercised in breach of the conditions prescribed in that behalf by the Act under which the order is passed, or that the order is not in strict conformity with the provisions of the Act.

Additional District Magistrate, Jabalpur v. Shivkant S. Shukla and Others[5]

The government appealed against the decisions of the High Courts. The cases involved forty-three prisoners, including four Members of Parliament. The Supreme Court's Constitution

[5] 1976 AIR 1207, 1976 SCR 172

Bench, comprising a majority of Chief Justice A. N. Ray and Justices M. H. Beg, Y. V. Chandrachud and P. N. Bhagwati (Justice H. N. Khanna dissenting) handed down an infamous decision:

> In view of the Presidential Order. Dated 27 June 27, 1975, under Clause (1) of Art. 359. no person has any locus standi to move any writ petition under Art. 226 before a High Court for *habeas corpus* or any other writ, order or direction to challenge the legality of an order of detention on the ground that the order is not under or in compliance with the Act or is illegal or is vitiated by mala fides factual or legal or is based on extraneous considerations. . . . Article 21 of the Constitution is the sole repository of rights to life and personal liberty against the State.

Justice M. H. Beg wrote: 'We understand the care and concern bestowed by the State authorities upon the welfare of detenus who are well housed, well fed, and well treated, is almost maternal.' The allusion to Indira Gandhi as the mother figure in this context must be noted.

Justice Y. V. Chandrachud wrote:

> The High Courts whose judgements are under appeal have, with the greatest respect, failed to perceive this limitation on the power of judicial review, though in fairness to them it must be stated that none of them has held that the declaration of Emergency is open to judicial scrutiny. But at the back of one's mind is the facile distrust of executive declarations which recite threat to the security of the country, particularly by internal disturbance. The mind then weaves cobwebs of suspicion, and the judge, without the means to knowledge of full facts, covertly weighs the pros and cons of the political situation and substitutes his personal opinion for the assessment of the Executive, which, by proximity and study, is better placed to decide whether the security of the country is threatened by an imminent danger of internal disturbance. A frank and unreserved acceptance of the Proclamation of Emergency, even in the teeth of one's own predisposition, is conducive to a more realistic appraisal of the emergency provisions.

Justice Chandrachud's deference to the Executive prompted him to describe the legitimate concern that the judiciary ought to have about the reasons given by the government for detaining its opponents as 'facile distrust of executive declarations'.

Justice H. R. Khanna, in his brave dissent (which he knew would result in denying him the office of Chief Justice despite his seniority), wrote:

> I agree with the learned Attorney General that if we are to accept his argument about the scope of the Presidential order of 27 June 1975, in that event, we have to accept it in its entirety and go the whole hog; there is no halfway house in between. So let us examine the consequences of the acceptance of the above argument. This would mean that if any official, even a head constable of police, capriciously or maliciously, arrests a person and detains him indefinitely without any authority of law, the aggrieved person would not be able to seek any relief from the courts against such detention during the period of Emergency. This would also mean that it would not be necessary to enact any law on the subject and even in the absence of any such law, if any official for reasons which have nothing to do with the security of State or maintenance of public order, but because of personal animosity, arrests and puts behind the bar any person or a whole group or family of persons, the aggrieved person or persons would not be able to seek any redress from a court of law. The same would be the position in case of threat of deprivation or even actual deprivation of life of a person because Article 21 refers to both deprivation of life as well as personal liberty. Whether such things actually come to pass is not the question before us; it is enough to state that all these are permissible consequences from the acceptance of the contention that Article 21 is the sole repository of the right life and personal liberty and that consequent upon the issue of the Presidential order, no one can approach any court and seek relief during the period of Emergency against deprivation of life or personal liberty. In other words, the position would be that so far as executive officers are concerned, in matters

> relating to life and personal liberty of citizens, they would not be governed by any law, they would not be answerable to any court, and they would be wielding more or less despotic powers.

Justice Khanna declared:

> I am, therefore, of the view that there is no sufficient ground to interfere with the view taken by all the nine High Courts which went into the matter, that the Presidential order of 27 June, 1975 did not affect the maintainability of the *habeas corpus* petitions to question the legality of the detention orders and that such petitions could be proceeded with despite that order.

And he concluded his judgement with these words:

> Before I part with the case, I may observe that the consciousness that the view expressed by me is at variance with that of the majority of my learned brethren has not stood in the way of my expressing the same. . . . A dissent in a court of last resort . . . is an appeal to the brooding spirit of the law to the intelligence of a future day, when a later decision may possibly correct the error into which the dissenting judge believes the court to have been betrayed [quoting the American Judge, Charles Evan Hughes].[6]

[6] In the *Puttaswamy v. Union of India* (2017) case, Justice Rohinton Nariman highlighted three significant dissenting judgments that later became the law: Justice Khanna's dissenting opinion became a cornerstone for the recognition of the right to privacy as a fundamental right in the *Puttaswamy* case. Justice Fazl Ali in *A. K. Gopalan v. State of Madras* (1950) dissented from the majority view that the state could detain individuals without trial. His dissent laid the groundwork for the later development of the doctrine of 'proportionality' in Indian constitutional law. Justice J. S. Verma's dissent in *Maneka Gandhi v. Union of India* (1978) emphasised the importance of personal liberty and the need for fair procedures. His views influenced the Puttaswamy judgment in expanding the scope of personal liberty and privacy. These dissenting judgments played a crucial role in shaping the legal landscape and were later recognised as correct interpretations of the Constitution.

Justice Khanna, in his autobiography *Neither Roses Nor Thorns*, narrates that he asked Niren De, the Attorney General, whether, given his submissions, there would be any remedy 'if a police officer, because of personal enmity, killed another man?' Justice Khanna recalls that the Attorney General's answer was unequivocal. Niren De said, consistent with his argument, 'there would be no judicial remedy in such a case so long as the Emergency lasts'. He added, 'It may shock your conscience, it shocks mine, but consistent with my submission, no proceedings can be taken in a court of law on that score' (2023, 85). Justice Khanna also records that he received congratulations from some persons in government for his 'bold' judgment. Niren De was one of them. Pulling aside Justice Khanna at a judges' party, the Attorney General said, 'Judge, may I express my admiration and congratulations to you for that great judgment'! (89).

Ram Jethmalini was among the distinguished lawyers who appeared on behalf of detained persons in the *habeas corpus* case. Before the judgment in this case was delivered, an arrest warrant under MISA was issued against Jethmalani, then chairman of the Bar Council of India, following his speech at the Palghat Lawyers Conference in Kerala on 25 January 1976. Several lawyers led by Palkhivala and Soli Sorabjee managed to get a stay on the arrest warrant. Jethmalani left India a day after the ADM Jabalpur judgment on 28 April 1976. He caught a flight to Canada and managed to get political asylum in the USA, becoming the first person to be granted asylum because of the Emergency.

The New York Times, on 30 April 1976, wrote, 'If India ever finds its way back to the freedom and democracy that were proud hallmarks of its first eighteen years as an independent nation, someone will surely erect a monument to Justice H. R. Khanna of the Supreme Court'.

It is said that the Owl of Minerva spreads her wings at the fall of dusk. Justice Y. V. Chandrachud, in a speech delivered on 24 April 2017, acknowledged that the *habeas corpus* judgment was flawed and that it was a mistake to uphold the suspension of *habeas corpus* during the Emergency. As an aside, his son, Chief Justice D. Y. Chandrachud, wrote in his judgment in the *Puttaswamy* case: 'The judgments rendered by all four judges constituting the majority in ADM Jabalpur are seriously flawed. Life and personal liberty are inalienable to human existence. They constitute rights under natural law'.[7]

Justice Bhagwati regretted the *habeas corpus* verdict thirty years later: 'I was wrong. The majority judgment was not the correct judgment. . . . I would agree with what Justice Khanna did. I am sorry (for the judgment)', he told *The Indian Express* in 2011. Bhagwati added, 'Initially, I did not favour the majority view. But ultimately, I do not know why I was persuaded to agree with them. I was a novice at that time, a young judge. . . . I was handling this type of litigation for the first time. But it was an act of weakness on my part' (*The Indian Express* 2011).

Constitutional Amendments During the Emergency

During the period of the Internal Emergency, when the Congress government of Indira Gandhi had more than a two-thirds majority in the Parliament, it rushed through five amendments to the Constitution.

The Constitution (Thirty-eighth Amendment) Act, 1975 came into force on 1 August 1975. It made the President's declaration of Emergency final and conclusive, meaning it could not be questioned in any court; likewise, with the power of the President, Governors of states, and Administrators of union territories to issue ordinances when the legislature is not in session. It expanded the Executive's power to remove recourse to courts for violating all fundamental rights, not restricted to the freedoms guaranteed under Article 19 before this Amendment. It clarified that the President could issue different proclamations on different grounds, even if a proclamation existed. These 38th Amendment clauses were repealed or revoked by the 44th Amendment Act (discussed in more detail below).

When the Constitution (Fortieth Amendment) Bill (that eventually became the Thirty-ninth Amendment Act) was tabled in Parliament, the Law Minister H. R. Gokhale said, 'the time has now come when we have to have a fresh look at the whole

[7] *Justice K. S. Puttaswamy (Retd.) and Anr. v. Union of India and Ors.*, (2017) 10 Supreme Court Cases 1, paragraph 110.

fundamental structure of the Constitution itself. The Constitution was framed years back when the situation was different. It was a document as a result of the compromise of different forces existing at that time'. He added that

> The Constitution is an instrument; it is a means to an end, and it is not an end in itself. If it is not to be an end in itself, as indeed it cannot be, I do agree that we all have to start an exercise of looking at the provisions of the Constitution to see that democracy, socialism, secularism, all these, are strengthened and adequately given effect to by a framework chosen by the people themselves.[8]

The Constitution (Thirty-ninth Amendment) came into force on 10 August 1975. The Amendment's primary feature was the insertion of Article 329A, which effectively removed the jurisdiction of courts, including the Supreme Court, over election disputes involving the Prime Minister and Speaker of the Lok Sabha, defying judicial review considered to be part of the 'basic structure and framework' of the Constitution. The Amendment provided that disputes relating to the election of the President and Vice-President shall be determined by a forum as may be determined by a parliamentary law. A similar provision was provided in the case of the election to either house of Parliament of the Prime Minister or the Speaker. Pending proceedings in respect of such election were made null and void. The Amendment envisaged a parliamentary law creating a new forum for the trial of election matters relating to the incumbents of the high offices, and the forum's decisions could not be questioned.

Another purpose of the Amendment was to protect specific legislation from judicial review. The First Amendment introduced the Ninth Schedule in 1951 to grant immunity to land reform legislation from judicial review. In 1975 the justification was that legislation for nationalising coking coal and coal mines for conserving these resources in the interests of the steel industry had been brought before courts because they were unconstitutional. So

---

8 https://eparlib.nic.in/bitstream/123456789/1508/1/lsd_05_14_07-08-1975.pdf *Lok Sabha Debates, 7 August 1975, Fifth Series, Vol. LIV. No.14. col. 59.*

also the case of sick textile undertakings which were nationalised in 1974. To prevent the smuggling of goods and diversion of foreign exchange, which affected the national economy, Parliament enacted legislation that was challenged in the Supreme Court and High Courts. All these laws – MISA, Representation of the People Act, 1951, the Representation of the People (Amendment) Act, 1974, and the Election Laws (Amendment) Act, 7 1975 – were included in the Ninth Schedule. The First Amendment had introduced the Ninth Schedule in 1951 to grant immunity to the laws contained in it from judicial review. The Constitution (Fortieth Amendment) Act, which came into force on 27 May 1976, added another 64 laws to the Ninth Schedule.

Election Appeal Taken Up after the Constitution (39th Amendment) Act

Even though the 39th Amendment precluded the Supreme Court from continuing its adjudication of the election dispute raised by Indira Gandhi's rival Raj Narain, it gave its verdict on Indira Gandhi's appeal on 7 November 1975.[9] The Bench comprising Chief Justice A. N. Ray and senior judges H. R. Khanna, M. H. Beg, K. K. Mathew and Y. V. Chandrachud, had started hearing the appeal in August 1975. Incidentally, these were the last five judges left in the Supreme Court who had decided the *Kesavananda Bharati* judgment. Four of the judges, except Justice Khanna (who agreed with the majority in *Kesavananda*, holding that the word 'amendment' could not mean destruction of the 'basic structure'), had written separate opinions in the *Kesavananda Bharati* case, rejecting the 'basic structure' doctrine.

Nani Palkhivala was the counsel for Indira Gandhi in her appeal to the Supreme Court vacation judge, Justice V. R. Krishna Iyer. The judge granted a conditional stay on the order of the Allahabad High Court, which permitted her to continue as Prime Minister. But after Indira Gandhi imposed the Emergency, Palkhivala withdrew as her lawyer. Indira Gandhi retained Jagannath Kaushal and Ashok Sen to argue her case. Shanti Bhushan, representing

[9] *Indira Nehru Gandhi v. Raj Narain* (AIR 1975 SC 2299)

Raj Narain (then lodged in jail), challenged the 39th Constitutional Amendment before the court in the same proceedings.

On 7 November 1975, the Supreme Court pronounced its judgment. All five judges wrote separate opinions. Chief Justice Ray, Justices Khanna, Mathew and Chandrachud declared the constitutional Amendment invalid, but held that the election amendment law was valid, reversing the Allahabad High Court's judgment and declaring Indira Gandhi's election valid. Justice Beg did not decide the validity of the Constitutional Amendment. He stated that the election law amendment was valid. Importantly, it was also noted that the 'basic structure' doctrine does not apply to ordinary legislation but only to constitutional amendments.

Chief Justice Ray did not directly rely on the 'basic structure' doctrine. He held that clause (4) of Article 329A, inserted by the 39th Amendment, in validating the election, has passed a declaratory judgment, not a law. The legislative judgment in clause (4) exercises judicial power. The validation of the election is not by applying legal norms. Nor can it be said that the election validation in clause (4) is by norms set up by the constituent power. He upheld Indira Gandhi's election by relying upon the amendments made in the election laws and set aside the High Court judgment against her.

Justice Khanna concurred with the Chief Justice's conclusion and upheld Indira Gandhi's election to the Lok Sabha. However, he relied extensively on the 'basic structure' doctrine. He said, 'This Court, in the case of Kesavananda Bharati, held by majority that the power of Amendment of the Constitution contained in Article 368 does not permit altering the basic structure of the Constitution. All the seven Judges who constituted the majority were also agreed that a democratic setup was part of the basic structure of the Constitution'. He added,

> I strike down clause (4) of Article 329A on the ground that it violates the principle of free and fair elections, which is an essential postulate of democracy and which in its turn is a part of the basic structure of the Constitution inasmuch as (1) it abolishes the forum without providing for another forum for going into the dispute relating to the validity of the election of the appellant and further prescribes that the said dispute shall not be governed by

> any election law and the validity of the said election shall be absolute and not consequently be liable to be assailed, and (2) it extinguishes both the right and the remedy to challenge the validity of the aforesaid election.

Justice Mathew took a nuanced view of the 'basic structure' doctrine regarding including the election laws in the Ninth Schedule. He said, 'Even after putting them in the Ninth Schedule, their provisions would be open to challenge on the ground that they took away or abrogated all or any of the fundamental rights and therefore damaged or destroyed a basic structure if the fundamental rights or right taken away or abrogated constitute or constitutes a basic structure'.

In *Indira Nehru Gandhi v. Raj Narain*, all the judges accepted the 'majority' verdict prepared by Chief Justice Sikri in the *Kesavananda* case. Most of the judges referred to the 'basic structure' doctrine to rule that the provisions of the 39th Amendment limiting judicial review, democratic governance and judicial independence, were unconstitutional. It was a landmark moment for judicial independence, affirming that the courts had the authority to protect democratic values against legislative overreach. The 39th Amendment's legacy is a cautionary tale about the fragility of democratic institutions and the need for vigilance in safeguarding constitutional values.

H. M. Seervai commented,

> Till we come to the Habeas Corpus Case, the attitude of the Supreme Court to preventive detention, even during an emergency, was almost impeccable. One would have thought that if the Supreme Court adopted that attitude during emergencies created by war or external aggression, the Supreme Court would more readily adhere to that attitude during an emergency created by "internal disturbance." However, in comparing two different periods of the Supreme Court's history, it is only fair to the Supreme Court to say that between 1964–66 and 1975–77 the climate had changed. (Seervai 1978, 75)

He mentioned some factors that might explain this change: the supersession of senior judges who held that Parliament did not have the power to amend the Constitution's 'basic structure'

(Justices A. M. Shelat, A. N. Grover and K. S. Hegde); the leaks about constitutional amendments intended to shake judicial nerves; press censorship even of judgments of courts; and an 'atmosphere of terror and fear' created by the mass arrests and maltreatment in prison (Seervai 1978, 75).

Soon after the decision of the court in the election case declaring the Prime Minister's election to the Lok Sabha as valid, on 10 November 1975, Chief Justice Ray constituted a Bench of thirteen judges to hear a review petition challenging the *Kesavananda* decision that Parliament could not amend the basic structures and framework of the Constitution. By then, eight other judges had been appointed to the Supreme Court. Justice Ray's appointment as Chief Justice had been controversial because he superseded three senior judges (who had ruled to limit Parliament's power to amend the Constitution in *Kesavananda*) to become the Chief Justice. A review petition needs a petition to review; it turns out that there was no petition to review in the first place.

On 10 and 11 November, Palkhivala argued that no case had been made to review the 'basic structure' doctrine. There had been only an oral request for a review and no sign that the courts had difficulty applying the theory. He narrated the consequences of the unbridled power of the government to amend if the limitation of 'basic structure' was removed. Justice Khanna, whose judgment coined the term 'basic structure', was to call it the finest performance by a counsel. Several observers believe Palkhivala reached the heights of advocacy not seen since. On 11 November, the Attorney General appeared and could not make the case for a review. Some judges accepted Palkhivala's argument on the first day, others on the next. On the morning of 12 November, Chief Justice Ray pronounced that the Bench was dissolved. The review of the *Kesavananda* ratio, that the 'basic structure and framework' of the Constitution was unamendable, was abandoned (Andhyarujina 2022). It is important to note that this was done within the first six months of the Emergency.

A New Constitution of India or the Constitution for Indira?

In October 1975 a paper titled 'Fresh Look at Our Constitution' was circulated with apparent official approval. It suggested a presidential form of government with the President enjoying virtually dictatorial powers. However, the government did not follow up on the recommendations in that paper. In 1976, Indira Gandhi appointed a committee headed by Swaran Singh to recommend constitutional changes, including a set of Fundamental Duties. The Report of the Swaran Singh Committee was followed up by enacting the Forty-second Amendment to the Constitution. The Amendment modified over 59 clauses and inserted several new articles, bolstering parliamentary authority and severely restricting judicial review. Articles 31, 39, 55, 81 and 83 were amended to limit judicial authority, while Articles 31D, 39A, 43A, 48A and 257A were introduced to expand the state's role in enforcing socio-economic obligations. The Amendment limited judicial review in cases challenging laws that purported to implement the Directive Principles of State Policy. It rendered them immune from judicial scrutiny, overturning the 'basic structure' doctrine.

The Forty-Second Amendment changed the Preamble by adding the words 'socialist' and 'secular' to the description of the Republic as 'sovereign and democratic'. The inclusion of 'integrity' after 'unity' reflected the government's anxiety over separatist tendencies arising from the growth of regional parties and movements favouring secession from the Union.

Originally, Article 31C protected laws that implemented the Directive Principles of State Policy specified in Articles 39(b) and 39(c), which concerned equitable resource distribution. The Amendment extended this protection to all the Directive Principles, granting them precedence over Fundamental Rights under Articles 14 (Right to Equality) and 19 (Right to Freedom of Speech and Expression). This meant laws promoting social and economic policies could override individual rights, effectively prioritising state interests over personal liberties.

In Part IV – A, the Amendment introduced a set of ten Fundamental Duties for Indian citizens under Article 51A: Respecting the Constitution, cherishing national heritage, promoting harmony, and protecting the environment. Though non-enforceable, these duties aimed to foster civic responsibility and align citizens' actions with the state's vision.

The Amendment expanded the government's emergency powers under Articles 352, 356 and 359: Article 352 redefined 'internal disturbances' as a basis for declaring an Emergency, developing the grounds for suspending Fundamental Rights. This redefinition allowed the central government to declare an Emergency in response to dissent, threatening democratic freedoms. Article 356 strengthened the President's power to dissolve state governments, weakening federalism and aligning state governance with central control. In Article 359 it allowed for the suspension of legal remedies to protect Fundamental Rights during an Emergency, giving the government unchecked power to curtail civil liberties. These provisions indicated a shift from a federal structure to a more unitary one, where states became increasingly subordinate to the central government. The emergency powers facilitated executive centralisation, effectively silencing dissenting voices and opposition.

One of the Amendment's most contentious aspects was its attempt to curb judicial review, particularly regarding the Supreme Court and High Courts. By adding Article 131A, Parliament granted exclusive jurisdiction to the Supreme Court to resolve questions of law involving the constitutionality of central laws, thus limiting the High Court's powers. Article 144A stipulated that Supreme Court rulings on constitutional validity required a two-thirds majority, intending to reduce the likelihood of adverse judgments against government laws.

The Amendment introduced changes to Article 368, reinforcing Parliament's authority to amend the Constitution. Article 368(4) and 368(5) stipulated that no constitutional amendment, including changes to Part III (Fundamental Rights), could be challenged in any court. This effectively insulated amendments from judicial review, undermining the 'basic structure' doctrine.

Moving Back from the Brink

Article 352 allows for extending the Lok Sabha's term during a period of Emergency. This provision extended the Fifth Lok Sabha term until March 1978. But just as she unilaterally declared a state of Emergency on 25 June 1975, on 18 January 1977, Indira Gandhi announced that the Fifth Lok Sabha would be dissolved and that a General Election would be held in March 1977. Press censorship ceased, and political prisoners were released. Indira Gandhi may have thought that the opposition was splintered and that elections would accentuate their divisions. She may have hoped that by winning the polls she could legitimise the Emergency before the international community and could also formalise Sanjay Gandhi's position in the Congress Party.

In the General Election held in March 1977, the people's verdict was more effective in acting against those responsible for the misdeeds and failures of the government than the judiciary during the Emergency. The judiciary follows election returns. Indira Gandhi's landslide victory in the 1971 election made the judiciary overlook her government's transgressions of the rule of law. The Janata Party emerged victorious, winning 295 seats. Morarji Desai became the Prime Minister, leading the Janata Party to form the government. However, the victory over the Congress party was short-lived. Still, the coalition government left a legacy by undoing many of the egregious amendments made to the Constitution during Indira Gandhi's regime.

The Forty-Third Amendment Act was introduced on 16 December 1977 (then called the 44th Amendment Bill) in the Lok Sabha and passed on 20 December 1977. The Rajya Sabha passed it on 25 December 1977. It came into force on 13 April 1978. It restored the jurisdiction of the Supreme Court, and the High Courts' jurisdiction regarding judicial review and the issuance of writs. It deprived Parliament of its special powers to make laws to deal with anti-national activities. It repealed six Articles (31D, 32A, 131A, 144A, 226A, and 228A) that had been inserted by the 42nd Amendment.

The Forty-Fourth Amendment Act also undid many changes made by the 42nd Amendment during the Emergency period. It was introduced in the Lok Sabha on 15 May 1978, and was passed on 23 August 1978, and by the Rajya Sabha on 31 August 1978. The President assented to the Amendment on 30 April 1979, when it came into force. The property right was removed from the list of fundamental rights and made a legal right under Article 300A.

The Amendment ensured that the power to proclaim an Emergency under Article 352 must be appropriately used and, after due consideration, subject to judicial review. Before the

44th Amendment Act 1978, an Emergency proclamation could be issued on the grounds of war, external aggression, or internal disturbance. Indira Gandhi used the internal disturbance provision. The 44th Amendment Act, therefore, introduced the expression 'armed rebellion' in place of internal disturbance. The President can proclaim an Emergency only after a written recommendation from the Cabinet and not at the request of only the Prime Minister. There was no parliamentary control, once a proclamation of Emergency was approved by it. But the 44th Amendment requires a special sitting of the Lok Sabha to consider disapproval.

Under the provisions of Article 358, Article 19 will be automatically suspended when an Emergency is declared based on war or external aggression. During an Emergency, enforcement of the rights conferred by Article 20 and Article 21 can no longer be suspended. Before the Act, enforcement of any or all of the Fundamental rights could be suspended when an Emergency was in force. This Amendment also overruled the Supreme Court's verdict in the *habeas corpus* case delivered in April 1976.

The 44th Amendment stipulated that any modifications in the basic structure of the Constitution can only be enacted if approved by a majority of votes in a referendum with at least 51 per cent voter participation. Article 38 was added to promote the welfare of the people in the Directive Principles of State Policy. Article 257A, which dealt with the power of the central government to deploy its military forces or other union forces to deal with a grave crisis, was removed.

The 43rd and 44th Amendments could be passed only after securing the support of the Congress party because the Janata Party government did not have a two-thirds majority in both houses of the Parliament. The Fundamental Duties, inserted by the 42nd Amendment under Part IVA of the Constitution, were retained. The additions to the Preamble were not altered. The new Directive Principles of State Policy added by the 42nd Amendment were unchanged. Specific subjects moved from the State List to the Concurrent List in the Seventh Schedule were not reversed. The extension of the duration of the President's rule in a state from six months to one year was not modified.

In November 1978, Indira Gandhi returned to Parliament from the Chikmagalur constituency in Karnataka, defeating her Janata Party rival, Veerandra Patil, by more than 70,000 votes. She was expelled from the Lok Sabha on 19 December 1978, sent to jail and released on 27 December 1979. The 1980 General Elections in India were held during 3–6 January. The Indian National Congress (Indira), led by Indira Gandhi, secured a landslide victory, winning 353 seats. This marked her return to power as Prime Minister. The Janata Party, the ruling party then, faced a massive defeat, securing only 41 seats.

Legitimisation of the 'Basic Structure' Doctrine

Minerva Mills v. Union of India[10] was decided on 31 July 1980. Chief Justice Y. V. Chandrachud, writing the majority judgement, upheld the power of judicial review of constitutional amendments. The judges, who concurred with the Chief Justice, ruled that a limited amending power is in and of itself a basic feature of the Constitution. The majority held that the Amendment to Article 31C, which prioritised Directive Principles over Fundamental Rights, was unconstitutional as it destroyed the harmony and balance between fundamental rights and directive principles. Justice P. N. Bhagwati, the fifth judge, dissented on this point.

Several cases after 1973 have legitimised the 'basic structure' doctrine, even though the ratio of the 11 opinions in the Bench comprising 13 judges in the *Kesavananda* case was unclear. But the doctrine has come in for criticism again by members of the Bharatiya Janata Party. The late Arun Jaitley, former Finance Minister of India, was a vocal critic of the 'basic structure' doctrine. He argued that the doctrine gives the judiciary excessive power over a democratically elected government. Jaitley famously called it the 'tyranny of the unelected', highlighting his concern that the judiciary could impose its philosophy over the people's will.

The Constitution gives the judiciary vast powers, more than most constitutions worldwide. Article 142 of the Constitution grants the Supreme Court the power to 'do complete justice' in any pending matter. This Article allows the court to pass any decree

[10] 1981 Supreme Court Reports (1) 206

or make any order necessary for ensuring that complete justice is done, providing the court with broad powers to make decisions that can fill gaps in the law and provide remedies beyond the limitations of statutory provisions. The exercise of power under Article 142 equips the judiciary to uphold the quintessence of constitutionalism, which is to place limits on the 'tyranny of the majority' in a parliamentary form of government.

Being mindful of the charge of the 'tyranny of the unelected', the Supreme Court recently laid down some guidelines for exercising its power under Article 141. In *High Court Bar Association, Allahabad v. the State of U.P.* [11] a five-judge Constitution Bench ruled that the court shall not nullify valid judicial orders passed in favour of other litigants in other jurisdictions. The powers of the court under Article 142 should not override substantive law. The court must respect litigants' substantive rights within its jurisdiction, preserving legal integrity. Article 142 cannot undermine the principles of natural justice. Litigants have a right to be heard before adverse orders are passed, including vacating stay orders, thus ensuring fairness.

Post-Emergency Executive Power

Many constitutional and legal provisions continue to enable the state to control individual liberties. The state of exception has become the norm, no longer an exception warranted by an Emergency. The Constitution allows for preventive detention under specific circumstances (Article 22). The National Security Act (NSA) and the Public Safety Act (PSA) grant the state powers to detain individuals without trial for extended periods, often on vague grounds like 'public order' or 'security of the state'.

The Unlawful Activities (Prevention) Act (UAPA) is an anti-terrorism law that allows the government to declare individuals and organisations as terrorists or unlawful, with stringent provisions for detention and limited scope for judicial review. Its broad definitions and powers can be, and have been, misused to stifle dissent. UAPA was substantially revised in 2008 in the wake of the terrorist attack in Mumbai in November 2008.

---

[11] 2024 INSC 150

Apart from changes to UAPA, making it more stringent, a new law was passed, the National Investigation Agency (NIA) Act, 2008. A separate cadre of the police force was carved out to tackle terrorist crimes.

The NIA had sweeping and vast powers and was directly under the control of the Ministry of Home Affairs (MHA) of the Government of India. Approximately 24,134 individuals have been charged under UAPA between 2014 and 2020. Data on the exact number of persons granted bail is not readily available, but there has been a gradual shift towards granting bail to UAPA accused in recent years. Only 235 individuals have been convicted under UAPA between 2015 and 2020. Most of those charged under UAPA remain in prison awaiting trial, and many are eventually acquitted.

The Armed Forces (Special Powers) Act (AFSPA) grants military personnel extensive powers in 'disturbed areas', including the use of lethal force and arrest without warrant. This has led to allegations of human rights abuses and limited accountability.

With advancements in technology, state surveillance has increased. Laws like the Information Technology Act and the interception provisions under the Indian Telegraph Act give the government substantial powers to monitor communications, often without robust oversight mechanisms. Under the Indian Telegraph Act, the government can intercept communications during a 'public emergency' or in the interest of 'public safety', terms which can be broadly interpreted.

The Prevention of Money Laundering Act (PMLA), 2002, has stringent provisions that allow confiscating property derived from or involved in money laundering. These provisions are excessively harsh and infringe on fundamental rights. The Act grants significant powers to authorities, such as the Enforcement Directorate (ED), to conduct searches, seizures and arrests. Critics argue these powers can be misused to target political opponents or individuals without sufficient evidence.

Some provisions of the Act violate principles of natural justice, such as the right to a fair trial and the presumption of innocence. Where the public prosecutor opposes the application, the court must be (1) satisfied that there are reasonable grounds for believing that the accused is not guilty of such offence, and (2) that he is not likely to commit any offence while on bail. Section 45 of the PMLA, which imposed these stringent conditions for bail, was held unconstitutional by the Supreme Court in the *Nikesh Tarachand Shah v. Union of India* case.[12] However, the government quickly promulgated an ordinance amending Section 45(1) to overturn the judgement.

Conclusion

The tensions between a 'sovereign parliament' and the judiciary's extensive power of judicial review began even before the ink was dry on the Constitution. The Statement of Objects and Reasons for the First Amendment, moved by Prime Minister Jawaharlal Nehru, explained,

> During the last fifteen months of the working of the Constitution, certain difficulties have been brought to light by judicial decisions and pronouncements, especially regarding the chapter on fundamental rights. The citizen's right to freedom of speech and expression guaranteed by Article 19(1)(a) has been held by some courts to be so comprehensive as not to render a person culpable even if he advocates murder and other crimes of violence. Another article in regard to which unanticipated difficulties have arisen is Article 31. Accordingly, the main objects of this Bill are to amend Article 19 for the purposes indicated above and to insert provisions fully securing the constitutional validity of zamindari abolition laws in general and certain specified State Acts in particular. [13]

The First Amendment overturned a decision of the Patna High Court striking down the Bihar Land Reforms Act, 1950, for violation of fundamental rights, especially the right to property in Article 31, without waiting for a decision of the Supreme Court. The other judicial decisions that it overturned were the Supreme Court's decision that the freedom of speech and expression

[12] AIR 2017 SC 5500

[13] Lok Sabha Debates (Part II), 16 May 1951, cols. 8818–8836 (Official Parliamentary Debates, Lok Sabha, 1951).

included the right to propagate ideas through circulars, striking down a ban on a communist journal in *Romesh Thapar v. Madras*, and the Court's decision that reservations based on religion, race and caste violated Article 15(1) of the Constitution, which prohibits discrimination in *Madras v. Champakam Dorairajan* (1951).

The early precedent of amending the Constitution whenever the Executive disagreed with judicial decisions led to the Fourth Amendment (1955) to clarify that the adequacy of compensation for land acquisition could not be questioned in court and expanded the scope of Article 31A to cover more categories of land reform. The Seventeenth Amendment (1964) further extended the protection of Article 31A to cover certain *ryotwari* lands and included provisions for compensation at market value for some categories of land. The Twenty-fifth Amendment (1971) introduced Article 31C, which provided that laws aimed at implementing certain Directive Principles of State Policy could not be challenged on the grounds of violating fundamental rights, including the right to property. The cycle of constitutional amendments culminated in the Forty-fourth Amendment (1978), which removed the right to property as a fundamental right by deleting Article 31 and introduced Article 300A, which made the right to property a constitutional right instead.

India may have entered the phase where the Executive does not need any formal declaration of Emergency or constitutional amendments to have its way. India has entered the era of 'autocratic legalism'. Scheppele writes:

> New autocrats are not just benefiting from the crisis of confidence in public institutions; they are attacking the basic principles of liberal and democratic constitutionalism because they want to consolidate power and entrench themselves in office for the long haul. . . . (T)he autocrats who hijack constitutions seek to benefit from the superficial appearance of both democracy and legality within their states. They use their democratic mandates to launch legal reforms that remove the checks on executive power, limit the challenges to their rule, and undermine the crucial accountability of institutions of a democratic state. (2018, 547)

In this chapter, it is impossible to evaluate the relevance of the arguments advanced by Scheppele to India. I will refer the reader to a comprehensive appraisal of the judiciary in contemporary times by Nandini Sundar (2023). She reminds us that the continuity in India of a 'state of exception' where the niceties of constitutionalism and fundamental rights do not bind the Executive is a colonial legacy. She correctly comments:

> India has also used colonial-era preventive detention, sedition, and emergency laws like the Armed Forces Special Powers Act (AFSPA) of 1958 on a consistent basis against its own people, especially in Kashmir and northeast India. . . . Victims of state-enabled and ruling-party-sponsored pogroms, as well as counterinsurgency operations (such as those in Delhi in 1984, Gujarat in 2002, Kandhamals in 2008, and the operation in Chhattisgarh, ongoing since 2005), have rarely got justice. In many of these cases, it is not just political backing but the deployment of legal "procedure" that is used to ensure impunity for perpetrators. (112)

The more things seem to have changed since the end of India's State Internal Emergency in 1977, the more they seem to remain the same.

References

Andhyarujina, T. R. 2022. *Kesavananda Bharati Case: The Untold Struggle for Supremacy between the Supreme Court and Parliament.* Lexis Nexus.

Delhi High Court. 1975. *Bharti Nayyar v. Union of India and Ors.* 15 Sept. <https://indiankanoon.org/doc/1149398/>

Khanna, H. R. 2023. *Neither Roses Nor Thorns.* Lucknow: Eastern Book Company. 30th Anniversary Edition.

Lok Sabha Debates (Part II), 16 May 1951, cols. 8818-8836 (Official Parliamentary Debates, Lok Sabha, 1951)

Scheppele, Kim Lane. 2018. Autocratic Legalism. *The University of Chicago Law Review* 85.2: 545–84.

Seervai, H. M. 1978. *The Emergency, Future Safeguards and the Habeas Corpus Case: A Criticism*. Bombay: N. M. Tripathi Pvt. Ltd.

Sezhiyan, Era, ed and comp. 2010. *Shah Commission Report: Lost and Regained*. Chennai: Aazhi Publishers.

Sundar, Nandini. 2023. The Supreme Court in Modi's India. *Journal of Right-Wing Studies* 1.1: 106–44. <https://escholarship.org/uc/item/313700c7>

The Indian Express. 2011. A Chief Justice of India Says "I Am Sorry", but 30 Years Too Late. 16 Sept.

3

Emergency and the Resistance Politics of Law: A Perspective from Andhra Pradesh

Kalpana Kannabiran

Exploring the 'Emergency Moment' in Andhra Pradesh

> Not in the manner of a dacoit, but more like a cat burglar, the Emergency crept into the political life of the country in the dead of night. The Emergency proclamation drafted by Siddhartha Shankar Ray with cunning barristry, was shrouded in secrecy with even important members of the union cabinet in the dark. Immediately after its approval by the then Prime Minister, it left No. 1 Safdarjung Road, climbed into a car and wound its way through the lonely Raj Path to Rashtrapati Bhavan, for the President's signature. A short while later, sated, it headed back towards the country. (Reddy, K. V. R. 1977, i, translation mine)[1]

What are the larger lessons of the 'Emergency Moment' for us? – in terms of our understanding of the state, of the meanings of life, liberty, protections and freedom under the constitution, the place of speech, voice and dialogue, and the *spatial rootedness* of justice (Philippopoulos-Mihalopoulos 2015). In this chapter, I focus on

---

[1] K. V. Ramana Reddy (KVR) (1927–98) was a political scientist, biographer and editor. A teacher by profession, he was founder secretary of VIRASAM (Revolutionary Writers' Association), and editor of its journal, *Arunatara*. KVR faced sedition charges and was imprisoned twice: during the Emergency, and as an accused in the Secunderabad conspiracy case. He is the author of two prison memoirs in Telugu – *Jaillo Moodnella Mucchata: June–October 1974* (Notes on three months in jail, 2011), and *Detenu Diary* (1977).

the judicial/legislative discourse around state action, that circulates in and around the Emergency Moment, using the methods of constitutional ethnography to understand 'the logics of particular contexts as a way of illuminating complex interrelationships among political, legal, historical, social, economic, and cultural elements,' as Kim Lane Scheppele argues. The idea is to draw attention to 'a set of repertoires that can be found in real cases and that provide insight into how constitutional regimes operate' (Scheppele 2004, 391). How might we signpost the constituents of the Emergency Moment with the Emergency at the centre – the midpoint in a manner of speaking? The idea of the *beforemath* renders the event and the *aftermath* intelligible and helps open out the historical trajectories and future directions of narratives, discourse and politics in the *longue durée*.[2] The continuum of the long Emergency Moment circulates around the event but breaches it in terms of memory, resistance, state practice, judicial discourse and futures (Hussain 2003).

Of critical importance in understanding this continuum is the aftermath – the rise of the Hindu right, immediately after, and, in a manner of speaking, from the embers of the Emergency of 1975, steering what began as a democratic resistance into forms of fascist politics.[3] This politics had regional specificities, and was, in the main, rooted, on the one hand, in the concentration of political power and interests in the regional propertied classes and the securing of Hindutva, on the other hand, through a violently stratified Hindu caste order that resisted any attempt at institutionalising social egalitarianism, with prominent leaders of the civil liberties movement, the Jan Sangh and the Janata party

---

[2] I borrow from Chinese American writer Yiyun Li (2022): 'In fiction as well as in life, oftentimes we attempt to reach backward from the aftermath of an event to the time before it, searching for clues and patterns'; 'If there is aftermath, there should be beforemath too . . .' (n. p.).

[3] The historical relationship between the career of Hindu nationalist ideology and Nazi propaganda, as also the Hindutva appreciation of Hitler and his *Mein Kampf*, is too well known and documented to need recounting here.

sliding seamlessly into the later leadership of the Bharatiya Janata Party. By the early 2000s, far from eschewing the authoritarian path represented by the Emergency (and far less redeeming the wrongs of Emergency), the programschrift of the 'New BJP' (Mehta 2022) under Narendra Modi, first in Gujarat and then nationally, used the Emergency playbook in institutionalising state and civic impunity in different spheres of national life (see Patel 2021), introducing denominational criteria for the determination of citizenship, eroding civil liberties and entrenching violent Hindutva in national politics.[4]

Against this backdrop, I focus in this chapter, on the specific ways in which the Emergency played out in one state – Andhra Pradesh (AP).[5] How do the issues highlighted in the national discourse on the Emergency compare with the specific experience of AP? What are the ways in which the AP experience informs and shapes the national debate? How might we piece together an assemblage of the Emergency experience – threading cases, fact-finding reports, court judgments and aftermath together, and opening out a vernacular archive that narrates the Emergency (and indeed the Emergency Moment) through the resistance to it, within courts and outside, always through the frame of law, because it is always a matter of life and liberty.

The specificity of AP needs to be mapped onto the Emergency, which was declared by Indira Gandhi on 25 June 1975. Less than two years later, in the Lok Sabha General Elections of March 1977, the Janata Party which took birth from a nationwide resistance to the Emergency led by Jayaprakash Narayan (JP), defeated the Congress and formed the union government with Morarji Desai as prime minister and Charan Singh as home minister. AP was one of five states in the country in which the Congress fared

---

[4] Narendra Modi was described early on by Ashis Nandy as someone who 'met virtually all the criteria that psychiatrists, psycho-analysts and psychologists had set up after years of empirical work on the authoritarian personality', with Nandy coming out of the interview shaken by the fact that he had, for the first time, 'met a textbook case of a fascist' (quoted in Patel 2021).

[5] All references to AP in this essay are to undivided Andhra Pradesh.

well, winning 41 out of 42 seats in the state. However, Neelam Sanjiva Reddy, the sole Janata Party candidate to win from AP was unanimously elected as the sixth President of India in July 1977, after serving as Speaker of the Lok Sabha for three months. Sanjiva Reddy had resisted the Emergency, joining forces with JP in 1975.

The resistance to the Emergency in AP was focussed on state violence and started within a day of Emergency being declared. In fact, this 'beginning' was on a continuum from the pre-Emergency resistance to curbs on free speech and political dissent that saw writers imprisoned and political activists sentenced to death, as I shall discuss later. Within the first three months of the new government taking charge in 1977, civil libertarians had persuaded the union government to constitute a commission of inquiry to investigate extra-judicial murders in the state – the only state in which this was done, and widely reported in the press.

James Manor's (1978) account of the 1977 election, especially his arguments that '[t]he Congress was aided by the fact that the rigors of the Emergency had hardly been felt by the vast majority of ordinary people in Andhra Pradesh' (794), and that Chief Minister J. Vengal Rao insulated the state from the potentially damaging initiatives from New Delhi (795), ignores the widely acclaimed work of civil libertarians in the state that called out the Vengal Rao regime's excesses during the Emergency, and fails to grasp the complexity of the processes at work during this period, a point I discuss briefly in a later section. Manor is not unaware that '[i]ndustrial labor and some tribal groups were directly affected and an estimated 800–850 persons were taken into detention' – 'in addition to about 250 people, mainly Naxalites, serving sentences or awaiting trial when the Emergency was imposed' (794, 794 fn. 26); that '[t]orture and murder were used by police in Andhra Pradesh, usually against Naxalites, to a degree unknown in any other state under discussion except Kerala' (795); and that the press was intimidated by 'police threats to editors and official pressure on nervous owners' (795). Yet, none of this enters his account of the deeply paradoxical election results when he re-asserts rather simplistically that 'such things were unknown to the vast majority of voters at election time' (795), focussing entirely on the power struggles and clashes of the landed and political elites.

Unintended though it may be, Manor's account of the 1977 election corroborates the civil libertarian assertion on the magnitude of state violence in AP during the Emergency. The Emergency was resisted in and through the courts by ordinary people, as I hope to illustrate later. The electoral success of the Congress in AP in 1977, in my view, cannot be explained adequately in terms of a popular consensus/public unawareness on the rule by Emergency in the state, nor can the symbolic significance of the single win by Neelam Sanjiva Reddy be ignored.

As there were no state elections at that time, the Congress remained in power in AP with J. Vengal Rao – who presided over the Emergency exceptionalism in the state – continuing as chief minister. In July 1977, the new union government tasked him with the responsibility of facilitating the probe against the repressive state action sanctioned by him between 1975 and 1977. He brought in advocate P. Shiv Shankar to represent his government (see Kannabiran, K.G. 2022, 99).[6] After the split in the Congress in January 1978, the newly formed Congress (I) came to power in the state in March 1978, with M. Chenna Reddy installed as chief minister, thus making for a seamless continuity in rule before, through and after the Emergency with Indira Gandhi at the helm of the party in government in the state, notwithstanding her defeat in the national election.[7] This long

[6] While he earned his stripes in this assignment and went on to become an influential minister in successive Congress governments and a staunch Congress loyalist, in an interview on camera three decades later for the documentary on K.G. Kannabiran, *The Advocate*, Shiv Shankar stated that (a) the encounters during Emergency were 'make-believe affairs and people were killed'; and (b) 'the [Bhargava] Commission felt, *and perhaps rightly so*, that it was sought to be scuttled' (cited in Kannabiran, 2022, 113, n. 5 & 6).

[7] K. G. Kannabiran filed his nomination in Medak for the 1980 national election when Indira Gandhi decided to contest from there, marking his resistance to the profound wrongs perpetrated under her watch during the Emergency. He withdrew shortly thereafter when S. Jaipal Reddy (Janata Party) and Keshav Rao Jadhav (Janata Party [Secular]) decided to contest. In what was her last election, Indira Gandhi won from Medak and retained the seat, giving up

Emergency Moment in AP resulted in the deep entrenchment of rule by exception in the state unlike in other states and cast its long shadow on successive governments. It did not end with the withdrawal of the Emergency, just as arbitrary arrests and detentions too preceded the declaration of the Emergency with revolutionary poets and writers preventively detained or killed in encounters in the late 1960s and early 1970s (Reddy, T. N. 1978; Manor 1978; Kannabiran, K. G. 2004).[8]

Rule *of* Law and Rule *by* Law

The Emergency Moment offers us an opportunity to reflect on the national and international strides of the relentless campaign against state impunity in the 1970s and its afterlives – as a way of re-inventing constitutionalism in the present. The judicial articulation of the distinction between 'rule of law' and 'rule by law' by the Supreme Court of India in *Navtej Singh Johar* in 2018, has been at the heart of civil liberties advocacy since the adoption of the Constitution in 1950, starting with the challenge to preventive detention by communist leader A. K. Gopalan: 'Rule of law requires a just law which facilitates equality, liberty and dignity in all its facets. Rule by law provides legitimacy to arbitrary state behavior' (Justice D. Y. Chandrachud, *Navtej Singh Johar*, para 5). However, it is also true that the phrase 'rule of law' encodes an analytical subtlety brought to bear on a fraught subject. Reflecting on the notion of emergency under colonial rule, Nasser Hussain (2003) points out importantly that while rule by law implies rule

Rae Bareli. (https://www.indiavotes.com/lok-sabha-details/1980/andhra-pradesh/medak/2911/27/7. Accessed on 24 June 2024). Jaipal Reddy rejoined the Congress after twenty-four years, in 1999: 'I left the Congress in protest against the temporary aberration of the Emergency; I have rejoined the Congress because I regard theocratic fascism (represented by the Sangh Parivar) as a very much long-term aberration and there is a remote chance of revival of the third front in the foreseeable future' (quoted in Swarup 1999 and Kidwai 2022a).

[8] For the ways in which the Emergency Moment found expression beyond the Emergency in different parts of the country, see the three volumes compiled by A. R. Desai (1986, 1990, 1991), K. G. Kannabiran (2022), and U. Baxi et al. (2024).

by the sovereign who enforces laws, rule of law suggests that laws themselves do the ruling:

> Eclipsing agents and action, the rule of law invokes a hermeneutic insularity, a ghostlike landscape where law rules and rules are law. . . . If the ethereal images of distance, mediation, and universality are embedded in the expression the rule of law, they are entirely opposite of the images associated with emergency: direct force, singular cases, final judgments, and so on. (29)

Moving this argument in a direction particularly relevant to the Indian experience of Emergency, Jaya Kasibhatla (2005) argues that constitutional emergency enables a specific form of 'democratic authoritarianism' where the arguments of both supporters and opponents of emergency are framed in terms of constitutionalism. In the resulting rhetorical impasse, '[t]he question of the legitimacy of the constitution is thus exiled from the debate altogether' (77).

Mindful of the complex intertwining of the law's rulings in 1975 and thereafter, the Emergency Moment in particular was subjected to a radical critique in the cases brought before courts in AP – in ways that interrogated the seamless continuity of colonial states of exception *and* the constitutional basis of democratic authoritarianism. Petitioners rejected judicial/administrative recourse to the palimpsest of exceptionalism rooted in colonial law, and in constitutional exceptionalism, pushing courts to re-frame the questions of life and liberty as also the meanings of state accountability under a rejuvenated constitutional commitment in independent India. Cases and incidents revealed the inner workings of criminal and lawless policing and opened out to view their strategies for counter-insurgency honed to perfection – surveillance, disruption, chilling effect, secrecy (Woodman 2021, 78–82).

Paradoxically, this period of heightened state violence also saw the unprecedented strengthening of social welfare and social justice programmes by a committed administration that acted autonomously and insurgently to further the rule of law and the goals of Articles 17 and 23 of the Indian Constitution. Between 1971 and 1977, but especially between 1975 and 1977, officers of the Indian Administrative Service in Andhra Pradesh led by the legendary S. R. Sankaran, focussed their energies on strengthening social welfare on the ground and tacitly mitigating the aggravated repression that had been unleashed by the police under instructions from the political leadership (Kannabiran, K. 2012, 217–30). The registration of the AP Social Welfare Fund in 1975; a slew of (136) government orders aimed at eliminating the micro-practices of untouchability in the state; and the drafting, passage and diligent implementation of the Bonded Labour System (Abolition) Act, 1976 (Central Act, 19 of 1976) speak to the ways in which the administration attempted to disengage everyday practices of democratic governance from an authoritarian regime. The success of this decoupling might perhaps account for the return of the Congress to power in the state despite its repressive rule.

In the sections that follow, I take a close look at the rule by exception in AP, drawing primarily on the work of K. G. Kannabiran (1929–2010), whose accounts of states of exception (Kannabiran 2004; 2022) stretch from the 1960s to the mid 2000s, and highlight the folding together of the norm and the exception in postcolonial India. There are in these accounts continuities in methods of (mis)rule, across different regimes that take easy resort to arbitrary rule, and the widespread use of the 'legality' of exception. Importantly however, across this political spectrum, he signposts the specific rupture a formal state of exception (like a declaration of internal emergency) brings to the interpretive powers of courts that deliberate on the empirical realities of justice and the Constitution in matters of liberty and life (or killable life, as it were) (Kannabiran, K. 2022, xxvi).[9] His disruption of precedents in advancing arguments put new axioms in place for a renewed

[9] Upendra Baxi (2024) also makes this important distinction when he observes that 'the Indian constitution does not contemplate undeclared emergency' (233), and goes on to examine the ways in which Indira Gandhi enacted the Schmittian notion of 'commissariat dictatorship', by claiming to stand between 'order and chaos' (235–36), asking the important question, 'What did 1975–76 do?' – in terms for instance, of birthing 'new forms of democraticity', 'human rights futures' and 'judicial activism' (238).

understanding of the rule *of* law – procedurally and politically – in and for the *longue durée*.

Emergency Jurisprudence in AP

K. G. Kannabiran identifies three aspects of illegal state action during the Emergency: arbitrary detentions; arrest and illegal confinement in detention camps ('eight to ten times more than official arrests admitted to'); and 'selective killing of those in illegal detention in encounters' (Kannabiran 2022, 90). His work on the Emergency cases addressed detentions, encounters and the death penalty awarded to Naxalite prisoners.

Challenging the Death Penalty

Two Naxalite leaders, Kishta Goud and Bhoomaiah, were sentenced to death for murder before the Emergency was declared. Kannabiran appeared in the High Court of AP against the death sentence and was active in the campaign demanding commutation. This was one of five political cases where the death penalty was awarded in AP in which he was directly involved to varying degrees – all cases that belonged to the beforemath of the Emergency. There was a vocal national and international campaign seeking commutation of their sentence led by Bhupesh Gupta, Chandra Rajeshwar Rao, P. Sundarayya, George Fernandes, K. A. Abbas, Mrinal Sen and Utpal Dutt, and supported by the American journalist Lawrence Lifschultz. Although CPI was an ally of Indira Gandhi during the Emergency, attempts by party leaders Mohit Sen, Bhupesh Gupta and Chandra Rajeshwar Rao to intervene with Mrs Gandhi failed: 'During the Emergency, she was not in a mood to listen to anybody, nor was she ready to show mercy to anyone' (Kannabiran 2022, 140).[10] Kishta Goud and

---

[10] Amnesty International's Secretary-General Martin Ennals raised the issue of capital punishment with the Indian Government for the first time in this case, through an appeal dated 22 November 1974; and on 5 December 1975 (4 days after they were executed) 'AI cabled its deep concern at the hanging' (Amnesty International Annual Reports 1973–74 in Desai 1986, 196, 201). This case went up to the Supreme Court which turned down the appeal: *G. Krishta Goud* (Justices A. C. Gupta and V. R. Krishna Iyer).

Bhoomaiah were executed in Mushirabad jail in Hyderabad on 1 December 1975, less than six months after the Emergency was declared. After this execution however, there was a sharp decline in the death penalty in political cases in AP – it was not awarded in any of the cases Kannabiran argued subsequently. In all these political cases involving Naxalite prisoners in AP, lawyers, judges and petitioners engaged in animated debate in court on whether 'political crime' (not carried out for personal gain) can be treated on par with 'ordinary crime' in matters of sentencing and punishment.[11] Alongside his opposition to capital punishment in political cases, Kannabiran defended death-row prisoners in AP and argued (with a fair measure of success) for commutation/acquittal in non-political cases as well – several of these in cases of gruesome crime where no lawyer was willing to appear, or where the accused were too poor to afford legal representation. The crux of his abolitionist position was that the death penalty had all the ingredients of premeditated murder (see Kannabiran 2022, 131–48), and there was no justification for courts to authorise the killing of persons under any circumstances. The politics of civil liberties in his understanding was capacious and guided by radical empathy in its articulation of the right to life.

Asserting the Right to Personal Liberty

On the question of personal liberty, the legal campaign against preventive detention that began with *A. K. Gopalan* in 1950

---

[11] This debate is reminiscent of B. G. Tilak's argument that agents like Khudiram Bose, 'though "misguided" betrayed no sign of "private grudge" or "mean spite", but demonstrated instead the "futility of ordinary methods of political agitation"' – and stripped of any self-interest . . . could in no way be categorised as an 'ordinary criminal' (discussed at length in Kapila 2021, 30). Kannabiran (see 2004, 27, 30, 55, 304–07) had studied Tilak's writing and the judgment in his case closely, since it often cast its shadow on the cases he represented in the 1970s, and certainly knew that the distinction between 'ordinary crime' and 'political crime' being debated in the 1970s' courts in AP had a long subcontinental provenance. For a discussion on this point in the case of *Intha Ramana Reddy* where Justice O. Chinnappa Reddy was the judge, see Kannabiran (2022, 142–44).

reached a peak around the Emergency in AP twenty-five years later. In the run up to the Emergency, Kannabiran argued the case of the detention of the Digambara poets Nikhileshwar, Cherabandaraju and Jwalamukhi in 1973 (*K. Yadava Reddy*). Justices O. Chinnappa Reddy and A. D. V. Reddy struck down detention orders issued under the AP Preventive Detention Act, 1970 as being violative of the constitutional guarantee under Article 22(5), and under Article 19(1)(d). In the words of Justice Chinnappa Reddy, it set right a 'retrograde step' and prevented 'the detaining authority from making capricious or mechanical orders. . . . It was absolutely essential for the detaining authority to found the order on clear and relevant grounds' (Reddy, O. C., (2008) 2023, 36).

And yet, during the Emergency, there were hundreds of cases of people preventively detained or arrested under MISA, starting with Advocate Pattipati Venkateswarlu on the day the Emergency was declared, and ending with the production of the fifteen-year-old Bhavani Shankarudu (who later became a leader of the Bharatiya Mazdoor Sangh) in court. Among the detainees were dissenters of all hues arrested 'even when the grounds of their dissent were valid' (Kannabiran 2022, 55): Naxalites, socialists, legislators from the CPI(M), activists of the Jamaat-e-Islami and RSS (Kannabiran 2022, 55–57; Manor 1978, 794–95). The challenge to the arbitrary and indefinite arrests revealed that the police were in routine possession of blank warrants to facilitate such arrests (Kannabiran 2022, 54). The cases Kannabiran brought before the court included *habeas corpus* petitions seeking production of countless persons illegally detained in camps and tortured – some of them shot dead in 'encounters'. The cases of custodial torture, custodial death, disappearances and encounters in AP during the Emergency were investigated by the Tarkunde Committee.

Investigating Encounters and Illegal Detentions: The Tarkunde Committee

The Tarkunde Committee was formed to investigate reports of extrajudicial murder of political dissenters by the police during the Emergency in AP in 1975–76, and was constituted by a diverse group of individuals mostly from Andhra Pradesh – all liberal intellectuals and advocates, all men – who were invested in the idea of India as a democratic country. Jayaprakash Narayan formally presided over the constitution of the committee and its announcement in April 1977 through the press, from his hospital bed in Jaslok Hospital, Bombay. The members from Andhra Pradesh were Balwant Reddy, M. V. Ramamurthy, Kaloji Narayan Rao, K. Pratap Reddy and K. G. Kannabiran. From the rest of the country, Arun Shourie, B. G. Verghese and Nabakrishna Choudhury. Justice V. M. Tarkunde was President of the Committee and Arun Shourie its secretary.

The press – the print media – supported the work of civil liberties in terms of reporting, investigating, facilitating investigations, cross-checking information received, identifying witnesses who might testify and standing with the committee in its commitment to protect civil liberties and end state impunity. The primary reports of this time are from the newspaper archives, English and Telugu.[12] In the era of an utterly compliant press and the rise of 'journalism as genocide', to use Suchitra Vijayan's (2016) words, the expansively inclusive approach of the publics to the question of the protection of civil liberties merits retelling. *Indian Express* and its Telugu imprint, *Andhra Prabha*, provided the most detailed coverage of every aspect of the work of the commission of inquiry. Between May and July 1977, reports in the papers detailed the terms of reference of the commission; published appeals to the public calling for witnesses to testify before the commission;[13] provided verbatim accounts of the animated debates in the legislative assembly between the opposition and the treasury benches on the fact that what are termed 'encounters' are in fact 'cold blooded murders' for which the government must be held

---

[12] Although Hyderabad has historically had a vibrant Urdu press, I have not been able to trace Urdu newspaper archives of the Emergency period, and therefore do not have information on the extent of coverage by the local Urdu press.

[13] 'Government Probe into Killing of Naxalites "Unacceptable"'. *Indian Express*, 18 May 1977, p. 5. 'Mr [Kaloji] Narayan Rao asked people to come out of their fear psychosis and give evidence against police atrocities so that the guilty could be brought to book'.

accountable; and asserted the need to give the commission powers to fix responsibility.[14] Members of the Tarkunde Committee held regular press briefings on the proceedings, and released interim reports to the press.[15] Kannabiran (2022, 95, for instance) also speaks of the ways in which journalists assisted in the work of the committee by tracing witnesses and gathering information from villages and neighbourhoods where people had been picked up, that would aid the committee, standing firmly on the side of truth even if it meant confronting a violent state.

The first interim report of the committee, based on extensive fact-finding, was released a month later and widely reported in the press.

> As far as Andhra Pradesh is concerned, on a rough count based on government statements and statements made by the accused in various conspiracy cases in courts, it would seem that 77 citizens are claimed to have been killed in "encounters" in this state alone during the Emergency. There is widespread apprehension that the "encounters" are staged, that in fact the citizens have been liquidated in cold blood by the police to terrorise potential dissenters in the state.[16]

In the first phase of its work, the Tarkunde Committee collected detailed evidence regarding three 'encounters' in which ten men (allegedly Naxalites) had been killed.[17] Of these the Committee had gathered conclusive evidence on two encounters in which four persons each had been killed; in the third there was adequate circumstantial evidence to challenge the official report of the

---

[14] 'Naxalite Issue: Panel Terms Assailed', *Indian Express*, 22 June 1977, p. 1.

[15] 'Cold Blooded Murder of 9 in Guntur: Second Report of Civil Rights Panel', *Indian Express*, 13 June 1977, p. 1. Banner headline.

[16] '"Encounters are Murders": Interim Report of Civil Rights Committee', *Economic and Political Weekly*, Vol. 12, Issue No. 21, 21 May 1977. https://www.epw.in/journal/1977/21/our-correspondent-columns/political-prisoners.html#

[17] 'Encounters' refers to fake encounters, i. e., extra judicial murder by the police with the active support of the government.

encounter. On the encounter in Giraipalli forest in Medak, reported to have taken place on the night of 24/25 July 1975, the Committee 'received evidence from a witness that he was no more than 50 feet from the four who were shot and was actually an eyewitness to cold blooded murder by police officials.'[18] They were tied to trees and shot. The four dead in this encounter were arrested on 15 July and were in custody till the time of their death: Janardhana Rao, Murali Mohan Reddy, Sudhakar and Ananda Rao. The eyewitness, who was also arrested and tied to a tree in the forest like the others, E. Bikshapati (1947–2020),[19] was let off and became the key eyewitness to testify on the details of this encounter:

> I was taken to Mulug police station. . . . In the evening at about 8.00 p.m. [24 July 1975] the police came . . . We . . . were all put into the police van . . . We were taken into the midst of the forest . . . The remaining four people were taken to the distance of 50 feet and were tied to trees by ropes from foot to chest, with the handcuffs on. A black cloth was tied over my eyes. The other four were also blindfolded. I heard S.P. directing to fire. I heard one of them refusing to 'fire'. Thereupon S.P. abused him in English. The people who were tied were raising slogans – 'Long live Mao, Long live the Revolution'. I heard the firing of guns six times. The S.P. approached me and said "you bastard you are lucky you are still alive" . . . After I was put into the van my blindfold was removed and . . . I found those four people with their heads hanging. . . .[20]

---

[18] '"Encounters are Murders": Interim Report of Civil Rights Committee', *Economic and Political Weekly*, Vol. 12, Issue No. 21, 21 May 1977. https://www.epw.in/journal/1977/21/our-correspondent-columns/political-prisoners.html#

[19] 'Toli taram people's war neta Bikshapati mruti: Girayapalli encounterku aayana pratyaksha saakshi' (Death of first-generation People's War leader Bikshapati: He was eyewitness to the Giraipally encounter) *Andhra Jyothi*, 6 August 2020.

[20] Testimony of E. Bikshapati submitted to the official Justice V. Bhargava Commission of Inquiry into Encounter Killings in Andhra

The second encounter took place in Chilakalagutta forest near Pakala lake on 31 October 1976. The four killed in this encounter were P. Rama Narsaiah (a Naxalite leader), Janaki Ramareddy alias Jani Reddy, Narayana and Srihari. The Tarkunde Committee heard from Jani Reddy's mother about these men being brutally tortured, their fingers chopped off and their bodies riddled with bullets. Witnesses spoke to the Committee of seeing the people being apprehended from their homes by the police; seeing them in police custody; and being transported along with them in police vehicles. The third encounter in Yellandu took place on the night of 5/6 November 1975. The two persons killed were Neelam Ramachandriah, a former Member of the Legislative Council and senior member of the CPI (ML) Chandra Pulla Reddy group, and Jampala Chandrasekhara Prasad, a leader of PSDU. A condolence motion was adopted by the Legislative Council on the former's 'demise': 'That this House places on record its deep sorrow at the demise of Sri Neelam Ramachandriah, former Member of the Andhra Pradesh Legislative Council and conveys its deep sense of sympathy to the members of the bereaved family.'[21]

On 15 June 1977, immediately after the lifting of the Emergency and the General Elections, there was a debate in the Lok Sabha on the release of political prisoners and the report of the Tarkunde Committee. The Union Home Minister Charan Singh provided detailed responses to members from all parties, in terms of state-wise figures, actions initiated towards release of prisoners, and inquiries into state excesses. The findings of the Tarkunde Committee led to the constitution of the Justice V. Bhargava Commission by the Prime Minister Desai to inquire into encounter deaths in Andhra Pradesh, after the question

---

Pradesh, on 30 July 1977. Quoted in Amnesty International, 'Political Killings by Governments: "Encounter" Killings in India', in Desai (1986, 248). Members of the Tarkunde Committee persuaded Justice V. Bhargava to visit the site of the encounter in the deep forest, which he did despite opposition from the police on security grounds. Details of this inquiry in Kannabiran (2022, 98–114).

[21] Andhra Pradesh Legislature. *Journal (Twenty-Fourth Session)* (From 29 January to 30 March 1976). Condolence Motion dated 18 March 1976. p. 69.

of whether law and order was a state subject was discussed. Members of the Committee insisted that '[w]hen there has been a gross violation of Article 21 of the Constitution and people have been brutally killed . . . [i]t is a premeditated murder of political dissenters. Therefore the central government must intervene' (Kannabiran 2022, 96).[22]

Public debates on state violence and police impunity in AP – among the people, in courts, and in legislatures – pointed to the fact that human lives (dissident lives, importantly) were placed at the centre of an understanding of democracy mindful of all the risks dissidents might pose to the government in power. These debates set a standard for democratic deliberation against which the decade 2014 and 2024 may be weighed. It also reverberates through mid-2024, when, despite a rhetorical continuity to its own 'seamless' history traced by the Congress Party leading the Opposition in Parliament, one witnesses the influence of this long resistance to exceptionalism and authoritarianism, in the Congress's resistance to 'theocratic fascism' (to use the late Jaipal Reddy's words).[23] Within this limited and evolving space, however, this democratic turn in national politics, incipient yet significant,

[22] The item titled 'Calling Attention: Large Scale Murder and Torture of Naxalites in Andhra Pradesh' (Lok Sabha Debates, 1977: pp. 217–24), reports in fair detail a discussion in the Lok Sabha on the Tarkunde Committee reports (see Kannabiran, K. 2022).

[23] The reference is to the Leader of the Opposition Rahul Gandhi's inaugural speech in Parliament on 1 July 2024, where the election symbol, the outward facing open palm, is re-valorised at this moment as the *abhayahasta*/*abhayamudra* – the hand that reassures and enjoins fearlessness and empathy in Hindu theology – connected in his interpretation to the open palm embodying similar values in different faiths on the subcontinent. At the time of its adoption by the Congress (I) in 1978, however, it was the 'panja', the echoes and symbolism of which are starkly different from '*abhayahasta*' in 2024 (Kidwai 2022b). It is important, however, despite the sharp shift, to register a caveat to the inherent limitations of this political strategy in articulating the complex and deep diversity in faith and practice of religion notwithstanding inclusive overtures, especially at a time when the political project of stratified citizenship is ascendant.

has also been haltingly and jaggedly signalled in courts, towards the middle of this decade, as I discuss in the next section.

Dissents – Political and Judicial

The Supreme Court in 2017 declared the right to privacy to be a fundamental right under the Constitution of India in *Puttaswamy*. In delineating the scope of this right, the nine-judge Bench resurrected what it called the 'Three Great Dissents' and unanimously affirmed (on hindsight) the rights of citizens to live lives free of surveillance and state interference, upholding the indivisibility and non-negotiability of fundamental rights, the right to liberty, autonomy and dignity. While a detailed discussion of this momentous decision is out of the scope of the present exercise, all three dissents bear retelling. One of the dissents so resurrected, and immediately relevant to our purpose, is that of Justice H. R. Khanna in the case of *ADM Jabalpur* (see Nariman 2021a: 147–91). The *Puttaswamy* court went as far as to say the judgment in ADM Jabalpur was 'seriously flawed' (para 119) and that '[t]he view taken by Justice Khanna must be accepted, and accepted in reverence for the strength of its thoughts and the courage of its convictions' (*Puttaswamy*, Justice D. Y. Chandrachud, para 120).

Justice Khanna's dissent in *ADM Jabalpur* flags the legal challenges mounted by conscientious resisters in different states in the country, and reiterates the arguments made before courts, whether or not the courts ruled in favour of the petitioners. As it turns out, the majority of opinions/decisions supported the Emergency, and the suspension of fundamental rights (in the high courts, as indeed in the Supreme Court).

Justice Khanna observed:

> I am unable to subscribe to the view that when right to enforce the right under Article 21 is suspended, the result would be that there would be no remedy against deprivation of a person's life or liberty by the State even though such deprivation is without the authority of law or even in flagrant violation of the provisions of law. (*ADM Jabalpur*, para 158).

This judgment was delivered on 28 April 1976, eight months after the first legal challenge to the Emergency in AP High Court. The Union and the states contended that in view of the 'Presidential order dated June 27, 1975 under Article 359 suspending the right of all persons to move any court for the enforcement of the rights conferred by articles 14, 21 and 22 of the Constitution, petitions for issue of writs of habeas corpus were not maintainable'. In particular, it was stressed that 'the right to move the court for enforcement of the right under Article 21 had been suspended' as '[t]he above mentioned presidential order was stated to be an absolute bar to the judicial security of the detention orders'. Nine High Courts in the country, including Andhra Pradesh, although undecided and far from unanimous on the remit of judicial scrutiny, nonetheless held that 'the Presidential order did not create an absolute bar to the judicial scrutiny of the validity of the detention' (para 140). K. G. Kannabiran (2022) reflects on this judicial equivocation and vacillation[24] in his discussion of the 'hundreds of cases' he argued in Hyderabad during the Emergency, of which *P. Venkataseshamma* was only the first.

The writ petition *P. Venkataseshamma v. State of Andhra Pradesh & Ors.*,[25] challenged the arrest of Advocate Pattipati Venkateswarlu under the Maintenance of Internal Security Act, 1971, on the intervening night of 25/26 June 1975. The petition was filed by K. G. Kannabiran, representing Pattipati Venkateswarlu's wife, the morning after his arrest. The President proclaimed Emergency on 27 June 1975, promulgated the *Maintenance of Internal Security (Amendment) Ordinance*, 1975, and the *Emergency-President's Order Regarding Suspension of the Rights*

[24] His experience of arguing the cases pointed to several instances of such vacillation – leading him to observe: 'In all the cases I argued, either my petition was dismissed or was referred to a full bench. I did not win any major victories, but what I did accomplish was an intense and long debate in courts in Andhra Pradesh on the Constitution and fundamental rights'; and in the case where blank warrants were recovered from a senior police officer in court and the officer publicly reprimanded by the judge, but 'the judge dismissed our petition. Although he knew it was an illegal arrest, he allowed it' (Kannabiran 2022, 54–55).

[25] *P. Venkataseshamma v. State of Andhra Pradesh & Ors*, AIR 1976 AP 1.

under Articles 14, 21, And 22 of the Constitution of India (G.O. Rt. No. 1650, General Administration [SC. D] 1st July, 1975). By the time Venkataseshamma's petition came up for hearing on 1 July 1975, all the presidential proclamations and orders were in place to hold citizens in a chokehold. It is important to recall excerpts from the judgment in the first case to challenge the Emergency in the country:

> Mr. Kannabhiraman, learned counsel for the petitioner, took time and raised additional grounds questioning the validity of the declaration under Cl. (1) of Article 359 of the Constitution and the validity of the First Amendment Ordinance in general and in particular clause (5) thereof by which Section 16A was introduced in the Principal Act. It is contended that this Amendment Ordinance is ultra vires of the powers vested in the President under Article 123 of the Constitution. This amendment "tampers with the basic structures or the forms of the Constitution' and is, therefore, void . . ." (*P. Venkataseshamma*, para 8)
>
> . . .
>
> Mr. Kannabhiraman for the petitioner, however, contends that a declaration under Article 359 does not authorise the making of laws which are violative of fundamental rights. Such laws are void in view of Article 13(2) of the Constitution . . . Any law which is violative of the provisions of the Chapter III of the Constitution being void ab initio, any action taken thereunder would ipso facto void and consequently the declaration made under Article 359 of the Constitution cannot stand in the way of the detenu approaching the Court to declare the detention to be illegal and without jurisdiction and obtain a writ of habeas corpus. (*P. Venkataseshamma*, para 27)
>
> . . .
>
> Mr. Kannabhiraman, learned counsel for the petitioner stresses that what are suspended by a declaration of the President under Article 359(1) are not the rights conferred under Part III of the constitution of India but only the right to move the Court to enforce the rights conferred by Part III. In other words according to the petitioner's counsel

> the fundamental right remains intact notwithstanding the declaration under Article 359(1) therefore the validity of the law on the ground of infringement of fundamental right can be questioned. The law which is void under Article 13(2) is non est and therefore the executive action purported to be taken thereunder is void Ab initio. (*P. Venkataseshamma*, para 31)

The writ petition was dismissed by the Andhra Pradesh High Court on 22 August 1975 with the court ruling that,

> neither the proclamation of emergency under Art. 352(1) of the Constitution nor the declaration of the President that the right to move courts for enforcement of any of the fundamental rights conferred by Part III of the Constitution is suspended, can be questioned in a Court of law. The proclamation of the President dated 25th June, 1975 issued under Art. 352 as well as the declaration of the President made under clause (1) of Article 359 on 30th June 1975 are, therefore, immune from attack. (*P. Venkataseshamma*, para 17)

A particularly interesting contrast is provided by two judgments delivered by Justice O. Chinnappa Reddy, in which Kannabiran appeared for the petitioners. The first was the case of the Digambara poets just before the Emergency, discussed earlier (*K. Yadava Reddy*). Speaking about the second – an Emergency case – Kannabiran (2022, 58–59) says:

> The case of senior advocate from Guntur, Jupudi Yagna Narayana was posted before the bench of Justice Chinnappa Reddy and Justice Jeevan Reddy. . . . I had a MISA case hearing that was coming up . . . at the same time that Yagna Narayana's case was to be heard. I asked him if he would argue his case himself. He was ready to do it, and said the law would be struck down by the evening. He felt, rather innocently, that since his case was to be heard by two progressive judges, they would definitely strike the MISA down. I cautioned him that what would be struck down was not the law but his writ petition. . . . The next day Yagna Narayana's writ petition was struck down. Progressive judges, without a thought, dismissed writ petitions of detenus. . . .

During the Emergency and after, Kannabiran steadfastly argued on the premise that, 'A constitution is a political document which gives legal content to a set of pre-existing rights, secured politically by peoples' struggles,' and did not accrue to citizens by virtue of their inclusion in the constitution (as courts, erroneously in his view, held) (Kannabiran 2004, 41).

Conclusion

What is resurrected by the Supreme Court in *Puttaswamy* is the history of the cases citizens brought to courts that asserted their right to life and personal liberty – notwithstanding their uneven reception by judges of that time. For, along with Justice Khanna, stands the unswerving assertion by petitioners and their lawyers in courts that fundamental rights shall not be suspended even under conditions of Emergency, a view that a miniscule number of judges across the country affirmed at that time. The minority view historically, in the matter of personal liberty especially, has presented the correct reading of the Constitution – as the Court pointed out in its resurrection of dissents, all importantly in the matter of personal liberty, retracing our steps right back to the inaugural constitutional moment of *A. K. Gopalan*. This also leads us to a more nuanced understanding of the tyranny of majorities and the consequences on citizens of such tyranny – connecting the Bench to legislatures and society generally. It is this aspect of *Puttaswamy* that helps us reclaim rights in the present that are illuminated by a resurrected past. Justice Rohinton Nariman, focussing on judicial dissent, observes: 'The dissenting judge reminds the people of India that they are lost only for the time being—the judgment in dissent will hopefully awaken a future generation of judges from the comatose slumber that the dissenting judge sees that the majority have fallen into' (Nariman 2021b, n. p.). Opening this out further, Justice B. V. Nagarathna, in her important dissent in the demonetisation judgment of the Supreme Court in 2023, reflects on the prospective significance of a declaration of the law on the validity of an action even after the action has been actualised – a reflection that bears immeasurable significance to the arguments presented in this essay:

> [T]his Court . . . has the competence to declare the law on a subject for posterity, even though no substantive relief may be given under the circumstances of a given case. . . . The effect of such declaration would apply prospectively. . . . [It] would only have the effect of deterring future measures from being carried out in a like manner, in order to save such measures, from the vice of unlawfulness.[26]

The 2017 eulogy of Justice H. R. Khanna by the Supreme Court of India (in *Puttaswamy*) and subsequent reflections on the value of judicial dissent, therefore, take us right back to the heart of the concerns K. G. Kannabiran voiced in his legal battles for the protection of civil liberties within courts especially during the Emergency, but also beyond those years: challenging Hindu majoritarianism in the citizens' tribunals on Ayodhya-Babri Masjid, 1992 and Gujarat 2002, and the Coimbatore bomb blasts case, 2006. His work on 'encounters' continued till the last case he argued in 2009 (*APCLC*).

The cases he speaks of in *The Speaking Constitution* (2022) and the large cohort of lawyers and human rights defenders he brought together to speak the constitution in courts and outside, especially in Andhra Pradesh, are catapulted into a rejuvenated articulation of the rule of law today, in the thick of the resistance to repressive right-wing governance, through the reinstatement of Justice Khanna's dissent, which is not merely symbolic or rhetorical. It is a re-statement by the Supreme Court, of the legitimacy of politics, of resistance to unjust rule, of the constitutional value of 'the courage of conviction', of the non-negotiability of fundamental rights even under authoritarian regimes, and even during a state of exception (whether *de jure* or *de facto*).

Finally, this resurrection of judicial dissents in *Puttaswamy* urges us to examine the relationship, historically in independent India, between political dissent and judicial dissent. For, political dissent has cascaded through the national election of 2024 in

---

[26] Justice B. V. Nagarathna in *Vivek Narayan Sharma & Ors vs. Union of India & Ors*. Writ Petition (C) No. 906 OF 2016, 2nd January 2023, Para 20.5. I am indebted to Upendra Baxi (2025) for drawing my attention to this aspect.

palpable ways. On the judicial side, three cases[27] illuminate this interconnectedness for us – the beforemath and the aftermath – and help us carve the space for politics in the judicial imagination: *Gopalan*, *ADM Jabalpur* and *Romila Thapar*. These cases visibilise political dissenters in a free, newly democratic state at one end; dissenters under internal Emergency at the centre; and dissenters in a state under a right-wing government where carceral governance and surveillance is normalised as everyday state practice at the other end, that is in the continuing present.

The Court's carnivalesque[28] resurrection of judicial dissent that had particularly to do with authoritarian practices of the state, is itself an intensely subversive act – a constitutional insurgency – that attempts to reinstate the right to resist, even as the surveilled land seems to shrink into a high security prison, under unbridled theocratic authoritarianism.

On the political landscape, the convergence of resistance has signalled a new grammar of politics – in several of the states, at the national level, and in the building of an expansive political community – that is diverse and plural. A consideration of whether and how these political formations or indeed these judicial moves will translate into and consolidate electoral transformations and deepened democratic processes in courts remains to be seen. Nevertheless, it foregrounds my central concern in this chapter that invites further probing: How do political dissent and judicial dissent illuminate each other on the question of personal liberty?

Through it all, 'the struggle for a better world . . . is its own reward.'[29]

---

[27] These are only three picked because of their immediate relevance to the Emergency Moment and the discussion in this essay. For a more detailed discussion on the relationship between political and judicial dissent see Kannabiran, Kalpana (2019).

[28] I borrow from Mikhail Bakhtin's work, especially on the *Dialogic Imagination*, as providing the sensibilities for comprehending the 'plurality of unmerged voices and consciousness, a genuine polyphony of fully valid voices' (cited in Dentith 1995, 40), as they emerge in court-talk around life and liberty.

[29] K. G. Kannabiran, undated note, c. 2007–08.

References

Baxi, Upendra et. al. 2024. *Of Law and Life: Upendra Baxi in Conversation With Arvind Narrain, Lawrence Liang, Sitharamam Kakarala, Sruti Chaganti*, Hyderabad: Orient BlackSwan, 2024.

Baxi, Upendra. 2025. A Legal Reckoning. *India Legal* (24 February): 16–29.

Dentith, Simon. 1995. *Bakhtinian Thought: An Introductory Reader*. London: Routledge.

Desai, A. R., ed. 1986. *Violation of Democratic Rights in India*. Vol. I. Bombay: Popular Prakashan.

———., ed. 1990. *Repression and Resistance in India*. Vol. II. Bombay: Popular Prakashan.

———., ed. 1991. *Expanding Governmental Lawlessness and Organized Struggles*. Vol. III. Bombay: Popular Prakashan.

Hussain, Nasser. 2003. *The Jurisprudence of Emergency: Colonialism and the Rule of Law*. Ann Arbor: The University of Michigan Press.

Kannabiran, K. G. 2004. *Wages of Impunity: Power, Justice and Human Rights*. Hyderabad: Orient Longman.

———. 2022. *The Speaking Constitution: A Sisyphean Life in Law* (edited, translated and with an introduction by Kalpana Kannabiran). New Delhi: HarperCollins.

Kannabiran, Kalpana. 2012. *Tools of Justice: Non-Discrimination and the Indian Constitution*. New Delhi: Routledge.

———. 2019. The Struggle is Its Own Reward. *Seminar* 721 (September): 29–38.

———. 2022. Introduction: Speaking the Constitution—A Biography of Civil Liberties in Independent India. In *The Speaking Constitution: A Sisyphean Life in Law*, ed. K. G. Kannabiran. xvii–lxi.

Kapila, Shruti. 2021. *Violent Fraternity: Indian Political Thought in the Global Age*. Princeton and Oxford: Princeton University Press.

Kasibhatla, Jaya N. 2005. *Constituting the Exception: Law, Literature and the State of Emergency in Postcolonial India*. Unpublished PhD dissertation, Duke University.

Kidwai, Rasheed. 2022a. *Leaders, Politicians, Citizens: Fifty Figures who Influenced India's Politics*. Hachette India.

———. 2022b. *Ballot: Ten Episodes that have Shaped India's Democracy*. New Delhi: Hachette India.

Li, Yiyun. 2022. In the Beforemath. *New York Review of Books*, 10 February.

Manor, James. 1978. Where Congress Survived: Five States in the Indian General Election of 1977. *Asian Survey* 18.8 (Aug.): 785–803.

Mehta, Nalin. 2022. *The New BJP: Modi and the Making of the World's Largest Political Party*. Westland Books.

Nariman, Rohinton F. 2021a. *Discordant Notes: The Voice of Dissent In the Last Court Of Resort*. Volume 1. New Delhi: Penguin. Apple Books.

———. 2021b. *Discordant Notes: The Voice of Dissent in the Last Court of Resort*. Volume 2. New Delhi: Penguin Allen Lane.

Patel, Aakar. 2021. *Price of the Modi Years*. Chennai: Westland.

Philippopoulos-Mihalopoulos, Andreas. 2015. *Spatial Justice: Body, Lawscape, Atmosphere*. Oxon: Routledge.

Reddy, K. V. R. 1977. *Detenu Diary* (Telugu). Kavali: Sarathi Press.

———. 2011. *Jaillo Moodnella Mucchata: June–October 1974* (Notes from 3 months in jail). Hyderabad: Jhanjha Publication.

Reddy, O. Chinnappa. (2008) 2023. *The Court and the Constitution of India: Summits and Shallows*. New Delhi: Oxford UP.

Reddy, T.N. 1978. *India Mortgaged: A Marxist-Leninist Appraisal*. Vijayawada: Tarimela Nagy Reddy Memorial Trust.

Scheppele, Kim Lane. 2004. Constitutional Ethnography: An Introduction. *Law & Society Review* 38.3 (Sept.): 389–406.

Swarup, Harihar. 1999. Homecoming after 24 yrs for Veteran Spokesman. *The Tribune*, 29 August. https://www.tribuneindia.com/1999/99aug29/edit.htm#1 Accessed on 24 June 2024.

Vijayan, Suchitra. 2016. Journalism as Genocide. *The Wire*. 30 March. https://thewire.in/communalism/journalism-as-genocide. Accessed on 15 April 2024.

Woodman. Connor 2021. Defending the 'Liberal-Democratic Order': The Strategic-Political Logic of Counter-Subversion In *Abolishing the Police*, ed. Duff Koshka (illustrated by Cat Sims). London: Left Book Club. 69–85.

Cases Cited

ADM Jabalpur v. Shivkant Shukla, AIR 1976 SC 1207.

Andhra Pradesh Civil Liberties Committee (APCLC) v. Government of Andhra Pradesh 2009(2) ALD 1.

G. Krishta Goud and Ors v. State of Andhra Pradesh and Ors (03.10.1975 – SC), (1976) 1 SCC 157.

Justice K. S. Puttaswamy & Ors v. Union of India AIR 2017 SC 4161.

K. Yadava Reddy, B. Bhaskar Reddy, A. V. Raghavachari v. Commissioner of Police, AP & State of AP, ILR 1972 AP 1025.

Navtej Singh Johar v. Union of India, AIR 2018 SC 4321.

P. Venkataseshamma v. State of Andhra Pradesh & Ors, AIR 1976 AP 1.

Romila Thapar & Ors. v. Union of India & Ors. Writ petition in public interest seeking the immediate release of activists raided and arrested in complete violation of their fundamental rights guaranteed under Article 14 and 21 of the Constitution of India. 29 August 2018.

Sessions Judge Nellore Referring Officer v. Intha Ramana Reddy 1972 CriLJ 1485.

State of Andhra Pradesh v. Intha Ramana Reddy and Anr. 1976, AIR 1977 SC 708.

Vivek Narayan Sharma & Ors v. Union of India & Ors. Writ Petition (C) No. 906 OF 2016, 2nd January 2023.

List of Abbreviations

AIR: All India Reporter

ALD: Andhra Law Digest

AP: Andhra Pradesh

CriLJ: Criminal Law Journal

ILR: Indian Law Reports

SCC: Supreme Court Cases

SC: Supreme Court

Acknowledgements

I am grateful to Peter R. deSouza and Harsh Sethi for detailed comments on earlier drafts. This essay draws on my larger ongoing work on the constitution-as-commons in independent India.

4

The Shah Commission Reports: A Tragic Moment and a Sinister Recurrence

Deepak Sanan

Introduction

What came to be called the Shah Commission was an inquisitorial body constituted under the Commission of Inquiry Act 1952. Here is its mandate:

> . . . for the purpose of making inquiry into a definite matter of public importance, that is, excesses, malpractices and misdeeds during the Emergency and in the days immediately preceding the said proclamation, by the public authorities, public servants, their friends and/or relatives and in particular allegations of gross misuse of powers of arrest or detention, maltreatment of and atrocities on detenus and other prisoners arrested under DISIR, compulsion and use of force in the implementation of the family planning programme and indiscriminate and high handed demolition of houses, huts, shops, buildings, structures and destruction of property in the name of slum clearance or enforcement of town planning or land use schemes in the cities and towns resulting inter alia, in large number of people becoming homeless or having to move far away from the places of their vocation. (First Report, March 1978, 1)

The terms of reference of the Commission, in a series of clauses, basically reiterated that the inquiry would relate to specific instances in the various areas just elucidated, with the addition that the Commission also recommend measures for preventing recurrence of such abuse of authority, misuse of powers, excesses and malpractices (ibid., 2). The Commission owed its popular nomenclature to Justice J. C. Shah, a former Chief Justice of India who was appointed as the Chairman (and sole member) of the inquiry commission.

The order of appointment stated that the Commission would inquire into complaints it received or matters that governments (at the central or state or union territory level) may bring to its notice. Its mode of functioning would follow the procedures laid down under the Commission of Inquiry Act (ibid., 2). The Commission itself clarified in its first interim report that it was meant to uncover facts and in doing so its role would be inquisitorial and not adversarial (ibid., 11). The Commission received around 48,500 responses to its call for people to write to it. Of these, 46,261 were taken on record as complaints (Final Report, August 1978, 218). These were further classified by the Commission into five categories (First Report, 3) on the basis of the Commission's understanding of each matter on three basic parameters: (1) whether they were within the terms of reference of the Commission; (2) whether they were of a serious nature; and (3) whether the Commission was in a position to inquire into them at its own level.

The Commission decided that if complaints were within its terms of reference (ToR), of a serious nature and within its capacity, it would try and enquire into these at its own level. In many cases, it called on the persons who could be considered to be victims or perpetrators or persons who otherwise might be in a position to throw light on the matter, to depose before it. Where persons appeared to be likely to be affected (adversely) by the inquiry, they were given an opportunity to call their own witnesses, cross-examine witnesses from the other side or advance arguments in support of their position. The Commission allowed persons deposing before it or those who were in effect called to defend themselves, to be represented by legal counsel (ibid., 3). Some of the persons called chose not to appear; or having appeared, raised objections to the Commission; or chose not to appear after a certain stage. Among the prominent persons in this category were Indira Gandhi, the former (and later again) Prime Minister, and some other persons close to her.

The actual classification of complaints into the five categories decided by the Commission was not necessarily on the lines it had envisaged. It became a somewhat discretionary exercise based on the understanding of the staff deployed for this purpose (Final Report, 220). Still, it enabled the Commission to complete its work in the tight time frame that was set for it. Of the complaints taken on record, 8,432 were not covered by its ToR. However, since 2,150 of these were considered to be serious, these were referred to the relevant government for further inquiry and action (218). The remaining 37,829 complaints were taken up by the Commission to be dealt with either at its own level or by reference to the relevant government at central, state or union territory level. For purposes of further understanding the nature of the complaints, in terms of the excesses mentioned in its ToR, the Commission placed all complaints into four categories: (1) those related to abuse of authority or misuse of power (15,990); (2) misuse of powers of arrest/detention and maltreatment of those detained (6,754); (3) compulsion and use of force in the Family Planning Programme (11,046); and (4) indiscriminate, high-handed or unauthorised demolitions (4,039). Instances of different kinds of excesses were reported from virtually every state and union territory in India, although the distribution was not an even spread. More complaints were received from the larger states, especially in the north, and relatively few complaints from the small states and union territories in the periphery of the country (Final report, tables on 218–20).

Of these complaints, as many as 28,771 (76 per cent) were sent to relevant governments for inquiry and action at their own level. Another 6,716 (almost 18 per cent) were also sent to relevant governments for holding proper inquiries and reporting back to the Commission. (In most cases, this did not happen by the time the Commission wound up after submitting its third and final report in August 1978.) In effect, there is data, about the extent to which the complaints were found to have been proved or not, only with respect to 2,010 (a little over 5 per cent of the total) complaints which were actually dealt with by the Commission at its own level. This showed that 586 complaints (29 per cent) were considered to have been wholly proved and 429 (21 per cent) were partially proved. (All percentages in this paragraph are calculated from information contained in Chapter XXIII of the Final Report, 2018–227).

If this can be considered a representative sample, it can be extrapolated to the total number of complaints that were considered to be within the ToR of the Commission. It would mean that there was some substance in 50 per cent of the complaints about excesses committed by functionaries of the state in the period that began a few days before the Emergency was imposed in June 1975, till it was lifted in March 1977. The Commission's findings are contained in three volumes: the first interim report submitted in March 1978, a second interim report in April 1978, and a final report in August 1978.

The Tragic Moment

The Shah Commission Reports are, at one level, a stark chronicle of a dark moment in India's much vaunted post-independence experiment with democracy. It is a narrative of occurrences of a time when the state donned an excessively authoritarian mantle and details a sombre sample of the excesses perpetrated, of the perpetrators and the victims. At another level, it is a lament, an attempt at explaining the systemic collapse of norms and values; and included some naïve suggestions to forestall such events, and a forlorn, unstated hope that such interludes could be avoided in the future.

The Emergency was Indira Gandhi's shock-and-awe response to the imminent threat of being forced out of office by an ongoing countrywide agitation which had been bolstered by the Allahabad High Court decision holding her guilty of electoral malpractice. It did not appear to have been thought through in any great detail barring the immediate agenda of muzzling the press, arresting and detaining leaders of the political opposition, and throttling any other source of dissent. It grew beyond ensuring this prime objective to the pursuit of a perverted vision of a country. This involved two ideas: halting the rapid growth of its population through a massive campaign to sterilise its adult citizens, and of beautiful cities where slums had been banished from sight. Accompanying all this was the abuse of authority to appoint loyalists to positions where they could be of use, and the harassment of all those who might fall foul of the powerful, for any reason at all!

Most arrests during the Emergency were carried out under two statutes, the Defence of India Act and Defence of India Rules (DISIR), and the Maintenance of Internal Security Act (MISA). The DISIR, enacted in 1962 in the wake of the Sino-Indian conflict, was draconian enough to justify almost any detention. MISA was amended in 1975 to make it even more difficult to question a detention in a court of law. It was no longer necessary to communicate to affected persons the grounds on which they were being arrested. The information could be declared confidential and not disclosed to the arrested, who would be denied an opportunity to be represented by legal counsel. In practice those in authority often did not even bother to specify any grounds for arrest while issuing detention orders. In many other cases these grounds were fabricated. As many as 34,988 arrests were made under MISA and 75,818 under DISIR during the Emergency. It was common practice to pick up individuals under these draconian statutes so that they would not be able to avail of commonly available judicial remedies even when alleged crimes were punishable under normal penal provisions. It was also common practice to rearrest individuals who managed to secure relief from the courts. Maltreatment of political prisoners was not unusual in overcrowded jails where they were held in close proximity to those accused or convicted of various crimes.

The Emergency saw the launch of a crash programme to intensify family planning. The Health Minister, Karan Singh, wrote a letter on 10 October 1975, stating that the population problem is so serious that some element of compulsion, in the larger national interest, was now necessary and a judicious mix of incentives and disincentives was desirable (Final Report, 153). The cafeteria approach to family planning was more or less abandoned in favour of sterilisation. The National Population Policy of 16 April 1976 encouraged states to legislate compulsory sterilisation after the birth of three children. The countrywide target for sterilisation in 1975–76 was 2.485 million and the achievement reported was 107 per cent. In 1976–77, the target was enhanced substantially to 4.255 million and the achievement reported was an astonishing 190 per cent! This level of sterilisation was obviously not voluntary. A slew of measures was adopted in various states trying to show performance to the powers that be in Delhi. These included denial of increments or promotion to government employees at various levels, denial of cards for entitlements under the public distribution system, and denial of various other services or approvals required from government; and this, in various places, extended to the use of coercive means to carry out forcible sterilisation.

Demolition drives were a countrywide phenomenon during the Emergency, but the scale in Delhi was unmatched. In the 30 months preceding the Emergency 1,800 structures were reported to have been demolished in Delhi, while this figure was 1,50,105 during the Emergency (Second Interim Report, 78). Three agencies were responsible for demolition in Delhi. The Delhi Development Authority (DDA), the New Delhi Municipal Committee (NDMC) and the Municipal Corporation of Delhi (MCD). As each agency vied to be seen as a superior force of destruction, due process and the rule of law became unnecessary and dispensable hindrances. Tens of thousands were evicted and dislocated to places with few or non-existent amenities and at great distances from where they had previously earned their livelihoods. In the most infamous instance of forcible demolition, police firing resulted in six officially acknowledged deaths in the Turkman Gate area of Delhi.

Government employees were expected to show exemplary levels of motivation, enthusiasm and efficiency in performing their duties, especially in relation to the core priorities of the government outlined above. Those considered to be recalcitrant (or who otherwise attracted the ire of the powerful) faced a number of punitive actions: 25,962 employees were compulsorily retired, 4,534 were terminated or dismissed, and 8,537 were superseded when they were due for promotion (Final Report, 36–38).

The Commission's views on why the Emergency resulted in such abuse of authority and excesses are expressed at many places in its Reports. At one stage it says that that there was a widespread subversion of the administration by those responsible: the politicians and the civil servants. Why did various persons give out orders that were ethically, morally or legally wrong, and why did others carry out orders that were beyond their call of duty? What was their motivation?

The Commission considered those for whom there was personal gain or advancement in performing acts that were ethically or morally (and often legally) questionable, as most responsible and deserving of punitive action. The Commission refrained from explicitly naming persons to be included in this category, since for various reasons it was not able to give adequate opportunity to them to defend themselves. However, there are sufficient indications about the persons who could be classified as those who acted for personal gain.

Apart from Indira Gandhi and her son Sanjay Gandhi, there were numerous politicians who were seen as having played important roles. In the central government, the most prominent were V. C. Shukla (Minister for Information and Broadcasting), Om Mehta (Minister of State for Home Affairs), Pranab Mukherjee (Minister of State for Banking and Revenue), Bansi Lal (initially Chief Minister of Haryana and later Defence Minister in the Union Cabinet) and Karan Singh (Health Minister). At the state level, numerous Chief Minsters like P. C. Sethi in Madhya Pradesh were seen as proactive in trying to curry favour with the centre, and at least one Home Minister (K. Karunakaran in Kerala) repeatedly overruled his civil servants in confirming detentions on unjustified grounds.

Among civil servants who went out of their way to please their political masters, the names that repeatedly crop up in the Reports include R. K. Dhawan (Additional Private Secretary to the Prime Minister), Krishan Chand (Lieutenant Governor [LG] of Delhi) and Navin Chawla (Private Secretary to the LG). Others of similar bent included P. P. Nayar (Joint Secretary, Justice), N. K. Singh (SA to the Commerce Minister), Jagmohan (Vice Chairman DDA), B. R. Tamta (MCD), Ailawadi (Member Secretary, NDMC), R. S. Mehtani (Private Secretary to Bansi Lal), D. Sen (Director, CBI), P. S. Bhinder (DIG Police, Delhi) and K. S. Bajwa (SP, CID Delhi). Numerous District Magistrates and police officers also went well beyond the call of duty in the enthusiasm and zeal they displayed in implementing questionable orders. Some of these persons may even have had a psychological bent that lent itself to malice or cruelty. The power they could wield in the Emergency presented an opportunity to pander to this aspect of their personalities. Examples of this would include uncalled for detention, refusal to grant parole even in case of serious illness or death of loved ones, pursuit of forced sterilisation, and eviction and demolition with scant regard for law and human rights. An instance that stands out is the allegation that Navin Chawla suggested that political prisoners be housed in sheds where the asbestos roofing would cause them to 'bake' in the heat and make them more amenable to recant their opposition to the regime!

It is this select group that saw personal gain in carrying out every order without regard to its legality and in anticipating the wishes of their masters, who most 'indulge[d] in short circuiting of administrative procedures, level jumping in chains of command and non-conformity with standard administrative norms and values' (Second Interim Report, 143, para 15.20). It is not surprising that both amongst politicians and civil servants, it was the relatively junior personnel who figured most in the list of names mentioned above, since they were the ones in a position to advance rather than those senior to them who had possibly reached the highest level they could aspire to.

It is also this group that was the initial progenitor of the all-pervading fear of adverse consequences that spread through the ranks of the administrative machinery. The fear was often genuine, generated by the threat to use the draconian MISA against the obdurate. It was furthered by the actions of those placed at a senior level who were often active participants (people like Krishan Chand, LG of Delhi). Others (like many cabinet ministers and secretaries of ministries/departments) became passive messengers or bystanders to the malign directions or orders which ought to have been resisted. This failure to stand up and question at a senior level furthered the fear syndrome. Self-protection was certainly one factor at play in choosing this easy way out. Another possibly was the fact that proximity to those in a position of authority breeds a certain personal familiarity with them that makes it difficult to demur or resist their wishes even when these are questionable from an ethical or moral or even legal standpoint. This phenomenon may also have been at play in the case of some close advisors to Mrs Gandhi who simply chose to move out of her immediate circle in this period and not visibly oppose the abuse of authority.

The absence of sanction or censure (and instead even appreciation) of wrongdoing by those at a junior level engaging in questionable actions, very soon resulted in arbitrary acts and abuse of authority becoming an acceptable norm. At the very least, unquestioning implementation or complicity in such actions became general practice. 'It came to be accepted as a new propriety and a new morality' (Final Report, 229). A very large number of district magistrates across India could, therefore, order unjustified detentions and oversee the demolitions and sterilisation campaigns which caused untold suffering, without experiencing any moral or ethical qualms. Senior officers in central ministries and state secretariats were able to turn a blind eye to the excesses even as they facilitated unjustified actions and even applauded excessive zeal or pulled up those who were more circumspect in their efforts in the field. In the Health Ministry, Gian Prakash (Secretary) and Sarla Grewal (Joint Secretary) were at the forefront of this kind of monitoring of family planning targets while seemingly oblivious to the coercive methods and forced sterilisations being carried out at various places.

It was not all bleak. The Commission singled out for special mention R. L. Misra, Joint Secretary in the Ministry of Home Affairs, as one who 'never gave in to the wrongdoings indulged in by the Delhi Administration even when his own Secretary had thrown in the towel' (Second Report, 143). There were others who tried to point out that proposed actions were not appropriate without necessarily taking up cudgels to defend right action. The Banking Secretary N. C. Sen Gupta who tried to resist the appointments in the RBI and in certain nationalised banks, was amongst them. The Commission also noted that 'even during the emergency there were several functionaries in the Government who stood up for what was right though the examples under this category were more in evidence among the lower functionaries than among the higher echelons' (Second Report, 144). But these were not the role models that the fence-sitters would choose to follow when the incentives favoured the norms of obedience, complicity and even 'anticipating the wishes of those in authority, however, illegal, immoral and incongruous with the basic tenets of administration such conduct may have been' (Final Report, 229).

The behaviour of those in positions of authority at various levels during the Emergency were a classic illustration of how theories of ethics tend to explain the why and how of ethically questionable behaviour becoming widespread in organisations and societies. Signals from the top can result in those who are relatively lower down the ladder seizing their chance to engage in level jumping. As the wrongdoers appear to prosper, a combination of fear of authority, desire to please and a normative change in the organisation (and in society as a whole) result in a fading of ethical concern – from a possible perception of wrong to complete insensitivity to such issues. Both self-preservation and self-promotion require adherence to these newly minted norms of propriety and morality, and almost everyone becomes part of the ethically blind herd, ushering in Hannah Arendt's justly famous characterisation of 'the banality of evil'.

The Commission made an attempt at addressing, at numerous places in the Reports, the ToR related to avoiding a recurrence of what had happened in the Emergency. Its prescriptions though appeared rather naive in the light of the ills it had diagnosed. It says at one place, '. . . in the final analysis this country will be governed well or ill by the competence and character of the government officer' (Second Report, 144). It highlighted the unhealthy commitment to the politician in power, and pointed out that government servants become committed to government when they instead need to be committed to the Constitution and the rule of law, and policies and programmes in conformity with these. Having said this, it wants government itself to safeguard/ protect officials from harassment and devise standard operating procedures for action in different situations! The Commission possibly was neither equipped nor given the time to make a detailed analysis for recommendations that could suggest the institutional architecture for sustaining democracy in line with the ideals of the Constitution. It ends its limited peroration on the subject with a pious hope: 'Solutions will be complex but the right solutions may be found if the exercise is undertaken at various levels with a steadfast desire and determination to reach them' (Final Report, 230).

The Sinister Recurrence

Reading the Commission Reports, almost five decades later, is a surreal experience. There is an uncanny resemblance to actions and events we are witnessing in contemporary times. The Commission noted about the Emergency: 'The nation was initially in a state of shock, and then of stupor, unable to realise the directions and the full implications of the actions of the Government and its functionaries' (Second Interim Report, 140). The description could so easily be used to describe the declaration of demonetisation one November evening in 2016 and its aftermath in the weeks that followed!

The Emergency regime used a sledgehammer approach to bludgeon the media into submission. The blanking out of all dissenting views through the censor and the direction to highlight favourably the rulers and their actions, was explicit. The control over the mainstream media being exercised today is more subtle but the results are similar. Reports, data and news that are considered unfavourable to the ruling dispensation usually suffer one of three fates: they either never appear in mainstream media, or are relegated to inconspicuous corners, or quickly vanish from view. The leader and his actions are thrust almost as conspicuously into the public eye, as in any Central Asian republic. Rumour ran rife as a result of the Emergency media policies, and in the absence of trusted sources, it was often believed to be true. The Commission mentions that in the infamous instance of the Turkman Gate firing, the official figure of deaths was 6 but it was a commonly held view that 400 were killed in the police firing. Compliance through fear increased even as trust in the rulers declined. Something similar is at play today as trust in the rulers and the credibility of mainstream media appear to be in decline. Social media gains greater acceptability amongst large sections and becomes the purveyor of facts and perceptions which are often of doubtful provenance.

The Commission brought out the manner in which law and procedure were violated in carrying out arrest and detention during the Emergency. It recorded flagrant instances of blank orders or fabricated grounds to punish those who had fallen foul of the powerful. Again, more subtlety is at play in the manner in which arrest and detention of those considered unacceptable is being carried out over the past decade. In the case of the law in relation to two critical Acts – the PMLA and UAPA – appropriate amendments and convenient interpretations by the Supreme Court require that the court has to be satisfied, before releasing an accused on bail, that a *prima facie* case of guilt is not made out by the prosecution. When combined with the fact that even statements before the investigating agencies can be used to incriminate the accused, the prosecution's task is easy and bail becomes an exception. Action under these Acts can become a recipe for almost indefinite incarceration. This when the conviction rates are 3 per cent for those arrested under UAPA between 2018 and 2020, and 0.05 per cent under PMLA until March 2022 (Radhakrishnan 2022).

Unlike the slapdash efforts during the Emergency, fabrication of grounds, for alleging serious offences, is now a sophisticated exercise. A case in point is that of planting incriminating material on the laptops of some of the Bhima Koregaon accused, accompanied by a concerted media campaign to paint them as anti-national elements and destroy their credibility. Similar smear campaigns and fabrication have besmirched the main accused in the North-East Delhi riot cases but without seemingly impairing public trust in the veracity of the allegations. As in the Emergency, often persons are not allowed to go free even if the courts grant bail. They are promptly arrested again on some other charge or by another agency. In the Emergency one form of harassment was to shift detainees to distant jails. In contemporary times, harassment often takes the form of flimsy cases being filed in distant locations and the accused being arrested and taken there for investigation. A noticeable difference between then and now is that the religion of the accused could impact the likelihood of securing bail.

The idea that population growth needs to be curtailed urgently has a contemporary resonance but with a twist! Population growth of one religious minority is projected as a threat by widespread fakery on social media and even insinuated through carefully curated reports with a veneer of academic respectability. Bulldozers used in dramatic fashion in the Turkman Gate demolitions during the Emergency are now normalised as a new concept of bulldozer justice. The absence or fabrication of due process for removal of structures in the cause of beautification evokes a sinister *deja vu* combined with a distressing focus of only punishing a certain minority for its alleged crimes.

Comparing the Commission's look at the jail conditions brings out a much worse contemporary situation in relation to undertrials. The Commission noted that on 1 January 1975 the jail population in India was 2,20,146 of which undertrials comprised 1,26,772 (57.6 per cent). Overall, the jail population was 120 per cent of the jail capacity of 1,83,369 and the conditions were quite miserable (Final Report, 135). In 2022 India had a prison capacity of 4.36 lakh, the number of actual prisoners was 5.73 lakh (131 per cent of prison capacity) of whom 4.34 lakh were under investigation/trial (75.8 per cent of all prisoners) (Bureau of Police Research and Development [BPRD]). Conditions have clearly worsened over the decades. However, while this increase in undertrials in jail was 8.4 per cent in a period of 37 years between 1975 and 2012, it has shown a sharp increase of 9.8 per cent in the 10 years since then.

The appointment of chosen persons in key positions follows a somewhat different trajectory than in the Emergency. Collegium recommendations for judicial appointments are often ignored if not considered palatable; dissent by the opposition member of committees selecting key regulators is overruled without a second thought; tenure extensions to the faithful have become routine. Regime control over institutions may seem less obvious and yet appears more overarching now than five decades ago. The Commission noted that fear was a pervasive, ominous presence, dictating behaviour in the Emergency. Now a culture of anticipating what is likely to be acceptable is an even more widespread norm of behaviour in the civil service and possibly the judiciary, than ever before. The difference between the Emergency and recent years is analogous to the distinction Arendt drew between authoritarianism and totalitarianism. The first only sought to crush dissent. This second seeks complete control over every institution and indeed, every individual. It seeks a hegemony over thought by even deciding what is taught and imbibed as knowledge by the young.

At one level, this gathering totalitarian moment in India is a reflection of a worldwide trend. The world is increasingly riven into two opposing camps, both inimical to the plurality that permeates the classical vision of liberal democracy. Why does it seem as if the heyday of liberalism, as expressed in our Constitutional values, has ended? The global explanation revolves around the acceleration of inequality in an era in which it was the liberal establishment that held sway. The liberal elite appeared to have gained materially even as it upheld equality as a core value being pursued by humanity. This seeming hypocrisy has been easy meat for attacks from both ends of the spectrum. For the right, immigration and Islam, as overwhelming threats to native culture, are additional weapons to decimate the squeamish liberal in the developed world.

Countries in Eastern Europe for a while, and more recently Italy, have seen the extreme right come to power riding this wave. In the Netherlands, France, Germany and Austria, the extreme right has made enormous gains. In many countries, elections are still an opportunity to throw out the establishment, represented by those in power, and it is not necessarily the right that always wins. Scholz edged out the post-Merkel Christian Democrats in Germany, a surprise for many. The Polish result and Labour booting out the Tories in Britain, are cases in point. But underlying all this is an increasingly polarised world. Both extremes on the right and left are gathering adherents, squeezing out the middle. Labour's victory did not see an increase in its vote share. Instead, it was the extent to which Nigel Farage's extreme right walked away with the traditional Tory support that enabled the huge Labour gains in Britain's first-past-the-post system. More evidence of polarisation can be seen in the 2024 election results in France and Trump's re-election in the USA. The right seems ascendant in many parts of the globe with even the Chinese Communists undergoing a nationalist, proto-fascist makeover under Xi. Russia, India and Turkey are other large countries where the extreme right has secured dominance. This is the picture at the end of 2024.

India's rightward shift has certainly been facilitated by both the moral and ethical bankruptcy of India's version of the liberal middle and the accompanying ethical fadeout in society. A singular illustration of this loss of values is the trajectory exhibited in the careers of the various individuals shown up as perpetrators, collaborators or conscience keepers by the Commission Reports. Among the politicians, it is interesting to note that not only did Indira Gandhi secure an electoral majority very soon after the Emergency, but a person like Pranab Mukherjee held important political offices all his life, finally ending up as the President and being conferred the Bharat Ratna, India's highest civilian honour. Among civil servants, to name just three: Navin Chawla went on to become the Chief Election Commissioner of India, N. K. Singh served in the Prime Minister's Office, as Member of Parliament and the Chairman of the Fifteenth Finance Commission, and Jagmohan served both as Governor of a state and a Union Minister. On the judicial side, while each one of the judges who negated individual liberty in the ADM Jabalpur case went on to become Chief Justices of India, there was no public office or recognition for the dissenting Justice H. R. Khanna. Similarly, High Court judges like Justices Aggarwal, Ranganathan and Lalit suffered because their orders were not palatable to the Emergency regime. Even the civil servants that the Commission lauded for doing their duty, are unsung heroes leaving little vestige in public memory.

Conclusion

Globally, the last three decades have seen the rapid growth of an epistemic community around the concept of transitional justice. With the end of the Cold War in 1989, it became possible internationally to view incidents of repression and abuse of human rights through a more universal lens rather than the ideological bipolarity that had marked the post–World War II decades. The decade of the 1990s saw some momentous instances of societies emerging out of authoritarian or even totalitarian situations. These include the end of apartheid in South Africa, the ethnic majoritarianism in the Balkans after the breakup of Yugoslavia, the genocide in Rwanda, and the end of civil war in Sierra Leone. This period saw the establishment of the International Criminal

Court as an attempt at an institutional framework for retributive justice (prosecution). This primary component of transitional justice draws inspiration from the Nuremberg or Tokyo trials of war criminals after World War II. Three other components come to be explicitly included in transitional justice: reparation for communities and individuals against whom atrocities were committed, amnesty for those who became instruments of perpetration, and truth telling as a reconciliation mechanism (Lawther et al. 2021).

As work on transitional justice became more extensive the field of enquiry widened. It has become clear that historically these moments are not unknown. Questions like 'who should be held responsible, what to do to right the wrongs that have been committed, and how to rebuild following struggle – have been central to every conflict that has been waged' (Quinn 2017, 11) in history. In the last century, dictatorship or military rule in Spain, Portugal, Greece, Argentina and Chile ended even before the emergence of transitional justice as a concept worthy of academic enquiry. In hindsight, the processes that these countries underwent, in the aftermath of the repression their people suffered, are being viewed through the prism of transitional justice. Somehow, India's post-independence moment of authoritarian repression and the attempt at dealing with it once democracy was restored, has been missed by the academic community engaged in broadening the understanding of transitional justice.

The Commission Reports are an early example that would fit well in the corpus of literature on transitional justice. It addresses concerns around retributive justice, reparation, amnesty and avoiding future events of like nature. The Commission was keen to limit the scope of retributive justice. In guidelines issued in July 1977, it said,

> The function of the Commission is not to record conviction but to determine culpability of individuals or groups. As far as public servants are concerned, they may be divided into the following three broad categories: (a) Those who may have simply acted in compliance with the orders or instructions given to them ; (b) Those who may have carried out the instructions a little [more] zealously

> than others; (c) Those who had exceeded or misused or abused their powers or authority for securing personal gain or for securing advantage to other individual(s)/ organisation(s). Public servants falling only in the third category would attract the critical attention of the Commission. (Second Report, 146)

It went on to say that,

> The Commission would like to reiterate that it would reckon its achievements not by the number or the seriousness of the punitive actions taken against persons who had transgressed the laws, but by the nature and extent of the remedial and ameliorative actions that follow this labours [sic] of the Commission. (Second Report, 146)

The work of the Commission emphasised reparation. In the case of family planning excesses, it recommended compensation, payment to those employees where justified dues had been held up and recanalisation where possible. In the case of demolitions, it recommended the constitution of special cells for ameliorative action by looking into individual cases. For the 25,962 employees who were prematurely retired, it sought review panels to reconsider cases and as a result 14,187 persons were reinstated. Out of 4,534 dismissed or terminated, 1,885 had been reinstated by the time the final Report was written (Final Report, 34–38). Analogous to the experience of the Truth and Reconciliation bodies that followed the South African case in the 1990s, the Shah Commission gave an opportunity of being heard to those who had suffered while ensuring that those who had inflicted suffering by their actions were present. Furthermore, the three volumes of the Report are peppered with observations and recommendations that seek amnesty rather than punitive action in most cases.

Is it the lack of follow-up action on the Report that has resulted in it being ignored by international scholars of transitional justice? It would be difficult to conclude this to be the case given the limited impact of even the most studied instances which are included in the corpus of literature on transitional justice. Perhaps it is only the scant attention that the Report has received within the country in the decades since the Emergency, that accounts for this lacuna.

The date that the Emergency was declared in 1975 has recently been christened as the 'Murder of Constitution Day' by the current regime in India. Ironical, given that in the last ten years, it has engineered a gradual process of totalitarian control that is likely to leave a far deeper imprint than the Emergency ever did. But it has done so in a manner so insidious that instead of widespread protest and dissent, every sinister move appears to have been normalised in the everyday life of the country. It is this that lends significance to the work of the Shah Commission. It is a record of repression, of abuse of authority, of a willing suspension of established norms of decent, fair and rule-based behaviour, that must be remembered so that every age can draw parallels and in so doing perhaps halt the normalisation of contemporary excess. In this context it is worth recounting what *The Economist* has to say in its obituary for Ángeles Flórez Peón, known as Maricuela, who died aged 105 on 23 May 2024. She was possibly the last living woman to have served in the socialist militia in the Spanish Civil War.

> For almost 40 years, under Franco's dictatorship, Spain had been made to forget the trauma of the civil war. The deep wounds that remained went untouched. Eventually there would be no one left who had actively defended the republic, a fervent socialist dream that lasted a mere eight years before it fell. But she remembered that fight with the vivid passion of the rebel she always was. When she became the last living militiawoman, the only repository of this history, it was her duty to tell it. A country without memory was a country without a soul. . . . What were a people, or a country, with no memory and no history? "Nada [nothing], nada, nada". (*The Economist* 2024)

References

Government of India. 11 March 1978. *Shah Commission of Enquiry Interim Report I.*

———. 26 April 1978. *Shah Commission of Enquiry Interim Report II.*

———. 6 August 1978. *Shah Commission of Enquiry Third and Final Report.*

Lawther, Cheryl, Luke Moffat and Dov Jacobs, eds. 2017. *Research Handbook on Transitional Justice.* Elgar Online. (downloaded via free access on 11/29/2021)

Quinn, Joanna R. 2017. The Development of Transitional Justice. In *Research Handbook on Transitional Justice*, eds. Cheryl Lawther et al. Elgar Online. (downloaded via free access on 11/29/2021)

Radhakrishnan, Vignesh. 2022. Data | UAPA, PMLA, Section 153A: Rise in cases, low on convictions. *The Hindu*, 10 September. <https://www.thehindu.com/data/data-uapa-pmla-section-153a-what-do-these-laws-have-in-common/article65871393.ece>

The Economist. 2024. Ángeles Flórez Peón, "Maricuela", made sure Spain did not forget its history. 4 July. <https://www.economist.com/obituary/2024/07/04/angeles-florez-peon-maricuela-made-sure-spain-did-not-forget-its-history>

5

Three Controversial Aspects of the Emergency Raj

Anand Kumar

The Emergency Raj

The imposition of the 'Emergency' is considered as 'the darkest hour' in the history of India since independence. It lasted from 26 June 1975 to 21 March 1977, and was termed as the 'derailment of democracy'. It lasted for twenty-one months where nearly 100,000 persons were jailed without trial, mostly under the Maintenance of Internal Security Act (MISA) and the Defence of India Rule (DIR). Strict censorship was imposed on the media. All fundamental rights were suspended. The Constitution was amended and extra-Constitutional centres of power mushroomed from the Prime Minister's Office to the local levels of governance. There was an increase in workers' lay-offs, reduction in bonuses from 8.33 per cent to 4 per cent, and severe restrictions on trade union activities. Nearly one crore common people were sterilised and 4,000 settlements of the urban poor were demolished through a nation-wide campaign which had no approval of either the parliament or state legislative assemblies. The elections to the parliament was postponed and the term of the Lok Sabha was extended. The balance of power between the legislature, the bureaucracy and the judiciary was no more.

There are three controversial aspects of the Emergency Raj which continue to remain significant in any endeavour to understand the drift and deviation from the democratic path:

(1) Was there an incitement to the armed forces to mutiny, and the police to rebel, leaving Prime Minister Indira Gandhi no other option except the declaration of internal emergency to prevent disorder and destabilisation?

(2) Was there no substantial resistance or protest against the Emergency Raj, except for a few insignificant episodes? It is claimed that when the Emergency was imposed, 'not even a dog barked'.

(3) The role of the socialists in the resistance was marginal except in 'the Baroda Dynamite Conspiracy' which involved twenty-five persons including the chairman of the Socialist Party, George Fernandes.

This chapter seeks to address some of the neglected aspects of these three controversial narratives.

The Charge of Inciting the Armed Forces and the Police

It all began with the first broadcast of Prime Minister Indira Gandhi declaring the Emergency on 26 June 1975. According to her,

> Certain powers have gone to the length of inciting our armed forces to mutiny and our police to rebel. The fact that our defence forces and the police are disciplined and deeply patriotic and therefore will not be taken in, does not mitigate the seriousness of provocation. The forces of disintegration are in full play and communal passions are being aroused, threatening our unity. . . . (*Times of India*, 27 June 1975)

It was contradicted by Jayaprakash Narayan in a letter from Chandigarh on 21 July 1975, where he was kept in detention soon after his arrest in Delhi on 26 June after the imposition of the Emergency. He writes,

> The burden of your song, as I have been able to discover, is that (a) there was a plan to paralyse the government, and (b) that one person has been trying to spread disaffection among the ranks of the civil and military forces. . . . As I am the villain of the piece, let me put the record straight. . . . About the plan to paralyse the government. There was no such plan and you know it. . . . As for the "one person" who is supposed to have tried to sow disaffection in the armed and police forces, he denies the charge. All that he has done is to make the men and officers of the Forces

> conscious of their duties and responsibilities. Whatever he has said in that connection is within the law: the Constitution, the Army Act and the Police Act. . . . (1977, 106)

Subsequently, in 'Why Emergency?', the paper placed before the Parliament on 21 July 1975, the Government laid great emphasis on JP's alleged incitement of the armed forces, the police and government employees, made in the course of his speech on 25 June 1975. But, according to the *Hindustan Times* report by Najmul Hasan, the highlight of JP's speech was his advice to Chief Justice A. N. Ray to abstain himself from the Bench when the prime minister's appeal came to be heard. The report continues, 'Mr. Narayan also called upon the army, police and Government employees not to obey any order they considered illegal. The Army Act lays down that the armed forces must protect the Constitution. If the Constitution is changed legally, it does not matter. But the army must oppose any unconstitutional changes'. On the police, JP is quoted as saying, 'I am not trying to arouse the police. But merely stating facts. After the police strike in Delhi, the Khosla Commission was set up to examine their grievances. It submitted its recommendations in 1968 but they have yet to be implemented. Even the Central and State Government employees' demands have not been conceded' (*Hindustan Times*, 26 June 1975).

Mrs Gandhi repeated her charge against JP about inciting the police and armed forces in a note to her special advisor P. N. Dhar (Dhar 2000, 309–10). At the same time, it is to be underlined that Mrs Gandhi told the NBC (USA), in an interview in September 1975, that there was no 'real' danger. After a few more months, the Prime Minister Gandhi changed her line and started talking about the 'subversion threat from abroad'.

Here are two reports from Reuters about her changed perspective. She spoke in a mass public meeting in Jammu on 28 March 1976 that 'some countries and some powerful people abroad were against India and looking for excuses to criticise it'. The prime minister also said that 'India faced increased external threat from all directions and she called for unity in the country to face the new challenges' (*India Abroad*, 2 April 1976).

In reality, there was an increase in the inflow of foreign capital (*Indian Express*, 13 December 1975). The Aid India Consortium pledged about $1,700 million in aid for 1976–77. The UK gave a 100 million sterling aid package, the Dutch gave $77 million in economic assistance, there was Rs 378 million worth wheat supply by Canada and the World Bank granted a $145 million loan to India. While speaking at a news conference in Moscow on 11 June 1976, after ending three days of talks and signing a joint pledge to strengthen friendship and cooperation between their countries with the Communist Party chief Leonid Brezhnev, Prime Minister Indira Gandhi accused 'the Western press' of launching a campaign of 'calumny, hatred and falsehood' against her following the declaration of the Emergency in the country (*India Abroad*, 18 June 1976). But it was not insignificant that the Prime Minister of France, Jacques Chirac, visited New Delhi, within seven months of the imposition of the Emergency, as the chief guest of the Republic Day on 26 January 1976, and India placed major orders for power, telecommunications, satellite equipment, railways, steel and petrochemicals. The global response to the Emergency has been succinctly summarised by Christophe Jaffrelot and Pratinav Anil (2021) by underlining the following two features: (1) foreign governments on both sides of the Iron Curtain had come to accept the Emergency in 1975; and (2) one of the reasons for the West's complacency, in spite of its national commitment to democracy, was that in the USA and Europe the Emergency was well thought of by the business world as the foreign capital benefitted under the Congress rule, both before and during the Emergency.

Let us get back to the issue of JP inciting the armed forces and the police to rebel on 25 June, leading to the declaration of internal emergency by the prime minister. According to Justice M. C. Chagla, former Chief Justice of the Bombay High Court,

> There was not a single statement in any of the resolutions suggesting that either they wanted to resort to violence or they wanted to take to illegal action. And the only piece of evidence on which the Prime Minister has been harping day in and day out is that JP said that soldiers and policemen should not obey illegal orders. This statement is legally sound. International organizations

> have approved that it is not incumbent upon a police officer or an army officer to carry out an order which is illegal. You know what happened in Vietnam when an American officer shot down 50–60 innocent villagers and was tried in America. What JP (Jayaprakash Narayan) said therefore, is legally sound. But he never called upon the army or police to revolt or to take up arms against the State. He was merely enunciating a legal proposition and he was moved to do so, because he found in Bihar policemen and soldiers shooting down innocent people and students.[1]

But the prime minister's message to the nation about the reasons for imposing the Emergency provided sufficient ground for the supporters of the regime to portray JP as a leader who was following in the footsteps of Hitler and Mussolini. At that time, there were 10,000 cinema theatres in the country where approximately 80 million persons were seeing documentary films put out by the Ministry of Information and Broadcasting, like *A Day with the Prime Minister*, *Indus Valley to Indira Gandhi* and *Thunder of Freedom*, every week. There were hints about the probability of a link between the political mobilisation against the government and the CIA (the notorious intelligence agency of the US). It was argued that strong measures ('bitter pill') against such instigators were necessary to prevent the possibility of any 'foreign-hand'-inspired coup.

It had an 'echo effect' even in the pro-government Sarvodaya circle. For instance, there was a conference of Sarvodaya workers, convened by the Bihar Bhoodan Silver Jubilee Committee at Rajgir with the purpose of gathering the anti-JP Sarvodaya workers in the state. Each one of the speakers justified the Emergency. Some of them claimed that JP had called upon the army to revolt and no democratic government could countenance that (Ostergaard 1985, 226–27).

---

[1] from a speech delivered by M. C. Chagla at the All India Civil Liberties Conference held by Citizens for Democracy, on 12 October 1975 at Ahmedabad. It was published in *Democracy or Dictatorship in India?* (Kumar n.d., 44).

On the other hand, it is important to contextualise the appeal of Jayaprakash Narayan to the police and armed forces. In fact, he had called upon the army and the police, for the first time, in the historical speech of 5 June 1974 at the Patna rally, to abide by their duties as codified in the Police Act and the Army Act, instead of allowing the people in power to use them as their tools. He stressed that it was their duty, including resorting to firing, if there was destruction and violence in the name of agitation and revolution. But it is not proper to use the army or police against peaceful protesters. He had reiterated in a public rally at Bhubaneswar on 31 March 1975 that he would not hesitate to give a call to the armed forces and police to revolt against the unjust and undemocratic orders of corrupt ministers and administrators: 'I have not given the call as the time for it has not yet come.' This speech received wide publicity and created an 'excited' reaction in the national press and the political community which compelled JP to clarify his point of view about the role of the armed forces. His references, he explained, had to be placed in their context. 'In the context of some sort of authoritarianism scuttling our democracy', the loyalty of the army was to the country, the flag and the Constitution; the army should not allow itself to be used by any party, government or party leader to further their interests (Ostergaard 1985, 186).

His much-maligned speech on 25 June 1975 at Ramlila Maidan in Delhi was only a reiteration of the Patna call of 5 June 1974 and the Bhubaneswar speech of 31 March 1976 (Jayaprakash Narayan, '*Sampurna Kranti Ke Liye Avahan*', in Dayal 2024, 289–311). It has to be remembered that there were many deaths due to police firing in several parts of Bihar, and the police had opened fire on the students' rally at Patna on 18 March 1974, on 19 March at Jamui (Munger) and on 20 March at Lakhisarai. There was imposition of curfew in 11 districts. At least 24 persons were killed and a few hundred injured in the state. Then there were police firings in three places in Gaya on 12 April in which 8 persons were killed (Dayal 2024, 8, 364). The situation was further complicated by the reports of the official enquiry committees justifying the firings (Ibid., 289–311, 305). Certain prominent leaders of the ruling party warned that army tanks may be used 'to control the growing unrest in Bihar'. It was no empty threat as the army was used in Gujarat to control the agitating students. It was also well known that there were a large number of people held in West Bengal under the DIR and MISA (both preventive detention laws introduced after the declaration of a state of emergency on 3 December 1971 at the time of 'the Bangladesh War' with Pakistan) for alleged involvement in extremist left-wing political activities or ffor being their sympathisers.

The mastermind of 'the West Bengal model', Chief Minister Siddhartha Shankar Ray, was known to be the main advisor of Prime Minister Indira Gandhi since the declaration of the internal emergency. Furthermore, Bansi Lal, known to be quite unscrupulous in misusing state power and government agencies as the Chief Minister of Haryana, was appointed as the new Defence Minister of India in December 1975. He was among the close advisors of Sanjay Gandhi, the new centre of extra-constitutional authority in the Emergency Raj.

JP was deeply disturbed by the incidents of mob violence, frequent police firings and the loose talk about bringing in the army. First, he asked the Sarvodaya activists to make field visits and try to find out the facts. Secondly, he appealed to the government and the state assembly to respond to the causes of the unrest and avoid resorting to use of force. But there was no change in the attitude of the state government. It alarmed and agonised JP. He shared his thoughts in a transparent manner with the student activists, Sarvodaya workers, and the people, by calling for '*Sampurna Kranti*' (Total Revolution) in a non-violent way.

There was also a personal side to this appeal. JP himself was subjected to unprovoked police violence during the Bihar movement on 4 November 1974 in Patna. He was also attacked by hooligans affiliated to the ruling party and its allies in the presence of the police in Kurukshetra, Ludhiana and Kolkata, during his tour of the country, in a short period of just one year since his call for *Sampurna Kranti*. He was compelled to abandon one of his meetings on 2 April 1975 in Kolkata where demonstrators belonging to the Youth Congress and the Chhatra Parishad surrounded his car and prevented him from getting out. Reporting this 'very ugly incident', *The Statesman* had commented on the strange inactivity of the police in a situation where the law and order was being defied before their eyes (3 April 1975).

On the other hand, there were government-supported rallies in Patna and the national capital and elsewhere, in support of Prime Minister Indira Gandhi who had been held guilty of corrupt electoral practices. The Patna rally on 11 November by the Communist Party of India (CPI) was described by the *Indian Recorder and Digest* as a 'grotesque demonstration of the Party's militancy'. It was followed by a 'Save Democracy Rally' of the ruling Congress Party in Patna on 16 November, led by the newly elected party president D. K. Barooah, with abusive slogans against JP and the Total Revolution movement.

It is unfortunate that the state and central governments tried to paint Jayaprakash Narayan as an irresponsible leader who was bent upon destabilising the nation by inciting the armed forces and the police. With the advantage of hindsight of the last five decades, it now looks like a childish attempt of a regime, with a growing legitimacy deficit, to try to justify (1) the imposition of the Emergency, and (2) the arrest of Jayaprakash Narayan and several thousand supporters of a movement for *Sampurna Kranti*. This proved to be counterproductive as it resulted in a nation-wide and global 'Free JP Campaign'.

Realities of Resistance against the Emergency

There are at least three, if not more, perceptions about resistance against the Emergency between 26 June 1975 and 21 March 1977. The first is commonly associated with a dismissive view of the protests, the satyagraha plans and other opposition endeavours, as if they were inconsequential. Surprisingly, there was prevalence of such a view in not only the pro-Emergency quarters but also among a substantial section of the anti-Emergency people. It was appropriately summarised by eminent journalist Prabhash Joshi, a close associate of Jayaprakash Narayan and an active Gandhian proponent of the *Sampurna Kranti Andolan* (Movement for Total Revolution). According to him,

> JP was disappointed that nothing was happening in terms of political movement or resistance when the emergency was imposed. Do you remember his famous

> statement? "Ganga will be on fire and the people will not tolerate it!" But that did not happen. Fighting a real, anti-establishment struggle is not in the RSS character. They are not a fighting force and they are never keen to fight. They are basically a compromising lot. They are never genuinely against the government, and this happened during the Emergency as well. Their cadre did not revolt. The Emergency went unchallenged. That is why, Mrs. Gandhi said, "When I imposed the Emergency, not even a dog barked." (Joshi 2005)

This assessment fails to explain the continuity of the Emergency rule for twenty-one months and the postponement of the Lok Sabha elections due in March 1976. The opposition leaders were in detention without trial. Curbs on the media remained as they were imposed on 26 June 1975. The protesters were being arrested and tortured by the police force. There was the additional fear of sterilisation camps and demolition drives.

The second perception is that there was a continuous opposition to the Emergency with the 'determined and indomitable youth belonging to the RSS [Rashtriya Swayamsevak Sangh]' as the backbone of the endeavour. It is further stated that the total number of people participating in the satyagraha organised against the Emergency was around one and a half lakh, where about 1 lakh and 37 thousand belonged to the RSS and Jana Sangh. Of these, about 7,000 were women, mostly from Maharashtra and Karnataka. About 150 to 175 participated from Delhi (Deshmukh 1979, 76–79). Two long news items from *The Economist* (London) and *Swaraj* (London) support this claim. According to another account from a similar source,

> Already since November 14, 1975, about 100,000 people have voluntarily courted arrest by defying public assembly and censorship laws. About 72 underground news sheets are in daily circulation. In city corporation, town municipality and village council elections in the state of Gujarat, the Congress has been defeated by the opposition four-party coalition. An opposition council, the Lok Sangharsh Samiti (peoples' struggle committee) is coordinating the struggle. There is resistance in 800 out of 959 districts in the country. (Swamy 1976, 20–21)

Akhil Bharatiya Vidyarthi Parishad (ABVP) has published a detailed account of the protest activities after the declaration of the Emergency on 26 June and the imposition of a ban on the RSS and twenty-four other organisations on 14 July 1975. It included joining the satyagraha organised by the Lok Sangharsh Samiti from 14 November 1975. It has recorded that a total of 4,500 activists of the ABVP were arrested and 650 members were put behind bars under MISA. A total of 11,000 members participated in the Lok Sangharsh Samiti protests and a similar number of ABVP members were engaged in the 'underground' activities. It also mentions names of victims of police atrocities, including Somnath who died in detention in Shivani, Madhya Pradesh (Kant et al. 2022, 321–40).

A third image of the resistance activities emerges from details available from the non-RSS, non-Jana Sangh sources. They include a ten-volume publication by the Government of Bihar edited by M. N. Karna, C. G. K. Reddy's *Baroda Dynamite Conspiracy: The Right to Rebel* (1977), *Anibani Ani Amhi* ('The Emergency and Us' in Marathi) edited by veteran freedom fighter and political scientist Usha Mehta (2005), *Vikas Sahyatri* edited by Sheodayal, and *Samved 13* edited by Kishan Kaaljayi. The self-immolation by the Sarvodaya worker Prabhakar Sharma (11 October 1976), satyagraha by veteran freedom fighter Bhimsen Sachar and others from Lok Sewak Sangh, fasting by K. Santhanam (a veteran freedom fighter and member of the Constituent Assembly), the long fast by the Sarvodaya author Vasant Nargolkar, the 'disappearance' of youth leader Rajan under police custody, torture of student leader Jasvir Singh, 'kidnapping' by a senior police officer of Prabir Purkayastha from the JNU campus and the arrest of senior journalist Kuldip Nayar were aspects that contributed to the complex narrative of the anti-Emergency protest activities. Anti-Emergency satyagraha by the Lok Sangharsh Samiti, under the convenorship of Gandhian Congress (O) leader Ravindra Verma, continuous daily satyagraha at Harmandir Sahib (Amritsar) by Akali Dal volunteers throughout the Emergency period, the Baroda Dynamite case, the decentralised 'underground' activities by student-youth activists, the intensifying of international criticism and growing opposition from Indians abroad, especially from the UK, USA and Canada, were the other significant components.

The apology letters by the top RSS leadership, the working out of a formula of reconciliation between the government and the opposition leaders, the refusal of JP and Morarji Desai to accept any solution other than the release of political workers, the abrupt withdrawal of censorship rules, the announcement of elections to the Lok Sabha by Prime Minister Indira Gandhi and birth of a new political formation, the Janata Party, that defeated the supporters of the Emergency rule, are also important parts of this puzzle.

There are several interesting features in this narrative. It was true that the declaration of the Emergency and arrest of a large number of leaders including Jayaprakash Narayan was a big blow which caused the receding of 'the JP wave'. There were spontaneous demonstrations for a few days in different parts of the country, but the police arrested the protesters and there were no further activities at the local level for quite some time, due to fear. But the Lok Sangharsh Samiti, which was formed to launch a people's campaign from 26 June, took quite some time to gather sufficient organisational strength to go for a sustained campaign. The recovery was helped by (1) the organising of an all-Bihar satyagraha on 2 October 1975 by the Chhatra-Yuva Sangharsh Vahini, Sarvodaya workers and opposition party supporters, which involved 2,000 arrests at 10 district headquarters, (2) formation of international support committees and their activities in the UK and the USA, and (3) the first all-India Civil Liberties Conference by the Citizens for Democracy on 12 October 1975 at Ahmedabad. The conference was presided over by former Chief Justice of India J. C. Shah and inaugurated by Justice M. C. Chagla. Eminent liberal leader Minoo Masani, socialist stalwart S. M. Joshi, jurist V. M. Tarkunde, parliamentarian P. G. Mavlankar and former Union Minister Mohan Dharia, were among the speakers at this well-attended programme.

Anti-Emergency movements were also helped by the news of protests in front of the Indian embassy in Washington DC (USA) on 30 June 1975, a full-page appeal by several eminent personalities in the *London Times* on 15 August 1975, support by the Amnesty International (particularly its Secretary-General

Martin Annals), and international tours by eminent Indians including Ram Jethmalani (President of the Bar Council of India), Subramanian Swamy (Member of Parliament), Leila Fernandes (wife of George Fernandes), Anand Patwardhan (filmmaker), Makarand Desai (former minister from Gujarat), C. G. K. Reddy (former socialist MP), and Devi Prasad (President, War Resisters International). These protests also appeared in print in *Satya Samachar* (a periodical of the Lok Sangharsh Samiti), *Resistance*, *Crusader* and *Pratirodh* (published by the socialist 'underground' network), *Swaraj* (a monthly published by the Free JP Campaign from London) and *Indian Opinion* (a monthly published by the Indians for Democracy from East Lansing, USA). Condemnation by the Socialist International, support by AFL-CIO (USA), and an appeal by 82 eminent Americans in *The New York Times* (4 March 1976) also helped.

The Free JP Committee was constituted in London on 27 June 1975 and included prominent British academicians, artists, publicists and peace activists. The committee was headed by the eminent friend of India, Lord Philip Noel-Baker (a Noble Peace Prize winner). Sarul Hoda, S. K. Saxena and Dharampal – three senior socialists of Indian origin with close contacts with JP – were also at the core of this. It was successful in getting support from the Socialist International, Amnesty International, International Transport Workers Federation and several trade union organisations. It may be relevant to remember that, in 1974, Indira Gandhi had asked Lord Fenner Brockway (UK), who was close to both Jawaharlal Nehru and Jayaprakash Narayan, to mediate between her and JP. Brockway had advised JP to accept Indira Gandhi's terms. However, after JP was arrested, Brockway publicly castigated Indira Gandhi and campaigned for JP's release (Visvesvaraya 2022).

Indians for Democracy (IFD) was newly established to promote awareness about the situation in India with over 20 active groups all over the US. It continuously informed the opinion-makers and the media about the Indian situation, which countered the formidable propaganda of the Indian regime in the USA. It was successful in getting support from the World Without War, AFL–CIO, American Friends Service Committee, and the University of

Chicago Students Union. The IFD was responsible for the Human Rights Walk from the Bell of Liberty in Philadelphia to the UNO Headquarters in New York, the petition to the UN Human Rights Commission, appearing before the US Congress hearings on India, and arranging lecture tours of visiting opposition leaders. The effectiveness of the work of the IFD can be measured by the fact that passports of four active members of the organisation – S. R. Hiremath, S. K. Poddar, Ram Gehani and Sharan Nandi – were impounded and the national scholarship of Anand Kumar (a PhD scholar at the University of Chicago) was cancelled (Reddy 1977, Ch. 9).

The satyagraha by the Lok Sangharsh Samiti was launched from 14 November, the birth anniversary of Jawaharlal Nehru, and lasted seven weeks. The satyagraha took place in nearly 3,000 locations and on over 500 occasions. Nearly 9,000 Satyagrahis were arrested. It was an impressive programme in terms of discipline, magnitude and duration. Prime Minister Indira Gandhi was informed about it by the convener Ravindra Verma through a formal letter dated 9 January 1976. But there were no reports in the media except coverage in the underground bulletins like *Satya Samachar*. The satyagraha was supported by the Akali Dal in Punjab.

Secondly, the Emergency-related measures, like the arrest of leading personalities, press censorship, ban on 26 organisations including the RSS, Jamaat-e-Islami, CPI-ML, Anand Marg etc., and significant constitutional amendments, caused fragmentation among the established blocks of sociopolitical activists. There were certainly five categories of response in most of the groups such as the Sarvodaya group, the socialists, the RSS and the Jana Sangh, the Marxists, the Congress parliamentarians, and human rights activists. These could be labelled as the (1) confrontationalists, (2) sympathisers, (3) mediators, (4) cooperationists, and (5) observers. There were a lot of back-and-forth movements over time among these categories. Acharya Vinoba Bhave is reported to have advised reconciliation in his meetings with Prime Minister Indira Gandhi on 7 September and again on 10 November 1975. Freedom fighter Achyut Patwardhan, Gandhian thinker Shriman Narayan, socialist leaders N. G. Gore and S. M. Joshi, and parliamentarian Krishna Kant were making efforts at mediation. The Communist Party of India led by S. A. Dange and Mohit Sen and a section of Sarvodaya leaders headed by Nirmala Deshpande, were among the cooperationists. On the other hand, a number of Congress parliamentarians moved from being 'observers' to join the 'confrontationalists' by establishing Congress for Democracy (CFD) under the leadership of Shri Jagjivan Ram, Hemvati Nandan Bahuguna and Nandini Satpathy after the Lok Sabha elections were announced on 18 January 1977.

Thirdly, there was an attack by the government on all such organisations and forums which had any association with JP's initiatives towards a non-violent revolution in India. It included the Gandhian Institute of Studies (Varanasi), Gandhi Peace Foundation (New Delhi), Association of Voluntary Agencies for Rural Development (AVARD), Sarva Seva Sangh, Lok Sewak Sangh, Mahila Charkha Samiti, and the Citizens for Democracy (CFD). The annual grants were withheld. Many of them were subjected to inquiries (Ostergard 1985, 222).

Fourthly, the act of going to jail helped only marginally in building morale. The anti-Emergency movement could not acquire the mass base it needed. The main reason why the old method of satyagraha did not succeed was the prevalence of fear, ill-treatment in police lock-ups and lack of publicity. Censorship of the press was so complete and the management of news so effective that the resistance activities went unnoticed. While it was widely known that several thousands of people were in jail, hardly anyone beyond the nearest relatives knew about who or how many had defied the Emergency regime.

Fifthly, there was a tendency to compromise with the Emergency regime within a few weeks of detention in significant sections of the opposition parties. For instance, the RSS Sar Sanghchalak Balasaheb Deoras wrote three letters to Prime Minister Indira Gandhi between 22 August 1975 and 16 July 1976. In November 1976, over 30 leaders of the RSS, led by Madhavrao Mule, Dattopant Thengadi, and Moropant Pingle, wrote to Indira Gandhi promising support to the Emergency if all RSS workers were released from prison. This has been verified separately by A. G. Noorani (2020, 404–05), Subramanyan Swamy (2000),

Ravi Visvesvaraya Sarada Prasad (Visvesvaraya 2010) and Prabir Purkayastha (2023, 143–44). There were negotiations between Chaudhary Charan Singh, Biju Patnaik, Om Mehta and Mohamed Yunus from 4 December 1976, and a letter was written by Patnaik to Minister Om Mehta on 1 January 1977 to take them further (Reddy 1977, 168–70). The DMK leader Karunanidhi had also agreed to cooperate with the Emergency Raj.

Finally, there was a territorial factor in the making of the resistance movement. According to JP himself,

> Be that as it may, except for Bihar there was no movement of its kind in any other state of India. In the UP, though committees had been formed, there seemed no possibility of a mass movement anywhere. And a satyagraha had started in April, it was far from becoming a peoples' movement. In other states though the struggle committees were formed, as the general election to the Lok Sabha was drawing near, the attention of the political parties was turned more towards the coming electoral struggle than to any struggle involving civil disobedience. . . . (JP's letter to Prime Minister Indira Gandhi, 21 July 1975)

This explains why out of a total of 1,10,806 persons arrested during the Emergency, nearly half were from UP (31,737), Maharashtra (15,272) and Bihar (10,107).

Role of the Socialists

There are no comprehensive narratives available about the role of socialists in the anti-Emergency protest and resistance. It may also be related to the fact that they were a fragmented fraternity during the 1969–74 period. There was the Socialist Party headed by George Fernandes as the chairman and Surendra Mohan as general secretary. But it had reservations about some aspects of the Bihar Movement. An influential section of the socialists, led by Raj Narain, Karpoori Thakur and Maniram Bagri, had merged in 1974 with several other smaller parties and formed Bharatiya Lok Dal (BLD) with Chaudhary Charan Singh as the President. They were deeply associated with the JP-led Bihar Movement in an unqualified manner. There was another stream put together by Omprakash Deepak, Kishen Patnaik, Sachidanand Sinha and

Indumati Kelkar as the Lohia Vichar Manch. It supported the Bihar Movement. A number of socialists had joined Congress (Indira) under the leadership of Prabhu Narain Singh and Jagdish Joshi. These fractures and splits had also impacted the labour organisations (Hind Mazdoor Sabha vs. Hind Mazdoor Kisan Panchayat), youth organisations (Samajwadi Yuvjan Sabha [Hyderabad] vs. Samajwadi Yuvjan Sabha [Banaras]) and other associations of the socialists.

But the socialists had a significant role in the pre-Emergency political turmoil for a variety of reasons, including an invisible bond of affinity with JP and deep admiration for his contributions in the 'Quit India' Movement of 1942 and his role in building the socialist movement between 1934 and 1954. In the immediate terms, Prime Minister Indira Gandhi was found guilty of electoral malpractices on 12 June 1975 which led to the opposition parties rallying together demanding her resignation on the basis of an election petition filed by socialist leader Raj Narain. There was a joint meeting of the national executive committees of the Akali Dal, Bharatiya Lok Dal, the Congress (O), the Jana Sangh and the Socialist Party on 21 June 1975, asking for the resignation of the prime minister. It also constituted a Programme Committee to mobilise public opinion and met, on 24 June in New Delhi, in the presence of Jayaprakash Narayan (the day before the imposition of the Emergency), to press further for Mrs Gandhi's resignation in the light of the conditional stay provided by the Supreme Court of India. This united body held a massive rally on 25 June 1975 in New Delhi where establishment of the Lok Sangharsh Samiti and its programme of weeklong nationwide mobilisation was announced.

The socialist students and political activists had a major role in the Bihar Movement from the very beginning. The president of Patna University Students Union, Lalu Prasad Yadav, was from the Samajwadi Yuvjan Sabha. The Bihar Chhatra-Yuva Sangharsh Samiti had a visible presence of socialists from different factions. The socialists were in the forefront of the political supporters of the students' agitation inside and outside the Bihar assembly, and outside Bihar, under the guidance of Jayaprakash Narayan after his arrival on the scene from 8 April 1974 until the end of the Emergency Raj on 23 March 1977.

In summation, the socialists were active in protesting against the Emergency rule. Their contribution was significant in three spheres: (2) organising the 'underground' resistance at the national level; (2) remaining 'uncompromised' in jails, and (3) mobilising international support. There were also significant narratives of courage from different parts of India including the case of the youth leader Hasmat Warasi (who died due to police torture in Indore), Kannada film actress Snehalata Reddy (who was tortured in jail in Bengaluru and died soon after her release), labour leader Lawrence Fernandes (tortured by police in Bengaluru), and student leader Jasbir Singh (who was tortured in police custody in New Delhi). There were several examples of courageous couples facing imprisonment, such as Madhu Dandavate–Pramila Dandavate, G. G. Parikh–Mangla Parikh, Shatrudra Prakash–Anjana Prakash, mother and son, Snehalata Reddy–Konark, father and daughter Raj Huilgol–Girija Huilgol, father and son Vishnudev Gupta–Jaishankar Gupta, father, mother and son Arjun Singh Bhadauria–Sarala Bhadauria–Sudhindra Bhadauria, and brothers George Fernandes–Lawrence Fernandes–Michel Fernandes and Kamalesh Shukla–Karunesh Shukla. I have recorded them here so that their resistance is noticed and their struggle is entered in the book of freedom. Further, Madhu Limaye's and Sharad Yadav's resignation from the parliament, in protest against the postponement of the Lok Sabha elections, is also a significant socialist action of defiance that cannot be ignored.

By all accounts, Karpoori Thakur and George Fernandes were two of the most effective socialist leaders of the resistance during the Emergency days. Ladli Mohan Nigam was another notable socialist leader who contributed towards coordination among the socialists without being arrested. He was charge-sheeted by the CBI in the Baroda Dynamite Conspiracy but remained untraceable during the Emergency. The police failed to arrest Karpoori Thakur throughout the period until the national elections were announced. He had made a dramatic appearance in a public rally led by Jayaprakash Narayan at Patna. Persuading the opposition leaders to unite, encouraging the leaders of the Bihar Movement, publication of resistance literature and guiding the socialist activists, were his major concerns. The 'open' letters of Karpoori Thakur to Acharya Vinoba Bhave (1, 2, 3, and 4) and *Indira Gandhi ke Sau Jhuuth* were significant among his booklets. One of his statements was published by the Committee for Freedom in India (Chicago), titled *Indira Gandhi 'Derailed'*. It was a systematic response to the official propaganda which claimed that 'had there been no Emergency today, chaos, anarchy and ruin would have ruled the country'. His statement opens with the following lines, 'There is neither war nor internal disorder nor financial collapse, and yet there is double Emergency in India: one in the name of war since December 3, 1971 and another since June 26, 1975, in the name of internal disorder.' His associates also arranged to publish *Behind the Bar* by JP and a famous speech by Chaudhary Charan Singh in the UP Vidhan Sabha.

Initially, Karpoori Thakur made the Terai region of Nepal his base and used to wear 'Daura Suruwal'. Then he shifted to Kolkata in September 1975. He travelled to Varanasi, Lucknow, Delhi, Bengaluru, Ahmedabad and Chennai. There is a description of his travelling in a third class compartment from Delhi to Ahmedabad to meet George Fernandes and another journey from Gorakhpur to Kathmandu by air to escape arrest. He also stayed in Hingalganj (Bangladesh Border), Siliguri, Barrackpur, Darjeeling and Dhenkanal. He established contacts with Jayaprakash Narayan, Charan Singh, Chandra Bhanu Gupta and George Fernandes. In Bihar, he was in communication with Kailashpati Mishra, Sachidanand Singh, Ram Vilas Paswan, Lakshmi Sahu, Mangani Lal Mandal, Shivnandan Paswan, Manjay Lal, Ramnath Thakur and Ajay Almast. In Bengal, he met Jyoti Basu, Pratap Chandra Chander, Abha Maiti, Dilip Chakravarti, Anil Bhattacharya, Nirmalendu De and Himanshu Halder, among others. He was also in touch with the leaders of the Forward Block and the Revolutionary Socialist Party.

George Fernandes was active in the resistance against the Emergency between 27 June 1975 and 10 June 1976 when he was arrested in Kolkata. A case was registered against him and 24 other associates which became famous as the 'Baroda Dynamite Conspiracy'. His co-accused, C. G. K. Reddy has written that, 'Mrs Gandhi unconsciously arranged a cross-section of India in the Baroda Dynamite Case. The accused hailed from several states – Bihar, Uttar Pradesh, Delhi, Madhya Pradesh, Gujarat, Maharashtra, Karnataka, Kerala and Andhra. They were drawn from all age groups. The youngest, Padmanabha Shetty was 21, and the oldest Prabhu Das Patwari, 68. They were from different social strata' (1977, 139). According to the chargesheet against him, 'Investigation showed that on the declaration of Emergency in the country on 25.6.75, George Fernandes A-1 went underground and decided to arouse resistance against the imposition of the same and to overawe the Government by use and show of criminal force'. In his reply George Fernandes wrote,

> . . . Dictatorship does violence to the spirit of man. It is neither legal, constitutional or even moral. It leaves the people no legal and constitutional means to fight it. And even then, to fight it remains an inalienable right of all men, of all those who believe in the sacredness, dignity and freedom of man. As Gandhiji said, given the choice between cowardice and violence to resist evil, he would not hesitate to choose, and he recommended that people choose, violence. While my belief in non-violence is a conviction, inherited from one of the greatest thinkers and humanist Dr. Rammanohar Lohia, I also believe, as Gandhiji believed, and no doubt Lohia himself believed, that injustice and evil should be fought wherever it raises its head. My fight against the dictatorship was born out of such convictions and it never entitled killing, or what the prosecution says, "criminal force". (Reddy 1977, 163–64)

The international support for anti-Emergency protests was another sphere of the socialist contribution. It helped in the internationalisation of the support for the restoration of democracy. It began with the contacts between the emissaries of George Fernandes and the secretary general of the Socialist International Hans Janitschek. *Socialist Affairs*, the official journal of the Socialist International, carried an article by George Fernandes in the July 1975 issue and several reports in the later issues. It also published a report put together by the Indian socialists, *Indira's India: Anatomy of a Dictatorship*, in English, German, French, Italian and Japanese (Reddy 1977, 55).

The anti-Emergency movement was substantially enhanced by the resolution of the bureau of the International calling upon the Government of India to end the state of emergency. It also expressed solidarity with the Socialist Party and other organisations fighting for democracy and socialism in India, and called upon all member parties to extend all support and assistance to the Socialist Party of India. The resolution facilitated contacts of the Free JP Campaign (UK) and Indians for Democracy (USA) with the socialist parties and the socialist trade unions of Austria, Belgium, Brazil, Canada, Denmark, France, Germany, Israel, Italy, Spain, Sweden, Switzerland, Yugoslavia and Japan. A joint protest by three eminent socialist leaders, Willy Brandt (Germany), Olof Palme (Sweden) and Bruno Kreisky (Austria), was one of the most significant outcomes of the efforts of the Socialist International. It also helped in bringing together a group of 82 eminent Americans issuing a public appeal for restoring human rights in India. It included Noble laureates like George Wald, Paul Samuelson and Linus Pauling. There were also eminent peace activists like Arther Ashe, Noam Chomsky, Joan Baez, Robert Pickus, Allen Ginsberg, Homer Jack and Michael Harrington. Famous India experts like Milton Singer, Bernard Cohn, McKim Marriott, Myron Weiner, Richard Park and Harold Isaacs also signed it. This unique effort was coordinated by Ved Mehta (author), Dorothy Norman (a biographer of Jawaharlal Nehru) and Sidney Hertzberg (a senior journalist).

Conclusion

The imposition of internal emergency was an unexpected situation in the course of democratic nation-building in independent India. In this unprecedented phase everybody was clueless about 'What is to be done?' and 'How is it to be done?'. Neither the ruling party nor the opposition had any answers. It inaugurated a new discourse of power which was later characterised as the 'first dictatorship in India' (Jaffrelot and Anil 2021). It was a decision made by Prime Minister Indira Gandhi in response to 'a sudden crisis of legitimacy deficit' arising from the Supreme Court refusal to her appeal for a total stay on the implementation of the Allahabad High Court judgement declaring her election to the Lok Sabha invalid.

This caused a political vacuum which promoted the rise of a number of extra-constitutional centres of power and authority. It is true that there was no spectacular resistance to the Emergency Raj. According to Jayaprakash Narayan, the people were shocked and terrorised by the country-wide arrest of most of the opposition leaders by the government. Still, it was a matter of shame that millions of men and women who were outside the jails passively witnessed the imposition of authoritarian rule, as there was no awareness about the democratic rights and there was little motivation to take the risk of resistance (Narayan 2015, 42).

But it is worth noticing that the Emergency Raj was significantly opposed in different ways by different sections of the society. In this chapter, three aspects of the resistance to the Emergency Raj are discussed and demystified: (1) the protest by Jayaprakash Narayan from jail about the much publicised charge of instigating the army and the police to rebel; (2) the civil disobedience organised by the Lok Sangharsh Samiti and its affiliates; and (3) the role of the socialists. On the basis of available evidence, it can be safely concluded that Jayaprakash Narayan tried to keep the doors of dialogue with the government open without compromising with the official narrative about the reasons which were presented to justify the imposition of the Emergency. Secondly, the record of resistance by the opposition parties was not overwhelming in terms of the expectations, nor insubstantial in the given circumstances of fear and lawlessness. Finally, there was diversity in the socialist resistance in their techniques and objectives, ranging from remaining firm in their resolve in jails to establishing 'underground networks' and internationalising the resistance work.

References

Ahmad, Noor. 2024. *Jannayak Karpuri aur Aapatkal Ke Din*. In *Jana Nayak Karpoori Thakur Janmashati Smaran-Granth*, ed. Ramashankar Singh. Nai Dilli: Samajwadi Samagam. 102–06.

Bhushan, Prashant. 1978. *The Case that Shook the Nation*. Gurgaon: Penguin Random House.

Prasad, Bimal. 1980. *A Revolutionary's Quest*. New Delhi: Oxford UP.

Brahmanand, ed. 1978. *Towards Total Revolution* Vols. 1–4. Bombay: Popular Prakashan.

Barik, R. K. 1977. *The Politics of JP Movement.* New Delhi: Radiant.

Baru, Sanjay, ed. 2019. *Democracy Interrupted.* Gurgaon: Penguin Random House.

Bhattacharjee, Ajit. 2005. *JP – Ek Jeevani.* Bikaner: Vagdevi Prakashan.

Chagla, M. C. 2016. *Roses in December.* Mumbai: Bharatiya Vidya Bhavan.

Chandra, Bipan. 2003. *In the Name of Democracy.* Gurgaon: Penguin.

Dayal, Shiva, ed. 2024. *JP Andolan aur Bharatiya Loktantra.* Mumbai: Pralek Prakashan.

Deshpande, Kusum. 2010. *Vinoba: Antim Parva.* Pawnar: Paramdham Prakashan.

Dhar, P. N. 2000. *Indira Gandhi, The Emergency and Indian Democracy.* New Delhi: Oxford UP.

Deshmukh, Nana. 1979. *RSS – Victim of Slander.* New Delhi: Vision Books.

Devasahayam, M. G. 2006. *JP in Jail.* New Delhi: Lotus/ Roli.

———. 2012. *JP Movement, Emergency and India's Second Freedom.* New Delhi: Vitasta.

Frank, Catherine. 2001. *Indira - The Life of Indira Nehru Gandhi.* Noida: Harper Collins.

Garg, Shravan. 1974. *Bihar Andolan: Ek Sinhavalokan.* Varanasi: Sarva Seva Sangh Prakashan.

Government of India. 1975. *Why Emergency.* New Delhi: Publications Division.

———. 1978. *Shah Commission of Inquiry Report.* 3 Vols. New Delhi.

Gyan Prakash. 2018. *Emergency Chronicles.* Gurgaon: Penguin.

Jayakar, Pupul. 1992. *Indira Gandhi.* Gurgaon: Penguin.

Jaffrelot, C. and Pratinav Anil. 2021. *First Dictatorship in India 1975–77.* Noida: Harper Collins.

Joshi, Prabhash. 2005. Not Even a Dog Barked. Tehelka, 2 July. (Interview by Amit Sengupta)

Kaaljayi, Kishan, ed. 2002. *Samved 13, Loknayak Ank.* Delhi.

Kant, Manoj, Pradip Rao and Umendra Dutt, ed. 2022. *Dhyeya-Yatra Vol. I*. New Delhi: Prabhat Prakashan.

Karna, M. N. 2016. *Bihar Andolan*. 10 Khand. Patna: Bihar Sarkar.

Kumar, Anand, ed. n.d. *Democracy or Dictatorship in India?* Chicago: Committee for Freedom in India.

Mehta, Vinod. 2015. *The Sanjay Story*. Noida: Harper Collins.

Mehta, Usha, ed. 2005. *Anibani Ani Amhi*. Mumbai: Granthali Prakashan.

Naipaul, V. S. 1976. *India: A Wounded Civilization*. New Delhi: Penguin.

Narayan, Jayaprakash. 1977. *Prison Diary*. Bombay: Popular Prakashan.

———. 2015. *Sampoorna Kranti*. Varanasi: Sarva Seva Sangh Prakashan.

Nayar, Kuldeep. 2017. *Emergency ki Inside Story*. New Delhi: Prabhat Prakashan.

Noorani, A. G. 2020. *The RSS: A Menace to India*. New Delhi: LeftWord Books.

Ostergaard, Geoffrey. 1985. *Non-violent Revolution in India*. New Delhi: Gandhi Peace Foundation.

Prasad, Sujata, and Bimal Prasad. 2021. *The Dream of Revolution*. Gurgaon: Vintage/ Penguin.

Purkayastha, Prabir. 2023. *Keeping Up the Good Fight*. New Delhi: LeftWord Books.

Rajeshwar Rao, Bhupesh Gupta, and Mohit Sen. 1975. *Emergency and the Communist Party*. New Delhi: Communist Party Publication.

Rajeshwar, T. V. 2015. *India: The Crucial Years*. Noida: Harper Collins.

Reddy, C. G. K. 1977. *Baroda Dynamite Conspiracy: The Right to Rebel*. New Delhi: Vision Books.

Sen, Mohit. 2003. *The Traveler and the Road*. New Delhi: Rupa.

Shah, Ghanshyam. 1977. *Protest Movements in Two Indian States*. Delhi: Ajanta.

Sheodayal, ed. 2014. *Vikas Sahyatri* (September). Patna.

Singh, Bajarang. 2018. *Ankhan Dekhi Bihar Andolan*. Nai Dilli: Prabhat Prakashan.

Singh, Ramashankar. 2024. *Apaatkaal men Karpoori Thakur Ki Bhumigat Sakriyata*. In *Jana Nayak Karpoori Thakur Janmashati Smaran-Granth*, ed. Ramashankar Singh. Nai Dilli: Samajwadi Samagam. 127–29.

Srinivasaraju, Sugata. 2025. *The Conscience Network: A Chronicle of Resistance to a Dictatorship*. Gurugram: Vintage.

Swamy, Subramanian. 1976. What is Happening in India? In *Democracy or Dictatorship in India?*, ed. Anand Kumar. Chicago: Committee for Freedom in India: 20–21

———. 2000. Unlearnt Lessons of Emergency. *The Hindu*, 13 June.

Tandon, Bishan. 2003. *PMO Diary*. New Delhi: Konark Publications.

Tiwari, Shankar. 2024. *Karpuri Thakur ka Nepal Pravas. Apaatkal Ke Dauran*. In *Jana Nayak Karpoori Thakur Janmashati Smaran-Granth*, ed. Ramashankar Singh. Nai Dilli: Samajwadi Samagam. 170–73.

Tripathi, Satyadev. 2024. *Apaatkal Ke Dauran Kapoori ji Ki Nepal Yatra*. In *Jana Nayak Karpoori Thakur Janmashati Smaran-Granth*, ed. Ramashankar Singh. Nai Dilli: Samajwadi Samagam. 187–88.

Ullekh, N. P. 2017. *The Untold Vajpayee*. Gurgaon: Penguin Viking.

Vasudev, Uma. 1977. *Two Faces of Indira Gandhi*. New Delhi: Vikas.

Visvesvaraya, Ravi Sarada Prasad. 2010. Emergency Chronicle. *Indian Express*, 23 Feb.

———. 2022. Why did Indira Gandhi Call for Elections in January 1977? *OPEN Magazine*, Jan.

6

The Economic Roots of the Emergency

Errol D'Souza

The Early Years after Independence

After Independence, India adopted an economic strategy that was based on a distrust of markets, export pessimism, and a belief in state control of the economy. Jawaharlal Nehru was influenced by the prevailing economic theories of the time that were anchored in the view that planning was the best way to industrialise a poor society (see Hirschman 1981). The Second Plan was the high noon of planning where the industrialisation of a predominantly agricultural economy was posited on the rapid expansion of the capital goods sector. Industrialisation was visualised as first building the capacity to produce goods that help to develop the complex of mining, metallurgical, engineering and electrical industries that were part of the capital goods sector itself – more coal that produced more steel that then produced more machinery and more transport and other industries that are related to one another. Once a sizeable industrial sector was established then it would be possible to have some of the goods produced there channeled to the consumption goods sector which would then expand output and raise the consumption levels of the economy.[1]

The strategy came under a cloud when India faced wars and the shock of two severe droughts in a row in the mid-sixties that

---

[1] India sought to produce its own capital goods rather than import as the thinking was that financing imports from the foreign exchange obtained by exports was not feasible since exports were predominantly of primary commodities that had inelastic demand and so were not predicted to have an expanding international market. Other countries such as South Korea that adopted a similar strategy changed gears and took advantage of expanding world trade.

made it dependent on American food aid. The disastrous defeat in the war with China in 1962 resulted in a huge budgetary cost to the government which found that it had a shortage of resources to fund the Third Plan. The idea of nationalising banks so as to mobilise resources for development was raised at that juncture[2] but was discouraged by finance minister T. T. Krishnamachari who argued that it was not likely to provide additional income to the government. The inflation rate almost doubled from 4.7 per cent in 1962–63 to 8.8 per cent in 1963–64 and stayed at that level the next couple of years. Foreign exchange reserves diminished and the balance of payments was in shambles. In the middle of 1965 Pakistan attacked in the Rann of Kutch and was beaten back. That year saw a second disaster in the failure of the monsoon and in September Pakistan attacked again in Kashmir. The wars and the drought adversely affected public finances and put a nail in the coffin of the Third Plan and planning was put on hold for three years.

Figure 1: Growth rate of Agriculture & TREND growth of Agriculture, Manufacturing and Gross Value Added (GVA)

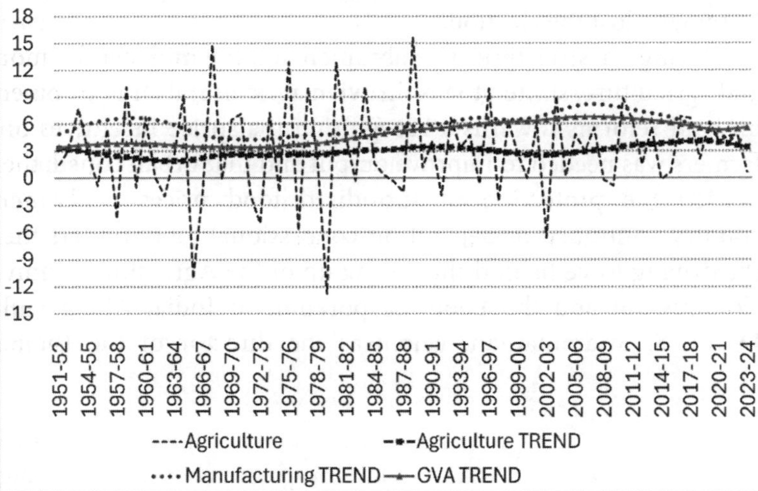

[2] Subhadra Joshi who was a senior member of the Congress party had brought a non-official resolution seeking the nationalisation of banks.

There was a sharp decline in agricultural output from a trend growth rate[3] of 3.3 per cent in 1951–52 to 2.1 per cent in 1965–66 (Figure 1). The population growth rate of 2.5 per cent per annum entirely canceled the average annual gain in food production and with slowly rising incomes there was a widening food demand-and-supply gap over the period. Only increasing infusions of PL 480 American food aid – 2 million tons in 1958, 4 million per year during 1960 to 1964 and 6 million in 1964–65 (a good year before the first bad drought) – suppressed a politically disastrous food price inflation. By 1965–66 Indian ministers and officials came around to the view that a new agricultural strategy was required.

In the political arena, in May of 1964 Jawaharlal Nehru died and Lal Bahadur Shastri became the prime minister in the midst of an intense succession battle. In January 1966, Prime Minister Shastri died in Tashkent where he had gone for peace talks with Pakistan. Indira Gandhi who was a member of Shastri's cabinet and who had refused the offer in 1964 of being made the prime minister was elected as the leader of the Congress Parliamentary Party owing to a Syndicate led by Congress party president K. Kamaraj who built a consensus in her favour against Morarji Desai who lost the election.

During Shastri's time, C. Subramaniam, the minister for food and agriculture, shifted the Nehruvian agricultural strategy based on land reforms towards a recognition that price incentives for farmers was needed to improve output and that urban consumers needed the protection of subsidised food prices whilst the country continued to depend on concessional food aid. He was the driving force behind the setting up of the Agricultural Prices Commission and the Food Corporation of India. Along with Dr M. S. Swaminathan, who was the director of the Indian

[3] Economists break up a time series of a variable Y_t at time t into a trend component T_t and a cyclical component C_t. That is, $Y_t = T_t + C_t$. The trend gives us the secular underlying component of the variable and indicates its long-run tendency.

Agricultural Research Institute, he is the architect of the green revolution[4] in India.[5]

With the monsoon failure of 1965 India requested for 7 mn tons of emergency food aid. The government committed to the intensive area programme in agriculture which would have priority on seed, fertiliser and other inputs. Subramaniam signed the Treaty of Rome which provided for increased investment in agriculture[6] and he emphasised the pivotal importance of an expanded fertiliser import target which required immediate US aid given the severe limits on the availability of foreign exchange.

The First Phase of Mrs Gandhi

When Mrs Gandhi took over as prime minister, Asoka Mehta joined the cabinet as the minister of planning. Mehta went to Washington for meetings with George Woods, the president of the World Bank, in March of 1966, where he made presentations on the country's revised agricultural and family-planning strategies and made promises of extensive liberalisation of the country's internal and foreign-trade regimes if the efforts could be funded with extra non-project aid[7] that was estimated to be $900 million

---

[4] This involved the introduction of new HYVs of wheat and rice that had begun to be available from internationally supported research facilities in Mexico and the Philippines which paved the way towards self-sufficiency in food in India.

[5] Instead of a civil servant Subramaniam put a scientist, Dr B. P. Pal, in charge of the Indian Council for Agricultural Research.

[6] That year Subramaniam went to Washington and met with President Lyndon B. Johnson and Orville Freeman, the secretary of agriculture. Later the same year, he met with Freeman in Rome and the Treaty of Rome provided for an increase in investment in agriculture by 40 per cent in the coming year and to be raised thereafter. Fertiliser production was to be actively promoted as part of the intensive area programme in agriculture.

[7] By 1958 acknowledging the foreign exchange shortage that had befallen India during the Second Five Year Plan, the US joined the World Bank in originating what became the Consortium of aid donors. As the largest aid donor, the US led the way in providing

annually – an increase over the $500 million a year. Woods agreed to raise this Consortium money and Mehta confirmed that India, consulting with the IMF, would go for a substantial devaluation. In late March 1966 Indira Gandhi herself landed in Washington and President Johnson promised food and other aid.

In early June 1966, just hours after the cabinet heard about it, minister of finance Sachin Chaudhuri announced a devaluation of the rupee from 4.76 to 7.5 to the dollar. There was an uproar. Politicians associated devaluation as a blow to national pride. Kamaraj called the decision as a sell-out to the Americans[8] and the Congress Working Committee, which was Indira Gandhi's own party, denounced her action. This was the beginning of her problems with the Syndicate and she began to give a leftward spin to her decisions so as to oppose the narrative that she was under pressure from the US. To indicate her independence, she attacked the Vietnam policy of the US as imperialist aggression which incensed Johnson. Johnson was already suspicious of the earnestness of the Indian development effort and had, from the spring of 1965, begun the practice of stalling food aid and meting it out a little at a time so as to keep up the reform pressure. There were distressing delays in the release of PL 480 food aid which was always less than that requested for. B. K. Nehru, India's ambassador to the US, would write in his memoirs (1997) that 'we lived from ship to mouth' and a delay in the arrival of a ship could mean 'starvation'.

The double drought, for a newly installed prime minister, was an act of god that radically subdued the effect of two important innovations in economic policy – the new agricultural strategy and the devaluation. The droughts camouflaged the effect of the

---

commodity or programme loans for the imports of types of goods such as steel, non-ferrous metals and types of equipment, and such loans came to be officially designated as 'non-project' from 1962 onwards.

[8] It is interesting that Kamaraj as president of the Congress party saw himself as part of a collective leadership and was upset that he had learned of the decision after it occurred, indicating a questionable view about the relationship between the party and the government.

agricultural strategy on the production of foodgrain and it caused scepticism in US policy circles that released food aid on the basis of programme implementation, whilst downplaying the effect of the drought. By the mid 1970s the Indian government and economic policy professionals and architects realised that despite the Green Revolution, the growth of agricultural production and per hectare productivity had not accelerated over the level achieved prior to 1965–66. Vaidyanathan stated that '... as against the target of 4–4.5 per cent a year, the trend rate of growth in crop production has been only 2.6 per cent a year since 1950–51' (1977, 1355). Figure 1 indicates indeed that the growth rate of the aggregate value added in agriculture declined from 2.9 per cent during 1951–52/1964–65 to near half that at 1.5 per cent during 1965–66/1974–75. This was because the agricultural strategy was restricted to a few crops such as wheat, bajra and maize; to a few regions in Punjab, Haryana, parts of UP and the southern states; and it got exhausted due to the restricted scope for increasing the acreage under crops and the acute inequality in the distribution of land and assets in the agricultural sector. Agricultural expansion was also restrained by the shortage of electricity for powering the quickly expanding number of electrified tubewells. With regard to the effects of the drought on devaluation, Bhagwati and Srinivasan (1975) found that if one separates the devaluation effects from the double drought's effects on exports, then the effects of the devaluation would have been positive and the effect on the trade gap would be, as was intended by the policy change, substantially narrowed.

The agricultural strategy and the devaluation could have played out positively but for the drought and the failure to follow through on financial aid from donors. The expectation of the scale of non-project assistance did not materialise.[9] In the May 1968 meeting of

[9] The first $900 million took time to stack together. Some members of the Consortium such as the Germans and Japanese were slow to meet targets and Johnson would not let the US commit its share till aid appropriations for the new financial year were completed. The package was committed only by November when there were less than five months remaining of the financial year.

the Consortium the commitment made by the members was way short of the target at $642 million. The financing style that relied on aid and domestic savings to fuel growth was affected by this experience. Indian policymakers found themselves vulnerable to arm-twisting which the Woods–Mehta deal had formalised and agreed on, as well as the minister of planning had committed to in good faith, and that the prime minister with a visit to the US had given her backing to. In addition, President Johnson's delay of food aid during a drought and his not responding to PL 480 requests for months towards the end of his term in 1968, motivated India to become more inward-looking and dirigistic at a time when it could have navigated the crisis in agriculture and continued with reforms that set the country on a more sustainable growth path. Reacting to the external vulnerability from donor leverage, the trade balance of the country, from 1967 till the first oil shock of 1973, was kept in close balance, the foreign exchange reserves of the country were enhanced, and the ratio of foreign borrowing to the government deficit was brought down.

The General Elections in 1967 were held in the backdrop of the devaluation and the drought. The Congress lost heavily in the northern states and many of its top leaders from the Syndicate were routed – Kamaraj, S. K. Patil, Atulya Ghosh – along with the presidents of the Congress party organisations in six states and chief ministers in four. The unprecedented drought and the spiralling inflation of agricultural goods that reached 18 per cent that year (see Figure 2) played a large role in the disenchantment of the people who found it difficult to manage their household budgets in obtaining essential commodities. It would be fair to say that Mrs Gandhi's first year in office was conceivably the worst faced by a prime minister since Nehru's in 1947, and was in the aftermath of war, back-to-back droughts and economic distress.

Subsequent to the 1967 election, Mrs Gandhi got Morarji Desai's cooperation by making him deputy prime minister and the finance minister. However, she did not consult him as a senior colleague while drawing up the list of cabinet members and, importantly, dropped Neelam Sanjiva Reddy who was a Syndicate member and had won his parliamentary seat from her cabinet.

Figure 2: Agricultural Inflation and Aggregate (GVA) Inflation

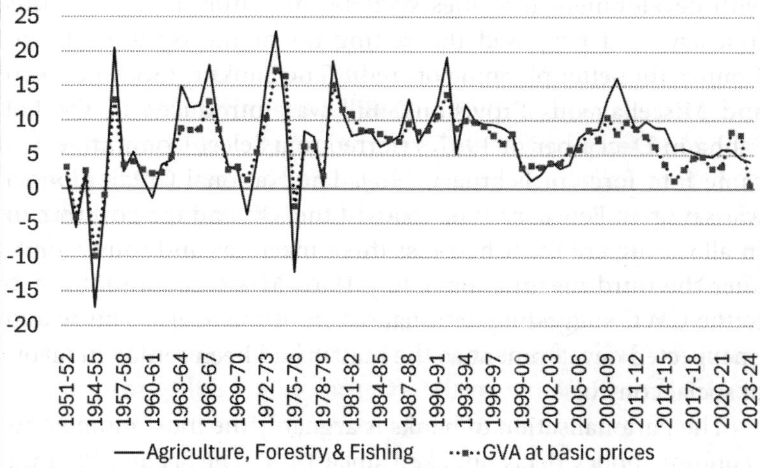

Naturally the meeting of the Congress Working Committee (CWC) in May 1967 had serious discussions on the economy and a decision was taken to have increased government participation in banking, foreign trade, insurance and foodgrain distribution. The Congress manifesto had made a promise about the social control of banks. While Y. B. Chavan, Kamaraj, and Jagjivan Ram were in favour of the takeover of private banks, Morarji Desai argued that they should be cautious as there was criticism about how inefficient the public sector was, and that there would be huge complications for the administration and a strain on the administrative resources of the government to efficiently run private banks in an integrated manner.[10] Morarji Desai carried the day at the next CWC meeting where nationalisation was rejected and it was delegated to the government to find measures that could channelise credit to development needs and explore ways to exercise control over banks through measures such as having a voice in the appointment of bank directors.

---

[10] The advisor in the finance ministry, V. A. Pai Panandikar, was asked by the CWC to conduct a study on social control over banks. The Panandikar Report was not made public.

In December of 1967, Morarji Desai made a statement in Parliament about the need for credit allocation in conformity with development priorities such as agriculture and small-scale industry, and proposed the setting up of the National Credit Council for better planning of credit. The Banking (Social Control and Miscellaneous Provisions) Bill was introduced in the Lok Sabha in December of 1967, referred to a Select Committee, and came into force in February 1969. The National Credit Council was set up in February 1968 to assist the RBI and the government in allocating credit. It had just three meetings and four months after the third meeting, on 9 July 1969, Mrs Gandhi sent a note to the CWC suggesting nationalisation of the banks. This was an unexpected development as the matter had been settled in favour of social control.

The nationalisation of banks is arguably the most momentous economic policy decision taken since 1947. The Second Plan was a landmark but, as we saw, it was quickly reversed in a decade with the Plan holidays and the new agriculture strategy. The effects of bank nationalisation manifested right through till the early 1990s. And importantly this bold economic measure had its basis in a bid to take political control of the party and to rebut the Syndicate. Even though Mrs Gandhi consulted leading economists like K. N. Raj and industrialists like G. D. Birla and J. R. D. Tata, the nationalisation decision was in essence political. I. G. Patel reports that she told him, 'For political reasons, it has been decided to nationalise the banks. You have to prepare within twenty-four hours the bill, a note for the Cabinet and a speech for me to make to the nation on radio tomorrow evening. Can you do it and make sure there is no leak?' (2002, 135).

On 3 May 1969, President Zakir Hussain died of a heart attack. The Syndicate nominated Neelam Sanjiva Reddy who Mrs Gandhi had kept out of her cabinet. She did not want him possibly because she was apprehensive that if Morarji Desai were to challenge her again Reddy might use his presidential authority to invite Desai to form the government.

Mrs Gandhi could not overtly challenge the Syndicate's decision. Instead she converted the political contest for power into an ideological battle. On July 9 she proposed nationalisation of Indian banks, a renunciation of the earlier agreement amongst the Congress party leaders to employ 'social control' of banks. The Parliament was slated to come back for a session on 21 July and she was unsure if she would have the majority in favour of nationalisation. She needed a presidential order before the Parliament resumed. Acting President Giri was to step down from his position on 20 July to contest the presidential election. She needed Giri to sign the ordinance by 19 July. She relieved Desai from the finance portfolio on 16 July. On 17 July she asked the RBI governor, L. K. Jha, to come to Delhi and help draft the legislation on nationalisation. The ordinance was readied for Giri's signature on time.

Mrs Gandhi then freed the Congress MPs from an obligation to vote for the Congress party candidate and said they could vote as their conscience guided them. Many voted for Giri who won a narrow victory for the presidency. This stung the Syndicate which expelled Mrs Gandhi from the Congress party on 12 November. The party broke up before the end of the year, and she formed the Indian National Congress (Requisition) or Congress (R). Though most Congress MPs stayed with Mrs Gandhi, they were not able to secure a parliamentary majority. To remain prime minister she had to rely on the CPI, the DMK and a handful of independent MPs.

The vulnerable experience of external assistance meant that domestic taxes would be required to finance growth. However, an economy that is predominantly agricultural and where the Constitution has reserved agricultural taxation for the states, cannot hope to gain revenues for the government from this source. Instead, with chronic food shortages that required an agriculture-led expansion, resources had to be directed towards agriculture. Financial repression that obligated banks to lend to the government at below market rates of interest was to increasingly become the means to finance the government budget along with direct recourse to credit from the RBI.

Nationalisation of banks also unfolded along with a leftward turn to economic policy with more stringent control over the private sector. Nationalisation was seen as standing up to the rich and as directing the flow of credit to priority users in agriculture and small-scale industries. The dissatisfaction with the economic circumstances arising from low growth and growing population pressure generated a feeling that poverty could not be reduced as a result of normal growth. Policymakers started to speak in terms of a direct assault on poverty. Many policies that are remnants of India's socialist past came into existence between 1967 and 1976. These included the Small-Scale Industry Reservation Act of 1967, Foreign Exchange Regulation Act of 1973, Urban Land Ceiling and Regulation Act of 1976, and Amendments to Chapter VB of the Industrial Disputes Act, 1976. In June 1970 the Monopolies and Restrictive Trade Practices Act was added to the list of socialist measures which, though propounded as a way of curbing monopoly power, became an instrument of corruption. Large business houses tactically captured authorisations for expansion and operation to keep out competition which worked at cross purposes to the purpose of the Act.

The growth rate of agriculture exhibited steady decline from 1951–52 to 1964–65 as can be seen from the dashed trend line in the graph of Figure 1. Thereafter the change in agriculture strategy paid off and offset the decline, with the growth rate improving to the level it was in the early 1950s. The average of the trend in agriculture growth from 1950–51 to 1964–65 is 2.48 per cent on a declining trend. The average of the trend in agriculture growth from 1965–66 to 1974–75 is the same 2.48 per cent, but this time on a rising trend as we can see in the graph. The stark difference between the two periods is in the *variability* of agriculture growth. The dashed lines showing the growth of agriculture depict that the lowest growth rate was of –4.5 per cent in 1957–58 and the highest was of 10.1 per cent in 1958–59 during the first period of fifteen years. In the subsequent period the variability was much higher with the lowest growth rate of agriculture at –11 per cent in 1965–66 and the highest at 14.9 per cent in 1967–68, and even the second highest (7.2 per cent in 1973–74) and lowest (–5 per cent in 1972–73) growth rates in the latter period were larger than the highest and lowest for the earlier period. With the share of agriculture equal to more than half that of the aggregate economy, such large variations due to weather shocks played havoc with the incomes that agents in the economy obtain and were the economic root of the turmoil the country experienced. The variation in agricultural output and associated inflation affected large masses of population who eked out a living from current and volatile agricultural incomes. A focus on the aggregate income and output of the economy conceals this variation as it grew at an average rate of 3.7 per cent from 1951–52 to 1964–65 and a marginally lower 3.5 per cent during 1965–66 to 1974–75 – indicative of the famous 'Hindu rate of growth' that was associated with India. Mrs Gandhi had a finger on the pulse when she declared *garibi hatao* as the vision for a country facing high variations in income and high inflation from intermittent drought.

Mrs Gandhi called for early elections in 1971 raising the slogan of *garibi hatao,* and won a handsome majority. The landslide victory for the Congress (R) was followed by repressive measures – the Maintenance of Internal Security Act of 1971 which sanctioned indefinite preventive detention, search and seizure of property without warrant, and wiretapping. Elections within the Congress (R) for office holders were discontinued and Mrs Gandhi appointed party officials and chief ministers of states. There was also the 24th Amendment of August 1971 that gave Parliament the authority to amend the Constitution, even the fundamental rights provisions, and the 25th Amendment of December 1971, which gave Parliament, rather than the courts, the right to determine the amounts of compensation to be paid when the government acquired private property. These were all indications of the populist dictatorship that was to follow.

Hardly had the government taken office in March 1971 when it was faced with the Bangladesh crisis, and it found itself busy with the task of finding means to maintain the flood of refugees. This was followed by the war with Pakistan and the termination of the US aid. The year 1971 also stands out as it saw the collapse of the par value system in international finance that had been the basis for world trade and payments since 1944 and resulted in India further devaluing the rupee. After four years of good weather the failure of summer and winter rains in 1972–73 resulted in a sharp decline in agricultural production. When OPEC raised oil prices fourfold in 1973 it resulted in a crisis with the import bill increasing by a billion dollars. Import prices of food and fertilisers went up, and the unprecedented bout of inflation of 1973 and 1974 followed.

The exceptional rise in prices and acute shortages of goods embittered the people since the recent election had stirred up expectations of a better life. Economic growth as measured by the growth rate of aggregate income was a mere 1 per cent in 1971–72, -0.3 per cent in 1972–73, a respectable 4.5 per cent in 1973–74, and again a dismal 1.2 per cent in 1974–75 – at a time when the population was growing at around 2.5 per cent. In fact, the per capita national income growth during the period 1971–72 to 1974–75 averaged a negative, –1.1 per cent, the *worst medium-term performance ever of the Indian economy*. The improved growth rate during 1975–76 of 7.1 per cent turned this negative figure to a paltry average growth of per capita income during 1971–72 to 1975–76 of 0.6 per cent – the lowest during the last seventy years of the Indian economy (Figure 3). It was also a period when the economy endured the *highest inflation rate India has ever witnessed* – 17.2 per cent in 1973–74 (Figure 2). At a time when growth was sputtering, inflation was rearing an ugly head. If one purchased a basket of agricultural goods for ₹100 in 1970–71, inflation implied that the same basket of goods would cost ₹165 in 1974–75 – an overwhelming increase in household budget payouts when real incomes were in fact almost frozen at the levels of 1970–71. This was due to the sharp increase in the prices of petroleum crude and crude oil products, and the relatively low supplies of essential consumer goods.

For three years, the country was rocked by violence, strikes, student agitations, gheraos and bandhs. Corruption and black marketing was rife. In the state of Gujarat where the Congress won 83 per cent of the seats in the 1972 state assembly elections, the chief minister, Chimanbhai Patel, lifted the regulations on the price of groundnut oil commonly used in cooking. The purpose was not to increase efficiency but to ensure substantial profits to oil traders who transferred part of it to the Congress party for its forthcoming expenses in the election in UP. By late December 1973 students in the state were protesting higher food bills in college dining halls. The ensuing riots and the *Nav Nirman* movement calling for the resignation of the chief minister and the way it spread to student protests in Bihar, and the rise of Jayaprakash Narayan (JP) and his advocacy of defensible violence to prevent injustice, is covered in other parts of this book.

Figure 3: Average Per Capita National Income Growth Rate

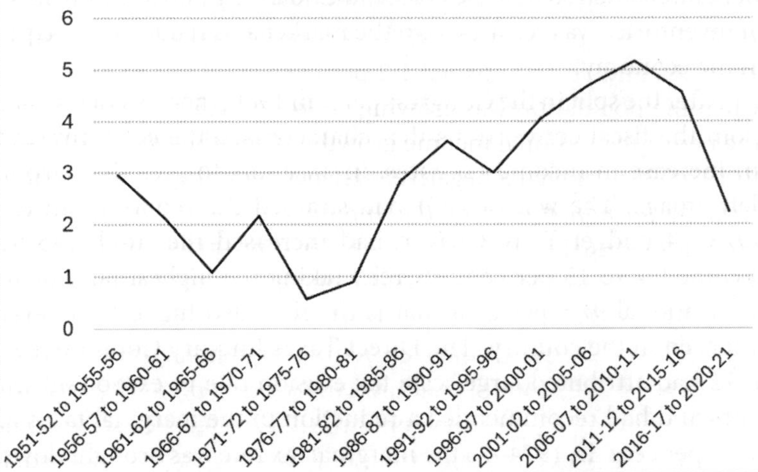

With inflation becoming an increasingly political issue an anti-inflation package was drawn up and announced in July 1974 in the form of three ordinances. The Additional Emoluments (Compulsory Deposit) Ordinance provided for compulsory deposit of the whole of additional wages and salaries and half of additional dearness allowance that affected nearly 18 million employees in the public and private sectors. The funds were to be frozen with the RBI and to be repaid with interest in five annual instalments. The Companies (Temporary Restrictions on Dividends) Ordinance limited the after-tax profits distributed by companies to 33.3 per cent of profits or to 12 per cent of the face value of shares, whichever was less. The Compulsory Deposit Scheme covered all income tax payers whose aggregate net annual income exceeded ₹15,000. This was set at a progressive rate[11] and the deposits were to be frozen with the RBI and repaid with

[11] The rate was 4 per cent of aggregate net annual income up to ₹25,000; 6 per cent plus ₹1,000 in the income slab of ₹25,001 to ₹70,000; and 8 per cent plus ₹3,700 on the excess of income that exceeded ₹70,000.

interest in five annual instalments. Union excise duties were raised on a number of items. There was also the imposition of a tax at the rate of 7 per cent on the gross interest earned by banks on loans, that would have an impact of raising the cost of borrowing. Operations against smugglers, hoarders and black marketeers were intensified so that the inordinate hoarding and accumulation of inventories was released into the market and reduced shortages in the economy.

After the split in the Congress party in 1969, there was a reversal from the fiscal conventions that characterised the economy and an increase in income tax rates, in an effort to give the party a 'left' image. The war of 1971 had strained the economy. In the 1973–74 budget Y. B. Chavan had increased the surcharge on income tax to 15 per cent, thereby taking the highest tax rate to an irrational 97.5 per cent that is the recorded highest rate ever imposed in the country. The Direct Taxes Enquiry Committee in 1971 had attributed large scale tax evasion due to exorbitant tax rates and had recommended a reduction in the marginal tax rate to 75 per cent. In 1974–75 the marginal tax rate was brought down to 77 per cent including a 10 per cent surcharge, and in 1976–77 it was reduced further to 66 per cent. It took much longer for fiscal authorities to realise that high tax revenues come from a wide tax base and not from high tax rates. Indirect taxes too were hiked on articles the government considered as being luxuries. And the budgetary expenditures were increasingly towards rural development.

The Emergency Years

George Fernandes called on workers of the Indian Railways to strike and demanded substantial increases in the salaries and bonuses of railway workers. He was outspoken about crippling the industry's ability to source raw materials and about bringing about economic chaos to knock down the government – to the extent of suggesting that the government would be brought to its knees if people starved when stranded trains could not transport food to them. From an economic stance it is clear that if he had succeeded and was then required to make good on the demand for increases in salaries and bonuses, the burden on the government budget – when there was already a downturn in economic activity and high inflation – would have led to economic chaos. The government on its part was excessively ruthless in the use of force where over twenty-five thousand workers were held without trial, and in the use of police brutality. JP called for a Bihar bandh in early October when the state was in the midst of floods in the north and a drought in the south, and people were in the midst of hardships; and as written in the *Times of India* 'frustrated politicians' used the bandh to 'spread anarchy' (4 October 1974).

Unlike in Gujarat where Mrs Gandhi had conceded to the demand to dismiss the chief minister and dissolve the state assembly, in Bihar she did not relent and used the police and military. In early January of 1975 a bomb killed railway minister L. N. Mishra in Bihar. He was the Congress party's principal fundraiser and had broken the railway workers' strike earlier. The turning point came in June 1975 when the High Court in Allahabad found that Mrs Gandhi's electoral campaign had broken electoral law in that her election agent had been a government employee and that the state government paid for high-quality loudspeakers and high rostrums to allow the diminutive prime minister to address election meetings from a dominating position. Her election was declared null and void, and the appeal made to the Supreme Court granted a stay with the condition that she could attend Parliament but not vote until her appeal was decided upon. She decided to impose the Emergency soon after. Thousands were rounded up and put into jail including her political rivals such as JP and Morarji Desai. She then proceeded to amend the Constitution so as to give herself unlimited power. The 38th amendment to the Constitution was passed in July, which barred judicial review of the Emergency. The 39th amendment did not allow for anyone to challenge a prime minister's election, and the 42nd amendment gave Parliament sweeping powers including the right to extend its term which it did by cancelling the elections due in 1976.

Declaring the Emergency in a radio address to the nation, Mrs Gandhi referred to the 'widespread conspiracy which has been brewing ever since (she) began introducing certain progressive measures of benefit to the common man and woman of India'. She announced that measures to relieve the hardships of various sections, including the poor and vulnerable, and those with fixed incomes, were under active consideration and that those would be announced soon. Five days later, the Twenty Point Programme was announced and held out the hope for the alleviation of poverty. It included implementation of land-ceiling legislation, a big increase in the allotment of house sites for the landless, a moratorium on rural debt to give relief to small and landless farmers and artisans, and the abolition of bonded labour. Such measures came under the jurisdiction of the states which had ignored them, and the Emergency gave an opportunity to the government in the centre the chance to address them. There were gains from the pursuit of these measures. By December of 1976, around 1.7 million acres of land were distributed among the landless as against 62,000 acres between 1972 and 1975. Over three million house sites were allotted in the first year of the Emergency. The monsoon too was bountiful and it resulted in a bumper harvest that exceeded for the first time the level achieved in 1970–71. Consequently there was a lid on prices and inflation actually turned negative. With strikes falling sharply and hoarding kept in check, there was an improvement in electric power generation and transport services, and the growth rate of manufacturing improved from the low of 2.1 per cent in 1975–76 to 8.8 per cent in 1976–77, 6.2 per cent in 1977–78, and 12.4 per cent in 1978–79. It again declined in the subsequent couple of years to −3.2 per cent, and 0.2 per cent during the Janata government phase. The first year of the Emergency resulted in a bumper food crop due to a good monsoon and this dampened agricultural inflation from the high of 22.9 per cent the previous year to −12.2 per cent in 1975–76. However, in the second year of the Emergency there was a drought again, and agricultural inflation was back at 8.4 per cent.

There has been a substantial debate in the 1980s on the slowdown in industrial growth in India during this period (see the summary in Varshney 1984). The periodisation most scholars used was from 1959–60 to 1965–66 where the growth rate of manufacturing was 6.9 per cent, and the subsequent period of 1966–67 to 1979–80 during which it declined to 4.3 per cent.[12]

---

[12] The data at that time was with reference to 1970–71 prices, unlike the 2011–12 prices we are reporting values for. At 1970–71 prices,

Figure 4: Gross Capital Formation (GCF) of Public Sector & Aggregate Gross Capital Formation as per cent of GDP at market prices

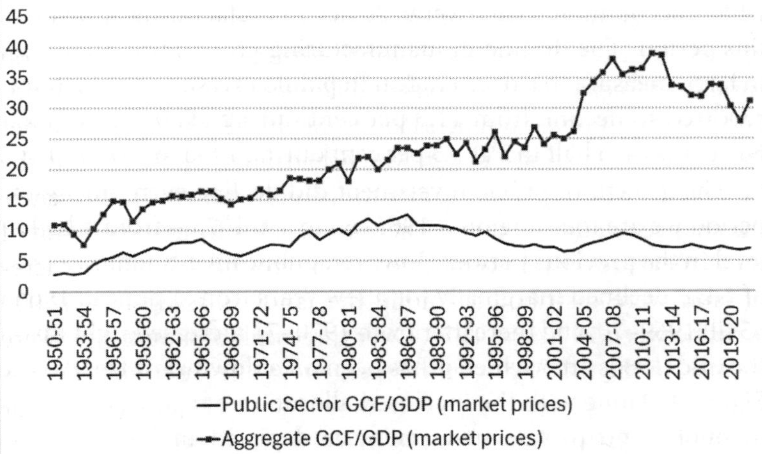

For the periodisation we have adopted, which captures the pre-Emergency period, the growth of manufacturing declined from 6.1 per cent during 1951–52 to 1964–65, to 4.5 per cent during 1965–66 to 1974–75. As can be seen from Figure 1, the year 1959–60 is like a turning point from which there was a deceleration of manufacturing growth right up to 1971–72. Thereafter there was an uptick to the growth rate. A word of caution – the data in Figure 1 is trend data which captures the longer run properties of the series[13] rather than the year-to-year fluctuations.[14] Apart from

---

the decline of the growth in the industrial sector was from 7.6 per cent during 1959–60 to 1965–66, to 5.5 per cent between 1966–67 and 1979–80.

[13] This is the secular underlying trend of the variable as described in footnote 4.

[14] There was substantial debate about the periodisation adopted. Ashok Desai was prescient in his view that the various authors were unduly influenced by the cyclical part of growth and that ten years hence it could well be that 1956–65 is regarded as one of high growth, and 1966–75 as low growth after which growth picked up pace. See Varshney (1984).

two years, 1968–69 and 1969–70 when annual manufacturing growth was above trend, for the other years in the 1965–66 to 1974–75 period annual manufacturing growth was below trend, which accounts for the overall lower manufacturing growth in this period. The decline in manufacturing growth was attributed in large measure to a deceleration in public investment which was reported to decline from 11.3 per cent during 1950–51 to 1965–66, to less than half this at 5.3 per cent during 1966–67 to 1980–81.

The growth of public investment did decline even during the period we are focusing on – 1965–66 to 1974–75 – from a higher level in the previous period. However, public investment as a ratio of GDP declined marginally for a few years from a peak in 1964–65 till 1969–70, and thereafter from 1970–71 increased right up till the mid-1980s after which it has been on a downward trend – see Figure 4. Along with the increased allocation of aggregate output to public and private investment as depicted in Figure 4, the trend growth of aggregate output (GVA) and of manufacturing increased from 1971–72 onwards as depicted in Figure 1. This is in line with research that public investment stimulates private investment in the Indian context.[15] The conundrum that scholars have expressed is, why is it that with high savings and investment rates the Indian economy was stuck in the Hindu rate of growth? Bardhan (1984) argued that a coalition of dominant interests – better-off cultivators, industrialists and bureaucrats – were using resources opportunistically for self-benefit rather than to build productive capacity. Isher Ahluwalia (1989) blamed the strangulation of industry by controls. And Francine Frankel (1978) expressed dissatisfaction that the state was incapable of mobilising additional resources to satisfy the demands being placed on it, which resulted in the supply-side constraints that inadequate public investments had been imposing on production. In the literature on economic growth, it is fundamental that increased savings and investment rates increase the rate of growth. Indeed, the literature on economic growth of the period

[15] This crowding in of private investment was noted even during the debates on the deceleration in industrial growth in the pre-1980s. See Varshney (1984).

emphasised that mobilising domestic savings and supplementing it with foreign aid was required by governments so as to overcome the deficiency of capital that characterised a developing economy. With savings and public as well as private investment growing, trend growth did improve to reach a maximum of 5.4 per cent in 2007–08 which is the year that private investment as a ratio of GDP too peaked. Public investment as a ratio of GDP increased till 1986–87 after which it declined - Figure 4. This increase in investment was not financed by standard income taxation or the taxation of goods and services but rather by the taxation of savings. This factor has been neglected in the explanations provided for low growth. Government expenditures from 1968–69 after bank nationalisation were increasingly financed through financial repression - the requirement that banks set aside a part of their deposits to fund government borrowing at administered interest rates which were below the market rate of interest.[16] This is the Statutory Liquidity Ratio or SLR requirement on banks in India, and the fraction of deposits so mobilised for government expenditure increased from 25 per cent in 1968–69 to reach a peak of 38.5 per cent in 1991–92 (Figure 5).

Financial repression results in savings being allocated to assets that would otherwise have been credit constrained and which have lower rates of return. This factor behind the low growth of the economy has not been given adequate attention (see D'Souza and Surti 2023). The period of the 1960s and 70s were, in addition to administered interest rates, marked by automatic monetisation of budget deficits by the RBI. Through the first four years of the 1970s money supply growth was 15 per cent when it had seldom crossed the 10 per cent mark before. Moreover, this period was marked by turbulence - a war with Pakistan which resulted in the government looking for means to maintain the flood of refugees

[16] The cost of financial repression is that it reduces the return to private saving and this could lead to a decline in savings. However, the nationalisation of banks essentially provided an explicit guarantee to depositors that all obligations of public sector banks will be fulfilled by the Indian government in the event of a failure, which dramatically improved the share of bank branches in rural areas, and increased the savings rate of the economy.

from Bangladesh, a drought in 1973, an oil shock in 1973 which resulted in a rise in import prices especially of food and fertilisers, the termination of US aid, and the breakdown of the Bretton Woods system. Whenever the government wanted resources to finance its expenditures it would take recourse to the RBI. The need to keep money growth in check meant that the RBI would keep raising the SLR so that the government would have the required resources, but now by taxing deposits in the banking system.

Figure 5: Statutory Liquidity Ratio for Indian Banks

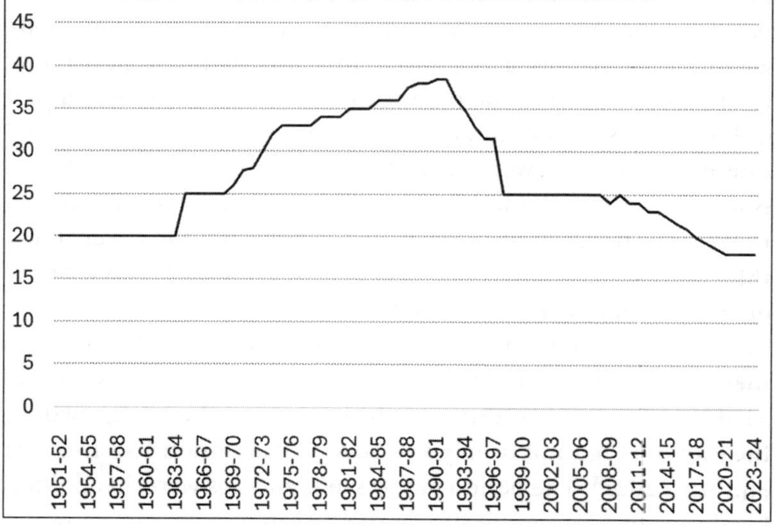

With a low ability to tax in an environment where agriculture is the dominant source of income, the government resorted to taxes on trade but more so on financial repression. We referred above to the high rates of direct taxation that were introduced only to be reversed as they led to evasion. Financial repression via increases in SLR was used by government to raise revenue due to the constraints on other types of taxes that could be imposed in a predominantly agricultural economy and with widespread poverty. The increases in SLR are depicted in Figure 5. Once an economy structurally transforms with manufacturing and services becoming a dominant component of aggregate income, a government can resort to a relatively broad tax base which results in a reduction on financial repression as a means of government revenues. The decrease in SLR, which was an important means of revenue generation in the first three decades after independence, accompanied this transformation of the economy. Even in 2023–24 the SLR is around what it was in 1951–52, which indicates its continued importance for funding the fiscal deficits of the government.

Mrs Gandhi had startled everyone by declaring an Emergency. On the night that the Emergency was declared Morarji Desai had predicted that she would never take the country towards dictatorship. 'She'll never do it – she'll commit suicide first', he is reported to have said (Jaffrelot and Anil 2020, 229). She again surprised everyone by calling off the Emergency and declaring elections. Perhaps the excesses of the Emergency unleashed by her son Sanjay Gandhi became too much to bear. The new National Population Policy that set high sterilisation targets to control population had overreached, with the number of sterilisations that were mostly forced reaching 8.2 million in the second year of the Emergency, more than double the target set. Sanjay had also embarked on a beautification drive of cities with a slum clearance programme that was implemented by demolition of structures and forced resettlement of large numbers of people. He had begun to establish contact with chief ministers of states without consulting his mother, had begun advocating a change in the Constitution and for a presidential form of government; and possibly to curb his adventurism and to delink him from some of his disreputable colleagues, Mrs Gandhi possibly felt that elections were the way to re-establish her eroding authority. We should recall that when she was re-elected in 1980 Sanjay wanted to become the chief minister of UP and had got the UP Congress legislature party to pass a resolution to elect him as their leader. She bluntly told H. R. Bharadwaj to inform his friend and her son that he cannot become chief minister and that if he insists, she will resign. Her support from the CPI was also on a rebound as it escalated its criticism of the family-planning measures and beautification drives. Perhaps the assassination of her cabinet minister and that of Sheikh Mujibur Rahman in August 1975 made her fear for her life, and she delayed calling for elections which she may have done earlier than she actually did. We do not know what the issues were that weighed in on her mind. She did receive feedback from the Intelligence Bureau that she would win the elections, but there is evidence too that she did not believe that. Perhaps what made her decide was the unpopularity with the excesses of the Emergency where people lost personal freedoms; or that as someone who had seen the freedom movement from close quarters and as the daughter of Nehru, she did not want to go down in history as a despotic figure. In March 1977, Mrs Gandhi was defeated in the elections. Morarji Desai became the prime minister and H. M. Patel, a retired bureaucrat, the finance minister.

A newly elected Janata government took the economy into a further tailspin. It continued with the trend of high market borrowing and in the budget of February 1979 the uncovered budget deficit was placed at ₹1,000 crore, but by the end of the fiscal year it had phenomenally increased to ₹2,700 crore. With the external shock in 1979 of the quadrupling of oil prices, India was in crisis again. When Mrs Gandhi was re-elected in January 1980 she inherited an economy that would have been familiar to her – foreign exchange reserves that had been wiped out, another drought, and inflation that was at the second highest level ever experienced in the country after the pre-Emergency period!

Concluding Comments

Severe droughts, wars, high inflation and economic distress in a predominantly agrarian economy inevitably had consequences, and the Congress party that was dominant since independence began to lose control over individual state legislatures which increased political instability. The passing away of Nehru with no clear successor led to factional infighting and the onset of alliances that were determined in part by personal ambitions of the major figures involved. The period may be identified as one where the preponderant concern of politicians was for self-preservation, and Mrs Gandhi was able to become the prime minister after some manoeuvring which resulted in a split in the Congress party. She accepted an alliance with radical groups in the party, and claimed that she was defending the poor against sectarian interests with the adoption of the slogan of *garibi hatao* and a return to the dirigiste policies of Nehru.[17] She adopted the strategy of going directly to the masses so as to augment her situation with respect to competing political elites. The opposition and JP, in turn, adopted a similar strategy of reaching out to the masses.[18]

This was a period of high inflation and low growth, and politics pivoted from a focus on growth to a politics of preservation and redistribution. The Emergency was a political counterpoint to the strikes and bandhs called by the opposition in response to the fragile economic situation of the times with a view to take political advantage. The increasing violence that had killed a cabinet minister and that could potentially be a threat to the life of the prime minister, and the loss of power with the High Court judgment that nullified the election result of the prime minister, would also have been a consideration in its declaration.

A redistributive politics focused on the poor was accompanied with a loss of dignity from the denial of liberty as the poor were forced to undergo sterilisation and forced evacuation, which would lead to a disenchantment of the poor from those who claimed to be their representatives. Fittingly, Mrs Gandhi was voted out of power when she ended the Emergency, on the basis of the promise of the Janata party of 'both bread and freedom' and the pledge that the representatives being voted for would act on behalf of their interests and be better able to absorb them into

---

[17] Shastri had sought to reform the Nehruvian approach with a more market-oriented approach to economic growth. With a limited section of large farmers reaping the benefits of rural development schemes, the gap with landless labourers and poor farmers increased. The industrial sector was unable to produce fertiliser and agricultural machinery in support of the amelioration of the rural economy, and the rural sector in turn did not have the economic capacity to generate a mass demand for manufactured consumer goods.

[18] When the agitations in Bihar in 1974 escalated into mass protests, JP announced his plan to paralyse the administration, introduce *Gram Swarajya*, and establish a people's government. His goal was to uproot corruption from political life and to create the conditions where people living below the poverty line would obtain basic necessities.

the democratic and growth process. That was not to be, and Mrs Gandhi was voted in again after the brief experiment of the Janata party.

In terms of the economy, the Emergency was a response to the highest inflation and lowest income growth the country had experienced since Independence. There was experimentation with extensive taxation and an anti-inflation package, and most importantly a shift towards a direct attack on poverty through the Twenty Point Programme.[19] The Emergency was also a political response of preservation of power as opposition political forces sought to obtain power during a period of instability. Those very forces, on coming to power, brought the economy back to where it was during the pre-Emergency era, and were unable to continue to enjoy electoral support.

References

Ahluwalia, Isher Judge. 1989. *Industrial Growth in India: Stagnation since the Mid-sixties*. Delhi: Oxford UP.

Bardhan, Pranab. 1984. *The Political Economy of Development in India*. Delhi: Oxford UP.

Bhagwati, Jagdish N. and T. N. Srinivasan. 1975. *Foreign Trade Regimes and Economic Development: India*. National Bureau of Economic Research.

D'Souza, Errol and Jay Surti. 2023. Public Bank Guarantees, Credit Allocation and Aggregate Investment. Mimeo.

[19] Drought and economic distress in a primarily agricultural economy resulted in earlier responses such as price-incentive strategies in agriculture and bank nationalisation so as to direct the flow of credit towards priority users. Financial repression was used during this adverse phase of the economy to provide the resources for public investment that crowded in private investment and as its share in GDP increased after 1970–71 till the mid-1980s, so did the growth in manufacturing as well as agriculture that also responded to price incentives. Public investment led growth was the policy from this period that sustained the growth of the economy till the late 1980s up to the time when the rising fiscal deficits spilled over into current account deficits and resulted in a currency crisis in 1991.

Frankel, Francine R. 1978. *India's Political Economy*. Princeton: Princeton UP.

Hirschman, Albert, O. 1981. *Essays in Trespassing*. New York: Cambridge UP.

Jaffrelot, Christophe and Pratinav Anil. 2020. *India's First Dictatorship: The Emergency, 1975–1977*. London: Hurst Publishers.

Nehru, B. K. 1997. *Nice Guys Finish Second: Memoirs*. Viking.

Patel, I. G. 2002. *Glimpses of Indian Economic Policy: An Insider's View*. New Delhi: Oxford UP.

Times of India. 1974. Bihar's Plight. 4 Oct.

Vaidyanathan, A. 1977. Performance and Prospects of Crop Production in India. *Economic and Political Weekly*, Special Number (August).

Varshney, A. 1984. Political Economy of Slow Industrial Growth in India. *Economic and Political Weekly* (1 September): 1511–17.

7

Emergency and the Fabled Foreign Hand: A Factual, Fanciful, or Fabricated Fear?

Varun Sahni

Perhaps due to the fading of public memory over time, it is not widely known today that India's second National Emergency, proclaimed by President V. V. Giri on 3 December 1971 upon the outbreak of war against Pakistan, was still in force when President Fakhruddin Ali Ahmed controversially declared the country's third National Emergency on 25 June 1975. Juxtaposing the two concurrently running states of emergency highlights the contrast between the contentious reputation of the third Emergency vis-à-vis the non-controversial nature of the second. Declaring a state of emergency on the grounds of 'external aggression' was not divisive; doing so for reasons of 'internal disturbance' clearly was. Evidently, an external aggression threatens the entire nation; an internal disturbance merely challenges the government of the day.

Sovereign territoriality, the juridical template upon which relations between states have been built and sustained for over three centuries, is predicated upon an 'inside-outside' dichotomy that distinguishes between a hierarchically ordered domestic realm regulated by legitimate authority relations and an international arena consisting of 'politics without government' that is driven solely by state interest and power differentials. History is messier than theory, however, and a neat dichotomy between inside and outside is not readily discerned in the historical record. This is certainly the case with the 1975–77 Emergency in India.

The purpose of this chapter is to examine whether factors and forces external to India featured in the decision to declare a state of emergency. In her letter of 25 June 1975 to the president recommending the imposition of Emergency, the prime minister had stated that 'there is imminent danger to the security of

India being threatened by *internal disturbances*' (TOI 2013; my emphasis). Likewise, the Proclamation of Emergency of 25 June 1975 had clearly declared that 'a grave emergency exists whereby the security of India is threatened by *internal disturbance*' (*Gazette of India* 1975, 1349; my emphasis). There was no mention of any sort of external threat to India's security in either the prime minister's letter or the Emergency proclamation. How important, then, was the external factor – the fear of the so-called 'foreign hand' – in the entire decision-making process in June 1975? As Paul McGarr points out, 'The spectre of a "foreign hand", or external intelligence activity, real and imagined, has occupied a prominent place in India's political discourse, journalism, and cultural production' (McGarr 2024, 5). In politics, perception is often more important than reality; indeed, at moments of situational crisis or systemic rupture, perception shapes reality. But how do we analytically capture this intangible and subjective factor? Whose perception matters?

International Relations theorist Kenneth Waltz (1954) famously articulated 'three images' through which an observer can seek to understand international phenomena: through the eyes of the statesperson or policymaker (the first image); through the lens of state/national interest and domestic policy impulses (the second image); or through the envisioning of systemic dynamics (the third image).[1] This chapter takes Waltz's three 'levels of analysis' as its point of departure to analyse whether the supposed foreign hand provides a plausible explanation of the Emergency proclamation of 1975. Since our intent is to understand the impact of the international system on India's domestic politics, we will reverse Waltz's levels by first analysing international systemic dynamics, then political developments within India, and finally the personal perspective of Indira Gandhi herself. This will be done sequentially in the three sections that follow. The chapter will

[1] Waltz's three levels of analysis have come to be known in the discipline of International Relations as respectively the Hobbesian, Kantian, and Grotian images for their respective emphases on human nature (*Leviathan*), the type of state (*Perpetual Peace*), or the form of the interstate system (*Mare Liberum*).

conclude with an assessment of the veracity of the foreign hand: did it have a factual basis, was it merely an unrealistic fantasy, or was it fabricated to justify the unjustifiable?

A Large but Weak Postcolonial State Navigates Systemic Bipolarity

In the period 1947–75, five features of India stand out in the international systemic context: its relative weakness despite its continental size; its unsettled regional setting; its low levels of development and its marginal role in the world economy; its unremitting quest for strategic autonomy; and its ambiguous nuclear status.

India became sovereign at a moment in world history when power was polarised between two large continent-sized states that presented radically different alternatives of how to best organise society, economy and politics. As a British colony, undivided India had contributed an army of 2.5 million men – the largest all-volunteer military force in human history – as well as an enormous fund of capital and natural resources to the Allied cause in World War II. Although this had given India a seat at the high tables that shaped the post-War order, as a colony India did not really have a voice at any of these tables. India was unable to secure a permanent UN Security Council seat at the San Francisco Conference even though a defeated ally, France, and a nominally independent and bitterly divided country, China, were included in the Big Five. For India, this truly was a 'near miss': barely two years after the San Francisco Conference (April–June 1945), India was finally free of its colonial status (August 1947). In systemic terms, India in 1947 was large but weak, postcolonial yet not revolutionary, more status-quo-oriented than revisionist: From being the 'brightest jewel in the British crown', and thereby a core area of interest to Britain's systemic hegemony, it became a peripheral actor in a marginal region. India's region, while far removed from the 'central theatre' of Europe with Berlin as its epicentre, was nevertheless an area of superpower competition, with the Western alliance moving quickly to enlist Pakistan in bloc-building to contain the Soviet Union in its southern flank.

India faced war due to unsettled borders and contested territories leading to two border wars against Pakistan (1947–48 and 1965) and one against China (1962). The war of 1947–48 was a partially successful defensive campaign, 1962 an unmitigated defeat, 1965 a tarnished stalemate, before Indira Gandhi gave the armed forces a free hand to conjure up a historic victory in the Bangladesh Liberation War of 1971. During the three decades between 1947 and 1975, South Asia as a region was neither peaceful internally nor cohesive externally. Or, to put the matter in active voice, India as the regional power was neither able to pacify its region nor make it cohere. The most plausible explanation of this signal foreign policy failure is that the Partition of India introduced a zero-sum political logic in the way the two successor states to British India, India and Pakistan, viewed the external world. No external presence in the region was ever perceived by both states in similar terms. Immediately after the victory of the Chinese Communist Party (CCP) in 1949, India tried to build strong ties with the Chinese Communist leadership while Pakistan was drawn into the US alliance structure to contain the Soviet Union and the PRC. India viewed the US alliance structure as a threat to the region, a perspective that Pakistan, as a US ally, obviously did not share. Later, as India's relations with China deteriorated, leading to the border war of 1962 between the two Asian giants, Pakistan's relations with China improved dramatically, culminating in the so-called 'all-weather friendship' that still exists between Beijing and Islamabad. Pakistan was one of the few countries with which China maintained close diplomatic and political relations even during the Cultural Revolution period. After the Sino-Soviet rift, India moved to cement its relations with Moscow, over time becoming a close friend of the Soviet Union. After the signing of the Indo-Soviet Treaty of Peace, Friendship and Cooperation in 1971, the two countries became virtual allies.

The Nehruvian tradition of foreign policy, which Indira Gandhi inherited, visualised the world in expansive frames: Cairo had greater salience than Colombo or Kathmandu; African decolonisation was more important than overcoming subcontinental ruptures; the road from Bandung led inexorably to Belgrade; systemic and global concerns (non-alignment, disarmament, NIEO) garnered far greater diplomatic energies and resources than the primary task of building a regional neighbourhood that was internally peaceful and externally coherent. Indian foreign policy during these years ranged far and beyond the immediate regional neighbourhood and presumed to reshape the world. Non-alignment, India's attempt to acquire policy autonomy in a rigidly bipolar world, was an innovative foreign policy that was both prudent (from a realist perspective) and ethical (from a normative perspective). As an attractive foreign policy option for the newly decolonised states of Asia and Africa, non-alignment soon transcended its Indian origins. India also had historical links with the region lying between Egypt and Iran, as it did with southeast Asia, specifically the Malay peninsula, most of eastern and southern Africa, and the islands and territories of the Anglophone and Dutch Caribbean, all with significant diaspora populations. However, India demonstrated little concern for persons of Indian origin living in other countries. When Indians in Burma faced persecution in the early 1950s, Nehru advised them to identify completely with the local population. The expulsion of the large Indian population from Uganda by Idi Amin in 1972, likewise, did not result in any meaningful reaction from India.

During these years India was fully a part of the developing world, which by the mid-1960s began to challenge the contours of the world capitalist system itself. In commodity groups in cocoa, copper, sugar and coffee, the countries of Asia, Africa and Latin America discovered their common cause, and the tricontinental 'Third World' was born. Two significant systemic developments in 1964 were the establishment of the United Nations Conference on Trade and Development (UNCTAD) as a permanent intergovernmental body of the UN General Assembly to deal with trade, investment and development issues, and the setting up of the Group of 77 (G77) as a caucus organisation of developing states to pursue common goals and develop leverage in UN deliberations. The year 1964 marks the beginning of a process of fundamental systemic reorientation, in which the centrality of the East-West political, ideological and military cleavages of the Cold War were gradually replaced by a North-South dichotomy drawn principally on economic and developmental lines. This process was accelerated by the early 1970s. The success of the Organization of the Petroleum Exporting Countries (OPEC), the most powerful commodity cartel in the 1970s, solidified the belief that a unified Third World coalition could force significant concessions from the industrialised countries. Third World countries participated enthusiastically in the Third UN Conference on the Law of the Sea (UNCLOS III), which began in 1973 (and was successfully concluded in 1982), and pushed for the formulation and promotion of the New International Economic Order (NIEO) in 1974, a diplomatic initiative in which India under Indira Gandhi's leadership was heavily involved.

India's birth as a sovereign territorial state was contemporaneous with the dawn of the nuclear age. From its earliest days as an independent state, India maintained and steadily expanded its nuclear establishment but maintained a policy of ambiguity with regard to developing a nuclear weapon. Under Indira Gandhi's leadership, India conducted its first nuclear test, a Peaceful Nuclear Explosion (PNE) codenamed 'Smiling Buddha', on 18 May 1974 in the Pokhran Test Range in Rajasthan. As Scott Sagan (1996, 68) has pointed out,[2] the timing of Smiling Buddha is puzzling: Despite its defeat in the border war against China in 1962, India did not conduct a nuclear test in the ten years after China tested a nuclear weapon in 1964, nor even before the coming into force of the Nuclear Non-Proliferation Treaty (NPT) in 1970 (which would have made India a legal nuclear weapons state), but then developed and tested just such a weapon less than three years after it dismembered Pakistan in 1971. Sagan (1996, 68) argues that a particular set of domestic politics – the existential

[2] In this article, Sagan famously proposes three models about 'why states decide to build or refrain from building nuclear weapons': the 'security model' suggests that states build nuclear weapons to increase national security against foreign threats, especially nuclear threats; the 'domestic politics model' views nuclear weapons as 'political tools used to advance parochial domestic and bureaucratic interests'; and the 'norms model' proposes that 'nuclear weapons decisions are made because weapons acquisition, or restraint in weapons development, provides an important normative symbol of a state's modernity and identity' (Sagan 1996, 55).

political crisis faced by Indira Gandhi in 1974 – provides a much better explanation for Smiling Buddha than national security compulsions. Whatever its motivation, a significant consequence of the nuclear test of 1974 was that India became the prime target of the interlocking treaties, ad hoc arrangements and suppliers' groups that in their conjunction constituted the multilateral non-proliferation architecture. US Secretary of State Henry Kissinger proposed the creation of the London Club, later the Nuclear Suppliers Group, in London in 1975, immediately after India's first nuclear test in 1974.

By 1975, there were therefore significant points of friction between India and the United States of America (USA). From the US perspective, India was a gadfly too large to ignore, that had been instrumental in setting up the Non-Aligned movement in 1961, had spearheaded the Third World movement to challenge the global economic order from 1964 onwards, had entered into a quasi-alliance with its enemy (Soviet Union) in order to dismember its client state (Pakistan) in 1971, and had detonated a nuclear device in 1974 in total defiance of the established nuclear order championed by the US. Troublingly for the US narrative, India was a liberal democracy in a profoundly undemocratic part of the world, but India had always had an ambiguous relationship with the Western market democracies and had never been a part of the Western security community; indeed, threats to India were never viewed by the West as threats to *democracy*. In 1975, the US and India truly were 'estranged democracies' (Kux 1994).

This is the bilateral context in which the US proclivity to meddle in the internal affairs of other states needs to be highlighted. In the 1947–75 period, US covert and overt intervention in other states included influence operations (1948–60 Italy, 1949–53 Albania, 1956–57 Syria, 1957–58 Indonesia, 1959–63 Iraq, 1961–65 Dominican Republic, 1965–66 Indonesia, and 1970–73 Chile), *coup d' états* (1949 Syria, 1953 Iran, 1954 Guatemala, 1960 Congo, 1963 South Vietnam, 1964 Brazil, 1966 Ghana, 1971 Bolivia, and 1973 Chile), assassination attempts (several on Cuba's Fidel Castro between 1959 and 2000), plots (the Bangkok Plot against Cambodia in 1959), invasions (1961 Cuba, Bay of Pigs/ Playa Girón), and terrorist operations (1961 Cuba, Operation

Mongoose). While some of these interventions failed, many succeeded, with some fundamentally altering the socio-economic and political trajectories of the intervened countries across four continents. In particular, the overthrow of Mohammad Mosaddegh in 1953 and Salvador Allende two decades later in 1973 resonated deeply in India, imparting a factual basis to the fear of the foreign hand in 1975.

Of course, the US was not the only superpower intervening in other countries during the Cold War years. The Soviet Union intervened with spectacular displays of power and purpose in Hungary (1956) and Czechoslovakia (1968), but also less dramatically in Congo (1960–65) and Yemen (1972). Why, then, were the bear's claws regarded as less threatening than the talons of the bald eagle? To understand why we must shift our gaze to the next level of analysis and consider India's domestic dynamics.

Domestic Politics and the Big Leap Leftwards

Born through a painful territorial vivisection, inheritor of a patchwork quilt of colonial provinces and presidencies and semi-autonomous feudal princedoms, and responsible for the fate of a continent-sized population characterised by immense socio-cultural diversity and widespread socio-economic deprivation, the domestic tasks of the Indian state in its first two decades clearly were pacification, consolidation and development. By the mid-1960s, the Indian state itself had started to change in significant ways. At the end of the Nehruvian period, and despite India's humiliating defeat at the hands of China in the border war of 1962, the Congress Party had remained in power, albeit temporarily weakened, and a political consensus still existed in the country. This broad-based consensus in India's public life could be attributed to several factors: cohesion flowing out of the freedom struggle, the experience of Partition at the moment of Independence and the determination that the country would not be divided ever again, the generation of 'tall leaders' spawned in the national liberation movement, the 'banyan tree' character of the Congress party, as also deliberate decisions to seek the 'middle ground' in domestic and foreign policy. Consensus was manifest in the policies of non-alignment and anti-colonialism in international relations, democracy and secularism in domestic politics, centralised planning and self-reliance in economic development, and egalitarian reform and affirmative action in the social sphere. Non-alignment in its initial years is best understood as the foreign policy analogue of the mixed economy at the domestic level: Sticking to the middle ground made choosing between the two superpowers unnecessary, and thereby prevented a rupture in India's public life. Admittedly, aspects of the national consensus outlined above were contested by the Jana Sangh, Swatantra party, and the Communist parties. Furthermore, this consensus masked the fact that the Indian state had turned steadily leftwards from the mid-1960s, and despite sporadic moves back to the centre, could be characterised as socialist for much of this period.

The leftward movement of the Indian state began with the *garibi hatao* ('Abolish Poverty') campaign by Indira Gandhi in the 1971 elections. Faced with an assault by the Old Guard/Syndicate within the Congress party, Indira Gandhi sought to change the discourse permanently in her own favour. In this endeavour, she largely succeeded. However, this phase of Indian domestic politics was not only about an individual leader; it was also about the creation of a new support base that could give the Congress party a permanent majority. The *garibi hatao* slogan, and the anti-poverty programmes with which it was accompanied, were designed to create a new coalition of rural and urban poor, with specific emphasis on the Scheduled Castes and Tribes and the religious minorities. Over time, the more liberal features of the Indian Constitution, especially some of the Fundamental Rights, were eroded while the socialist tendencies in the Directive Principles of State Policy were progressively strengthened.

The movement leftwards domestically had its external cognate. In 1971, faced with the certainty of war against Pakistan, the possibility of an Islamabad-Beijing axis and a pronounced US tilt towards Pakistan, India signed a Treaty of Peace, Friendship and Cooperation with the Soviet Union. This period of Indian foreign policy was marked by diplomatic moves aimed at strengthening Third World solidarity and pushing a revisionist agenda in various multilateral forums. Thus, the foreign policy thrust of the early

1970s was the outcome not only of inimical external developments but also of the domestic changes in India since the mid-1960s.

During the 1947–75 period, the Soviet Union was covertly active in India's domestic politics in a systematic and concerted fashion. We know two facts from the Mitrokhin Archive: (1) 'The Third World country on which the KGB eventually concentrated most operational effort during the Cold War was India' (Andrew and Mitrokhin 2014, 312), and (2) by the early 1970s 'the KGB presence in India became one of the largest in the world outside the Soviet bloc' (Andrew and Mitrokhin 2014, 321). The KGB was a major source of funding for the Communist Party of India (CPI) (Andrew and Mitrokhin 2014, 313) from the late 1950s. It conducted covert active-measures operations in support of Krishna Menon 'probably in the hope that he would become Nehru's successor' (Andrew and Mitrokhin 2014, 314–15) and later sought to support the prospects of Gulzarilal Nanda and Lal Bahadur Shastri in an effort to ensure that Morarji Desai did not succeed Nehru (Andrew and Mitrokhin 2014, 316). During the 1966 elections the KGB had sought to engineer a left-wing alliance between the CPI and the Communist Party of India, Marxist (CPM) *against* Indira Gandhi and the Congress party (Andrew and Mitrokhin 2014, 317). After the July 1969 bank nationalisation, Moscow pushed the CPI to support Indira Gandhi (Andrew and Mitrokhin 2014, 318) and backed the Mohan Kumaramangalam thesis that 'since the CPI could not win power by itself, as many of its members and sympathizers as possible should join the Congress, make common cause with "progressive" Congressmen and compel the party leadership to implement socialist policies' (Andrew and Mitrokhin 2014, 319).

Since India did not restrict the number of Soviet diplomats and trade officials in India, there were always many officially covered positions available to the Soviet covert agencies for their operatives in India, including Soviet intelligence officers expelled from other countries (Andrew and Mitrokhin 2014, 321). Oleg Danilovich Kalugin, onetime head of counterintelligence in the KGB, recalled that the KGB had 'scores of sources throughout the Indian government – in intelligence, counter-intelligence, the Defence and Foreign Ministries, and the police' (Quoted in

Andrew and Mitrokhin 2014, 321). Kalugin adds: 'It seemed like the entire country was for sale; the KGB – and the CIA – had deeply penetrated the Indian government. After a while neither side entrusted sensitive information to the Indians, realizing that their enemy would know all about it the next day' (Quoted in Andrew and Mitrokhin 2014, 322). Most damning of all, Kalugin opined that the KGB was more successful than the CIA 'partly because of its skill in exploiting the corruption which became endemic under Indira Gandhi's regime' (Andrew and Mitrokhin 2014, 322).

However, the mirror clearly had two faces during the Cold War. Two books published *after* the Emergency claimed that the CIA had had access to the highest reaches of the Indian state in the 1960s and early 1970s. The first book was the memoirs of US Senator Daniel Patrick Moynihan in which, recalling a review that he had ordered as the US ambassador to India, Moynihan claimed that the CIA had only twice interfered directly in India's domestic affairs by covertly channelling money to the Congress party in order to help defeat the Communist party in state elections in Kerala and West Bengal (Moynihan 1978, 41). The bombshell was Moynihan's allegation that in one of the two instances CIA funds had been handed over to Indira Gandhi herself when she was a Congress party official, an allegation that Indira Gandhi dismissed as 'mischievous, malicious and baseless' (cited in McGarr 2015, 289). A few years later, Seymour Hersh alleged that Morarji Desai, Indira Gandhi's political archenemy, 'was a paid informant for the CIA and was considered one of the Agency's most important "assets"' (Hersh 1983, 450). Allegedly, Desai had been on the CIA's payroll for $20,000 per annum during the Lyndon Johnson and Richard Nixon administrations and was regarded as a 'star performer' by the Agency, an allegation that Desai rejected as 'sheer madness' (*Indian Express* 1983) and 'a sheer mad story' (D'Alessio 1985). Desai filed a $100 million libel suit against Hersh in 1985 but both the judgement in 1989 (*Justia Law* 1989) and the appeal (*Justia Law* 1992) went against him, largely on procedural rather than substantive grounds. When the Hersh allegation became public in 1983, it was instantly linked to the Moynihan allegation of 1978. Instead of reflection, introspection, and preventive action against future penetration by foreign espionage agencies, the public debate got divided on bitter partisan lines, as evidenced in the parliamentary debate on 26 August 1983 (Parliament Digital Library 1983).

Thus, there was clearly more than one foreign hand active in India in 1975. That Soviet covert activities were ignored, tolerated, perhaps even encouraged as a counter to the CIA, can best be explained by the leftist orientation of the Indian state during these years: Moscow was widely seen as a friend, not foe.[3] But the 'greatest successes of Soviet active measures in India remained the exploitation of the susceptibility of Indira Gandhi and her advisers to bogus CIA conspiracies against them' (Andrew and Mitrokhin 2014, 336). To understand this factor, we need to understand the personality of India's leader, who was at once hugely popular and highly insecure.

Pride and Paranoia: The Perplexing Personality of Indira Gandhi

One of Indira Gandhi's leading *bête noire*, Henry Kissinger, who had long and influential careers in the mutually dissonant worlds of power and knowledge, reportedly remarked: 'As a professor, I tended to think of history as run by impersonal forces. But when you see it in practice, you see the differences personalities make' (quoted in Isaacson 1992, 13). Or, as Fred Greenstein has observed in more academic language, 'politics is a matter of human behaviour, and behaviour . . . is a function of both the *environmental situations* in which actors find themselves and the *psychological predispositions* they bring to those situations' (Greenstein 1987, 7; my emphases). Understanding the psyche and personality of Indira Gandhi becomes relevant because, as Surjit Mansingh has pointed out, 'By a combination of her own choice and the default of others, Mrs Gandhi was as prominent in

[3] Although not universally so. Jayaprakash Narayan noted in his diary on 21 July 1975 that the promulgation of Emergency 'was a Soviet plot' in which the deeper plan 'hatched by the Soviets was to take effect at the point of transition from social democracy to Communist dictatorship, at which point Indira was to be replaced by a Soviet stooge' (Quoted in Jayakar 1995, 284).

foreign as in domestic politics' (Mansingh 1984, 18). Jayantanuja Bandyopadhyaya remarks that, 'With her built-in sense of personal insecurity, her eternal mistrust of people, and her inevitably authoritarian political style, Mrs Gandhi was psychologically incapable of operating through the normal institutional channels for the administration of the foreign policy' (Bandyopadhyaya 1980, 341). Furthermore, 'Her suspicion of the bureaucracy below her was as great as her mistrust for the political leaders around her' (340)

Indira Gandhi's toughness and strong survival instinct developed as a young woman isolated in a Swiss sanatorium in war-torn Europe, movingly revealed in a conversation with Pupul Jayakar: '. . . my life was so hard that something had to develop to help me to meet that hardship' (quoted in Jayakar 1995, 106). Her toughness was revealed with full force on the eve of the Emergency: 'The greater the pressure mounted by the Opposition on her position as Prime Minister, the more defensive and abrasive were her speeches to the crowd. She spoke of plots against her, of anti-national forces wanting to destabilize the country, of the hand of foreign governments' (Jayakar 1995, 273). But her toughness had its roots in insecurity and loneliness: 'Indira Gandhi frequently referred to her childhood as "insecure'; she is most often described as "lonely"' (Mansingh 1984, 19). Ashis Nandy attributes these personality traits to her 'unending search for total security and total acceptance' (quoted in Mansingh 1984, 19). In the words of Mansingh again: 'Indira Gandhi erected defences for herself against being encroached upon by the outside world' (Mansingh 1984, 20).

The Mitrokhin Archive provides a fascinating glimpse into Soviet attempts to take advantage of Indira Gandhi's personality from the early 1950s onwards. During Indira Gandhi's first visit to the Soviet Union in 1953, the KGB kept her under 'continuous surveillance' but 'also surrounded her with handsome, attentive male admirers' (Andrew and Mitrokhin 2014, 316). However, 'Soviet attempts to cultivate Indira Gandhi during the 1950s were motivated far more by the desire to influence her father than by any awareness of her own political potential' (317). As her insecurity and paranoia grew, the KGB carried out many active measures 'which claimed to expose CIA plots in the subcontinent. . . . persuading Indira Gandhi that the Agency was plotting her overthrow' (326). She was 'also easily persuaded that the CIA, rather than the mistakes of her own administration, was responsible for the growing opposition to her government' (326).

According to former Indian intelligence officer B. Raman, 'She feared that the US intelligence was trying to destabilize her Government as a punishment for her action in East Pakistan. She started seeing the hand of the Central Intelligence Agency (CIA) everywhere . . .' (Raman 2007, 39). However, Raman then qualifies his statement:

> Her fears were not totally imaginary. . . . the PSYWAR Division of the CIA mounted a vicious disinformation campaign against her projecting her as a Soviet surrogate. All sorts of false stories regarding her were disseminated . . . that she had agreed to give base facilities to the Soviet Navy in the Andaman and Nicobar Islands and in Vizag, . . . that experts from the KGB, . . . , had played a role during Operation Bluestar in June 1984. . . . (Raman 2007, 40)

It is clear from contemporary accounts and subsequent analysis that no single event contributed more to Indira Gandhi's sense of paranoia of the foreign hand than the assassination/death/suicide of Salvador Allende Gossens, President of Chile, on 11 September 1973, during the military *coup d'état* that overthrew his elected government.[4] About the cause of Allende's death,

---

[4] Some observers, analysts and biographers suggest that even more than the *coup* against Allende, Indira Gandhi was traumatised by the assassination of Sheikh Mujibur Rahman, Prime Minister of Bangladesh, along with almost his entire family on 14 August 1975. According to P. N. Dhar, 'Intelligence reports to overthrow Mujib's government in Bangladesh added to her fears' (Dhar 2000, 254). In the words of Katherine Frank, 'Indira was devastated by the news of the assassination of Mujib and his family. And for once her belief that the CIA was implicated in their deaths was probably correct. . . . she interpreted his assassination as an omen of what could happen to her and her own family' (Frank 2001, 389). Andrew and Mitrokhin remark, 'The assassination of Sheikh Mujibur Rahman and much

James Dunkerley remarks that 'the uncertainty about his wounds and who inflicted them is the subject of sharp controversy': 'the military junta which deposed the president declared him a suicide whilst most of his supporters on the left subscribe to the view that he was shot down by his assailants' (Dunkerley 1992, 14). US Secretary of State Henry Kissinger had insisted in September 1973 that the US had played no role in the Chilean *coup d'état*. On 8 September 1974, less than a year later after the *coup*, news leaked that the CIA director, William E. Colby, had admitted to the US Congress in a top-secret hearing that the Nixon administration had in fact authorised more than $8 million for covert activities in Chile between 1970 and 1973, in order to 'destabilize' the 'Marxist' government of Salvador Allende and make it impossible for him to govern (Hersh 1974). Just two days after Colby's congressional testimony became public, US Ambassador to India Moynihan sent a cable to Kissinger reporting that the Indian Prime Minister had reminded a large audience in Madras that she had been ridiculed when she had spoken of an outside hand in Allende's killing, but that the foreign conspiracy in Chile was now confirmed (Moynihan 1974). He further quoted Indira Gandhi as telling the Madras crowd that 'reactionary forces, helped from outside, were using the current difficulties to whip up the people against the government and in this context it had become necessary to make India strong' (Moynihan 1974).

In November 1973 Indira Gandhi told Fidel Castro at a banquet in New Delhi, 'What they [the CIA] have done to Allende they want to do to me also' (Andrew and Mitrokhin 2014, 326). Her belief that the CIA 'had marked her out for the same fate became something of an obsession' (Andrew and Mitrokhin 2014, 326). P. N. Dhar, who served as her principal secretary during those tumultuous

---

of his family on 14 August further fuelled Mrs Gandhi's conspiracy theories. Behind their murders she saw once again the hidden hand of the CIA' (Andrew and Mitrokhin 2014, 328). However, the Mujib assassination happened almost two months *after* the Emergency had been promulgated, so the events in Bangladesh in August 1975 were at most a *post facto* validation of Indira Gandhi's fears of the foreign hand.

years, writes that 'Indira Gandhi herself had apprehensions of foreign involvement in the affairs of the country on the pattern of what happened in Chile. . . . Since she was herself high on Nixon's hate-list, she became apprehensive of what she called "the foreign hand"' (Dhar 2000, 254). Katherine Frank also mentions Nixon's 'hate list': 'She knew she was high up on Richard Nixon's hate list, and she was genuinely afraid that she would be overthrown and destroyed in the same way Chile's CIA-backed General Augusto Pinochet had staged a coup against Salvador Allende in 1973' (Frank 2001, 374–75). It is indeed true that the hatred that Nixon and Kissinger had for India and its leader cannot be ascribed to Cold War realpolitik alone, but rather emits a distinct stench of racist loathing mixed with personal antipathy: We know from the White House Tapes that, in their Oval Office conversations about India, they referred to Indira Gandhi specifically as a 'bitch' and an 'old witch', and Indians in general as 'bastards' (Kissinger 1979, 848; FRUS 1971a; FRUS 1971b).

On the eve of the Emergency decision, Indira Gandhi's confidants and advisers could point to the contrast between Jayaprakash Narayan's visit to the US in 1971, when he was campaigning for the Bangladesh freedom movement and was consequently treated with 'total indifference', with the 'praise showered' upon him during his US visit of 1974, when 'he was campaigning against Indira Gandhi, whom the Nixon administration wanted to punish for her defiance in 1971 and for the explosion of a nuclear device later' (Dhar 2000, 254). Dhar also mentions a US consular officer named Peter Burleigh 'who was constantly in touch with the agitators', which was seen as evidence of US involvement in anti-Indira agitations (Dhar 2000, 254). 'The enemy was diverse, but it was led by the 'fascist' JP movement, backed, Indira maintained by "a foreign hand"' (Frank 2001, 382).

But along with the paranoia came a certain measure of pride, both in herself and in the country she led. 'She was convinced that India would self-destruct if she relinquished power' (Frank 2001, 375). For all the Soviet exploitation of her fears of CIA subversive activity, 'At no time did Indira Gandhi accept the argument often propounded by Washington, and implicit in Moscow's proposals for Asian collective security, that the security interests of India or any other regional state could be served by an enhanced presence of either great power' (Mansingh 1984, 19). Furthermore, 'Where Nehru had articulated India's national interests in high-flown phrases of world peace and cooperation, Indira stressed national security, territory, and prestige as integral parts of national interests' (Mansingh 1984, 26). It is this admixture of pride and paranoia that makes Indira Gandhi's personality truly perplexing and fascinating, and made her so vulnerable to fears of the foreign hand.

Veracity of the Foreign Hand

So, in conclusion, did the fear of the foreign hand have a factual basis, was it merely an unrealistic fantasy, or was it fabricated to justify the unjustifiable? Our analysis across three distinct levels of analysis – the dynamics of the bipolar international system since 1945, the leftward trajectory of Indian politics since 1969, and the personal preferences and prejudices of Prime Minister Indira Gandhi since the mid-1950s – would suggest that there is no single answer to the question contained in the subtitle of this chapter. It is a fact that the US had intervened both overtly and covertly in the internal affairs of many countries since 1898 – as indeed had the Soviet Union since 1919. It is also a fact that the CIA had for many years sought to discredit Indira Gandhi and strengthen political forces opposed to her. Finally, it is also a matter of historical record that Nixon and Kissinger, neither of whom had any qualms about intervening forcefully in other countries when it served US interests, personally loathed Indira Gandhi.

There was, nevertheless, also a fanciful aspect to the fear of the foreign hand. Indira Gandhi clearly overplayed that card by attributing to the foreign hand every manifestation of dissension and opposition to her government. But another fanciful aspect was to ignore India's sheer size. With a population of 623.5 million in 1975, India was 56 times larger than Chile in 1973 (population of 11 million) and 34 times larger than Iran in 1953 (population of 18 million). Even Indonesia, the largest country in which the US has ever successfully intervened, had a population of 101 million in 1965, one-sixth of India's population in 1975. Aside from trivial funding and influence operations, for either of the two superpowers to have intervened in India in 1975 would have been a colossal undertaking with no guarantee of success.

Finally, the foreign hand was also an artful fabrication to justify rupturing a quarter-century of liberal democratic politics by the imposition of Emergency. Clearly, allegations of the foreign hand conveniently allowed Indira Gandhi to brush aside even valid criticisms and critiques of corruption and maladministration. If the threat was external, why the need for an *internal* Emergency? Neither the prime minister's letter to the president on 25 June 1975, nor the formal proclamation of the Emergency in the dying moments of that fateful day, had made any mention of foreign threats. Was Allende merely a fig leaf, as would be Mujib two months later, both used quite cynically to strengthen Indira Gandhi's hold on power? Could it be, all protestations and portrayals to the contrary, that the Emergency was about regime survival, not national security?

Unsatisfactory though that might well be, this chapter does not throw up a definite, let alone a definitive, conclusion. Claims of the foreign hand in 1975 were at once genuine, illusory and instrumental. History does not fit into crisp conceptual categories. Each level of analysis throws up a valid and coherent story. The membrane between inside and outside is permeable. Half a century on, intellectual probity impels us to recognise that there is more than one convincing narrative about the initiation of the 1975 Emergency.

References

Andrew, Christopher, and Vasili Mitrokhin. 2014. *The KGB and the World: The Mitrokhin Archive II*, 2nd edition. London: Penguin.

Bandyopadhyaya, Jayantanuja. 1980. *The Making of India's Foreign Policy: Determinants, Institutions, Processes and Personalities.* Bombay: Allied Publishers.

D'Alessio, F. N. 1985. Former Indian Prime Minister Questioned in Libel Suit, Associated Press, Chicago, 30 April.

Dhar, P. N. 2000. *Indira Gandhi, the 'Emergency', and Indian Democracy.* New Delhi: Oxford UP.

Dunkerley, James. 1992. *Political Suicide in Latin America and Other Essays.* London: Verso.

Frank, Katherine. 2001. *Indira: The Life of Indira Nehru Gandhi*. London: HarperCollins.

FRUS. 1971a. Conversation Between President Nixon and the President's Assistant for National Security Affairs (Kissinger), Washington, DC, 26 May 1971, *Foreign Relations of the United States, 1969–1976*, vol. E-7, Documents on South Asia, 1969–72, Document 150, [National Archives, Nixon Presidential Materials, White House Tapes, Recording of Conversation between Nixon and Kissinger, Oval Office, Conversation No. 505–4], accessed on 29 August 2024 from https://history.state.gov/historicaldocuments/frus1969-76ve07/d135.

———. 1971b. Conversation Among President Nixon, the President's Assistant for National Security Affairs (Kissinger), and the President's Assistant (Haldeman), Washington, DC, 5 November 1971, *Foreign Relations of the United States, 1969–1976*, vol. E-7, Documents on South Asia, 1969–72, Document 150, [National Archives, Nixon Presidential Materials, White House Tapes, Recording of Conversation among Nixon, Kissinger, and Haldeman, Oval Office, Conversation 615–4], accessed on 29 August 2024 from https://history.state.gov/historicaldocuments/frus1969-76ve07/d150.

Gazette of India. 1975. Notification. *The Gazette of India*, Extraordinary, Part II, Section 3, Sub-section (i), No. 169, New Delhi, 26 June: 1349.

Greenstein, Fred I. 1987. *Personality and Politics: Problems of Evidence, Inference, and Conceptualization*. Princeton: Princeton UP.

Hersh, Seymour M. 1974. C.I.A. Chief Tells House Of $8-Million Campaign Against Allende in 70–73, *The New York Times*, 8 September: 1, accessed on 12 May 2024 from https://www.nytimes.com/1974/09/08/archives/cia-chief-tells-house-of-8million-campaign-against-allende-in-7073.html.

———. 1983. *The Price of Power: Kissinger in the Nixon White House*. New York: Summit Books.

Indian Express. 1983. Sheer Madness, Says Desai, *Indian Express*, New Delhi, 3 June: 1.

Isaacson, Walter. 1992. *Kissinger: A Biography*. New York: Simon & Schuster.

Jayakar, Pupul. 1995. *Indira Gandhi: A Biography*. New Delhi: Penguin.

Justia Law. 1989. *Desai v. Hersh*, 719 F. Supp. 670 (N.D. Ill. 1989), US District Court for the Northern District of Illinois, July 14, 1989, accessed on 5 September 2024 from https://law.justia.com/cases/federal/district-courts/FSupp/719/670/1437743/.

———. 1992. *Morarji Desai, Plaintiff-appellant, v. Seymour Hersh, Defendant-appellee*, 954 F.2d 1408 (7th Cir. 1992), US Court of Appeals for the Seventh Circuit, Argued Dec. 5, 1990, Decided Jan. 28, 1992, Rehearing and Rehearing En Banc Denied March 26, 1992, accessed on 5 September 2024 from https://law.justia.com/cases/federal/appellate-courts/F2/954/1408/128191/#fn1.

Kissinger, Henry. 1979. *White House Years*. Boston: Little, Brown and Company.

Kux, Dennis. 1994. *India and the United States: Estranged Democracies 1941–1991*. New Delhi: Sage Publications.

Mansingh, Surjit. 1984. *India's Search for Power: Indira Gandhi's Foreign Policy 1966–1982*. New Delhi: Sage Publications.

McGarr, Paul M. 2015. "Do We Still Need the CIA?": Daniel Patrick Moynihan, the Central Intelligence Agency and US Foreign Policy. *History* 100.2 (340): 275–92.

———. 2024. *Spying in South Asia: Britain, the United States, and India's Secret Cold War*. Cambridge: Cambridge UP.

Moynihan, Daniel P. 1974. The United States as a Counter-Revolutionary Power – The Case of India and Chile, confidential cable from US Ambassador in India to the Secretary of State, 10 September, accessed on 26 February 2024 from https://wikileaks.org/plusd/cables/1974NEWDE12063_b.html.

Moynihan, Daniel P. with Suzanne Weaver. 1978. *A Dangerous Place*. Boston: Little, Brown and Company.

Parliament Digital Library. 1983. *Calling Attention to Matter of Urgent Public Importance: Reported allegations made by Mr Seymour Hersh in his recent book The Price of Power against former Prime Minister of India, Shri Morarji Desai*, 26 August 1983, accessed on 22 October 2024 from https://eparlib.nic.in/handle/123456789/835159?view_type=search.

Raman, B. 2007. *The Kaoboys of R&AW: Down Memory Lane*. New Delhi: Lancer Publishers.

Sagan, Scott D. 1996. Why Do States Build Nuclear Weapons? Three Models in Search of a Bomb. *International Security* 21.3: 54–86.

Sen, Suhit K. 2019. *The Paradox of Populism: The Indira Gandhi Years 1966–1977*. Delhi: Primus Books.

Times of India (TOI). 2013. Emergency Papers Found. *The Times of India*, 30 June, accessed on 20 October 2024 <https://timesofindia.indiatimes.com/home/sunday-times/deep-focus/emergency-papers-found/articleshow/20839450.cms>

Walker, R. B. J. 1993. *Inside/Outside: International Relations as Political Theory*. Cambridge: Cambridge UP.

Waltz, Kenneth N. 1954. *Man, the State and War: A Theoretical Analysis*. New York: Columbia UP.

Acknowledgement

The research assistance provided by Rupal Rupali is gratefully acknowledged.

This chapter, written while my father was battling through his final illness, is dedicated to his memory.

8

Resistance Journalism during the Emergency

Pamela Philipose

Those twenty-one months of unfreedom coming twenty-eight years after India had gained its freedom were perceived as an ominous sign of the flaws in its democracy. The promulgation of an internal emergency on 25 June 1975, upended a foundational aspiration of the independence movement: freedom of speech and expression for every citizen. On the midnight of 15 August 1947, Jawaharlal Nehru had alluded to this aspiration when he spoke about India's tryst with destiny as a moment when 'the soul of a nation, long suppressed, finds *utterance*'. His daughter, Indira Gandhi, as prime minister, signaled a premature end to that tryst by clamping down on 'utterance' during an interregnum that saw the complete suspension of democratic rights. Greatly perturbed by a verdict delivered by the Allahabad High Court on 12 June 1975, on a long pending election petition which had disqualified her from the membership of the Lok Sabha, she pressed what her close advisor P.N. Dhar was to later describe as the 'panic button' (2000, 262). With this one move, she silenced the full spectrum of her critics, from opposition parties and combative trade unions to an increasingly argumentative press.

Print Media in the Mid-1970s

The mid-1970s was a period when print capitalism in India was thriving. Its success was driven by a new keenness within the post-independence generation of the middle class to follow the news cycle in order to understand better their lived realities and develop a sense of self autonomy. Only newspapers could claim to be relatively independent of the government in that period, with both radio and television coming under tight government controls.

The salience of newspapers, especially those owned by an indigenous capitalist class, was buttressed by several significant developments over the earlier decade. The 1967 General Election had challenged the Congress's one-party rule for the first time in its history, leading to the party splitting in 1969. It has been argued that during those years it was the press, rather than parliament, that was perceived as the more credible forum for national discussions and debate. The government, on its part, tried to rein in the big newspapers by introducing policies such as reducing newsprint imports citing a foreign exchange crisis. In 1972, however, the Supreme Court of India, in *Bennett Coleman v. Union of India,* by overturning a newsprint control policy that the Government of India had brought in earlier that year,[1] struck a blow for large newspapers. The petitioners had made the case that their right to free speech and expression was violated by the policy which authorised a 20 per cent increase in newsprint allocation only for newspapers of less than ten pages. Their main argument was that this move discriminated against newspapers which had more than ten pages and therefore amounted to 'newspaper control'. Four judges of the five-judge bench hearing the case were persuaded by this line of reasoning.

A healthy momentum of growth saw India emerge as among the world's largest publishers of dailies, with circulation figures standing at 9.34 million in 1976, behind only the USSR and Japan. Strikingly, while English language newspapers enjoyed a preeminent position in the period immediately after independence, they had now been overtaken by language publications, with those in Hindi, Marathi, Urdu and Malayalam emerging as the top sellers. At the same time, English language dailies held pride of place in terms of their individual circulation. The *Indian Express*, as a multi-edition English language daily, accounted for 403,927 copies, followed by the *Times of India* with 346,733 copies (Pendakur 1988).

These big newspapers were controlled by urban elites and read largely by urbanites as only a fraction of their numbers reached

---

[1] *Bennett Coleman v. Union of India,* https://indiankanoon.org/doc/125596/

rural India. For Mrs Gandhi, it was the newspaper-owning elite and their city-based, middle-class readers who came to be perceived as her principal threats, not the anonymous millions in the hinterland. Young people, galvanised by the Navnirman movement, were on the streets; railway workers under the banner of All India Railwaymen's Federation, led by the fiery socialist leader George Fernandes, had brought the country to a standstill a year earlier through a nation-wide strike. Meanwhile, Jayaprakash Narayan's Total Revolution seemed to have arrived at the doors of Delhi. These were the forces – all of which drew their power from newspaper coverage – that Mrs Gandhi now sought to silence by gagging the press. She was driven by a strong sense of self-conviction. As she explained to visiting British civil servant W.G. Archer in March 1976, '"Total freedom" (of the press and public opinion) will be fatal to India' (see Guha 2000).

The system set up to achieve this objective had many dimensions, three of which are noteworthy.

First, and most important, was an array of punitive legal instruments. Not only were existing laws, like the Indian Penal Code, the Criminal Procedure Code, the Sea Customs Act, the Indian Telegraph Act and the Indian Post Offices Act, available to the regime; newly minted ones were now primed for instant deployment. Among these was the Prevention of Publication of Objectionable Matter Act (PPOMA), which first came in through the ordinance route and was rushed through Parliament in February 1976. It was considered as 'more draconian' than laws in force during the colonial period (Bhargava 2005, 64). 'Objectionable matter', as laid down in the new law, could be anything ranging from exciting disaffection against the government to publishing scurrilous material.

Simultaneous with the passing of the draconian PPOMA were laws that repealed protective legislation like the Parliamentary Proceedings (Protection of Publication) Act, which had been passed in 1956 by the then information and broadcasting minister Feroze Gandhi and sought to protect the right of journalists to report on discussions in Parliament without fear. The Press Council, an institution set up in 1966 to protect and self-regulate journalistic practice, was also dismantled through legislation.

The second dimension of the coercive system was the constitution of a formidable cadre of officers whose primary function was to surveil, report on and restrain the press. They included in their ranks innumerable censors who were to ensure that not a word that sought to criticise the ruling dispensation, or its prime leaders, passes into cold print. To provide muscle to their efforts was the ever-present threat of incarceration, referred to colloquially as the 'midnight knock', given the propensity of the Indira Gandhi police to make their arrests under the cover of darkness. The jails were already crowded thanks to the mass arrests of political activists, but there was always room to accommodate the obstreperous journalist.

The third important aspect of the system was controlling any reportage by the international media that sought to discredit the regime. Like autocrats who had preceded and followed her, Mrs Gandhi was extremely sensitive to how she was perceived by the world. Foreign correspondents could only function in the country if there was no doubt about their 'friendly attitude' to the government. Those whose publications carried any objectionable report could face deportation (Bhargava 2005, 64). Lawrence Lifschultz of the *Far Eastern Economic Review* was threatened with such a fate if his dispatch on Kuldip Nayar's case appeared in print. Those who refused to sign a censorship agreement with the regime were given notice to leave. Consequently, Mark Tully of the *BBC*, Peter Hazelhurst of the *Times*, London, *Newsweek*'s Loren Jenkins and the *Daily Telegraph*'s Peter Gill, had to pack their bags at short notice (Kapoor 2015, 59). Foreign publications that carried stories deemed hostile, such as the *Newsweek* cover story of 7 July 1975, captioned 'Indira's iron fist', or the *Economist*'s take on Sanjay Gandhi under the headline, 'The Son Also Rises', were banned in India. By the end of the emergency, seven correspondents had faced expulsions, while twenty-seven others were banned from entering India (Bhargava 2005, 53).

The architecture of censorship during the Emergency followed that set down in the Central Censorship Order, 1976, which drew its power from the Defence of India Rules, 1971, and came into force on 26 June 1975. Under it 'no news, comment, rumour or other report relating to any action taken under certain provisions of the Defence of India Rules, or any action taken under MISA, could be published unless it was previously submitted to the Censor (called 'authorised officer') for his scrutiny and his permission was obtained' (Sorabjee 1977, 11). Other clauses laid down that no news or report could be published nor any comment made on the Emergency, the presidential order, the suspension of Habeas Corpus, the place or conditions of detention of persons arrested under MISA, or – interestingly – the family planning programme. The imposition of presidential rule in the Indian states of Tamil Nadu and Gujarat without the censor's prior scrutiny and permission was also soon tagged to the themes proscribed by the government.

The Press Information Bureau chief was appointed chief censor. He was the principal authority and all the other authorities had to follow the guidelines either he or any officer of the central government laid down. Despite this elaborate schema, there was little uniformity. According to the 'Government of India White Paper on Misuse of Mass Media' brought out by the Janata Party government in 1977 following Mrs Gandhi's electoral defeat, what was cleared by a censor in one place was often found to be objectionable and punishable by another elsewhere. Pre-censorship orders, too, were arbitrarily imposed on recalcitrant editors.

This structure to oversee censorship appears to have been quite distinct from the circle of bureaucrats who advised Indira Gandhi on press matters, headed by H.Y. Sharada Prasad, information advisor to the prime minister. Prasad himself appeared agnostic about the Emergency, going by his private correspondence. In a letter to Natwar Singh, then serving as India's deputy high commissioner to the United Kingdom, dated 20 July 1975, he confessed to a feeling of how little he really knew which 'has overwhelmed me in the last three weeks' (Singh 2021).

The System and Its Captors

It took a brief while for this arrangement of interlocking policies, laws and officials to fall into place. There were initial attempts by editors and reporters to strike back at the empire through the publication of empty spaces where editorials should have been.

Sometimes cat-and-mouse games were played with the censors, through the use of texts written by incipient sesquipedalians and tucked away in spaces like the third editorial. Lofty Tagorean quotes about the mind being without fear; photographs that spoke eloquently like the Raghu Rai image of a man pushing a cycle with two children and a woman following them, surrounded by policemen, to show 'normal life in Chandni Chowk'; or even creative advertisements such as the one that appeared soon after the declaration of the Emergency announcing the death of 'O'Cracy, D. E. M., beloved husband of T. Ruth . . .', sneaked passed the searching eye of the expurgator.

But all this soon came to an end. The capitulation of the journalistic community to the writ of the autocrat became the dominant description of the era. L.K. Advani's remark – 'You were asked only to bend, but you crawled' – was a much cited one. Books and memoirs written subsequently went on to reinforce this assessment. Ajoy Bose and John Dayal in their book on the Emergency, *For Reasons of State: Delhi Under Emergency*, remarked that the press was 'a willing slave that enthusiastically accepted its fate' (Dayal and Bose 1978, 176). Christophe Jaffrelot and Pratinav Anil were also damning in their assessment: '. . . the resistance appears uneven and unimpressive. . . . In a word, then, the Emergency was dictatorship by consent. Resistance never came anywhere near toppling the regime. Democracy was restored at a time of Mrs Gandhi's, not her critics', choosing' (Jaffrelot and Anil 2020, 256).

There is virtue in such assessments. Never having personally experienced the coercive apparatus of the colonial state at first hand, many towering journalists of those times were torn between an inchoate desire to resist and an abiding fear of the unknown. At what point then do editors and the serried ranks under them, who pride themselves on their courage and political understanding, allow themselves to become ciphers?

During the Emergency most mainstream newspaper proprietors, ever conscious of the material dimension of a possible government crackdown, such as the withholding of government advertisements and newsprint allocations, needed just a nudge from the central government to fall in line. The Bennett Coleman

& Co. Ltd, owner of the *Times of India* – the country's largest selling newspaper at that time – was a prime example with the *Times* board deciding 'that the paper would not oppose the Emergency, because whatever their opinion of the matter, the law was to be followed and this was the law at that point of time' (Ghosh 2016).

As a trainee journalist functioning from the commodious common newsroom that the *Times of India* shared with its subsidiaries in Bombay, I could personally sense an unsettling trepidation on the day after Emergency was declared. One of the striking developments of 26 June 1975, that I remember, was a meeting that Khushwant Singh, then editor of the *Illustrated Weekly of India*, had called. We gathered at the centre of the newsroom to hear him vow in his deep baritone that he would fight censorship and suspend the publication of his magazine until it was lifted.

Years later he wrote about that experience: 'The *Times of India* offices were in pandemonium. . . . I was determined to resist and thought if editors of other papers published by Bennett Coleman and Co. would form a united front against censorship we would succeed in making the government change its mind against the press' (Singh 2009, 2). In that account he was particularly critical about the stance taken by other editors. 'I expected Sham Lal, editor of the *Times of India*, to become our leader. He bluntly refused to do so. Sham Lal's number two, Girilal Jain, resident editor in Delhi, went one better by lauding the emergence of Sanjay Gandhi as the new leader' (2). Inder Malhotra, the third most senior editor in the Bombay office, would later recall that 'a few of us proposed that if we couldn't speak against it, we wouldn't support it either, and that was the final position the paper took' (quoted in Ghosh 2016).

The irony of course was that while Khushwant Singh himself suspended the *Illustrated Weekly* for three weeks, it wasn't long before he too came to perceive the virtues of Sanjay Gandhi and went on to feature him prominently in the magazine on at least three occasions during the Emergency. This included a cover story on 15 August 1976, based on an interview Singh had conducted with Sanjay, which bore the title, 'The Man Who Gets Things Done'.

Sham Lal, the editor that Khushwant had criticised so bitterly, did none of this–neither the protest nor the panegyrics. When asked by an interlocutor on the morning of 26 June 1975, as to what his next editorial would be, he is said to have tersely replied: 'I'll be writing on potato cultivation in Lahaul' (Rahman 2015). Sham Lal waited until Mrs Gandhi was defeated to write an acerbic double-column editorial against the Emergency (Kapoor 2015, 53). His one stance of protest was to desist putting out any piece that carried his byline for the duration of the Emergency.

There were several prominent editors who chose to be loyal to Indira Gandhi, and publicly so, including Chalapathi Rau of the *National Herald*, a newspaper supported by the Congress party. In fact, Rau would often be called upon to draft pieces for Mrs Gandhi, including a refutation to a statement issued by 500 international politicians and intellectuals who had brought out a six-column advertisement in the *Times*, London, beseeching the world not to let 'the light go out on Indian democracy' (Nayar 1977, 124). There was Edatata Narayanan of the CPI-leaning *Patriot*, who argued that the press had invited trouble upon themselves through irresponsible and partisan writing. Narayanan disliked Jayaprakash Narayan but allowed his reporters like John Dayal and Ajoy Bose, who later became chroniclers of the Emergency, a free rein and they made full use of it to expose the regime to the extent they could. There were several others senior journalists too who either came out in support of the prime minister or kept their counsel and followed the censor's orders.

The naked fear in the newsroom reflected in what was published. Newspapers came to read like each other, filled with 'ineffectual government handouts of the Ministry of Information and Broadcasting. Most of the reports were equivalent to government propaganda' (Ghosh 2016).

This rather unedifying history would appear to prove Advani right. The reality, however, was far more complex. The courage and fortitude of innumerable, often faceless, journalists, essayists, and litterateurs, who took on the Emergency system, have been forgotten, overlooked, or even erased in the intervening period of half a century. Some who were forced to go through severely punishing times were often let down by their institutions. The family of K. R. Sundar Rajan, a *Times of India* assistant editor picked up and taken to Arthur Road Jail, Bombay, shortly after the promulgation, was suddenly left without resources because his newspaper stopped paying his salary. It was only with the support of colleagues that the family could get through their ordeal (Rajan 2021). The newspaper also refused to reinstate him once he was released.

Comparisons may be odious but the Emergency generation of journalists, it could be argued, showed far more resoluteness and resistance than did their later-day counterparts when another authoritarian regime emerged four decades later under the leadership of Narendra Modi. They also had a far more informed understanding of the role journalism has to play in a republic when democracy is under threat. The country was spared the blatant kowtowing to power by media professionals seen today under the Modi regime. This despite the present generation of scribes knowing full well the harms the 1975 Emergency had visited on their profession.

Revisiting the fortitude, even audacity, that many journalists exhibited, even as the growing shadow of Mrs Gandhi's dictatorship loomed over them, is therefore a valuable undertaking.

Pushing Back against the Behemoth

One of the most definitive accounts of the bewilderment, anxiety and outrage in the immediate aftermath of that midnight constitutional coup came from the editor of a major newspaper in the capital, the *Hindustan Times*. B. G. Verghese, in his autobiography, *First Draft*, recalls returning home on the early morning of 26 June, after putting out a supplement on the midnight announcement. He suspected that it would be a long day and he was right. Slowly the impacts of the Emergency were becoming discernible: electricity supply to the major newspapers had been cut in Delhi as well as in states like Madhya Pradesh and Punjab, while *Motherland*, the Jana Sangh organ, had been shut down. Incidentally, while a few copies of the *Hindustan Times*' late-night supplement made it into print, the *Statesman* had no luck:

> The rotary was about to get started when a flash message on the tickers announced the imposition of pre-censorship on all news and comments relating to the arrests and the internal situation. . . . Hurriedly the rotary was stopped. The *Statesman* sent its supplement page-proof to the PIB office for clearance. But by the time it was returned with names of the arrested leaders deleted and their pictures crossed out, the power supply to the office was cut. The supplement could not be printed. (Nayar 1977, 61–62)

In his office Verghese found the staff depressed, with the younger ones more obviously angry. The consensus among his colleagues was that no editorial should appear in the next day's issue and ways to beat the censor by allegory, quotations, puns, sarcasm and through innuendo were discussed. But there was a problem: the *HT* management and union were strictly opposed to any sabotage of the newspaper by way of protest. A strategy was then drawn up discreetly among the editorial staffers: material for composing would be delayed with the edit page editor made to appear deep in work. Finally, as the deadline for the front page neared, the edit page with the missing editorial would be released. In the hurry to get the newspaper out on time, the blank space where an editorial should have been, would escape scrutiny. The ruse worked. 'Nobody noticed anything amiss. The papers were bundled and sent by conveyor to the delivery window, there to be loaded in taxis going to Dehra Dun, Ambala, Agra and other destinations, and then our own vans for distribution in the city. . . . Readers, next morning, 'read' our blank editorial. They understood' (Verghese 2010, 215).

As an interim show of resistance, the 'blank editorial' spoke loudly. It is interesting to note how widely the strategy was adopted by publications across the country before the days of instant digital communication. In Delhi, apart from the *Hindustan Times*, the *Statesman*, the *Indian Express* and the *Financial Express* also carried blank editorials, as also papers elsewhere like the Indore-based Hindi daily, *Nai Duniya*. Another popular measure was to carry a quote in support of freedom by a well-known thinker or politician on the front and editorial pages.

Such initial acts of defiance soon came to an end – even Mrs Gandhi's earlier quotes on press freedom were disallowed. The Union Minister of Information and Broadcasting V. C. Shukla, who on 28 June had replaced I. K. Gujral, the previous incumbent who was perceived as too lenient,[2] signaled the state's intent. In his first meeting with editors in Delhi, he observed that the Emergency ushered in a new era: 'In future, no "confrontation" would be permitted between the press and the government . . . this meant the end of dissent and protest' (Verghese 2010, 212).

Indeed, the system made sure that those who crossed red lines would pay a price. Mrs Gandhi is believed to have personally insisted that Verghese be dismissed as editor. In September that year *HT*'s proprietor, K. K. Birla, sacked his editor peremptorily (Puri 2015). According to the grapevine, he did it on the staircase although Verghese himself does not clarify this in his account.

Meanwhile, there was another show of defiance from another corner of Delhi. Kuldip Nayar, editor, Express News Service, issued a call to all journalists in Delhi to come for a meeting to discuss the Emergency at the Press Club of India on 29 June. Although attendance at this meeting was not impressive – about a hundred turned up according to Nayar's estimate – a resolution did get passed which deplored censorship and appealed to Mrs Gandhi to reverse the decision. It also demanded the release of Jagat Nara of *Hindi Samachar*, Jullunder (Jalandhar), and M. R. Malkani of *Motherland*, who had been arrested. Nayar sent copies of the resolution to the president, the prime minister and the information minister (Nayar 1977, 78). Nayar was arrested a month later. It made world news. The *New York Times* carried a report datelined 26 July, under the headline, 'India Arrests One of Her Most Important Journalists'.

But Nayar was not easily intimidated despite the privations of jail. He would later recall that the first lunch the state served him – rotis and dal – came with flies in the food. He thought he would boycott the meal but one sensible prisoner advised him that he had better eat otherwise he would have to go hungry. Once freed,

---

[2]Retrieved from https://indianexpress.com/article/opinion/editorials/june-29-forty-years-ago-new-ib-minister/

Nayar immediately travelled across the country to capture the mood on the ground, a practice he followed up on the following year as well. The conclusion he reached was unambiguous: 'However submissive almost everyone was, very few people had accepted authoritarian rule' (Mansukhani 2024).

It is an observation that could just as well have been made for many journalists working through the Emergency, although editors like Verghese, Nayar and Nihal Singh of the *Statesman* were never submissive. Singh later wrote about his encounter with Minister Shukla, in January 1976, in the latter's office. The previous day's *Statesman* had been called for and the minister wanted to know why it had Egyptian president Anwar Sadat as the first lead, along with other foreign news on the front page. Singh did not bother to prevaricate: 'Mr Minister, your censorship laws permit you to tell us what not to print, but if you want to tell us what to print and how to print it, you will have to devise new laws' (Singh 2011, 119).

Unsurprisingly, the *Statesman* was one of Shukla's major targets and he ensured that government appointees were made to join the newspaper's board which led to a lengthy case being argued in the Calcutta High Court. What helped was the editorial independence of the management. C. R. Irani, its managing director, was totally opposed to the Emergency and was known to play 'a cat-and-mouse game with Shukla, staying at a friend's house (when he was in Delhi) and not answering his phone' (Kapoor 2015, 58).

It was the *Indian Express*, however, that faced the full blast of Mrs Gandhi's displeasure right from the very start. The *Statesman* came to be categorised as 'Hostile', in the list that Shukla drew up to classify newspapers by their attitude, but the *Express* was considered 'Continuously Hostile' (Ananth 2020). Every retributive measure of punishment was deployed against the newspaper from that infamous power shutdown on day one and the sealing of its press, to board fixing, pre-censorship, and inquiries into alleged malpractices. Yet, the newspaper kept up its critical reporting as much as it could. During the Turkman Gate evictions, ordered at Sanjay Gandhi's behest, which had taken place amidst police firing and fatalities, the most incisive report was that of the *Express*. Reporters standing on its rooftop, which overlooked Delhi's largest cemetery for Muslims, could spot the bodies being brought for burial (Dayal 2023).

The retributive actions against major newspapers in the capital and its well-known editors had an all-India resonance, even in those days of strict censorship, but there were many other editors who had conducted themselves with exemplary fortitude but were far less known. Their publications were often modest in size and catered to regional language readerships. Among their number were also small self-published but prestigious journals which did not have much national recall.

Among those banned almost immediately were the Urdu daily *Hayat-e-Millat*, and the Marathi language *Marmik*; the Tamil daily *Nathigam*, based in Madras, and the Trivandrum-based Malayalam daily *Thaniniram*. Two major RSS publications, the *Organiser* and the *Panchjanya*, came under the net, and even sundry ones like the film magazine *Mother India*, and *Confidential Adviser*, with its semi-pornographic content.

If the editor, three trustees and five employees of *Sadhana*, a Marathi publication, in western India, found themselves arrested and their press seized; the editor of *Dainik Sambad*, a newspaper brought out from Agartala in the east, had remarkably similar experiences ('Government of India White Paper'). In the south, Cho Ramaswamy, who edited the *Tughlak*, also faced the heat. He had to visit Shastri Bhavan in Delhi so often to deal with censor's cuts, that at one point he is reported to have laid his salary on the table of the censor and said, 'This belongs to you. You are the editor!' Fortunately for him, he was spared jail time.

One of the curiosities of the era was the tough treatment accorded to publications of very modest circulation. Perhaps this was because they were edited by eminent personalities with differing ideological views but large reserves of courage. Among them were *Opinion*, published by A. D. Gorwala; *Himmat* by Rajmohan Gandhi; Nikhil Chakravartty's *The Mainstream*; M. R. Masani's *Freedom First*; and Romesh Thapar's *Seminar*, a monthly with a subscription of around 2,500. All of them, sooner rather than later, came up against the full might of the state precisely because of the moral authority they commanded. All of them waged bitter confrontations with the authorities and had their presses shut down. Most were issued pre-censorship orders.

They responded to the harassment in differing ways. Gorwala approached the Bombay High Court for his right to publish and when his newsletter was banned, produced a cyclostyled newsletter in its stead; *Himmat* bought its own press with financial help from its contributors in order to keep going; Masani challenged the pre-censorship orders against *Freedom First* in the Bombay High Court; while *Bhoomiputra*, a modest quarterly published from Ahmedabad, sought similar relief in the Gujarat High Court, after being set upon for publishing M. C. Chagla's speech on civil liberties. *Mainstream*'s Chakravartty continued to defy the censor for as long as he could in the face of personal chastisements from Shukla, but unrelenting pre-censorship orders finally forced him to shut down his weekly from December 1976 to January 1977. For Thapar, too, pre-censorship was the tipping point: he chose to close *Seminar* rather than give up on his right to free expression. Many other prestigious publications opted for a similar course, like the satirical magazine, *Shankar's Weekly*, on 31 August 1975, because, as its founder famously remarked, 'dictatorships cannot afford laughter' (Kapoor 2015, 55).

Several cartoonists of those times would have fervently endorsed this observation, given that their work constantly came up against the censor's veto. Abu Abraham's pocket cartoon in the *Indian Express* dated 4 July 1975, with the catchline 'Don't you think we've got a lovely censor humour', came back with the stamp, 'Not to be published'. For some unfathomable reason however, one of Abraham's most brilliant cartoons, which caught the zeitgeist of the times, made it to front page of the *Indian Express*. Dated 19 December 1975, it showed President Fakhruddin Ahmed in his bath tub signing a document. The speech balloon went, 'If there are any more ordinances, just ask them to wait' (Gopalakrishnan 2024).

Satire and irony of this kind may sometimes have escaped the censors but in time the regime had its way. Behram Contractor was able to smuggle in a lampoon on Mrs Gandhi's twenty-point programme, by publishing a piece on a six-point programme to change the diet of South Indians in *Femina*, the women's magazine from the *Times of India* stable, but he gave up the effort soon enough and stuck to writing about cricket and mangoes: 'the only subjects considered safe during the era of censorship' (Jaffrelot and Anil 2020, 359).

There were unfortunately few instances of newspapers banding together in solidarity to challenge Mrs Gandhi's Emergency although occasionally there were attempts to share experiences. The Navjivan Trust press was sealed for six days when it published a booklet on the *Bhoomiputra* case. *Milap*, a Bhavnagar-based monthly, in its issue of August 1975, reproduced a news item from the *Bhoomiputra* about how another newspaper, *Maitri*, had been shut down for reporting on Vinoba Bhave's indefinite fast. What followed was a series of predicaments. Its editor made the unwise move of seeking an explanation for this from the authorities which led to not only the confiscation of back issues, but the homes of local subscribers being raided, the press being seized, and the editor and owner of the press thrown into jail (Bhargava 2005, 62).

The geographical spread of these publications would indicate the extent of Mrs Gandhi's coercive net, and her determination to quell dissent on a pan-Indian scale. Publications in some states like Tamil Nadu, then under the Dravida Munnetra Kazhagam government of K. Karunanidhi, before it was dismissed in January 1976, were constant irritants to the Indira Gandhi regime. 'Of the nine publications subjected to pre-publication censorship by September 1975, at least three were in Tamil' (Jeffrey 2000, 190).

It could be claimed that the impacts of the Emergency were less intense in southern India. In a recent paper, Christophe Jaffrelot and Pratinav Anil observed that the contrast between north and south India, was striking. They attributed this partly to the character of the dominant party and the ruling chief ministers, but added that the 'diverse geography of the Emergency further complicates an already complex version of authoritarianism' (Jaffrelot and Anil 2021, 5). A closer look at neighbouring Kerala, a Congress-friendly state, would indicate that the 'lesser intensity' was also because many newspapers chose to support the central government's diktats without demur. One of the cases of torture during the emergency that attracted a great deal of attention in Kerala was that of an engineering student, Rajan, who was arrested on 1 March 1976 and subsequently died of torture inflicted by the Kerala Police. His body was never found, leading his father, T. V. Eachara Varier, to file no less than eight cases in different courts to get to the truth of his son's disappearance. The issue acquired political resonance across the country, with Malayalam newspapers taking sides on the issue. Varier in his memoir, *Memories of a Father*, made special note of the way the *Malayala Manorama, Veekshanam,* the Congress mouthpiece, and Communist Party of India's *Janayugam*, took stances against both him and his son (Varier 2004).

The Government White Paper provided a broader view of the pan-Indian dimensions of this crackdown. It noted that 253 journalists/editors were arrested during the period of the Emergency; 100 of whom were taken into custody lasting at least one year under MISA, with another 60 under the Defence and Internal Security of India Rules. The accreditations of 51 correspondents were also withdrawn ('Government of India White Paper').

Postcards from the Underground

One of the most enthralling aspects of this story was the presence of a thriving underground press which flourished largely through the agency of the trusty cyclostyling machine. Prabir Purkayastha, in his book, *Keeping Up the Good Fight: From Emergency to the Present Day*, describes the modus operandi adopted to challenge the Emergency by members of the CPI(M)-backed Students Federation of India (SFI) in Jawaharlal Nehru University: a cyclostyled broadsheet, called *Resistance*. 'We decided to buy a cyclostyling machine, cut the stencil on a typewriter and cyclostyle the pamphlets ourselves. . . . We would distribute these pamphlets at night, and this activity continued throughout the Emergency' (Purkayastha 2023, 101).

Cyclostyling was one way to generate outlawed literature, but there were others too including the handwritten inland letter form, Photostats and typed sheets. Together they created a silent river of bulletins and newsletters that flowed below the censor's gaze and circulated crucial information. In this way 'one learnt of Kuldip Nayar's arrest, the lathi charge and arrests at Raj Ghat on Gandhi Jayanti, the expulsion of foreign correspondents', recalls C. H. Pahlada Rao, writing about the underground news networks in Karnataka. It emerged, he pointed out, from 'a vast network of exchange of information operating at the local, regional and national levels. Though these information centres were vulnerable, the sympathy which a resistance struggle evoked among the common people was their armour' (*The Pen in Revolt*).

In Karnataka when the RSS organ *Vikrama* was shut down and its editor, Be. Su. Na. Mallya, arrested under MISA, the large army of Sangh sympathisers fell to the task of preparing handwritten news using carbon sheets:

> Everything was done clandestinely. We used other names like Kahale, Jyoti, for our newspapers which had to be printed. I also used to post the newspapers which were printed under pseudonyms. But had to strategically post them, as all posts together would raise suspicions. I posted a few in one post box and the next few in another post box on the next street. ('Satyagraha in Karnataka')

Amiya Rao and B. G. Rao in their reminiscences (in *Pen in Revolt*) of underground publishing in Delhi recall that information flows were so strictly controlled during this period that residents of Defence Colony did not know of atrocities having taken place barely a few kilometers from them, even after three months had passed. This sorry state of affairs prompted them to bringing out a bulletin of uncensored news items. Their sources were many, including most importantly, political prisoners. Their first two issues had reports on how the Bihar government kept all prisoners deemed to be Naxalites in fetters, and how once six prisoners had been shot dead when they were brought to the jail gate at Bhagalpur.

Among the most poignant documents that were circulated underground was a letter written by Gour Kishore Ghosh, a journalist who wrote for the *Ananda Bazar Patrika*, to his thirteen-year-old son. In it he explained to the boy why he had shaved his head in protest over the loss of his right to write and why he would keep his head bare until his freedom was restored. He faced a quandary, he confided to his son: 'On the one hand, I have to think of you, your security; on the other hand, I have to think of myself, of my self-respect as a man. . . . It is this dilemma that torments me every day' (in *Pen in Revolt*). The letter touched a chord because it reflected the existential crisis that so many faced and it found a ready readership through the underground press. But once it appeared in print in *Kolkata*, a Bengali monthly, Ghosh was promptly jailed – a possibility that he had alluded to in the letter.

Resistance, as we have seen, came in various forms and from various quarters. But ultimately, as L. C. Jain states in his autobiography, *Civil Disobedience: Two Freedom Struggles, One Life*, 'it was the crackdown on these multiple freedoms that turned the tide of opinion even amongst those who were supportive of the Emergency. The turning point was the relentless muzzling of the press' (Jain 2011, 195). If the gagging of the press was a central pillar of Mrs Gandhi's Emergency, the opprobrium it brought within India and across the world was a major reason for its subsequent withdrawal. The results of the 1977 General Election provided abundant evidence of the groundswell of silent outrage.

A Postscript

The period following the Emergency has been seen by many commentators, especially within the media, as a moment when the Nehruvian dream of 'utterance' found expression. B. G. Verghese argued that 'If India won Independence in 1947, it won freedom in 1977. The dangers of centralized state power were plainly apparent, and the new trend was to encourage decentralization, non-governmental initiatives and wider popular participation. The media was a major beneficiary of the new ethos' (Verghese 2003, xx). He also pointed out that there was now a growing political and social consciousness and investigative journalism came into its own. 'The "people" had restored democracy. What was happening to them? There was an awakening interest in issues of equity and other social concerns—the little man, the grass roots, the environment, the consumer. There were now more players in the field and more voices heard on and off stage . . .' (xxi).

Jaffrelot and Anil believe that such a view was overdetermined, even over-romanticised. The Emergency proved to be the period when the Sangh Parivar gained a new legitimacy, leading to the mainstreaming of Hindu nationalism. Simultaneously, new neoliberal nostrums began to strike a chord. With the growing rejection of statism, industrialists sensed an opportunity to consolidate their voice within the media and outside it. They add, 'In the years that followed the last vestiges of working-class politics were imperiously wiped out from the republic' (Jaffrelot and Anil 2021, 13).

Even the belief that the new-found media 'freedom' would prove to be sustainable was quickly belied. The Emergency may have ended but 'central and state governments continued to experiment with ways to control the press . . . breaking the nexus between "big business" and newspapers went out of fashion. . . . (This) resulted from an understanding that big newspapers could be politicians' friends' (Jeffrey 2000, 191). Decades later, under the regime of Narendra Modi, the nexus between big business and the media – once excoriated by media functionaries and the public – now began to be actively enabled and encouraged, even as laws to control the media came to be enacted. The remarkably supine mainstream media that emerged as a consequence quickly acquired the moniker of '*godi* media' (lapdog media).

A poem, 'Yet', written by Ramen Sarkar when the Emergency was on, captures in a few lines the sheer egregiousness of the assault on freedom of speech during those dark days of the seventies, even as it keeps alive the hope that somewhere, somehow, the raised fist of resistance would prevail. When the moon defies the blackout and climbs the sky, the poet asks, 'who goes to arrest it?' (Perry 1983, 271). The question confronting the poet and, by extension, the journalist, is a completely different one today: What happens to us when the moon, instead of climbing the sky, prefers – whether in pursuit of power or in fear of arrest – to lurk in the murky darkness instead?

References

Ananth, V. Krishna. 2020. India's Free Press is Still Tormented by the Laws Brought by the Emergency. *The Wire*. 25 June. Retrieved from https://thewire.in/history/emergency-free-press

Bhargava, G. S. 2005. *The Press in India: An Overview*. New Delhi: National Book Trust India.

Dayal, John. 2023. The Powerful Loudness of a Blank Space. *PUCL*. 26 June. Retrieved from https://pucl.org/manage-writings/the-powerful-loudness-of-a-blank-space/

Dayal, John and Ajoy Bose. 1978. *The Shah Commission Begins*. Hyderabad: Orient Longman.

Dhar, P. N. 2000. *Indira Gandhi, the 'Emergency', Indian Democracy*. New Delhi: Oxford India Paperbacks.

Ghosh, Jhumur. 2016. Indira Gandhi's Call of Emergency and Press Censorship In India: The Ethical Parameters Revisited. *Global Media Journal* 7.2. Retrieved from https://www.caluniv.ac.in/global-mdia-journal/Article-Nov-2017/A4.pdf

Gopalakrishnan, Gokul. 2024. Recalling the Political Genius of Iconic Cartoonist Abu. *The Wire*. 12 April.

'Government of India White Paper on Misuse of Mass Media, August 1977'. Retrieved from https://publicarchives.wordpress.com/wp-content/uploads/2014/09/white-paper-on-the-misues-of-mass-media-during-the-internal-emer.pdf

Guha, Ramchandra. 2000. Indira Gandhi and the Indian Emergency. *The Hindu*. Retrieved from https://ramachandraguha.in/archives/indira-gandhi-and-the-indian-emergency-the-hindu.html

Jaffrelot, Christophe and Pratinav Anil. 2020. *India's First Dictatorship: The Emergency, 1975–77*. New Delhi: HarperCollins India.

———. 2021. Interpreting the Emergency. *Heidelberg Papers in South Asian and Comparative Politics* 79. Retrieved from https://hasp.ub.uni-heidelberg.de/journals/hdpapers/article/view/13789

Jain, L. C. 2011. *Civil Disobedience: Two Freedom Struggles, One Life*. New Delhi: The Book Review Literary Trust.

Jeffrey, Robin. 2000. *India's Newspaper Revolution: Capitalism, Politics and the India-language Press 1977–99*. New Delhi: Oxford UP.

Kapoor, Coomi. 2015. *The Emergency: A Personal History*. New Delhi: Penguin Viking.

Mansukhani, Raju. 2024. Emergency Declared. *The Statesman*. 25 June. Retrieved from https://www.thestatesman.com/opinion/emergency-declared-1503313439.html

Nayar, Kuldip. 1977. *Emergency Retold.* New Delhi: Konark Publishers Pvt. Ltd.

Pendakur, Manjunath. 1988: Mass Media During the 1975 National Emergency in India. *Canadian Journal of Communication* 13.6: 32–48. Retrieved from https://cjc.utpjournals.press/doi/full/10.22230/cjc.1988v13n6a3159

Perry, John Oliver, ed. 1983.*Voices of the Emergency: An All India Anthology of Protest Poetry of the 1975–1977 Emergency.* Bombay: Popular Prakashan.

Puri, Anjali. 2015. Why More of Us Should Regret B. G. Verghese's Demise. *The Business Standard.* 1 January. Retrieved from https://www.business-standard.com/article/current-affairs/why-more-of-us-should-regret-b-g-verghese-s-demise-115010100036_1.html

Purkayastha, Prabir. 2023. *Keeping Up the Good Fight: From Emergency to the Present Day.* New Delhi: LeftWord.

Rahman, Masseh. 2015. Crawling Through the Emergency. *Outlook*, 24 June. Retrieved from https://www.outlookindia.com/national/crawling-through-the-emergency-news-294674

Rajan, Mohan Sundar. 2021. Remembering the Emergency. *Deccan Herald*, 21 June. Retrieved from https://www.deccanherald.com/opinion/remembering-the-emergency-999631.html

'Satyagraha in Karnataka during Emergency'. 2023.*Vishwa Samvada Kendra*.25 June. Retrieved from https://vskkarnataka.org/satyagraha-in-karnataka-during-emergency/

Singh, Khushwant. 2009. *Why I Supported the Emergency: Essays and Profiles.* New Delhi: Penguin.

Singh, Natwar. 2021. A Letter from Sharada Prasad. *The Sunday Guardian*, 3 April. Retrieved from https://sundayguardianlive.com/news/letter-sharda-prasad

Singh, Nihal. 2011.*Ink in My Veins – A Life in Journalism.* New Delhi: Hay House India.

Sorabjee, Soli J. 1977.*The Emergency, Censorship and the Press in India, 1975–77.*London: Writers & Scholars Educational Trust.

The Pen in Revolt: Underground Literature Published During the Emergency. Retrieved from https://1975emergencyindia.wordpress.com/wp-content/uploads/2017/04/the-pen-in-revolt.pdf

Varier, T. V. Eachara. 2004.*Memories of a Father*. Asian Human Rights Commission, translated from the Malayalam by Neelan. Retrieved from https://www.scribd.com/doc/100326924/Varier-Memories-of-a-Father-of-Rajan

Verghese, B. G., ed. 2003. *Breaking the Big Story: Great Moments in Indian Journalism*. New Delhi: Penguin/Viking.

———. 2010. *First Draft: Witness to Making of Modern India*. Tranquebar.

9

Chronicle of a Repression Foretold: JNU in the Emergency and After – University Restructuring in a Global Context*

Ravi Arvind Palat

Phalanxes of riot police storming Hamilton Hall in New York's Columbia University which had been occupied by pro-Palestinian student activists on May Day 2024[1] was eerily reminiscent of 'at least three rings' of 'gun totting helmeted troops wearing bullet proof jackets and carrying heavy shields' (Hashmi 2020) surrounding Periyar and Kaveri hostels on the JNU (Jawaharlal Nehru University) New Campus on 8 July 1975 and carting off several students and the general secretary of the JNU Karamchari Sangathan to jail as part of the roundup of activists opposed to the declaration of the Emergency.[2] Though the politics behind these police invasions of university spaces were different, they both raise issues regarding the relationship of the university to the wider world and the broader political issues of the day.

Starting with the experience of the Emergency in JNU, this is a meditation on changes in university education since the 1980s

---

* Non-incriminatory thanks are due to Pulapre Balakrishnan, Peter deSouza, Harsh Sethi, and Romila Thapar for their comments and suggestions on earlier drafts.

[1] Over 2000 university students all across the United States were arrested by May 2024 in connection with protests over the Israeli invasion of Gaza (*New York Times* 2024 ; Srinivasan 2024)

[2] The exact number of students arrested during the raid of JNU hostels remains a matter of dispute ranging from 17 to 60 (Banerjee 1978 ; Prakash 2019: 22; Batabyal 2014: loc 6345); (Selbourne 1977,166–67; Tripathi 2016).

globally, with special reference to India. After discussing JNU during the Emergency and its immediate aftermath, we look at the restructuring of universities since the 1980s as neoliberal policies sought to transform them into training institutes for a 'knowledge' economy rather than educating people to be critically engaged citizens. In India, the demand for credentials to participate in a 'knowledge' economy led to an explosive growth of tertiary institutions without adequate funding or infrastructure, leaving them more vulnerable to manipulation and attacks by the government. Increasingly frequent arbitrary acts undermine institutional autonomy and shared governance. These patterns are now being paralleled in the United States as the shift to a post-industrial age has led to high inequalities in income and wealth, and rich donors now call the tune even in elite universities as the middle-class contracts.[3]

Idea of JNU

Despite depictions of universities as 'ivory towers' insulated from the material pressures of quotidian life, the very function of higher education is to critically question existing social, political and economic arrangements; it inevitably leads to dissent, protest and disruption. Reading about and discussing historical and contemporary conditions in the world necessarily implies questioning structures of power, privilege and hierarchy; challenging even the epistemological foundations of knowledge.[4] Perhaps more than in the West where before the 'democratisation' of higher education after the Second World War, the modern university was for the elite,[5] its correlate in the periphery

---

[3] Limitations of space preclude a discussion of the growing gap in income and wealth world-wide but see (Milanovic 2016).

[4] The radical student movements of the 1960s, by invoking the demands of Black and ethnic minorities, of women, of national liberation and socialism, challenged the intellectual foundations of the Western academy and existing power structures and led to the reconfiguration of disciplines.

[5] At the outset of the Second World War, there were merely a 150,000 students collectively in Great Britain, France and Germany (Hobsbawm 1992, 56). As applicants to Harvard were largely from

constituted students as a political category at least since the early twentieth century because what they read of European history and philosophy did not correspond to their realities.[6] It is this that prompted Sir Frederick Lugard, the British governor of Nigeria who had served earlier as chancellor of the University of Hong Kong, to warn that the educated African be inoculated against the 'Indian Disease' (Mamdani 2016, 71; see also Nair 2019, 43–44).

In this regard, the public university in India was a microcosm of the society at large. While stark inequalities persisted in primary and secondary education, with the rich sending their children to well-endowed private schools where the language of instruction was English, and the poor to state and municipal schools to be educated in local languages, only the extremely rich could send their children to universities overseas (Chaudhuri 2019, 82–82). The university, then, was the only site where all sectors of society were represented in a more egalitarian form than anywhere else. 'The public university is thus a unique and historically unprecedented space', writes Satish Deshpande, 'from the point of view of the democratization of society' (2016, 33). JNU was created as a new type of university in India: it was the first university to be created by an Act of Parliament and was designed from the outset as a national institution; its mandate was not to replicate courses in other universities but to create new academic structures and processes to inculcate a critical outlook among students, and to create knowledge relevant to India. As a

wealthy families, it accepted 85 per cent of applicants in 1940, but as conditions changed this figure dropped to 3.4 per cent in 2021 (Haselby and Stoler 2021).

[6] I draw here on Fabio Lanza (2010) who argued that students as a political category (rather than a social classification of all those who studied) were constituted at Peking University especially during the 4 May 1919 movement (see also Chen 2024). In India, protesting the partition of Bengal, students of Calcutta's Eden College burnt an effigy of the Viceroy, Lord Curzon, in 1905, and the first recorded student strike was at the King Edward Medical College in Lahore in 1920 with students protesting the discrimination between English and Indian students. It was followed by widespread student involvement in the freedom struggle in colleges across the country (Tripathi 2021).

national university, its charge required that it draw students from all over the country. Rather than affiliating colleges in south Delhi to the new institution, it was set up primarily as a postgraduate university with a small undergraduate component to lighten its sobriety. Key to the JNU being a national university was a unique admissions policy instituted in 1974 which combined written tests with an interview, which awarded points for socio-economic deprivation (for regional, economic and social disadvantages), and included students in the admissions process. Indeed, it was student pressure that led to the establishment of this distinctive admissions policy (Batabyal 2014, ch. 7; Kumar 2016; Prakash 2019, 25–27). Its national character promoted an unmatched degree of socialisation – especially when in the 1970s, people from South India were popularly referred to as 'Madrasis' elsewhere in Delhi!

Rather than replicating syllabi and curricula of other universities in the country, the JNU was explicitly created to critically approach existing knowledges; drawing on the latest intellectual trends, it was to be interdisciplinary and have centres of study rather than traditional departments; and by adopting a semester system in which courses were to be re-thought rather than merely chopping year-long courses in half, many centres of study attempted to structure courses around intellectual issues through the tutorial system, questioning intellectual paradigms instead of merely disseminating information; students were to be assessed continuously instead of only by an annual examination; and from the outset it had a faculty-to-student ratio that was the envy of universities elsewhere (Batabyal 2014; Prakash 2019).[7] Its legendary first vice chancellor, Gopalaswami Parthasarathi or GP as he was known, was insistent 'that the university is a place for advancing knowledge and not just handing out degrees . . . for asking questions, raising doubts about the information given, and by critical questioning of any subject. . . . It is the one institution in every society that has the right to do this' (Thapar 2018). From these orientations, where its faculty enjoyed the autonomy to create innovative courses, it attracted students who thrived in its

[7] In 1975, it had 800 students and 200 faculty (Prakash 2019, 27).

exciting intellectual atmosphere.[8] It generated a very distinctive political culture on the Left – with not only the student wings of the Communist parties but also a critical Marxist tradition, the Marxist Forum, and an important liberal strand, the Free Thinkers. Students managed their own affairs including running their own union elections conducted by an elected election commission (Kumar 2016). In constituting students as a political category, the radical tradition ensured that student fronts of right-wing national parties were marginalised. It was inevitable that the hard political and economic environment of the early seventies – oil price hikes, failed monsoons, the Vietnam War, calls for a New International Information Order, presence of some 10 million refugees from Bangladesh, a hostile US administration blocking assistance from the World Bank and terminating its own aid (Raghavan 2016) – would lead to sharp critiques of the government.

JNU and the Emergency

These concerns impinged on public universities across the country with particular urgency – as witnessed by the JP-inspired student movement in the Hindi belt – and when the Emergency was declared just before midnight on 25 June 1975, along with leading opposition figures, student activists affiliated with the JP movement at Delhi University were also rounded up by the police and detained (Index on Censorship 1976; Kapoor 2019). Since the major national parties did not then have a strong presence in JNU and the JP movement's association with the Jan Sangh and RSS had tainted it in the view of many, students there were not immediately arrested.

This provided a vital breathing space to activists at JNU – the dominant political group on campus, the SFI, issued pamphlets and notices against the Emergency, not in its own name but in the name of the 'Resistance.'[9] Activists cyclostyled pamphlets in the dead of night and placed them in the hostel messes, the library and

[8] For a contrast between faculty autonomy at JNU and centralisation in Delhi University, see (Loomba 2019, 136).

[9] http://sfijnuunit.blogspot.com/2015/06/emergency-files-01-police-raid-in-jnu_24.html. For pamphlets issued by the JNU Resistance

elsewhere.[10] The SFI also moved those most likely to be arrested off-campus and those who remained on campus were moved to different rooms each night and locked in till daybreak (Hashmi 2020). Thus, the police raid on the Periyar and Kaveri hostels on 8 July provided slim pickings even though the sitting general secretary of the Jawaharlal Nehru University Student Union (JNUSU) could not evade capture and detention.[11]

The university administration swiftly moved to make membership in the student union 'voluntary', to impose a 'Code of Conduct' – as happened in 2024 at Columbia and other universities in the United States faced with anti-Israeli protests (Bazelon and Homans 2024) – and to deny admission to eleven students who had been academically qualified. One of these students was D. P. Tripathi, the JNUSU president, applying for admission to the MPhil programme. Egregiously, he was denied admission even before he had sat for the entrance examination. Since Tripathi was thus not formally a student, a meeting of the union – called the JNUSU Student Council – chaired by Ashok Lata Jain, a student councilor from the School of Social Sciences, was convened and it called for a three-day strike from 24 to 26 September 1975 to protest these acts, the first such collective protest in the country since the Emergency was proclaimed (Yechury 2020). She was immediately expelled. While the strike was going on, the prime minister's daughter-in-law, Menaka Gandhi, a student in the School of Languages, came to attend a German class and Tripathi asked her not to cross the picket line, reportedly saying: 'You are one of us, Mrs Gandhi, Junior!' Furious at this, Mrs Gandhi Junior left the campus and soon after, Prabir Purkayastha, a student

(and for other pamphlets, manifestos, press statements, etc.) see https://www.flickr.com/photos/parchaproject/

[10] Prabir Purkayastha (2016) states that due to the dangers faced by small cyclostyling shops, the JNU SFI unit bought a small cyclostyling machine.

[11] In part, since the police made the mistake of encircling the Godavari Hostel for women students first, many activists in the other two hostels were able to make their getaway before the police came to their hostels (Yechury 2024).

mistaken by the police for Tripathi, was kidnapped in broad daylight in a gangster-movie-style operation and incarcerated for fourteen months (Prakash 2019, 14–18, 29–30, 337; Selbourne 1977, 167; Tripathi 2016; Yechury 2020; Purkayastha 2020: 338; Plys 2020, 152–54). Interestingly, the only resolution passed by the Jawaharlal Nehru University Teachers' Association (JNUTA) against the Emergency was the one condemning this kidnapping (Purkayastha 2016).

In conditions when open resistance to the Emergency would be immediately squashed by the police, students adopted innovative forms of resistance:

> Sometimes we had poetry readings in the hostels, recite revolutionary poems against dictatorship, against oppression . . . and this will be read in all hostels simultaneously. Now how do you organize picketing or strike? You cannot organize them in the traditional way . . . [as] that would expose people and make the police to enter. So you work out silent ways so there would be students on the lawns, reading books, and if someone is walking into a building, going to class, you quietly stop them and explain to them . . . why there is a protest. (Tripathi quoted in Plys 2020, 153)

Likewise, when a faculty supporter of the Emergency proposed a resolution supporting the government's action at a general body meeting of JNUTA, the opposition sidelined it by noting that any discussion of the Emergency was illegal. It was followed by a suggestion that the association observe a moment of silence in mourning – with no mention of what was being mourned (Mukhia 2020, 334). Similarly, when a government minister came to the university to give a talk, students opposed to the Emergency sat in the front rows and as soon as the minister began to speak, they all rose up and left the room (Purkayastha 2016; Yechury 2024).

Nevertheless – despite honorable exceptions like Romila Thapar, S. Gopal, Krishna Bharadwaj, André Béteille, Raj Krishna, T. N. Madan, Mrinal Datta Chaudhuri, V. M. Dandekar, and a few others – the intelligentsia was generally quiescent, surprising even Mrs Gandhi. Béteille (1978, 944) argued that the politics of the Emergency rendered the distinction between 'progressive' and 'reactionary' inoperative as some 'progressives' supported the Emergency while some who opposed it were 'notoriously reactionary'. JNU faculty member and chairman of the University Grants Commission, Professor Satish Chandra, congratulated the government for restoring 'peace' to universities because, he said, prior to the Emergency, 'teachers' associations' were behaving like 'trade unions' (quoted in Jaffrelot and Anil 2020, 338–39; Chandra 2003, 169, 230–35)! Bipan Chandra (2003, 173) writes that 'people' were 'tired . . . of students' and teachers' strikes and agitations' and that after the Emergency was imposed, 'Calm was restored on the campuses as students and teachers went back to classrooms, and examinations were held on time'. He also claimed that there was no concerted effort by the government 'to interfere with courses, teaching, or research' (Chandra 235). But this is disingenuous on at least two grounds: First, because academic publications take a long time between article or manuscript submission and final publication after reviews and revisions, and the span of the Emergency – twenty-one months – was too short to have an impact, in contrast to newspapers and magazines. Second, the climate of fear and intimidation led to varying degrees of self-censorship (Béteille 1978, 945). Unlike the case of Delhi University, not a single JNU faculty member was arrested (Ram 1978).

These conditions necessarily fractured the Left unity that had been forged on campus by the SFI and the AISF as the latter supported the Emergency, and a large number of the faculty supported, or were affiliated with, the CPI. However, a general acceptance of the intellectual project of the university meant that supporters of the government did not attack or tell on those opposed to it; that there was respect for academic scholarship and the diversity of perspectives as well as strong friendships crafted in a small university across political divides (Patnaik 2020, 178; Tripathi 2016). Even if elements of the campus community, most notably the founding chair of the Centre for Political Studies, Professor Rasheeduddin Khan – also a nominated Rajya Sabha MP – supported the government, they helped students who were in trouble (Selbourne 1977, 309–10; Chenoy 2020, 231–32). As a consequence, there was a posse of undercover police agents posing as students to spy on oppositional activity.

Soon after the Emergency was lifted and a new government elected, JNUSU launched a campaign against the vice chancellor, B. D. Nagchaudhuri, who had implemented Emergency policies and banned the Union, expelled students and overruled admissions on political grounds. In October 1977, he was barred from the campus by the JNUSU and in return he closed the campus *sine die* – a closure that ran for forty days during which students manned the library and kept it open all day and night – without the loss of a single book – and ran the hostel messes (Yechury 2020; Kumar 2016).

However, close upon its heels, the personal friendships and intellectual camaraderie that held the campus together, despite political and ideological differences, began to unravel, as more and more students began enrolling in JNU not for scholarly or intellectual reasons but to stay cheaply in its hostels as they prepared for UPSC examinations. After the Janata Party government came to power, Kuldeep Kumar (2016) claims that political power and money became factors in JNUSU elections. In 1983, over a minor disciplinary action against a student,[12] there was a gherao of the vice chancellor, the rector and the registrar for some fifty hours in the vice chancellor's house, till the police intervened. This led to attacks by students on the houses of hostel wardens and several professors, burning books and vandalising vehicles. This incident had also pitched the student union, headed then by Nalini Ranjan Mohanty of the Students for Democratic Socialism, against the faculty, many of whom were threatened along with their families. The earlier respect for intellectual differences was now becoming frayed (Batabyal 2014, ch. 13; Nair and Ghosh 2020). It was especially unfortunate that this coincided with an increasing communalisation of Indian politics – ranging from the Khalistan movement and the ethnic conflict in Assam to the rise of the BJP

[12] A student, who abused a hostel warden and his family and was transferred to another hostel, was led back to his former room by the JNUSU president who broke the lock (Batabyal 2014, loc 7037–96; Nair and Ghosh 2020, 343).

– and with far-reaching economic changes including the closure of mills in Mumbai, Kanpur and Ahmedabad.

The violence in 1983 substantially transformed JNU. Its earlier admissions policy based on prior academic performance, results of a written examination and interview were abandoned for a straight-forward written exam administered in various centres across the country and proctored by its faculty rather than by an outside agency. There were no longer any direct student involvement in the admissions process. One important fallout of this was that without the interview, the faculty could no longer spot inherent talent among applicants who were not very articulate in English (Batabyal 2014, loc 7417).[13]

The Neoliberal University

Tertiary education was also undergoing a fundamental restructuring across much of the world at this time, though they were accented differently in various locations as world-wide economic and political trends were refracted by local structures of education, positions in the global hierarchy of wealth and social conditions in each country. In most cases, these pressures led to a shift away from a broad-based education to a narrower vision of training for employability in a 'knowledge' economy; a dilution of shared university governance by faculty, students and administrators; and increasingly greater political interference in university curricula.

Economic crises had undermined university funding in the Anglosphere while Structural Adjustment Programs imposed by the World Bank on universities in Africa, the Caribbean and Latin America devastated educational institutions there. Fearing continued electoral losses, the Democrats in the United States, and Labour parties in Australia, New Zealand and the United Kingdom tacked to the right, casting competition and the market as the only legitimate principle of human activity, seeing human

[13] Atiya Habeer Kidwai (2020, 46) recalls that when Ashok Lata Jain interviewed for admission at the Centre for Regional Development, she broke down in tears when the first question was in English and she had to be assured that her lack of fluency in English would not be held against her.

beings as competitive, profit-and-loss calculators rather than as citizens with inalienable rights and obligations. Within the sphere of education, what this meant was to treat education as creating human capital rather than forming citizens who are trained in understanding the broader problems of power and social responsibility that had undergrid the liberal arts curriculum in the academy (Brown 2015; Palat 2024).[14]

Sharp declines in government funding often compelled academics in Africa to work as contract researchers for scholars in the 'Global North' (Mamdani 2018). Since India was not as highly indebted as Latin American, African and Caribbean states in the 1980s, economic pressures impinged on the Indian government only in the early 1990s when it was compelled to ship much of the country's gold reserves in the dead of night to Japan, Switzerland and the UK (Mody 2023, 256–57), devalue the currency and adopt business-friendly de-regulation of the License Raj. The subsequent demand for credentials as the growing importance of computers and information technology reconfigured knowledge as a factor of production, led to an explosive growth of universities. The central government established seventeen new Indian Institutes of Technology (IITs) between 2001 and 2016; seven Indian Institutes of Science Education and Research between 2006 and 2016; and twenty-one new All India Institutes of Medical Sciences between 2012 and 2020 (Jalote 2021, 13).[15] Aggregate enrollments in the tertiary institutions exploded from 4,900,000 in 1991 to 32,300,000 in 2013; the number of universities by almost four times, from 184 to 723; and the percentage of the 18–23 age group attending these institutions soared from 8.1 per cent to 23.9 per cent (Deshpande 2016, 33).

---

[14] In India, a report commissioned by two leading industrialists – Mukesh Ambani and Kumaramangalam Birla – on privatising education bluntly stated that university education is not a universal right and it should follow the principle of 'user pays' (Chandra 2019, 70).

[15] https://en.wikipedia.org/wiki/Indian_Institutes_of_Science_Education_and_Research;https://en.wikipedia.org/wiki/All_India_Institutes_of_Medical_Sciences

The speed and scale of university expansions were, unfortunately, not matched by the allocation of appropriate resources and infrastructural development. Over the last two decades, the allocation of central government funds to education – despite the creation of new central universities and national institutions – has not exceeded 3.5 to 4 per cent of government expenditure for primary, secondary and tertiary education. More than 50 per cent of these funds between 2015 and 2018 were allocated to the 3 per cent of students who study at the ninety-seven IITs, Indian Institutes of Management (IIMs) and the National Institutes of Technology (NITs). The IITs which account for 1.18 per cent of the students in higher education receive 26.96 per cent of central government expenditure on education (Hasan 2020, 33).

Consequently, many of the new universities and colleges were inadequately funded and ill-equipped to train students for a 'knowledge' economy and routinely churned out unemployable graduates. In the rush to establish universities, moreover, little attention was paid to improve the curricula and infrastructures of primary and secondary schools (Thapar 2015, 34–35). It is not surprising then that between 2011 and 2016, the unemployment rate for college graduates more than doubled from 4.1 per cent to 8.4 per cent, and when the Indian Railways advertised 63,000 vacancies in 2018, it received 19 million applicants (Slater 2019)! Hence, even as a credentialling mechanism, the experiment failed.

In much of the Anglosphere, extensive measures, 'metrics' or academic audits were implemented to gauge the effectiveness of academic departments – often quantitative standards rather than qualitative ones (Shore and Wright 1999). A search of terms like 'accountability', 'metrics', 'performance indicators', or 'benchmarks' on the Google Ngram Viewer which trolls through scanned publications and books indicates that their occurrence increases sharply around the mid-1980s as decision-makers sought to replace seemingly subjective judgements with seemingly objective criteria. On the surface this may seem perfectly unobjectionable: what could be wrong in holding departments and schools accountable by measurable criteria? Yet, the metric often replaces the goals that these measures ought to serve.[16]

Unsurprisingly, the emphasis on metrics changed the management of universities. Rather than senior academics serving for fixed terms in administrative posts and then returning to their faculty positions, now the universities are run by academic executives who move between institutions. When 'moonlighting academics' served temporarily in management posts, they shared the ethos of the faculty, and it was hard for university presidents and provosts to ignore faculty opinions. However, as they have been replaced by permanent managerial satraps – "deans, deanlets, deanlings' in Benjamin Ginsberg's (2011, 2) nice phrase – it has weakened the shared professional ethos within the university, and faculties and schools are restructured for financial rather than intellectual reasons (Mulhern 2020, 121). Part of the responsibility for this lies, of course, with the faculty because of the greater importance placed on research and publications which creates more obstacles to them serving fixed terms in managerial posts. The progressive resort to contingent academic labour has also 'reduce[d] the institutional voice of the established academics and increase[d] the power of the manageriat' (Collini 2017, 42).

The prominence of managerialism – with university presidents' cabinets staffed primarily by non-academics as only the vice-president for academic affairs is likely to have had significant classroom experience – has led universities in the United States to discount hallowed traditions like respect for academic freedom and the sanctity of tenure. This accounts for administrators at Columbia University, for instance, violating procedures established after 1968 and arresting students occupying the Hamilton Hall (Hirsch 2024). When the police were also summoned a few weeks earlier, on 18 April, to clear a protest encampment on the Columbia

[16] Jerry Muller (2015; see also Collini 2017, 45) cites the chilling example of surgical report cards used in some states in the US to rate the efficiency of surgeons and serve to calibrate their salaries. This pressured surgeons to concentrate as much as possible on procedures with high survival rates and tended to avoid needier patients who had less chances of survival but may nevertheless have been saved. Thus, more 'patients died, but the metrics improved'.

University campus, the police themselves acknowledged that the demonstrators were peaceful![17] As the New York University history professor Steven Hahn wrote to that university's president, Linda Mills, the indiscriminate arrests of students had a parallel in 'the darkest days of McCarthyism, when self-regarding liberals rushed to do the dirty work of the rightwing political police and tormentors who laughed as dissidents were fired, blacklisted, and personally ruined by their one-time colleagues' (Iqbal 2024).

A very different structure of educational institutions and sociopolitical conditions in India refracted these global trends. Administrators continue to be recruited from the faculty and quantitative metrics do not have the same salience they have in the Anglosphere, but political pressures on what is included (or excluded) from the curriculum is often more intense. Governments across the political spectrum projected a managerial and administrative vision of higher education, quite unlike the innovative vision that had led to the creation of the JNU. The UPA regime's Central Universities Act of 2009, establishing sixteen new central universities conferred autocratic powers on vice chancellors who were charged to 'regulate and enforce discipline among the students and the employees'; members of student's councils were to be 'nominated on the basis of merit'; and there was no provision for elections to any statutory body. Additionally, disputes relating to conditions of appointments were precluded from judicial review (Bhattacharya 2019, 174; Chaudhuri 2019, 77). Though many of the new central universities were set up in rural areas to ease access, the absence of infrastructure paradoxically restricted access as they charged higher fees than the older universities (Bhattacharya 2019, 158). Given their location in rural areas, university administrations appropriated 'local feudal modes of functioning' as when the vice chancellor of the Central University of Jharkhand ordered the suspension of a lecturer for having invited one of her former professors –

[17] New York Police Department's chief of patrol, John Chell, told reporters that the demonstrators were 'peaceful,' did not resist arrest and 'were saying what they wanted to say in a peaceful manner' (Bellafante 2024).

M. N. Panini, a retired JNU Professor of Sociology – to give a lecture (Bhattacharya 2019, 159–60; Jaffrelot 2019, 181).

The first NDA government had termed interpretations of Indian history that challenged the periodisation of Indian history as Hindu, Muslim and Modern as 'anti-Hindu' and 'anti-national' (Thapar 2016, 20). The second NDA government propounded a narrow and exclusionist interpretation of 'Hindu' as manifested by its Citizenship Amendment Act of 2019 which provided an accelerated pathway to Indian citizenship for migrants from Afghanistan, Bangladesh and Pakistan excluding Muslims. The appointment of Mamidala Jagadesh Kumar as JNU's vice chancellor in 2016 signaled a qualitatively more intrusive attempt by the Narendra Modi government to reconfigure JNU, and tertiary education more generally.[18] Professor Kumar drastically slashed research budgets – by almost 50 per cent over three years – reduced enrollment by 84 per cent, overrode university guidelines on appointments and promotions, arbitrarily replaced chairs of academic centres and deans of schools, and tried to punitively delay or refuse to pay pensions to faculty who opposed his policies (Jaffrelot 2019, 176–77; Iftikhar 2020; Mahaprashasta 2018; Press Trust of India 2021).

In violation of standard procedures, the vice chancellor's appointment of faculty affiliated to the ruling party – and the increased presence of ABVP on campus – meant that though the Left orientation of student politics did not substantially change,[19] now a section of the students and faculty openly sided

[18] Other instances include a 139-day strike by students at the Film and Television Institute of India to protest the appointment of a board filled with BJP members in 2015; against police brutality against protests at Jadavpur University (2014), Punjab University (2015) and Banaras Hindu University (2017); and the Occupy UGC movement in protest against a decision eliminating research fellowships (2015) (Martelli and Ari 2018, 289; Sundar 2018, 53).

[19] Between 1974 and 2017, twenty-two SFI candidates were elected as JNUSU presidents; they were followed by AISA (student wing of the CPI-ML) eleven times; one each by the AISF, NSUI and ABVP; and eight by other organisations or independents. There were no JNUSU

with the government and attacked other students and breached the solidarity that the campus had largely exhibited during the Emergency (Purkayastha 2020, 340). This was most evident on 9 February 2016 when JNUSU held a meeting to condemn the hanging of Afzal Guru who had been convicted of participating in an attack on the Indian Parliament in 2001, a meeting that had been banned by the JNU administration at the behest of the ABVP. Though capital punishment could have been opposed on a variety of grounds – philosophical, ethical, religious – and in a university context could have been a 'teaching moment', it was termed an 'anti-national' event and a police raid on campus led to the arrests of scores of students who were then assaulted by lawyers when they were produced in the Delhi courts at Patiala House. Other JNU students and faculty, as well as journalists, were also subject to physical assaults (Marvel 2016; Azad et al. 2016; Jaffrelot 2019, 178–79; Thapar 2016; Singh and Dasgupta 2019). Nothing remotely like this had happened to JNU students during the Emergency!

Professor Kumar's disregard for established university procedures was paralleled by Columbia University President Nemat Shafik summoning police to clear student protests in April and May 2024 (Hirsch 2024). Almost at the same time, on the opposite coast of the United States, the administration of the University of California at Los Angeles refused to act for hours as an armed mob laid siege to a student and faculty encampment protesting the Israeli attacks on Gaza. Further, at UCLA

> Days before the . . . attack, campus officials had allowed off-campus protestors—seemingly supported by a collection of outside donors—to erect a massive screen-and-speakers installation to inflict an audio-visual assault on the camp at all hours of the day and night. . . . When nearby classroom buildings were rendered out of service as a result . . . , the administration did little more than shrug its shoulders and fecklessly assert its commitment to the right to protest. (Makdisi 2024)

---

elections between 2008 and 2012 because its election procedures did not conform to the recommendations of the Lyngdoh Committee (Martelli and Ari 2018, 269, table 1; Martelli and Parkar 2018).

In elite private universities in the US, rich donors have increasingly ridden roughshod over faculty governance and in many states, with Republican governments, tenure for faculty has been under threat and even eliminated and the teaching of subjects like Critical Race Theory and certain books banned (Crespo and Weld 2024; Sugrue 2024; Mudde 2024). Ironically, then the JNU appears to hold a mirror to their future for some universities in the Global North in a post-industrial age, just as students from the periphery constituted themselves politically before their counterparts in the core!

An Uncertain Future

To sum up, JNU was created at a time when the need for a critically engaged citizenry was accepted by elites almost everywhere. The public university was also perhaps the most democratic space in India as it was 'the only site . . . where all major social groups (including the women of each group) [came] together in more or less egalitarian conditions' (Deshpande 2016, 33). Unlike older established universities in the country, most of which had been established during colonial rule, where students were seen as passive consumers of knowledge, JNU was created as a different kind of university: designed to inculcate critical thinking and to produce knowledge relevant for the country rather than to be an imitation of Oxford or Cambridge. It was primarily a postgraduate university where faculty had considerable autonomy to create new, innovative courses of study and it had a low faculty-to-student ratio.

The exciting intellectual atmosphere at JNU attracted students who were critically engaged in the political, economic and social issues of the day, and from its very inception these issues dominated the agenda: JNUSU pushed for the university's distinctive admissions policy and student union elections were characterised by high-level discussions on imperialism and the Vietnam War, Stalin v. Trotsky on socialist construction in the USSR, and the strategy for a revolution in India. A shared respect for intellectual excellence held the small university community together despite ideological differences.

The Emergency was a sharp rupture as it shattered Left unity on campus and police raids and arbitrary arrests forged a resistance movement even though many of the faculty remained largely silent with, of course, some notable exceptions. At the end of the Emergency when JNUSU demanded accountability from the vice chancellor and senior administrators who had used the Emergency to undermine the student union, distort the admissions process and expel students for political reasons, they closed the university, and the union demonstrated its maturity by running the library and the hostel messes for over a month.

In the 1980s, as geopolitical conditions in the world and in the country changed, and industrialisation slipped down the hierarchy of wealth and cut the ground from under labour unions, the nature of university education began to change. After the Second World War, the extension of a liberal arts tertiary education to a broad segment of the society, especially in the United States, had been 'nothing short of a radical democratic event, one in which all became potentially eligible for the life of freedom long reserved for the few' (Brown 2015, 185).[20] In the Anglosphere, as economic constraints cut government expenditure on education from the late 1970s, universities became more expensive and entry became more restricted. The emphasis shifted from broad-based criteria for critical citizenship to employability as universities were transformed from educational institutions to credentialling factories for a 'knowledge' economy which did not value intellectual excellence: after all Bill Gates, Steve Jobs and others were all college dropouts.

In India too, especially after liberalisation in 1991, there was a rapid increase in the number of universities without adequate funding or infrastructure, again to serve a 'knowledge' economy even as employment opportunities for graduates did not keep pace. At JNU this trend was reflected in the creation of professional schools – a School of Engineering and the Atal Behari Vajpayee

[20] Liberal arts, a phrase that came into usage in the fourteenth century, was, Raymond Williams (1985, 179) noted, 'predominantly a class term [which identified] the skills and pursuits appropriate . . . to men of independent means and assured social position, as distinct from other skills and pursuits . . . appropriate to a lower class'.

School of Management and Entrepreneurship. De-regulation of the economy also led to progressively larger numbers of students – especially from the rich and upper-middle classes – leaving for universities overseas, and thereby diluting the democratising character of universities in India.[21]

The broadening of university education and of the middle class had also created a new paradigm shaped by the movements of 1968 in the Anglosphere: students created themselves as a political category and engaged in direct action that was seen as legitimate by university authorities and government administrations. Widening income inequalities, shrinking middle classes and diminishing well-paid employment opportunities steadily eroded these conditions. In the United States, protests against the Israeli invasion of Gaza ruptured the paradigm shaped by the movements of 1968: university administrations no longer condoning occupation of buildings and other forms of direct action by activists (Polgreen 2024; Bazelon and Homans 2024). Many U.S. universities suspended chapters of Students for Justice in Palestine and Jewish Voice for Peace which had spearheaded campus demonstrations, and imposed new codes of conduct and restricted entry to campuses. Earlier, campus protests against right-wing provocateurs had led conservatives to claim that universities were liberal bastions, clamping down on the freedom of speech. Protests against the Israeli invasion of Gaza have further restricted permissible speech as campus administrators sought to shield themselves from legislative blowback: NYU even amended its Non-Discrimination and Anti-Harassment policy to include 'Zionism' as a violation (Lennard 2024; Blinder 2024). No longer, it seemed, was free speech foundational to universities! At the same time, though names and photos of protestors were plastered on trucks that circulated around campuses, these were

[21] In 1995–96, 31,743 students from India went to study in the United States; in the first 10 months of 2023, 760,000 went overseas, and some 1.5 million Indian students were studying abroad (*Economist* 2024); http://www.usinpac.com/immigration-blog/indian-students-to-the-us-have-nearly-doubled-in-10-years/; https://learningenglish.voanews.com/a/record-numbers-of-indian-students-study-at-us-universities/7523101.html

not denounced as bullying by university administrators who were themselves the target of anger from wealthy alumni and donors. Everywhere, the neoliberal university hollowed out shared governance between faculty, students and administrators.

A few years earlier in February 2016, when JNUSU organised a meeting protesting the execution of Afzal Guru, a Kashmiri separatist convicted of participating in the 2001 attack on the Indian Parliament, students in the university were cast as anti-national. Rather than using the occasion to question capital punishment, Kashmiri separatism and nationalism more broadly (see Azad et al. 2016), students were seen as seditious and in 2024 a movie was released: *JNU: Jahangir National University* with the tagline 'Can one educational university bring down the nation'. Its title also reflected the Hindutva contention that non-Hindus were second-class citizens or even a fifth column. The movement had come full circle: envisioned as a national university by an Act of Parliament some sixty years ago, and creating an enviable reputation for itself through its intellectual excellence and socially engaged student politics, the second NDA government now groundlessly alleged that it was 'anti-national'! Freedom of expression and critical inquiry was once again under threat. There could be no clearer illustration of how the idea of a university had been deformed, travestied and distorted.

References

Azad, Rohit, Janaki Nair, Mohinder Singh and Mallarika Sinha Roy, eds. 2016. *What the Nation Really Needs to Know: The JNU Nationalism Lectures*. New Delhi: HarperCollins.

Banerjee, Sumanta. 1978. JNU and the Political Power Game. *Economic and Political Weekly* XIII (9 September): 1542–44.

Batabyal, Rakesh. 2014. *JNU: The Making of a University, 1964–1989*. Delhi: HarperCollins.

Bazelon, Emily and Charles Homans. 2024. The Battle over College Speech will Outlive the Encampments. *New York Times*. https://www.nytimes.com/2024/05/29/magazine/columbia-protests-free-speech.html?searchResultPosition=8.

Bellafante, Gina. 2024. What Columbia Should Have Learned From the Protests of 1968. *New York Times*, 26 April.

Béteille, André. 1978. Intellectuals and the Indian Emergency. *International Social Science Journal* XXX.4: 944–46.

Bhattacharya, Debaditya. 2019. Of Feudal Intellectual Capital: The History of New Provincial Universities. In *The Idea of a University: Histories and Contexts*, ed. D. Bhattacharya. Abingdon: Routledge. 155–78.

Blinder, Alan. 2024. New Training and Tougher Rules: How Colleges are Trying to Tame Gaza Protests. *New York Times*, 24 August.

Brown, Wendy. 2015. *Undoing the Demos: Neoliberalism's Stealth Revolution*. New York: Zone Books.

Chandra, Bipan. 2003. *In the Name of Democracy: JP Movement and the Emergency*. New Delhi: Penguin.

Chandra, Nandini. 2019. The Surplus University. In *The Idea of the University: Histories and Contexts*, ed. D. Bhattacharya. Abingdon: Routledge. 63–92.

Chaudhuri, Supriya. 2019. The Crisis of the Public University. In *The University Unthought: Notes for the Future*, ed. D. Bhattacharya. London: Routledge. 74–90.

Chen, Jack W. 2024. On the Event, Politics, and the University. *Positions Politics*, 3 August. https://positionspolitics.org/jack-w-chen-on-the-event-politics-and-the-university/

Chenoy, Kamal Mitra. 2020. My Story of JNUTA. In *JNU Stories: The First 50 Years*, eds. N. Bhattacharya, K. Chakrabarti, S. Gunasekaran, J. Nair, and J. L. K. Pachau. New Delhi: Aleph Book Company. 230–33.

Collini, Stefan. 2017. *Speaking of Universities*. London: Verso.

Crespo, Andrew Manuel and Kirsten Weld. 2024. The Harvard Corporation Tries to Kill Faculty Governance. *Chronicle of Higher Education*, 5 June. https://www.chronicle.com/article/the-harvard-corporation-tries-to-kill-faculty-governance?sra=true.

Deshpande, Satish. 2016. The Public University After Rohith-Kanhaiya. *Economic and Political Weekly* LV.11 (12 March): 32–34.

Economist. 2024. Brainy Indians are Piling into Western Universities. 20 June.

Ginsberg, Benjamin. 2011. *The Fall of the Faculty: The Rise of the All-Administrative University and Why It Matters*. New York: Oxford UP.

Hasan, Zoya. 2020. The Crisis of India's Higher Education. In *Education and the Public Sphere: Exploring the Structures of Mediation in Post-Colonial India*, ed. Suresh Babu G. S. Abingdon: Routledge. 27–39.

Haselby, Sam and Matt Stoler. 2021. It's Time to Break Up the Ivy League Cartel: Democracy Requires Something More than a Handful of Super-Rich Universities. *Chronicle of Higher Education*, 28 May. https://www.chronicle.com/article/how-meritocracy-became-trickle-down-education.

Hashmi, Sohail. 2020. My Days in Tihar Jail: JNU and the Emergency of 1975. https://delhiwithsohailhashmi.wordpress.com/2020/06/25/my-days-in-tihar-jail-jnu-and-the-emergency-of-1975/.

Hirsch, Marianne. 2024. How a University Administration Relinquishes Its Educational Mission. *Columbia Spectator*, 6 May. https://www.columbiaspectator.com/opinion/2024/05/06/how-a-university-administration-relinquishes-its-educational-mission/.

Hobsbawm, Eric J. 1992. The Crisis of Today's Ideologies. *New Left Review* 192 (Mar–Apr): 55–65.

Iftikhar, Fareeha. 2020. JNU Spending on Security Up, Research Budget Down. *Hindustan Times*, 7 October. https://www.hindustantimes.com/delhi-news/jnu-spending-on-security-up-research-budget-down/story-XYRxiddp16Ma24phZHuCPL.html.

Index on Censorship. 1976. India: Arrests at Delhi University. V.1: 76–77. https://www.tandfonline.com/doi/abs/10.1080/03064227608532505.

Iqbal, Razia. 2024. I Teach Democracy at Princeton. Student Protestors are Getting an Education Like No Other. *Guardian*, 4 May.

Jaffrelot, Christophe. 2019. *Modi's India: Hindu Nationalism and the Rise of Ethnic Democracy.* Princeton: Princeton UP.

Jaffrelot, Christophe and Pratinav Anil. 2020. *India's First Dictatorship: The Emergency, 1975–77.* London: HarperCollins.

Jalote, Pankaj. 2021. *Building Research Universities in India.* New Delhi: Sage.

Kapoor, Coomi. 2019. How Arun Jaitley, Then 22, was Arrested During the Emergency Crackdown and Lodged in Tihar Jail. *Scroll.in*, 24 August. https://scroll.in/article/934458/how-arun-jaitley-then-22-was-arrested-during-the-emergency-crackdown-and-lodged-in-tihar-jail.

Kidwai, Atiya Habeeb. 2020. Heady, Informal, Inclusive: The Early Years. In *JNU Stories: The First 50 Years,* eds. N. Bhattacharya, K. Chakrabarti, S. Gunasekaran, J. Nair, and J. L. K. Pachau. New Delhi: Aleph Book Company. 44–49.

Kumar, Kuldeep. 2016. JNU: Republic of Ideas. *Frontline*, 2 March. https://frontline.thehindu.com/cover-story/republic-of-ideas/article23593918.ece.

Lanza, Fabio. 2010. *Behind the Gate: Inventing Students in Beijing.* New York: Columbia UP.

Lennard, Natasha. 2024. College Administrators Spent Summer Break Dreaming Up Ways to Squash Gaza Protests. *The Intercept*, 27 August. https://theintercept.com/2024/08/27/zionist-nyu-gaza-campus-protests/

Loomba, Ania. 2019. Of Utopias and Universities. In *The Idea of the University: Histories and Contexts*, ed. D. Bhattacharya. London: Routledge. 130–42.

Mahaprashasta, Ajoy Ashirwad. 2018. Allegations of Political Bias in Faculty Hiring the Latest Battle in the JNU. *The Wire*. https://thewire.in/education/allegations-political-bias-faculty-hiring-latest-battleline-jnu.

Makdisi, Saree. 2024. For Whom is Campus Safe to be? *Los Angeles Review of Books*, 10 May. https://lareviewofbooks.org/article/for-whom-is-campus-to-be-safe/.

Mamdani, Mahmood. 2016. Between the public Intellectual and the Scholar: Decolonisation and Some Post-independence Initiatives in African Higher Education. *Inter-Asia Cultural Studies* XVII.1. 68–83.

———. 2018. The African University. *London Review of Bools* XL.14, 19 July. https://www.lrb.co.uk/the-paper/v40/n14/mahmood-mamdani/the-african-university.

Martelli, Jean-Thomas and Bariş Ari. 2018. From One Participant Cohort to Another: Surveying Inter-Generational Political

Incubation in an Indian University. *India Review* XVII.3: 263–300.

Martelli, Jean-Thomas and Khaliq Parkar. 2018. Diversity, Democracy and Dissent: A Study on Student Politics in JNU. *Economic and Political Weekly* LIII.11, 17 March, https://www.epw.in/engage/article/diversity-democracy-dissent-study-student-politics-JNU.

Marvel, Ishan. 2016. How the ABVP Brought the State into JNU. *The Caravan*, 2 March. https://caravanmagazine.in/vantage/how-the-abvp-brought-the-state-into-jnu.

Milanovic, Branko. 2016. *Global Inequality: A New Approach for the Age of Globalization*. Cambridge, MA: Harvard UP.

Mody, Ashoka. 2023. *India is Broken: A People Betrayed, Independence to Today*. Stanford, CA: Stanford UP.

Mudde, Cas. 2024. Why are US Campuses Facing an Orgy of State Repression in the 'Land of the Free'. *Guardian*, 30 April. https://www.theguardian.com/commentisfree/2024/apr/30/us-campus-peace-protests-overreaction-gaza.

Mukhia, Harbans. 2020. Reminiscences. In *JNU Stories: The First 50 Years*, eds. N. Bhattacharya, K. Chakrabarti, S. Gunasekaran, J. Nair, and J. L. K. Pachau. New Delhi: Aleph Book Company. 331–35.

Mulhern, Francis. 2020. In the Academic Counting-House. *New Left Review* 123 (May–June): 115–32.

Muller, Jerry Z. 2015. The Costs of Accountability. *American Interest* XI.1 (3 August). https://www.the-american-interest.com/2015/08/03/the-costs-of-accountability/.

Nair, Janaki. 2019. The Provocations of the Public University in Contemporary India. In *The University Unthought: Notes for a Future*, ed. D. Bhattacharya. Abingdon: Routledge. 41–61.

Nair, Janaki and Ranjan Ghosh. 2020. May 1983: An Irreverent Memoir. In *JNU Stories: The First 50 Years*, eds. N. Bhattacharya, K. Chakrabarti, S. Gunasekaran, J. Nair, and J. L. K. Pachau. New Delhi: Aleph Book Company. 343–48.

New York Times. 2024. Where Protesters on US Campuses Have Been Arrested or Detained. 3 May.

Palat, Ravi Arvind. 2024. World-Systems at 50: A Provisional Balance-sheet. *Journal of World-Systems Research* XXX.1: 451–69.

Patnaik, Prabhat. 2020. Recollections of JNU. In *JNU Stories: The First 50 Years,* eds. N. Bhattacharya, K. Chakrabarti, S. Gunasekaran, J. Nair, and J. L. K. Pachau. New Delhi: Aleph Book Company. 177–80.

Plys, Kristin Victoria Magistrelli. 2020. *Brewing Resistance: Indian Coffee House and the Emergency in Postcolonial India.* Cambridge: Cambridge UP.

Polgreen, Lydia. 2024. Columbia, Free Speech and the Coddling of the American Right. *New York Times,* 19 April. https://www.nytimes.com/2024/04/19/opinion/columbia-protests-israel-gaza-crackdown.html?searchResultPosition=2.

Prakash, Gyan. 2019. *Emergency Chronicles: Indira Gandhi and Democracy's Turning Point.* Princeton: Princeton UP.

Press Trust of India. 2021. JNU Teachers' Association Demands Immediate Release of Pension to Retired Faculty Members. *The Wire,* 12 November. https://thewire.in/rights/jnu-teachers-association-demands-immediate-release-of-pension-to-retired-faculty-members.

Purkayastha, Prabir. 2016. Prabir Purkayastha Speaks on Freedom and Emergency at Freedom Square, JNU. https://www.youtube.com/watch?v=nwShH4wuWNw.

———. 2020. JNU Under Emergency: Then and Now. In *JNU Stories: The First 50 Years,* eds. N. Bhattacharya, K. Chakrabarti, S. Gunasekaran, J. Nair, and J. L. K. Pachau. New Delhi: Aleph Book Company. 337–41.

Raghavan, Srinath. 2016. Decoding the Emergency. *Seminar* 677. https://www.india-seminar.com/2016/677/677_srinath_raghavan.htm.

Ram, Mohan. 1978. JNU Under Emergency. *Economic and Political Weekly* XIII.28 (15 July): 1124.

Selbourne, David. 1977. *An Eye to India: The Unmasking of a Tyranny.* Harmondsworth: Penguin.

Shore, Chris and Susan Wright. 1999. Audit Culture and Anthropology: Neo-Liberalism in British Higher Education. *Journal of the Royal Anthropological Institute* V.4 (Dec): 557–73.

Singh, Mohinder and Rajarshi Dasgupta. 2019. Exceptionalising Democratic Dissent: A Study of the JNU Event and its Representations. *Postcolonial Studies* XXII.1: 59–78.

Slater, Joanna. 2019. India's Railroads had 63,000 Job Openings. 19 Million People Applied. *Washington Post*, 4 January.

Srinivasan, Amia. 2024. If We Say Yes. *London Review of Books*, XLVI.10, 23 May. https://www.lrb.co.uk/the-paper/v46/n10/amia-srinivasan/if-we-say-yes.

Sugrue, Thomas J. 2024. College Presidents Behaving Badly. 6 May. https://www.chronicle.com/article/college-presidents-behaving-badly.

Sundar, Nandini. 2018. Academic Freedom and Indian Universities. *Economic and Political Weekly* LIII.24: 48–57.

Thapar, Romila. 2015. To Question or Not to Question? That is the Question. In *The Public Intellectual in India*, ed. R. Thapar. New Delhi: Aleph Book Company. 1–40.

———. 2016. Targetting Institutions of Higher Learning: Fear of the Intellectual. *Economic and Political Weekly* LI.10 (5 March): 19–21.

———. 2018. The Man Who Built JNU Understood What a University Stands For—The Freedom to Question and Debate. *Scroll.in*, 3 July. https://scroll.in/article/884499/the-man-who-built-jnu-understood-what-a-university-stands-for-the-freedom-to-question-and-debate

Tripathi, Devi Prasad. 2016. JNU's Ethos is Being Eroded. interviewed by A. Phadnis. *Business Standard,* February 20. https://www.business-standard.com/article/opinion/jnu-s-ethos-is-being-eroded-dismantled-d-p-tripathi-116022000744_1.html.

Tripathi, Santosh K. 2021. Higher Educational Institutions and India's Struggle for Independence. *Shodh Sanchar* XI 41 (January–March): 178–83.

Williams, Raymond. 1985. *Keywords: A Vocabulary of Culture and Society*. New York: Oxford UP.

Yechury, Sitaram. 2020. The Sort of Police Deployment You See Now is Unprecedented. interviewed by S. Nair. *The Hindu,* 17 January. https://www.thehindu.com/society/the-sort-of-police-deployment-you-see-now-is-unprecedented-sitaram-yechury/article30585927.ece.

———. 2024. JNUSU 1977–78: Restoring Students' Rights After Emergency. *Newsclick,* 27 September. https://www.newsclick.in/jnusu-1977-78-restoring-students-rights-after-emergency.

10

Internal Disturbances: Poetry and Prophecy 1975–77

Rukmini Bhaya Nair

History does not repeat itself; rather, it *rhymes*.[1] We will try to test the truth of this popular variant of the hypothesis attributed to Karl Marx in his *18th Brumaire of Louis Napoleon*[2] by applying it to the poetry written in a variety of Indian languages during the fraught years of the Emergency. Rhyme has always been an attribute of poetry – but what does it mean to say that 'history rhymes'?

Let's begin with a contemporary snippet: 2024 was a year of pitched election battles across the globe, with at least sixty-five countries going to the polls,[3] India being the largest, and most polycentric, of these democracies. It was at this time, in the months leading up to our elections, that the Modi government declared 25 June *Samvidhan Hatya Diwas* (the Day of Murder of the Constitution).[4] This was the BJP's rhetorical riposte to

[1] Mark Twain, attributed, with confoundingly little evidence. See https://quoteinvestigator.com/2014/01/12/history-rhymes/

[2] Karl Marx, paraphrased and attributed: 'History repeats itself the first time as tragedy and second as farce.'

[3] See essay: 'The Ultimate Election Year: All the Elections Around the World in 2024' in *Time Magazine*. https://time.com/6550920/world-elections-2024/

[4] We find representative reports in a variety of newspapers and online newscasts such as the following in the *Deccan Herald*: 'In what is seen as a response to the Opposition I.N.D.I.A.'s campaign centred around Constitution that damaged the BJP's prospects, the Narendra Modi government on Friday declared June 25 as "Samvidhan Hatya Diwas"' (Day of Murder of Constitution). https://www.deccanherald.

the Opposition's (I.N.D.I.A.) campaign, in which the freedoms guaranteed by the Indian Constitution were a central theme. But a piquant irony arises at this point: if the Constitution of India had indeed been 'murdered' on 25 June 1975, it followed that it had already been moribund for nearly fifty years! Indeed this violent metaphor of 'murder' in itself repeats, or rhymes with, another powerful 'obituary' that appeared in the Bombay edition of the *Times of India* a few days after the Emergency was imposed. It read: '*O'Cracy, D. E. M., beloved husband of T. Ruth, loving father of L. I. Bertie, brother of Faith, Hope and Justicia, expired on June 26*'.[5] So are rumours of the death of the democracy in India true or greatly exaggerated? Does our revered Constitution now wear a permanent tag around its neck, saying 'Wanted: Dead or Alive'? And on what bog-like grounds did we stand in 2024 when so many voted for an ideal that had been 'declared dead' more than once? Were we – are we still – in a realm of walking ghosts, ventriloquism, coroners and/or coronations; of salamander-like regeneration, of rhetorical malfeasance – or what? This, to my mind, is exactly the sort of paradox that poets, in their Shelleyan role as 'the unacknowledged legislators of the world', revel in.

Think again now of the word 'rhyme'. As Marx understood well, present events can echo past ones, past records can prophesy future histories, and literary genres like tragedy and farce can mimic each other down the ages. Marx may have been neither a poet nor the originator of the metaphor that history rhymes, but he was well aware that 'echoic mentions' (Sperber and Wilson 1986) turn history into a text, or texts, that can be ideologically interpreted to great effect. Consider the Indian Constitution, for example. It leads off with the ringing phrase 'India, that is Bharat'. This is a classic case of textual 'rhyming', or an echo-effect,

---

com/india/centre-to-observe-june-25-as-samvidhaan-hatya-diwas-congress-hits-back-with-june-4-as-modi-mukti-diwas-3103240

[5] See Manu Joseph, 'How Indians Protest,' *The Times of India*, 20 May 2007. Retrieved 10 November 2018; and Granville Austin, *Working a Democratic Constitution: The Indian Experience* (Oxford University Press, 1999), 295.

when two nouns refer to the same entity.[6] Not much fodder for debate here, one would have thought. Yet, we continue to observe extended controversies in the political sphere today over the provenance of the terms 'India' and 'Bharat', in which the former is identified with the worldview of an English-speaking elite, while the latter is associated with citizens who supposedly do not share that privileged upbringing. Such are the subtle – and not-so-subtle – ways in which small, seemingly insignificant, language matchsticks can become sparks that set alight large affective fires. In order to understand how language functions as an emotional barometer that measures with unexpected accuracy the political climate of an age, we turn in this essay to a neglected but prescient source – Emergency poetry. The essay's last section, 'Internal Disturbances', presents a number of striking poems from that time but even the limited lines from the poem below, which anticipates with such panache our present polarisations, offer a revealing curtain-raiser.

> India that is Bharat
> India the land that died 5000 years ago
> Will India rise in its sudras and live in their labour?
> Will India be India
> and cease to be Bharat? ('India—India' by Mahabaleshwara Katrahalli, translated P. Rama Moorthy; in Perry 1983, 107)

[6] Technically, these language structures are known as 'noun phrases in apposition'. For instance, in the phrase 'Peter deSouza, editor of a 2025 volume on the Emergency', both the name and the descriptive phrase following it are taken to refer to the same person. However this would not necessarily preclude faux arguments about whether someone with such a 'non-Indian' name is qualified to write on the Indian Constitution, and so forth. Such rhyming routines are, of course, also very familiar to us in everyday conversational routines: for example, if somebody introduces a woman as 'my sister, whom we call Bunty, although her real name is Mumtaz', we assume, in context, that the noun phrases 'my sister', 'Bunty' and 'Mumtaz' refer to the same person. This is a three-part illustration of how nouns in apposition work as 'rhymes' that ordinary language users handle with sophisticated ease.

Stephane Mallarme famously described poetry as 'the language of a state of crisis' (see Nair 2009). Nowhere is this insight more foregrounded than during the Emergency. At the time, an un-orchestrated chorus of poets writing in languages as diverse as Bengali, Gujarati, Hindi, Kannada, Malayalam, Telugu and Urdu comes together to make the point that when prose loses its tongue, it is the duty of poetry to speak. In the paragraphs that follow, we shall explore the many ways in which poets speak into a void of silence during that rhyming, still terrifyingly resonant, couplet of years: 1975–77. Perhaps we should, however, preface our reading of the specific outpouring of poetry during the Emergency with a more general argument about the role that poetry seems to play in the articulation of our cultural anxieties.

A Defence of Poesy[7]

Poetry, a marathon runner across temporal tracks and geographical continents down the ages, has always been supported by the sturdy legs of rhythm and rhyme. This makes it a winner

---

[7] '"The lawyer says what men have determined, the historian what men have done. The grammarian speaks only of the rules of speech, and the rhetorician and logician, considering what in nature will soonest prove and persuade, thereon give artificial rules, which still are compassed within the circle of a question, according to the proposed matter. The physician weighs the nature of man's body, and the nature of things helpful or hurtful unto it. And the metaphysic, though it be in the second and abstract notions, and therefore be counted supernatural, yet doth he, indeed, build upon the depth of nature. Only the poet, disdaining to be tied to any such subjection, lifted up with the vigor of his own invention, doth grow, in effect, into another nature, in making things either better than nature brings forth, or, quite anew, forms such as never were in nature, as the heroes, demi-gods, cyclops, chimeras, furies, and such like; so as he goes hand in hand with nature, not enclosed within the narrow warrant of her gifts, but freely ranging within the zodiac of his own wit. Nature never set forth the earth in so rich tapestry as diverse poets have done; neither with pleasant rivers, fruitful trees, sweet-smelling flowers, nor whatsoever else may make the too-much-loved earth more lovely; her world is brazen, the poets only deliver a golden."'

in what one might call the ‘Empathy Stakes’ for at least three deep evolutionary reasons. First, poetic recitation is a *memory tool* that precedes writing, only invented about 5000–7000 years ago, by an estimated 20,000 years. In the early dawn of human speech, in prehistory as well as in later, documented history, the best way to store valuable information was in fact in robust oral vats. This is one of the chief reasons why even medical treatises like the *Caraka-Saṃhitā* (from 2 BCE to 6 CE) are composed *in verse*. Back then, it was by far the best way to remember, and to teach, the prescriptions (no pun intended) of the text. Millennia later, poetry remains a mnemonic device in widespread use. Not only does it serve to introduce young children of all communities to the wonders of the world long before they learn to read and write but it constitutes a prime route to *political persuasion*. Recall here the applause a parliamentarian gets when s/he recites an Urdu verse or a line from the *Cilappatikāram*, or Shakespeare. Or think back to videos that record the mesmerising hold of skilled orators like Narendra Modi over their audiences. Each of these examples constitute solid evidence for the coproduction of history and poetry for millennia – right up to the present.

These observations bring us to our second point: poetry, song and story are among the best generic means to bring a sudden lump to the throat. One might be a complete sceptic

---

‘“Even among the most barbarous and simple Indians [Author’s note: Sidney means Caribbeans, not Indians of either subcontinental or native American lineage, but little does this fact seem to matter in the early modern blossoming of the colonial imagination] where no writing is, yet have they their poets, who make and sing songs (which they call *areytos*), both of their ancestors’ deeds and praises of their gods—a sufficient probability that, if ever learning come among them, it must be by having their hard dull wits softened and sharpened with the sweet delights of poetry; for until they find a pleasure in the exercise of the mind, great promises of much knowledge will little persuade them that know not the fruits of knowledge.”’ Sir Philip Sidney (*A Defence of Poetry*, aka *An Apology for Poetry*, written circa 1580, published posthumously 1595). See https://www.poetryfoundation.org/articles/69375/the-defence-of-poesy and https://en.wikipedia.org/wiki/Are%C3%ADto

about populist rhetoric, one might have sought over a lifetime to emulate an Orwellian disdain for nationalist chest-thumping – and yet find it impossibly hard to resist the raw appeal of, let's say, national anthems that gets entire populations to proudly rise to their feet in public ceremonials (Nair 1996, 2024). Likewise, 'alternative national anthems' such as Muhammad Iqbal's *Sare Jahan Se Achcha* somehow manage to wipe away the longstanding adversarial stances associated with another historically 'rhyming pair', India and Pakistan, for at least a few magical moments. Even us deracinated academics largely unmoved by poetry's meretricious seductions appear a little embarrassed in public about our inability to appreciate it, staring modestly down at our toes until the moment of sudden verbal assault has passed. That is the power of poetry: it is an *evolutionary emotion-booster* imprinted in our brains. From mothers' lullabies to thunderous political speeches, our affective reaction to the poetry tends to be knee-jerk, autogenetic.

We come now to our third and final point in defence of poetry. Perhaps the greatest strength of poetry is its deceptive *cloak of weakness*. Poetry is a 'feminine' form easily dismissed by serious strategic thinkers. The great patriarchs who negotiate arms-deals, conduct secret border-security dialogues, highhandedly impose populist diktats (ranging from bank-nationalisation under Indira Gandhi to demonetisation under Namo) with little public debate – and, now in the twenty-first century, maintain armies of trolls, and deftly manipulate AI algorithms that can create major swerves in public opinion – obviously don't give a toss for the delicate Muses Erato and Calliope. They believe they have immensely more powerful weapons to hand. And we should not forget, by the way, that women can be patriarchs, too. For all her inspiring stature as India's Durga, Indira Gandhi, unlike her father who died with Robert Frost's poem 'Stopping by the Woods on a Snowy Evening' propped up on his desk, showed few signs of vulnerability to poetic inducements. One is hard put to find a single reference to a poetic source in the entire corpus of her speeches. Yet, it could well be, I suggest, that Indira severely underestimated poetry and literature as forms of what one might call 'counter intelligence', especially during the Emergency.

Handcuffed to History

Just one more brief pit-stop before we get to the poems which are the main subject of this essay. Global readers of literary texts know of the Emergency not through the local poetry written in India's many languages but through two major works of fiction: Salman Rushdie's *Midnight's Children* (1981) and Rohinton Mistry's *A Fine Balance* (1995).

The opening paragraph of Rushdie's Booker Prize-winning novel begins:

> I was born in the city of Bombay . . . once upon a time. No, that won't do, there's no getting away from the date: I was born in Doctor Narlikar's Nursing Home on August 15th, 1947. And the time? The time matters, too. Well then: at night. . . . On the stroke of midnight, as a matter of fact. Clock-hands joined palms in respectful greeting as I came. Oh, spell it out, spell it out: at the precise instant of India's arrival at independence, I tumbled forth into the world. There were gasps. And, outside the window, fireworks and crowds. A few seconds later . . . in that benighted moment . . . thanks to the occult tyrannies of those blandly saluting clocks, I had been mysteriously handcuffed to history, my destinies indissolubly chained to those of my country. (Rushdie 1981, 1)

Rushdie has since remarked: 'The one thing you learn as a historian is just how fragmented and ambiguous and peculiar the historical record is' (Rushdie 1989). Literature as a genre could, in this sense, be characterised as an attempt to heal the wounds of history and to bind together its ambiguous fragments. In the 'magic realist' passage above, recording the *namaste* greeting of midnight clocks at the exact hour of Indian Independence, we observe how Rushdie metonymically universalises the individual biological fact of being born in a particular city, Bombay, in a particular year, 1947, by presenting it as a national, and then as the universal and joyous cosmopolitan experience of gaining freedom. Yet, this national birth results in him being 'mysteriously handcuffed to history' forever, now and in the future (see Nair 2003, 2009). It is this realisation that they were in fact the prisoners of history that the poets of the Emergency, to whose voices we shall shortly come, most poignantly express.

Rohinton Mistry adopts a somewhat similar stance to Rushdie's in his massive 'realist', rather 'magic realist', novel of 641 pages titled *A Fine Balance*, closely rivalling the 672 pages of *Midnight's Children*. Mistry's style and emotional tenor are quite different from Rushdie's. His vision is tragic, whereas Rushdie's, despite the travails faced by his protagonist, is ultimately buoyant. However, Mistry's focus on a single character whose fate is determined by the historical events of the Emergency, is similar.

Mistry has said: 'Before I start writing I know I have at least one character who I want to work with' (Richards 2003). In *A Fine Balance*, that character is Maneck, whose suicide at the very end of the novel in the city of Bombay, also the city that Rushdie places front and centre in *Midnight's Children*, seems to snuff out the 'balance', a virtue that Mistry seems to value above all. As he puts it, 'you cannot draw lines and compartments, and refuse to budge beyond them. . . . You have to maintain a fine balance between hope and despair. . . . In the end, it's all a question of balance' (Mistry 1995, 231). The final, bleak message of Mistry's novel is that the Emergency destroyed that 'fine balance' in the lives of many ordinary people across India, including Maneck's, who sees no reason to live after he has lost his friends and his community has been irreparably damaged. Mistry's act of expiation for the brutalities imposed, as I see it, is his massive novel, teeming with believable and moving portraits of 'the common man' and of Dina, an uncommon, courageous woman.

A salient fact that we should also note about both these famous novels is that they were published several years after the Emergency: Mistry's in 1995, on the 20th anniversary of the Emergency, and Rushdie's, in which Emergency occurs as a harrowing episode but not the central theme of his book, in 1981. We might thus say that these are literary accounts that 'look back', rather than 'look at' a synchronous present when history takes an unexpected turn right before one's horrified eyes. The poets of the Emergency, writing in the exact rhyming years 1975–77 are, in this sense, up-close eye-witnesses to a crime of history, just as W. H. Auden anticipated when he deliberately placed an exact date just beneath the title of his acclaimed poem, 'In Memory of W. B. Yeats', mourning the death of the poet William Butler Yeats.[8] That date was February 1939, when the Allies and the Axis powers were limping, each gravely wounded, towards the killing fields of World War II. Auden's implication seems to have been that only the poets, not the politicos, were up to the tasks of healing the wounds of history at that devastating time when a phalanx of 'living nations wait[ed], each sequestered in its hat[red]'. Here is an extract from his poem:

> Follow, poet, follow right
> To the bottom of the night
> . . .
> In the prison of his days
> Teach the free man how to praise.

Many of Auden's themes – 'intellectual disgrace' and the traumas of nationhood; hate, pity and healing; imprisonment and freedoms; and even the metaphor of the 'barking dogs' of Europe – are, as we shall see in the next section, repeated in poetry of the Emergency (for example, the Tamil poet Pillaipandian writes, 'At midnight the rabid dog pouncing on my mother lapped up blood . . . Courageous dog kin appeared with their eyes as stones. Howled all around, they were mauled to pieces'). It almost seems as if there is some sort of locally indexed, but universally understood, response to historical crisis that it is the urgent duty of poets to voice. Again, parallel rhymes and parallel disturbances?

Internal Disturbances

The response of leading newspapers to the declaration of the Emergency is by now part of national legend. When President Fakhruddin Ali Ahmed imposed the 'just-a-few-moments-before-midnight' Emergency[9] under Article 352 of the Constitution on

---

[8] This point about the unusual placement of a date underneath the title of a poem was specifically noted by Edward W. Rosenheim, back in 1966 in *College English*. See references.

[9] It appears significant that President Ahmed did not choose the exact hour of midnight for his Emergency declaration. That might have been a 'rhyme too far', given the history of postcolonial India.

the advice of his Prime Minister, Indira Gandhi, informing citizens that *the security of India is threatened by internal disturbances*, the reaction was immediate.[10] The first edition of the *Indian Express* consisted, for example, of a blank page instead of an editorial, while *The Financial Express* carried Rabindranath Tagore's poem: *Where the mind is without fear, and the head is held high.* If that 'blank page' signalled a mute but dramatic protest against the 'freedoms of speech' imperilled by the Emergency, Tagore's poem did the opposite. It prophetically spoke out from a time of resistance to colonial rule to the crisis of the Emergency in the present. Those two strategies, of mutinous silence and poetic outspokenness, effectively 'rhymed' at the time.

Today, we are back at another 'rhyming' moment when we are charged with 'redeeming' – Nehru's word – the now half-a-century-old Emergency. What does the Emergency mean to us today? The poems we are about to read are a guide. They were written less than forty years after India gained independence and, overall, express, not just the shock of the Emergency but a deeper unspoken sense of disappointment and disenchantment over the loss of the vital dreams of freedom envisioned in 1947. These poems, just a small selection of many hundreds of poems,

---

Generations of Indians are as familiar with Jawaharlal Nehru's 'Tryst with Destiny' speech as the world is with Lincoln's 'Gettysburg Address'. We need no reminding but here are the first few lines of that superbly poetic speech: *Long years ago we made a tryst with destiny, and now the time comes when we shall redeem our pledge, not wholly or in full measure, but very substantially. At the stroke of the midnight hour, when the world sleeps, India will awake to life and freedom. A moment comes, which comes but rarely in history, when we step out from the old to new, when an age ends, and when the soul of a nation, long suppressed, finds utterance . . .* In short, that fragment of language, the 'midnight-hour', had been claimed. It would be almost sacrilegious to rhymingly claim it again. This is one of those undercover moments in the Emergency where nuance won over notoriety – a poetic victory of sorts.

[10] See '40 Years Of Emergency: When newspaper published poems, remained blank' https://www.indiatvnews.com/news/india/40-years-of-emergency-when-newspaper-published-poems-52026.html

speak powerfully for themselves and I will not burden them with unnecessary commentary, except to make two brief interventions.

First, I want to draw attention to the fact that 'Emergency poetry' is not confined to any one region. It literally emanates from the 'four corners' of India. Even the miniscule sample in this chapter has poems from no less than thirteen languages: Hindi, Punjabi and Urdu from the north of the country; Kannada, Malayalam, Tamil and Telugu from the south; Assamese, Bengali and Oriya from the east; and Gujarati, Konkani and Marathi in the west. It is therefore a real pity that, owing to copyright restrictions, we can only reproduce two to four lines from the poems quoted. I am sure in my heart that the poets in question, many now long dead, would themselves have been far more generous; they would not have wanted their voices constrained by commercial legalities. They would have intuitively realised that not only has poetry represented the mnemonics of knowledge since early in the pre-history of communication but that it at once stands as a witness (*sākṣī*) to historical 'truth' and a preeminent symbol of freedom (*svarāj, āzādī*). In a volume dedicated to the myriad kinds of violence inflicted by the Emergency and the various sorts of future hope that were courageously voiced at the time, I am therefore struck by a profound irony. In the present paired 'rhyme' between then and now, violence is being done and hope is being crushed once again as these literary bodies of 'Emergency thought' are robbed of their healing wholeness. How might we address the dire possibility that these texts will perforce be lost in the mists of history simply because they are too hard to retrieve and must be severely gutted when they are perchance recovered? Such a situation appears to me to pose an ethical challenge for the contemporary politics of publishing in a 'post-truth' era where the discursive space for print media is shrinking, as is the preservation of hope embodied by the freedom of the arts to speak unfettered. How should we, as a beleaguered, underdefined, global community, withstand this perhaps less grave but nevertheless serious, 'emergency' that must, to some extent at least, concern all the contributors, including the publishers, to the current volume? But back, for the time being, to the lessons of the past.

Second, I must record a real debt of gratitude to two 'foreigners', an American academic and a British scholar, who saw the great value of this poetry. This poetic 'corpus' – a word not without irony under the circumstances – was a national outcry but it was also a record of dissent that could be of worldwide significance, which is why they worked so hard to have it lovingly translated in the moment. If I have any say in the matter – which of course I do not – I would forthwith reprint *Voices of Emergency* today for readers of another generation, caught up in the many grim emergencies generated by the twenty-first century, personal and political. The book's extensive and excellent Foreword (Selbourne) and Preface (Perry), in conjunction with the poems' own raw resonance, offers us all an affective education that we sorely need.[11]

---

[11] Perry and Selbourne's Bombay based, 1983 Popular Prakashan publication is, we note, dedicated 'In gratitude and hope' to 'all people who recognise poetic expressions of feeling during the Emergency have meaning beyond words and place and time'. On a personal note, I became acquainted with one of the book's authors, J. O. Perry, after I saw a very generous review by him of my *Ayodhya Cantos* (Penguin 1999) in *World Literature Today*. Here is an extract from that review by this dedicated critic from faraway Tufts University who kept a fierce eye open for new books of poetry from the subcontinent, right up to the moment he passed in 2016: 'It is difficult in a short space to convey Nair's range of sophistication from street-smart to erudite, the depth and flexibility of her poetic tones and languages, key indices of the lived-with intelligence as well as the witty acuity and technical mastery to be found throughout these lyrical yet trenchant poems. . . . If Nissim Ezekiel gave Indian English poetry a model of formal rigor and incisive thought and Jayanta Mahapatra created an imaginative realm fusing immediate sensation and personal meditation, Rukmini Bhaya Nair now shows how both profoundly serious social issues and intimate personal moments can be imaginatively probed through the disciplined exercise of sensitive intelligence, passionate inquiry and unflinchingly open-minded, readily self-critical discernment. . . . Her technical and intellectual mastery of a hitherto unexplored area of poetic possibilities here establishes a new level of achievement for this genre. A new pace-setting level of poetic achievement in India.' Today, so many years later, I still treasure John's words.

And now the poems. In a circular fashion, we will begin with Gujarat – Gandhi's state – in western India, not only because of its dominant place in the national imagination, especially post-2002, but because some of the most powerful poems in Perry and Selbourne's volume emerged from the state of Gujarat. We will then return to the west of India at the end of this chapter after we have heard voices from other parts of India, all anguished, all defiant. Chandrasen Momaya's lament is characteristic. He tells us that he is a poet 'who has not seen the conflicts of yester years' but being a witness to the 'horrors' of the Emergency, he now faces an existential crisis: 'I am a poet who . . . has ceased to be a poet / And become a testimony to voices that are choked and shrieks that rent the air' ('Cessation of a Poet' by Chandrasen Momaya, translated from Gujarati by Mansukhlal Jhaveri; in Perry 1983, 25). The 'cessation' of poetry in favour of 'testimony' then rhymes with a second poem from Gujarat, which seems to anticipate the 'garbage can' vocabulary that we heard most recently and virulently in the American elections of 2024. This constitutes one reason why I think it would be well worth rereading this repository of poetry today. It is just so full of cautions for the present. The second poem from Gujarat explains that the poet, Badal, was arrested under the Maintenance of Internal Security Act (MISA) because he was found 'exploring' a prohibited site. This was the 'garbage can' for 'Democracy / Dumped by our rulers there' ('Arrest' by Badal, translated from Gujarati by Mansukhlal Jhaveri; in Perry 1983, 10).

We could have stayed in Gujarat for the rest of this chapter and gained a great deal, but part of the impulse of this brief chapter is to give the reader a sense of the widespread nature of the poetic protest against the Emergency. So we move now to another part of India: the north. In many ways, we still instinctively think of Delhi, located in the north as an epicentre of the Emergency, given that it saw some of the most violent assaults (forced vasectomies, the bulldozing of 'unauthorised' settlements, the political opposition being scrubbed out) on freedoms that had hitherto been taken for granted. The first of the Delhi poems, 'Abbatoir' graphically describes the 'ogre' enforcers of the Emergency as 'twin apparitions' who appear 'in the dead of the night', the first one 'dyed in an ink deeper even than the night's'. 'The other, a grotesque-breasted ogress of a mountainous height. / Then, a he-ogre shouts unfamiliar gibberish down the pits of my sensitive ears' ('Abattoir' by Vinod Sharma, translated from the Hindi in a Delhi newspaper, by Keshav Malik (1976); in Perry 1982, 3. The three figures in Sharma's terrifying poem are: Bansilal, minister of defence, Indira Gandhi and Sanjay Gandhi).

The second Delhi poem, also in Hindi, is by a political figure that almost everyone will recognise.

> Though we break, we will not bend. Darkness itself challenges us.
> . . .
> As the mythical Angad once more Plants his foot.
> Here we take our stand.
> The powers of darkness challenge us and we may break,
> but never bend.
>
> ('Determination, from Prison 1976' by Atal Bihari Vajpayee, translated from Hindi in *Dharmayug*, June 1977, by Ajit K. Mishra, Kamla Dutt and John Oliver Perry; Perry 1983, 46)

Also from the north, in Urdu, emerged some of the sharpest of criticisms aimed at the craven silence of Indian 'intellectuals' during the Emergency and the pen's utter inefficacy. A deep contempt expressed for every body-part – 'hands, eyes, ears, lips' – of these spineless mortals in 'Confessions' and in 'Museum' below.

> Our sole request is
> The spinal cord not snap
> And we don't give up
> The habit of crawling.
> ('Confession of India's Intellectuals' by Shaheryar, translated from Urdu in memory by Dr S. M. H. Rizir and John Oliver Perry; in Perry 1983, 35)

> Only one tongue—a dagger—still wags
> Only one pen—a tyrant's—still moves.
>
> ('Museum' by Mohammad Hasan, translated from Urdu in *Asri Adab* [Oct. 1979], by the poet; in Perry 1983, 136)

And finally, the last stop in the north records the post-midnight swoop of 'Black Marias' in Punjab, and a sinister 'pounding on the door and the rattle of chains'. Would these constitute the 'internal disturbances' that President Fakhruddin Ali Ahmed said necessitated the almost-midnight declaration of the Emergency, one wonders – or was it another sort of 'disturbance', more alien and more ambiguous?: "This was not a first journey. / But how disturbing that moment after midnight' ('Disturbing Moment' by Mrityubodh, translated from Punjabi by the poet for *Dissenting Voices* (1977); in Perry 1983, 51).

The east of India is represented in this essay by poetry in three languages: Assamese, Bengali and Oriya. Like the Hindi poem 'Abattoir', this Assamese poem identifies individuals. It is also steeped in blood. The adjectives 'devilish' and 'poisonous' are used – but this is not a poem of condemnation. Rather, it is an elegiac poem, a poem about the loss of springtime, a poem that mourns the loss of young comrades from all over India.

> The innocent fawn totters and dances Just before the hunters.
> The antelope, the deer and the hare: Rabin, Snehalata, and Rajan
> . . .
> In exchange for your blood
> We are preparing the country's liberation.
> ('Rabin, Rajan, Snehalata[12] and Others' by Chandra Kataky, translated by the poet from the Assamese *Souvenir of All Assam Students Union*, 9 August 1977; in Perry 1983, 171)

In Bengal, which shares a limited but troubled border with Assam, the response to the Emergency is varied, ranging from mythological to contemporary pressures. Irony is a hallmark of these 'rhyming dialogues' – as in the two poems below. Sankha Ghose's poem begins with the personified mountain range, Vindhya, complaining to the mythological sage Agastya, that he has put her to a great deal of trouble. Agastya then replies to his

[12] Rabin Kalita (of Assam?), Snehalata Reddy in Karnataka, and Rajan in Kerala died during or after from Emergency imprisonment.

'dear Vindhya' that he will surely take appropriate action once the time comes. We shall now let this poem's abbreviated, but still compelling, lines speak for themselves.

> "I'll restore everything with honor
> when I've looted the honeycomb."
> Vindhya, on that assurance, now . . .
> is most polite even to snails.
> ('Agastya's[13] Journey' by Sankha Ghose, translated by Lila Ray from Bengali, in *Chaturanga*, Winter 1976; in Perry 1983, 8)

The next poem, by Samsur Anowar, records a by-no-means-mythological but recognisably modern conversational moment during the Emergency when a poet invited to read his poems requests that they 'should not be taped'. Anowar says he is 'alarmed' by this incident for bio-cosmic reasons and proceeds to ask a hard-to-answer, counterfactual 'what-if?' question in response.

> What if . . . birds suspended their singing because
> their voices are recorded or streams . . .
> cease their flowing when their babbling is enscrolled?
> ('A Poetry Reading is Arranged' By Samsur Anowar, translated from Bengali by Lila Ray in *Krittibas*, April 1976; in Perry 1983, 163)

The poem from Odisha, bordering Bengal, returns us to a theme that has persisted from the Emergency to the present: the wounding of our Constitution. The author describes his poem as a 'folk farce', recalling the second coming of history as farce, à la Marx; his tone, however, is that of Emile Zola who wrote the famous letter titled *J'Accuse...!* holding the French government to account for its anti-Semitism in the case against army officer Alfred Dreyfus. Baikuntanath Patnaik accuses the Indian Government of 'looting by force' the 'freedom of sixty crore'; he refers to Gandhi, in ironic Churchillian terms, as a 'half-naked pauper' under the Emergency government, and he ends defiantly 'As Hitler has gone, so you must go!' These words have a harsh ring; they are extreme, but

[13] Patron saint of Dravidian brahmins; who first took Vedic teachings south beyond the Vindhya Mountains.

can we honestly say they do not resonate in a twenty-first-century world dominated by so many authoritarian populist leaders?

Ask yourselves—you slaves of power!
Aren't you the beasts of your greedy burden?
In the heat of history, power melts like rotten snow;
As Hitler has gone, so you must go!
('Emergency Operation of the Indian Constitution' by Baikuntanath Patnaik, translated from Oriya by Dilip Naik, in *Jhankar*, October 1977; in Perry 1983, 66)

The poems below, from the four southern states of India, begin with another concept that is a hardy perennial in democratic politics – not the Constitution this time, but electoral politics. In a historically fraught time such as the Emergency, Kovai Vanam wisely – and punningly – advises us on the 'end(s)' of elections. He enquires whether our common goal is just 'Victory through elections!'. Or, should our votes be much more self-reflexive, since 'what we give', in the end, are 'not our ballots but tickets of admission': 'To what we ourselves / Represent' ('On the End of Elections' by Kovai Vanam, translated from Tamil by A. Manoharan, in *Sila Ethiroligal* or 'Emergency Poems', April 1977; in Perry 1983, 151).

Then, like the Assamese poem by Chandra Kakaty, K. V. Raman Reddy's ironic 'All's Well', written in Telugu, in quite another corner of the country, speaks of life in a real, as well as metaphoric, prison cell. It contrasts the resilience of those who 'dream the dream of Revolution' with the sleepless 'loneliness' of the prison guards who are forced to proclaim *Sab Theek Hai* (all's well) when it clearly is not. The disparity between embattled truth and manifest falsehood that Reddy focuses on is a constant refrain in this poetry and goes well beyond a narrow critique of the Emergency to a world full of amplified lies – a theme, once again, that seems to speak plangently to us in our twenty-first-century present.

Nightly . . . we dream the dream of Revolution.
. . .
Poor police guards
lonely unfortunates
who cannot sleep

> but hourly call out
> "Sab tik hai—All is well."
> ('All's Well' by K. V. Ramana Reddy, translated from Telugu by Chekuri Rama Rao, in *Jailu Kokila* (1977); in Perry 1983, 8)

Another telling 'historical rhyme' that links colonial rule to the circumstances of the Emergency is evident in the following Malayalam poem by Vyloppilli Shreedhara Menon. The great power of this poem consists in its identification of the commonplace rhetorical device of agreement (see Kornprobst 2012). This trope justifies ceding authority to tyrants because they 'make the trains run on time', even if the fact is that they do no such thing! Such blind rhetorical acceptance, Menon skilfully suggests, can often confine a whole populace within authoritarian language prisons that let in no light – and allow no insight.

> In the bus the passengers' gossip goes around:
> "What great peace we now have everywhere!"
> . . .
> The retired county officer is at last contented:
> "All things are secure as when the British ruled."
> ('As When the British Ruled' by Vyloppilli Shreedhara Menon, translated from Malayalam by K. Ayyappa Paniker; in Perry 1983, 10)

The final poem from the south of India we shall read is by P. Lankesh. Written in Kannada, this philosophically acute poem continues to explore the leitmotif of deception, doubt, and other barriers to understanding ('dear friends, your poems have reached me but will they reach our people?') that the previous poem by Menon pinpointed. Those dominant colours – red and black – in his poem do indeed signal the perpetration of violent injustice but, at the same time, Lankesh leaves us with a sliver of hope as he envisages a future in which 'perhaps these poems will stir into life the minds of some listeners'. As I see it, these long-ago poems are indeed fulfilling this exact function at this exact moment. They are stirring into life the minds of listeners.

> Dear Friends,
> . . .
> Surely we poets aren't the big sinners

We aren't enormous liars...
But when... the earth its proverbial patience
Then perhaps these poems
Will stir into life
The minds of some listeners.
('Red Poems of Black People' by P. Lankesh, translated from Kannada in *Red Poems* by P. Rama Moorthy and John Oliver Perry; in Perry 1983, 4)

And finally, we return to the west of India: to a poem from the large Gujarat-adjacent state of Maharashtra, followed by one from the tiny state of Goa to the south-west of Maharashtra.

The Emergency phenomenon of forced vasectomies may be most associated with Delhi but Sandanand Rege's poem is a reminder that the contagion of bad ideas spreads faster in times of tyranny ('everyone in my alley has got it done'). Fear and conformity are the twin enforcers of 'the law' at such times and liberty is a goner. The nameless protagonist of this poem is a 'bachelor', yet the absurd ethos of the Emergency dictates that 'if someone becomes pregnant', he thinks, 'they'll hold me responsible'. That is why he runs to the Family Planning Clinic, gasping: '"Perform Vasectomy on me"' ('Joke in a Clinic' by Sadanand Rege, translated from Marathi by the poet; in Perry 1983, 110).

The next poem from the state of Goa, written in Konkani, emphasises the historical importance of India's freedom movement ('with untold sacrifices and countless struggles, the brave people of this nation won its liberty!'). Subsequently, though, came 'the evils we are in today'. Yet, like Lankesh and so many other Emergency poets, Cyrano Valles leaves open a door to hope 'after darkness and confusion dissipates', he prophesies, 'the bright sun of Democracy will once again shine'. Amen to that!

Will all these sacrifices of our forefathers
Have been in vain as we and future generations
Become hereafter slaves of a dictatorship forever? ...
But never lose hope of regaining our liberty!
('Song of Liberty' by Cyrano Valles, translated from Konkani by the poet; in Perry 1983, 198)

We conclude with a short poem written by a Parsi in the shared, hybrid tongue that we have all in fact used in the current volume (Perry and Selbourne call it 'Indo-Anglian'). Jimmy Avasia's piece, simply titled 'Emerging', captures a chiaroscuro thought that also struck me as I started on my chapter: namely, the etymological 'rhyme' between the concepts of 'emergency' and 'emergence', separated from each other by just a single, final phoneme. A political Emergency such as that imposed in 1975 is dire but it also shocks us into reassessing democratic freedoms that we may have taken for granted. Avasia's poem movingly emphasises that the citizens of India 'awoke' one sudden day to find that '*we*' were 'free to do what *they* wanted' [italics mine]. The tussle between the freedoms of speech and action previously assumed and the draconian new norms 'emerging' from the 'Emergency' powers imposed by the government of the day, are effectively captured here in Avasia's subtle use of the pronominal system of English. The story of 'we, the people' and 'they, the perpetrators' comes alive through his use of extremely commonplace language, turning the Emergency into a universal phenomenon that anyone at all might one day experience. This was a time, Avasia indicates, when 'ideals collapsed' before the public eye, yet 'nobody spoke'. An unnatural silence replaced everyday conversational exchanges. A version of 'the truth' was selected by the authorities but the consequences of their choice affected everyone – and not in a good way. Questioning itself, a basic mode of human thought, was imperilled. The couple of attenuated lines below, constrained by editorial requirements, make the point via a succinct rhyme: 'On the way to an answer they selected a truth / but all suggestion of question died en route' ('Emerging' by Jimmy Avasia, Indo-English in *Kavi*; in Perry 1983, 67).

Overall, despite bouts of utter despair such as Avasia's, the collective memo from the agonistic Emergency poetry we have just read seems to be that an emergency, however dark, presages an emergence into a more luminous future, however distant. Poetry as a genre, we have argued in this chapter, is symbolic of the entire gene-pool of language. This universal language resource reveals our self-images to us most clearly at times of crisis when all our senses are jolted. Emergency poetry, in particular, written across

India's many languages, reveals how a political force majeure can stir people into a realisation of their common humanity. An oeuvre that 'rhymes across time', it functions as both rebuke and reminder; it mediates the hidden affective gulf between those soaring aspirations and depths of despair that we are prone to as a species. We would thus do well to heed these perspicacious messages as we confront the clamorous challenges of our own times.

References

Austin, Granville. 1999. *Working a Democratic Constitution: The Indian Experience*. New Delhi: Oxford UP.

Kornprobst, M. 2012. How Rhetorical Strategies Reproduce Compromise Agreements: The Case of the Nuclear Non-Proliferation Regime. *Government and Opposition* 47.3: 342–67.

Mistry, R. 1995. *A Fine Balance*. Toronto: McClelland and Stewart.

Morey, P. 2004. *Rohinton Mistry*. Manchester: Manchester UP.

Nair, R. B. 1996. Bombay's Balzac. *Biblio: A Review of Books* 2: 2–15.

———. 2003. The Linguistic Qualities of the *Satanic Verses*. In *Salman Rushdie: From Midnight's Children to the Satanic Verses*, ed. D. Smale. London: Palgrave Macmillan. 80–87.

———. 2009. *Poetry in a Time of Terror: Essays in the Postcolonial Preternatural*. Oxford and Delhi: Oxford UP.

———. 2011. The Nature of Narrative: Schemes, Genes, Memes, Dreams and Screams! In *Religious Narrative, Cognition and Culture: Image and Word in the Mind of Narrative*, ed. A. W. Geertz, and J. S. Jensen. London: Equinox Series in Religion, Cognition and Culture. 17–146.

———. 2016. Narrative: Self, Poetry and Politics. In *Demo(s): Philosophy-Pedagogy-Politics*, ed. H. Letiche, G. Lightfoot, and J. L. Moriceau. Rotterdam: Sense Publishers, supported by the University of Utrecht, 35–52.

———. 2024. Coronavirus Spacesuits: Or, Hard Times as Launching Pads for Literary Travel. In *From Canon to Covid: Transforming English Literary Studies in India*, ed. A. Multani et al. London: Routledge. 45–59.

Perry, J. O., ed. 1983. *Voices of Emergency: An All India Anthology of Protest Poetry of the 1975–77 Emergency*. Mumbai: Popular Prakashan.

Richards, Linda L. 2003. Interview with Rohinton Mistry. *January Magazine*. https://www.januarymagazine.com/profiles/mistry.html.

Rosenheim, E. W. 1966. The Elegiac Act: Auden's 'In Memory of W. B. Yeats'. *College English* 27.5 (February): 422–25.

Rushdie, S. 1981. *Midnight's Children*. London: Jonathan Cape.

———. 1989. Interview on the Bandung File, *Channel 4*, 14 February.

Sperber, D., and D. Wilson. 1986. *Relevance: Communication and Cognition*. Oxford: Basil Blackwell.

Publisher's Acknowledgements

All poetry quotations from *Voices of Emergency: An All India Anthology of Protest Poetry of the 1975–77 Emergency*, edited by John Oliver Perry, published by Popular Prakashan, 1983, are reproduced courtesy of the publisher.

11

Many Meanings of Freedom: The Dandawate Prison Letters

Gyan Prakash

Throughout modern history, incarceration has served as the nursery for introspections and ruminations on life and politics. Most famously, Antonio Gramsci penned his thoughts on Italian history and on the conditions of hegemony in capitalist societies, in his *Prison Notebooks*. Nehru wrote *Glimpses of World History* for his daughter Indira and his classic nationalist text *The Discovery of India* in British jails. Understandably, such writings dealt primarily with the public and institutional conditions of politics and society. But imprisonment also produced deeper reflections on freedom. Arthur Koestler, writing about his imprisonment in Spain during the Spanish Civil War said, 'I have never been so free as I was then'. Facing death, 'we were free—men without shadows, dismissed from the ranks of the mortal; it was the most complete experience of freedom that can be granted a man' (1942, 203–04). The revolutionary Bhagat Singh used his experience of incarceration to think expansively on the boundaries of freedom. Hindi novelists in the 1930s and 40s focused on the experience of imprisonment to identify freedom not just in the public sphere of politics but also in the familial and private sphere of love and intimacy.[1]

This essay explores such reflections on freedom during the twenty-one months of Indira Gandhi's 1975–77 Emergency regime that locked up over 110,000 political leaders, activists and ordinary citizens. I ask if the experience of being placed behind bars stimulated introspection on the meanings of freedom not

---

[1] For an insightful reading of Bhagat Singh and Hindi novelists, see Govind 2014.

only in terms of institutions, not simply as matters of legal and political status, but also as something more profound? Did this introspection produce a greater dedication to democracy and the value of equality in the sense that Ambedkar had in mind? Did the discourse on freedom stop at the door of party politics, or extend to explore its existential meanings? I ask these questions with regard to the remarkable set of letters exchanged between the socialist leader Madhu Dandavate (1924–2005) and his wife Pramila Dandavate (1928–2002).

'Writing letters is a hugely calming activity in the loneliness of the prison. These letters are meant for other people of course, but they are also a great way to hear oneself think, to hear oneself sort out one's own feelings and thoughts.' This was Madhu reflecting on letter writing in one of his letters to Pramila, his wife and comrade in politics.[2] Madhu, a Member of Parliament elected from Maharashtra, was arrested on 26 June and lodged in Bangalore jail for eighteen months. Pramila was taken into captivity on 17 July 1975, and was held in the Yerawada Central Prison, near Pune. During their time apart, the two wrote to each other weekly, exchanging nearly two hundred letters.

Politics is understandably prominent in the Dandavate prison letters. Both were seasoned political activists. Madhu became politically active in the 1942 Quit India movement, which brought the socialists, including JP, to the public stage as an inspiring new force. While earning graduate and postgraduate degrees in physics in Bombay, Madhu was drawn to the socialists. When they parted ways with the Congress after independence and formed the Socialist Party in 1948, he joined them. He taught as a professor of physics while participating in political activities. In 1971, he was

---

[2] Madhu Dandavate to Pramila Dandavate, 6 December 1976. This letter is part of the collection, Documentation of the Emergency Period in India, Center for Research Libraries, Chicago, containing hundreds of letters and other documents. The letters between the Dandavates are in rolls 2 and 3. All subsequent citations are from this collection and will only mention the date of correspondence. I am immensely grateful to Irawati Karnik for her translation of the letters and poems from Marathi into English.

elected to the Parliament from a Maharashtra constituency, a feat he went on to repeat for five consecutive terms.

Pramila was also a political activist, who found her socialist calling first in the Rashtra Seva Dal, an organisation of volunteers founded in the 1940s by Sane Guruji, a revered figure in Maharashtra. It promoted social change, secularism and a decentralised socialist agenda. Participation in its activities brought her into the circle of socialists in Bombay, including Madhu. With senior socialist leader S. M. Joshi acting as the matchmaker, she married Madhu in 1953 and became his partner in politics. Elected in 1968 to the Bombay Municipal Corporation, Pramila made her mark in the fiery protests by women against price rise in the early 1970s. As thousands of women took to the streets, shaking their wooden rolling pins to remonstrate the rising cost of food, a trio of leaders – Mrinal Gore, Ahilya Rangnekar and Pramila Dandavate – emerged as the face of this new militant movement. Not surprisingly, all three women were put behind bars during the Emergency.

Given this background, politics was the language of communication between the couple. Aware that their letters were censored, they exchanged information about arrested colleagues in code. Being placed behind bars was 'getting married', Indira was 'mother-in-law', her son Sanjay Gandhi was 'the prince', satyagraha was 'going on pilgrimage', and Jayaprakash Narayan (JP) was 'Prabhavati's husband'. They were forthright in their opposition to the Emergency and Indira. Their imprisonment did not bend them. They were confident that the propaganda disseminated by the censored and controlled newspapers could not forever place a lid on the truth. Madhu assured her of it by quoting Emile Zola: 'If you shut up the truth and bury it under ground, it will but grow and gather to itself such explosive power that the day it bursts, it will blow up everything in its way.'[3]

Prison made Madhu and Pramila draw from their intellectual resources to sustain their defiance. The letters frequently drew on writers, poets, philosophers and political leaders to articulate the couple's steadfast defence of freedom. Their intellectualism was rooted in their background of having grown up in educated

[3] Madhu Dandavate to Pramila Dandavate, 1 March 1976.

Maharashtrian brahmin families. Madhu's father was a civil engineer and his mother was a social worker. His grandfather was a man of literature, who translated classical Sanskrit works into Marathi, and the household library contained literary works and the writings and speeches of Gandhi, Nehru and other nationalist leaders. Surrounded by books, Madhu developed an early aptitude for the world of ideas, which the college years in Bombay developed further. He read Marx, who kindled his interest in social justice that was to stay with him for the rest of his life. So did his interest in literature and classical music, both Hindustani and Western. Like him, Pramila also grew up in an educated family. Her father was a well-known gynaecologist, and she completed her high school in Bombay. An interest in art led her to complete a graduate degree from the famed J. J. School of Art. She became a teacher in an art school, and also plunged into politics that brought her into the company of socialist intellectuals including Madhu.

It was no accident that the Dandavates' intellectualism led to a commitment to socialism. Maharashtra boasted a long tradition of the intelligentsia's involvement in social reform. It was here that Jyotiba Phule in the nineteenth century and B. R. Ambedkar in the twentieth century had mounted sweeping critiques of caste hierarchy. While these offered radical challenges from below, brahmin intellectuals such as M. G. Ranade and G. K. Gokhale pushed for change from above, conjoining nationalism with social reform. Notwithstanding this spectrum of ideological and political positions, Maharashtra's intelligentsia enjoyed a rich history of engagement with social critique. The Dandavates were heirs to this tradition. So were several other leading socialists, who were also Maharashtrian brahmins. But so also were numerous right-wing ideologues, including Savarkar, the RSS founding members, and Gandhi's assassin, Nathuram Godse.

The Socialist Party was an organisation of intellectuals. This was both its strength and weakness. Ideas, not opportunism, drove the commitment to socialism. But differences over ideas and principles produced bitter conflicts. Since its founding in 1948, the history of the socialists in India is riddled with splits and mergers. But in times of adversity, such as imprisonment, intellectualism was a source of strength. Early in her imprisonment, Pramila wrote that she was devouring one book after another. After reading an inspiring Marathi book by P. Narhar Joshi titled *The Great Prison*, she wrote:

> Whenever great people have been arrested, it has proved to be a boon for mankind. Excellent literature, poetry as well as thought were born in prisons. Great people have always been ready to undergo any test, to face any challenge in order to be able to stand by what they believe in, their commitment in life and for upholding the truth. No power in the world can curb their energy. The book filled me with tremendous enthusiasm. I do have some experience when it comes to prisons. But this book has inspired me doubly. I feel like there is some meaning to my life. Nana, I am a simple and small human being. But you are truly made of the stuff of the great people. I am certain that you won't just read but that you will also write. This forced vacation will give birth to great, eternal literature through you, I am sure of it.[4]

As if on cue, Madhu told her that after two and a half months of research he had finished drafting two chapters of a book on Marx and Gandhi.[5] It was not 'great literature' but it was a comparative analysis of the two paths to revolution, one based on class struggle and the other on individual change in human beings. Speaking of the experience of writing, Madhu wrote: 'Amidst the roses on the table and the *champa* [frangipani] flowers on the trees, the pen moves in speed and smoothly.' Then he quotes from Byron's *Don Juan*:

> There's music in the sighing of reeds
> There's music in the gushing of a rill
> There's music in all things, if men had ears
> Their earth is but an echo of the spheres.

Madhu had found in Byron a way to identify even in the confines of the prison an underlying and universal human spirit expressed in the musical rhythm of the pen on the page, in the blossoming of flowers. All was not lost. He tried to lift Pramila's spirit:

---

[4] Pramila Dandavate to Madhu Dandavate, 10 July 1975.

[5] Madhu Dandavate to Pramila Dandavate, 3 October 1975. The completed book was published as *Marx and Gandhi* (1977).

> 'Your last letter had a shadow of sadness over it. You said that our home and life together would be completely destroyed by the time we get out of here. And you don't know if you have the strength and persistence to do it all, all over again. Your comment felt exceedingly hopeless to me. We have always carried our life together on our backs. As long as our spine is in place, who can possibly touch our life together?"

There was nothing wrong with their spines. As their exchanges make clear, there was no question of resigning to the Emergency's suppression of democracy. But incarceration sparked reflections on the broader goals of JP's Total Revolution. Pramila would often return to it, exploring its meanings. Clearly, it meant something more fundamental than the usual institutions of democracy – party politics, elections, freedom of the press, etc. She wrote: 'Our society needs a cultural revolution in the true sense.'[6] She wrote this while decrying religious observances as counter-revolutionary, and casting doubts on those activists who mouthed the slogan of Total Revolution while espousing religious ideologies. For her, revolution in a 'true sense' implied breaking free from religion; it meant a culture unbounded by religious dogmas and rituals.

Underlying this commitment to revolution was a staunch advocacy of freedom. Like Madhu, she frequently turned to Marathi poetry to express her thoughts on freedom. She sent Madhu two Marathi poems. She transcribed one called *Bhinta* (The Wall) by the famous poet Mangesh Padgaonkar that was published in a special 1976 Diwali issue of the magazine *Marathawada.*[7]

> There is a wall around me.
> A wall around you
> Walls everywhere you look
> Walls all around

The poem proceeds to expound on the many types of walls, those of fear that are invisible and suffocating. It rails against walls of surveillance that engender fear and enforce conformity, the limiting walls that deny freedom of speech, and entrench societal

---

[6] Pramila Dandavate to Madhu Dandavate, 24 January 1976.

[7] Pramila Dandavate to Madhu Dandavate, November 30, 1976.

divisions, and walls that demand discipline and expression of support, to be 'hailed'.

She transcribed a second poem called *Mukt* (Free) by Kusumagraj, a noted Marathi poet.

> A cage is broken
> And the free bird
> With the blood from its wounded wings
> Draws red winding lines . . . .

The poem lauds the bird's 'blood-soaked' joy and pride as it breaks free from the cage even in the face of death.

Expressing captivity and freedom at the level of phenomenological experience, the poems spoke to their existential conditions of incarceration. The public sphere of freedom could be read in them, but their power derived from the poetry's attention to something bodily, a sensory experience of confinement and breaking free. The deeply intertwined experiences of public and personal incarceration could be read in the dense, compacted language of poetry.

At the personal, existential level, the separation forced by their incarceration in two separate jails was hard on both. Madhu acknowledged a note of sorrow in his letters but thought that this was perhaps because the pangs of sadness are more keenly felt than the feelings of happiness.[8] He invoked Shelley's 'To a Skylark' to explain the desolate mood of his letters: 'Our sweetest songs are those that tell of saddest thought.' Continuing in this vein, he reflected on the ordinary criminals sentenced to life imprisonment in the Bangalore Jail. Their lives filled him with pathos:

> When the life imprisonment prisoners water the rose bushes on the premises, they shed their tears into them as nourishment and see the reflection of those tears in the smiling, blooming fragrant flowers. In the winter cold, these flowers dry and wither away and these prisoners think about when they will step out after having completed their sentence and wonder about whether the society will see their forever tarnished lives the same way.

[8] Madhu Dandavate to Pramila Dandavate, 24 November 1975.

Even prisoners condemned to life imprisonment were not without recourse. They could find creative freedom in their tears to nurture plants.

Like the prisoners who found a creative resource in their tears, he was also free to imagine. 'We have the liberty to build the towers of our imagination while staring at the skies through the day; and the freedom to paint vivid dreams of tomorrow in the darkness of the night.' Besides, you could cope with the misery of imprisonment, as he did, by reading and writing. There was also his beloved classical Hindustani music broadcast over the radio, and the scent of flowers in the prison garden. 'I had the fortune to listen to Sunil Bose's Raga Bihag and Jayjaywanti on national radio. I woke up still intoxicated by the fragrance and the music and sat down to write to you. Roses – Jayjaywanti – Pramila and the beautiful picture was complete!'[9]

The talk of roses did not soothe the pain of separation that Pramila felt. 'You wrote "Jayjaywanti – Rose – Pramila and the picture is complete". But the flowers in your flowerpot gave you the gift of fragrance, which made you forget the thorns and lulled you to sleep with the memory of the fragrance.'[10] Separation was a thorn and she was not shy about expressing the pain it caused. She wrote frankly of her longing for him. The prison suffocated her. 'No matter how much we laugh on the outside, no matter how playful we are, my mind seems to be flailing about like a fish out of water.'[11]

Both read books and listened to classical music on the radio to ease their time in prison. Music, she wrote, broke the shackles of routine and re-energised and refreshed her. Then, there were letters to be written and received. 'Have you ever written letters to me so regularly in life before?' Pramila asked.[12]

> Early on in our marriage, I remember you would go away on long tours and wouldn't write to me for months. I'd be ready to cry. The only place I got to read anything about

[9] Madhu Dandavate to Pramila Dandavate, 27 September 1975.

[10] Pramila Dandavate to Madhu Dandavate, 5 October 1975.

[11] Pramila Dandavate to Madhu Dandavate, 22 December 1975.

[12] Pramila Dandavate to Madhu Dandavate, 8 June 1976.

> you was in the newspapers. I would feel so embarrassed when someone asked about you. I would have nothing to tell them. But now look at us! You write me every Monday without fail. Thanks to the Emergency!

They wrote about the books they read. Madhu read *Boundless Sky,* an anthology of Rabindranath Tagore's writings, and recommended that she immediately get hold of a copy. She, in turn, recommended Dale Carnegie's *Lincoln, the Unknown* for its portrayal of how the American President carried the weight of a deep personal sorrow all his life. She described Irving Stone's *The President's Lady* as beautiful and so moving in its depiction of the injustices suffered by Rachel, Andrew Jackson's wife, that she wept as she closed the book.

Letters were not just a way of maintaining contact or exchanging information but also the means to express love and affection without the benefit of physical proximity. Politics, books, poetry and music served as languages to communicate their feelings. Rapturous descriptions of nature frequently enlivened their exchanges. Pramila wrote: 'These days we have heavy rains here. I have always loved the rain. The atmosphere looks cleaner. The earth (whatever little we can see of it) looks like a freshly bathed young woman. The moment the sky clears up, all my favorite birds flap their wings clean and start chirping away.'[13]

Pramila could also invigorate the disembodied text by telling a story:

> One particular sparrow was having quite an interesting time just a few days back. Most of the other sparrow couples were busy getting ready to welcome their young ones into the world but this one was still busy with romance with her male sparrow. She was quite a special one. Then one day, she saw herself in the mirror. That was it. She couldn't stop looking at her reflection and wondering who it was. She would spend so much time tapping it with her beak, looking at herself from the top, from the side, every which way possible. She would spend hours trying to figure out who was behind the mirror. We even put the mirror flat on the table but she

[13] Pramila Dandavate to Madhu Dandavate, 8 June 1976.

> still wouldn't let it go. She was so jealous of the "other" sparrow in the mirror that whenever the male sparrow flew close, she would do everything in her power to send him away. But she just refused to rest. When we put the mirror away, she found the one on the wall. She would spread her wings and would try to attack it. When we covered it with a cloth, she still couldn't stop hovering around it, worrying about the "other" sparrow. We felt a little bad for her but also couldn't help laughing at her. I told her, "If you spend so much of your time worrying over the 'other woman' in the mirror, your man will get tired and actually go get himself another wife." She would wake up every morning and come sit by the mirror. We have no idea how the male sparrow finally managed to distract her. But one day, I saw the two of them sitting close together quite cozily. These days, they seem to be working towards building a nest.

In Pramila's storytelling, you can read expressions of the intimate self; and you can observe a capacity to identify the delusions of self-reflections in which the self could appear as an image of the other. Imprisonment placed constraints on this intimate self but did not crush it. The self, confined and troubled, found expression in the storytelling of sparrows. Being placed behind bars did not crush it. If anything, the self's awareness was intensified. She reproached Madhu for being emotionally restrained. 'We do a public reading of your letters,' she told him, because 'they aren't written to your wife but to your co-revolutionaries'. For 'even though your letters are beautiful, barring perhaps a sentence or two, they are entirely objective. There is hardly anything subjective in there.'[14]

In fact, Madhu could also be 'subjective'. In a letter, he remarked that the past twenty-three years of their married life had passed in a rush. 'As though in revenge for that, we have been forced into this solitude at the prison. The tranquility has made it possible to immerse oneself in the memories of the last twenty-three years.'[15] Then he turns to poetry to express his feelings.

---

[14] Pramila Dandavate to Madhu Dandavate, 18 February 1976.

[15] Madhu Dandavate to Pramila Dandavate, 18 October 1976.

When the fire simmering down below
Is brought billowing to the top by memories
My skin comes alive with the thought of you
And the distance hurts . . .

He wonders when they will meet again. 'But the very next moment my heart tells me that we do not want to accept meeting each other under conditions that make us feel helpless and insulted. And as these thoughts linger in my mind, I am reminded yet again of something else Kusumagraj said': 'I don't want the pathetic intimacy of cowards / I would rather endure being apart from you!' 'Whenever it is that we are released from prison, we will be stepping out with a refreshed mind. The life in prison will motivate us with new energy to continue our twenty-three-year journey together for many more years to come.'

Pramila too could dream of the future, but she also fondly remembered the past. She reminded him of 22 October, their wedding anniversary, and recalled what her mother had asked when Madhu first came home. 'There are so many young men around you. Which corner did you pick this one out of?' Little did her mother know, Pramila wrote, that she had picked a diamond. 'After these twenty-two years, if someone asked me, I would choose exactly the same partner and the same journey. But I won't do the "*vatsavitri*" pooja [the traditional Hindu patriarchal tradition of husband worship]!'[16] Her love for Madhu was not that of a traditional wife but that of a modern woman, a partner in the shared journey of politics.

Prison intensified her awareness of their relationship, and she was not afraid to admit that her heart pined for him. She repeatedly implored him to apply for a transfer to the Yerawada prison, or at least seek permission from the government to allow him to visit her. When he did apply for permission, she was overjoyed.

> I received your letter on Thursday and I have actually been daydreaming constantly. This kind of behaviour isn't becoming of our age. But I keep imagining our meeting (in prison). Even though you have only sent in an application to the central government as of now. But

[16] Pramila Dandavate to Madhu Dandavate, 17 October 1975.

> I keep dreaming of it happening. My mind has never wandered all this time. But now it takes effort to keep it under control. There are so many young girls around me that I have to be careful not to let them sense my state of mind.[17]

Sadly, when the court ordered in April 1976 that Madhu be allowed to visit her, the government added a cruel stipulation that he reimburse the cost of the security escort. Of course, there was no question of accepting the humiliating condition. 'No matter how eager I might be to meet you, you know I cannot compromise my principles for any kind of personal gain. And if you were to think otherwise, I wouldn't be able to bear it.'[18] Madhu agreed with her, and the meeting did not happen. She was crushed. 'On the one hand it feels like it was the right thing to do. But on the other, I feel saddened when I remember the lines in your letter: "We will meet when we get released – of course, if we get released!" You wrote it quite casually but I cannot digest it that casually.'[19]

In fact, she did not. In a letter she wrote in June 1976, Pramila began by noting that his telegram misspelt his name as Madhur (sweet) Dandavate. 'I said, yes, he is sweet.' After this tender remark, she expressed her determination to stay strong in spite of the pain of separation. But the letter ended with the question: 'When will this night end?'[20] And a month later: 'How many days will you survive on a limited patch of sky? When I wander around the prison during the day, watching different birds and the changing colors of the sky, I wonder about which piece of it you are stuck with. When will this never-ending night lead to dawn?'[21] Madhu was also disappointed by their aborted meeting but took it in his stride as the political reality of the Emergency. He did not dwell on it. Instead, his mind turned to the larger political meaning of their condition. Thus, on 9 August, a week

---

[17] Pramila Dandavate to Madhu Dandavate, 17 January 1976.

[18] Pramila Dandavate to Madhu Dandavate, 1 May 1976.

[19] Pramila Dandavate to Madhu Dandavate, 17 May 1976.

[20] Pramila Dandavate to Madhu Dandavate, 9 June 1976

[21] Pramila Dandavate to Madhu Dandavate, 29 July 1976.

after she wrote about the 'limited patch of sky' under which he was confined, Madhu wrote about the day's meaning. Remembering that 9 August was the day the Quit India movement was launched, he quotes the famous verse from Faiz Ahmad Faiz:[22] 'This stained tainted light, this night bitten dawn / That we were waiting for, this is not that morning.'

The turn to Faiz to reflect on the struggle for independence from British rule encapsulated what their time in prison afforded. Time moved slowly in prison, allowing for reflections on the quotidian life. An anniversary of a celebrated date in the freedom struggle brought to mind Faiz's biting commentary on the tragic conjoining of Independence and Partition. A prisoner's tending of flowers, the sight of nature bathed in monsoon showers, hearing Hindustani classical music, and the dalliance of sparrows, triggered philosophical ruminations on life, love and freedom. In their time in prison, poetry, literature and philosophy became the means for meditations on politics and history. If captivity tested and intensified their commitment to freedom at the personal, existential level, it also impelled them to explore and reaffirm the meaning of public freedom. The capacity to express love for each other went hand in hand with explorations of freedom beyond its legal and political meanings. Total Revolution appeared inextricably related to the need for a cultural revolution. Time spent in prison allowed Madhu and Pramila to envision their personal and political lives enmeshed in and enriched by history, culture and philosophy.

Returning to the Time of Politics

While Pramila and Madhu spent their time in prison on philosophical thoughts, another time of politics was at play. JP was released on 12 November 1975 from the Chandigarh hospital where he had been confined. Admitted to Jaslok Hospital in Bombay and diagnosed with kidney failure, he set about bringing together the opposition parties.[23] Since the parties represented in

---

[22] Madhu Dandavate to Pramila Dandavate, 9 August 1976.

[23] A blow-by-blow account of these unity efforts is in Limaye 1994, chapters 7–12.

these discussions had been part of the JP movement, the unity move was logical. In May 1976, JP gave an interview in Bombay to confirm that the formation of a new united party was 'around the corner' (Narayan 2010, 585).

When the news of the alliance reached those lodged in prison, the reaction was not universally positive. Pramila wrote to Madhu expressing her reservations and asked why he had changed his views.[24] She argued that it was meaningless to form a party with the sole aim of contesting elections. Clinging to her thoughts in the prison, she wrote: 'Only if we are prepared to sacrifice the politics of elections until the atmosphere becomes conducive to democracy, can we hope for a sincere struggle towards a party with a future.'[25] Perhaps in reference to a speech Madhu had given in prison recanting his earlier views on the RSS and stating that the organisation was the closest to Gandhi's ideals, she wrote:

> Gandhiji's commitment to Hinduism was inclusive, his idea of Hinduism was a secular one. And these people who rely on religious bigotry and hatred . . . what do the two ideas have in common? If while forming a new party, the old parties refuse to let go of their shortcomings, if they refuse to self-analyse, if they refuse to put an end to sycophancy, then the new party that forms will simply be a product of all the flaws from before. How can it be infused with a new energy, how can it be capable of a total revolution?

She had not gone to prison just for a parliamentary alternative to Indira but for Total Revolution.

Pramila was not alone. The veteran socialist leader S. M. Joshi received letters from imprisoned party activists expressing their disappointment with the plan to join the 'rightists' and 'communalists'.[26] Madhu had apparently also expressed his

---

[24] Pramila Dandavate to Madhu Dandavate, 4 March 1976.

[25] Pramila Dandavate to Madhu Dandavate, 21 June 1976.

[26] Letter from Narendra, Naini Jail, to S. M. Joshi, 6 June 1976. Documentation of the Emergency Period in India, Microfilm Roll no. 7.

doubts. N. G. Goray, the senior socialist leader responded to these doubts. The plan for the unification of opposition parties should cause no surprise, he told Madhu. It was, after all, the culmination of what the JP movement was leading towards prior to the imposition of the Emergency. Of course, he had no illusion that his comrades would wholeheartedly welcome it. He had not forgotten the history of socialists. 'We shall always remain divided, hesitant, ready for the maximum sacrifice, but always absent and divided when the culmination of the process comes in sight.'[27] Madhu threw in the towel. He wrote to Pramila explaining his change of heart. At the urging of all the parties, JP had gone ahead and announced the decision for a united party. If they were to withdraw or object at this stage, JP's credibility would suffer. 'If there is no "parliamentary alternative" left, then we will have squandered away everything.'[28]

Prison had served as a time for reflection on the meaning of freedom, both in the public sphere and in personal relationships. But then pragmatic politics took over as rumors floated that Indira was likely to dissolve the Lok Sabha and announce fresh elections. The structure of parliamentary politics did not allow the politics of freedom that the imprisoned Dandawates had explored. 'Total Revolution' took a backseat to forming a united opposition party. The imprisoned political leaders who had resorted to insurgent poetry, literature and philosophy to explore and extend the meanings of freedom, resigned to its restricted meaning in party politics. Succumbing to the structural pressure of party politics was a choice they made, he more readily than her, although they could have chosen differently. They could have shown the spine they demonstrated when thrown behind bars, stuck to the more philosophically expansive idea of freedom that they discovered in prison, but chose to bend to the pressure of party politics. In this respect, Gandhi offers an exemplary case of the politics of moral commitment. Ambedkar is yet another example.

---

[27] N. G. Goray to Madhu Dandavate, 19 April 1976, Documentation of the Emergency Period in India, Microfilm Roll 7.

[28] Madhu Dandavate to Pramila Dandavate, 5 July 1976.

But in 1977, practical politics won over moral commitments. Determined to 'defeat that woman',[29] JP took the lead in bringing together the non-communist opposition parties. This was not easy. Not everyone was convinced that a cadre-based political party like the Jana Sangh could be trusted to dissolve its identity in the new party while retaining its student and trade union organisations. The discussions brought up ugly jockeying for advantage in the proposed united organisation. Personal ambitions of leaders roiled the talks. JP's authority prevented the clash of views and personal and party ambitions from completely derailing the unity talks. Also critical was the shared experience of imprisonment that convinced leaders of different parties to continue to seek unity even if it meant sidelining the wide-ranging ideas of freedom and social transformation that some of them had explored in jail.

What clinched it was the announcement by Indira Gandhi on 18 January 1977 that national elections would be held in March. On 23 January, the Bharatiya Lok Dal, Jana Sangh, Swatantra Party and the Socialist Party announced that they were dissolving their individual identities to form the Janata Party. It demanded the release of arrested leaders and activists and removal of restrictions on the press and political meetings, and Indira complied. Madhu had already been freed, arriving at Dadar Station in Bombay on 1 January 1977 to a rousing welcome by over two thousand supporters who carried him on their shoulders 'like a champion wrestler'.[30] Three weeks later, Pramila's long night came to an end on 21 January. The Socialist couple, now united, immediately plunged into the Janata Party's election campaign against Indira. The wider reflections on freedom were forgotten.

References

Dantavate, Madhu. 1977. *Marx and Gandhi*. Bombay: Popular Prakashan.

---

[29] JP's parting remark to M. G. Devasahayam, the Chandigarh District Magistrate entrusted with his confinement in the PGI Hospital. See Devasahayam 2012, 224.

[30] Madhu Dandavate to Pramila Dandavate, 10 January 1977.

Devasahayam, M. G. 2012. *JP Movement: Emergency and India's Second Freedom*. Delhi: Vitasta, 2012.

Documentation of the Emergency Period in India. Center for Research Libraries, Chicago.

Govind, Nikhil. 2014. *Between Love and Freedom: The Revolutionary in the Hindi Novel*. Delhi: Routledge.

Koestler, Arthur. 1942. *Dialogue with Death*, tr. Trevor and Phyllis Blewitt. New York: The Macmillan Company.

Limaye, Madhu.1994. *Janata Party Experiment, Volume* I. New Delhi: B.R. Publishing Corporation.

Narayan, Jayaprakash. 2010. *Selected Works: Vol. X*. Delhi: Manohar Publishers.

12

Reading [in] the *Mulahiza*

Mahmood Farooqui

When I first went into Tihar as an undertrial I was put up in what is called there the *mulahiza* or the newcomers' ward. The Urdu word *mulahiza* means to present something, for inspection, etc. It functions in Tihar, and in other jails in India, both as a verb and noun. Every newcomer must have his *mulahiza*, which means that his records, medical investigations and family details must be entered into thick, large registers that appear to date back to the time of World War I. As one inmate later quipped, the questions that are asked upon arrival – name, father's name, mother's name, caste, etc. – remind you of the Pandas at cremation ghats. Even the tone is the same. In the *mulahiza* ward, everybody, by definition, was a first-timer and we had similar fears and thoughts. Everyone around me, every day, seemed to oscillate between 'Why me?' and 'I'm finished'. And they were right to feel so. It all looked deeply despairing from where we were. Why me? And what did I do to deserve this? What did my family do to deserve this? By this, we meant not so much the deprivation of food, sleep, comfort, family, friends, recreation or freedom, but the ignominy, humiliation and insult that we incessantly faced. We were woken up at 5 am to shouts of *oye uth, bahar nikal,* accompanied by various abuses including Delhi's favourite BKL, by the warders and inmate munshis. We were hectored to stand in a queue for the morning prayer, further hollered at when we stepped out for our court dates, which included five different stages of security checks and registration of names, with digested and unselfconscious tones of insult at each stage. The beauty of this whole enterprise was that nobody in the administration, in the police, or even inmates thought this remarkable. How else were you supposed to address the dregs of society? However, this constant verbal belittling desperately grated on us, especially those of us who came from slightly better-off backgrounds.

Nothing in your past can actually prepare you for the present. No matter how many tortuous moments you may have spent, no matter how many times you may have tossed on a bed of thorns, no matter how many hours/eons of tenterhooks you may have lived through, the pain of the present always lies in the present. I felt it then. It was alive. It was pulsating. It was unprecedented. And each time it wounded me with fury as if it was the first time I was experiencing pain. There is never any preparing for pain, no immuring oneself from it, and there is no getting used to it. However, no matter how intense, despair is not life threatening. Agony cannot be computed in medical terms; there are no agony-meters. I often wondered in those days about people with life threatening diseases and compared my situation to theirs and then mocked myself for this absurdity.

For it was impossible to wallow too long in one's personal misery. We were densely packed, in ten barracks, around a small central yard, with each barrack containing nearly fifty people. The lucky ones lay horizontally, against the wall, the others in the aisles. There were always too many people and too much noise, which reminded me of the French writer Jean Paul Sartre's words – 'hell is other people.' Everyone was miserable, but undoubtedly some were more tortured than others. There was an eccentric old man in my barrack who would speak to nobody and nobody would speak to him, although, since his *phatta* or bed was right by the door, everybody passed him by. He sat on his haunches and made notes at odd hours of the day. He would arrange and rearrange scraps of paper, and sometimes scribble furiously. He grumbled, sometimes mumbled to himself, and hung out by himself. I occasionally spoke to him, would buy him chai or registers and papers. I learnt that his name was Vijendra Singh.

One day he confided that his bhabhi had slapped Sections 323/326 and *larai jhagre ka case* on him and his wife had been forced to support her. He sometimes made megalomaniac claims which showed his neurosis. One day he told me that, *Modi ka ye jo project hai, ye meri den hai.* He didn't specify which project he meant but he was sure that he had given Narendra Modi the idea for it. He also repeatedly asked whether his wife could unilaterally divorce him without his knowledge. Despite repeated reassurances to the contrary, he continued to torture himself. One day he asked me if it could help him in anyway if he converted to my faith! A few days later he said that he was in deep trouble as his wife's boyfriend, who was a Sardarji, now worked at the *chakkar*, the main Jail office, as a compounder. His enemies had infiltrated the prison so he was now afraid of stepping out of the ward. It was for the same reason that he declined my advice to see the jail psychiatrist who might have issued him some antipsychotics. He repeatedly asked me to translate his story into English and to send it to the media; otherwise, all he could see was death at every corner. Later I learnt that his wife sometimes came for *mulaqat*. I tried to counsel him by saying, 'After all your wife comes to meet you here and expresses concern for you, supports you; you have to trust her and appreciate that.' He would nod but soon doubt, that pernicious virus, would kick back in and he would be despondent again. One day he complained to a visiting deputy superintendent about harassment in his barrack. His tormentors were hauled up, abused, beaten, by the lathi-wielding *sevadars* or inmate volunteers, all in the name of justice. It was terrible business both ways. There is nobody so meek that he can't oppress someone. His thin, gaunt, needy appearance, and my inability to help him, got on my nerves, every day.

After a few weeks, our barracks were shuffled. The many little adjustments we had all made to get our individual *grihasthis* going, fell away. In the new barrack there were new neighbours, new *bhais*, who cornered the fans, and new rules for drinking water and visiting the toilet. It was like being displaced from one's home and being shunted to some new place. My earnest new *phattewar*, i.e., neighbour with his sleeping place adjacent to mine, Ghulam Mustafa used to drive a rickshaw near Badarpur. He would earn ₹280 daily, and had two daughters and a son. He became embroiled in robberies through some friends. They would waylay passengers and rob them, in shared autos, often after drugging them. One day two cops invited him to a police station on the pretext of using his help for an investigation, and handcuffed him there. They tortured him, forced him to identify the other autowallas, and then forced him to turn an approver in their case. After they had extracted his confession and nabbed the others, they implicated all of them in an accident case in faraway Kapasehra and several other false cases. His charges included Section 328, looting people after giving them drugs, and Section 365, for kidnapping, as well as murder. He slept next to me, knocked out, and would squeeze me tight against the person on the other side, while I hated being touched. He knew no scriptures but prayed fervently. If he found me reading the Quran he would come and sit next to me, eager and sincere like a child, without understanding a word of what I read, which was in English. I realised that what he was after was the *barkat*, the power of the incantation, the power of the chant, and therefore the incomprehensibility of the language in fact added to its charm and potency, the basis on which his faith rested. He was striving to listen closely to something that he didn't fully understand, didn't understand at all in fact, but the strain of doing so in a loud, noisy room, full of distractions, made it an arduous and pious task, which probably assured him that he would earn some merit. Prayer and worship calmed him, gave him strength and hope, as it did for many others there.

I met all kinds. There was an Afghan boy who had been arrested for stealing mobile phones. He had no Hindi and no *mulaqat* and no lawyers, and yet would sometimes burst into song and dance. One day he caused much mirth at the office when he said, '*ham peechhe se Afghan hain, aage se bees saal se Hindustani hain*' – We are Afghans from the rear, but Hindustanis from the front. He often chased me to buy him *laung* (clove) from the small shop that stayed open for a few hours, which was called the 'dry canteen'. *Laung* was an antidote to smoking; and the ingratiating and obsequious air with which he sidled up to me embarrassed me. But I also admired his spirit, and his ability to make himself merry, and others, in that god-forsaken place.

Few meaningful conversations took place around me. By that I don't mean philosophical or intellectual exchanges. I mean simply the emotional conversations that provide consolation or hope. Instead, most talk was banter; the word *bakwas* is apt for it. It was all *bakwas* talk or *masti* talk when it was entertaining, or just *timepass* when it was not. *Timepass*, whether in Ludo, TV, voluntary work, or in prayers was of course the thing we were all after, for after all, we had been sent in to do time, even if it was time which was doing us. But I understood the value of *bakwas* too. People could hardly speak of their relatives or friends or family, or the life they had left behind, or their losses or suffering, since everybody was in the same boat. What was left to us therefore was impersonal small talk. But one has to respect the value of *bakwas*. It helped you talk; it helped you listen; it helped you pass time. Above all, it gave you an impression of being normal, of being alive, of being in an ordinary space, a casual place that was not necessarily a jail. It helped break through the confines of this confinement. In that space, my presence as an exotic director, as an entertaining storyteller, or somebody deemed to be famous, was certainly a greatly enlivening moment for many. Therefore, I was incessantly accosted, which accentuated my misery manifold.

The *deorhi* was the main hub of the jail. It was where the superintendent sat, as did his deputies, and where the undertrial and convict offices lay. As the name implies, it was a vestibule, with two imposing tall gates, which were never fully opened, and never ever together. We always entered and exited through little side gates when we went for our court dates or when we had work there. Every time we stepped back inside, we had to go through frisking, pass two x-ray machines and then strip ourselves naked behind a screen. The *deorhi* security was supervised by men from the Tamil Nadu Special Police, who were all called TSP in Tihar. Their forbidding manner was aggravated by their lack of Hindi. They would say, mechanically sometimes, *pant khol, kachha utaar*. Sometimes they made you squat, repeatedly, or turn around. It wasn't that private either. Sometimes they would handle two or three inmates together. Every time we exited the *deorhi* we were strip-searched. Even on occasions when I was summoned inside to meet the superintendent or his deputy, or later even the director general, I had to suffer this ritual humiliation.

Through my stay in prison, I went through this hundreds of times and always with the same sense of mortification. My body was repeatedly exposed to the disciplinary regime of a power that was superior to me. If retribution be the cardinal principle of justice, then I paid my dues two hundred times over, within the first month, regardless of my culpability. Who is to say whether an impersonal gaze, an official command, is less degrading than a personal one? Was I not powerless to resist, was I not a victim of a brute force too, with a real gun-and-baton-wielding authority behind this coercion. Was one's subjugation to this coercion any less worthy of notice or sympathy than the injustices that prevail outside? Wasn't this impersonality, this robotic and dispassionate command, more cruel, more despotic, more fierce even – not once, not twice, but many many times over? Wasn't this routinisation itself more sinister, more evil, than an act of excess or greed? There was a superior power there, and absolutely no question of my being able or entitled to any resistance whatsoever. The hold of the state's punitive and disciplinary powers over my body was absolute and complete.

But equally, being there, sharing those stories, watching men who were far more woebegone than me, would perforce lessen the momentousness of my own fall. Every second story was one of deep despair, usually more horrid than mine. There was a Chinese man there, or Vietnamese; I couldn't tell. Nobody could, but he was widely believed to be Chinese. He was reportedly caught smuggling 7 kilograms of gold. He was a sight. Didn't speak to anybody, obviously, but did hellos with a select group of people, many of whom were Africans. Every time a jail official held a meeting he would step forward and try to say something. The moment he stood up, a ripple of anticipated mirth swirled through the crowd which turned into laughter at the incomprehension of the official. Ritually then, a Nigerian would be called up who was supposed to understand his sign language. I don't know if he did; I am positive he did not. But he gave the most reasonable explanation possible by using common sense. He always said, 'He is saying he wants a Chinese interpreter.' How difficult was that to understand. How much common sense was required to arrive at this? Yet at each meeting the same ritual was repeated. I couldn't even begin to fathom his isolation. What degree of alienation can possess a man who is imprisoned in a place far away from his country where nobody understands his language, where he cannot communicate with anyone, cannot even say aloud the names of his loved ones to anyone, where nobody calls him by name and where any passer-by could mock him? I knew that he understood mockery for sure as I saw him react sharply to snide remarks. Mockery has a universal expression.

I had been on bipolar medication for years before I was sent inside. Initially I was too dazed to do anything to help myself. Besides, everybody around me was equally depressed. However, my wife's persistence eventually forced the administration to ensure that a psychiatrist examined me and I was put on antipsychotics. It was a laborious, cumbersome process to get them issued every week. They could not be handed to us so we had to go to the main internal office, the *chakkar*, to consume them on the spot. Tihar is a highly bureaucratic jail so everything required permissions, applications, signatures and counter-signatures by the assistant superintendents, the deputy superintendents, the superintendent, the warder, the ward inmate munshi and so on and so forth. I was too demotivated to help myself, even after my medicines began to be issued; also it was not a given that I would be allowed out every day as the whim of the warder determined everything. Recourse to psychiatric drugs was described in Tihar as *dimagh ki dawai* and was looked down upon, particularly in my case, since I was supposed to be a powerful person.

On my first evening out, I met a big lumbering man with a shabby appearance. Over time I learnt that his name was Sharafat and that he used to work in HUDCO, a well-regarded public sector undertaking. He was quite well spoken, and had a smattering of English too. He told me that when he first came inside, they put him in the mental ward – i.e., the Drug De-Addiction Centre ward – where they pack all the drug addicts. For the first month he prayed to God every night that he should not wake up in the morning, and every morning he used to shriek at finding himself still alive. One day I found him eagerly waiting for me as if we had an assignation. He took out a set of papers with some figures and crude drawings. He asked me whether I could translate something into English and then told me that his wife was murdered, and the Police had shown a *tawa* as the murder weapon. However, it was not possible in this case because in his family and hometown the *tawa* used for cooking was convex, and not concave as shown in the evidence. He wanted me to write an application disputing the recovery of the tawa and a butter knife. Thus, I learnt that he was there for the murder of his wife. God, what an ordeal, irrespective of whether he was culpable or innocent. And what a forlorn life. Except for an occasional visit from his brother nobody came for him. I wondered where would his children, if any, be? Was there anyone to look after him, and did he have anything to return to? What a lonely existence and with all sorts of noises in his head, with his strange *salwar*-like pajamas, his t-shirts, his gigantic but always tottering frame, the slow, shuffling gait. How did he rise up from the floor where we all slept; how did he get up from the Indian-style overflowing latrines?

Due to a combination of several circumstances, it took me nearly two weeks to discover that the little shop, known as the dry canteen, also sold registers and pens. I bought them by the dozen and began to furiously write every day, sometimes for hours, amidst disruptions and screaming. I was also desperate to get books from home. The superintendent asked me to put down a list of books which I wanted, which I did, but nevertheless the application was somehow never complete enough. It always lacked a signature or a stamp. So I was thrilled when one day I discovered the jail library. The library was in a different ward, ward no. 11, also known as the IGNOU ward, after the open university that promotes distant learning. I had heard some accounts of it, that it was the best ward there, meant for artists and musicians and those who wished to pursue education. When I saw it, I realised that it certainly looked more spacious and more peaceful than anything I had seen in jail before. However, I was stunned when I entered the library. I have written about the joys of discovering the extraordinarily well-supplied library of jail no. 3 of Tihar elsewhere.[1] In the library I found many delights. Among them was Kuldip Nayar's account, *In Jail,* of his time in Tihar during the Emergency. I devoured it and found that there were both similarities and vast differences in Tihar from his time. He wrote about the widespread corruption, which seemed to be of a much higher order than when I was there.

He writes about the 'money order services' that functioned in jail where an inmate could send a note home and the warders

[1] https://www.catchnews.com/author/mahmood-farooqui-2179.html

would smuggle in cash for which they charged a percentage of the money. It was rather high – 33 per cent – but the delivery took only twenty-four hours! There were businessmen who could have thousands of rupees delivered to them, could use the telephone and could freely leave the jail premises, on occasion even travelling to faraway places like Calcutta (Kolkata). But more than the businessmen, he writes, it was the smugglers jailed in Tihar who were the lavish spenders. Their food came from Moti Mahal and their whisky from Connaught Place. They had not only wine but also women, and not just the so-called 'call girls'. The women would apparently be brought in when 'the Sahiblog' went home for lunch, and their empty offices became 'recreation rooms'. There were also 'slaves', that is, boys between ten and eighteen employed as 'helpers', who cooked, washed utensils, cleaned rooms, fetched water and did other chores.

This was the background which made the Supreme Court pay serious attention to a number of petitions, letters and complaints which reached it from Tihar. There were many inmates who acted as helpers to other well-off inmates in my time. They were called 'shooters', and they would wash, clean, fetch things and perform chores in return for money, or canteen food, or, the most coveted of all, Tihar's black gold, tobacco. But in general, it was much more difficult to get the 'facilities' that Nayar described. Non-vegetarian food, cigarettes and alcohol were all at such a high premium that I was not sure if anybody actually enjoyed these things inside. But then, I only knew one corner of one jail in Tihar – so what did I know?

However, once I gained a fuller access to the library, I felt chuffed and fortified. I began to read and write. There was not enough light in the barrack, so I would sit outside to read, amidst the spit and sputum and flies. It was there that I read Dickens and Tolstoy. But I couldn't sit outside for five minutes without someone coming to talk to me or pry into my register. I offered notobrety, i.e., a celebrity who was notorious. I was an object of curiosity, and further so because I wrote, or read, in public, in English, and of course I was also somebody who could listen and console, so I offered a sight to most. Later I read about the sense of consolation that this same library provided to many of my predecessors in Tihar. Afzal Guru, Kobad Ghandy, the Tihar-trained advocate Shahid Azmi who was assassinated in Mumbai, the journalist Iftikhar Gilani, and the young man Mohammed Aamir who was wrongly accused of terrorism and spent nearly fourteen years inside before penning his memoir,[2] all found great solace here.

I found in the library some scribbles by Afzal Guru in a book by former judge and jurist V. M. Tarkunde's *For Freedom*. Later I learnt about Justice Tarkunde's stellar role in fighting for the inmates during the Emergency. The Emergency exposed all voices critical of the government, left, right and centre, to prison as well as government excesses. The civil liberties movement in India, which had begun in the early 1970s, took off in a big way after the Emergency was lifted, as even those on the left who were until then sceptical of constitutional values, became aware of the importance of civil rights and political liberty. The formation of the APDR in West Bengal was further catalysed by the Civil Rights Report presented by Justice Tarkunde who examined the political encounters in Andhra Pradesh and concluded that most of them were cold-blooded murders. The People's Union for Civil Liberties and People's Union for Democratic Rights, which remain active in our period, were born in this period.

The imposition of the Emergency in 1975, the suspension of civil liberties and democratic rights, including Habeas Corpus, and the mass arrest of political opponents, seemed to justify the Naxalites who had called Indian democracy a sham. The historian Ranajit Guha has cautioned against reading the Emergency as a radical deterioration in the state of Indian democracy and stressed that 'nothing has been well with Indian democracy ever since its inception'. He has suggested that the Emergency was merely a climatic act 'in a process going back to the very circumstances of the birth of the Indian republic'. Yet, it is also undeniable that the Emergency witnessed mass incarceration for the first time in independent India. Thousands of students, ordinary citizens and

---

[2] *Framed As a Terrorist: My 14-Year Struggle to Prove My Innocence*, https://speakingtigerbooks.com/authors-name/mohammad-aamir-khan/

middle-class professionals joined hands with leaders of established political parties to protest against the Emergency and experienced prison for the first time. The prison population in West Bengal alone jumped to a hundred thousand. Governments in different states treated the new entrants to prison differently. In some places like Tihar, makeshift camps and barracks were set up. In others, the overcrowding aggravated the already terrible conditions. In all places, however, politicians who had held office or had been elected to state or central legislatures, were treated deferentially.

In Tihar, no one is now regarded as a political prisoner so there are no rights or privileges for them as such, unlike during the Emergency. I read about the separate ward they had made for senior opposition leaders in Tihar during the Emergency, and how the confabulations to create the Janata Party actually took place here. In his extraordinary prison memoirs, Ram Singh, who was arrested for being a Naxalite, and spent thirteen years in prison, writes about political leaders who were confined in the Fatehgarh Jail in UP.[3] Many of them enjoyed a high life in prison. They had bedding facilities, mosquito nets, cleaner linen, and their headcount was not humiliating. They received better rations, including non-vegetarian food amounting to a quarter kilo of mutton every day. A rookie inmate or *kaccha* was provided to a superior-class prisoner, also sometimes known as *safaiyya*. The *safaiyya* would collect ration from the kitchen/store including mutton or fish. Sometimes they would make ₹400 or ₹500 just by selling off this mutton. Ram Singh was surprised that during the cold war between the Emergency prisoners and jail officials, the loyalty of the common prisoner lay with the cruel jailors who had never treated him any better than a beast. The ordinary prison inmates cursed the *politicals* and stole things from them to please their masters. With the connivance of such people, protestors and political prisoners in the jail were frequently thrashed and the matter disposed of by reporting such incidents as common brawls. Also, during the Emergency, some seventy-five Naxalite prisoners were killed in jails in UP.

---

[3] *13 Years: A Naxalite's Prison Diary*, https://navayana.org/products/13-years/?v=c86ee0d9d7ed

It was difficult, in fact impossible, for local police to gain entrance into Tihar. In Delhi, the police and the jail cadre are two different services, and so the role of the police stops outside the gates of Tihar. However, in many other states, the prison officers, especially senior officers, are appointed from the state police cadre. This made a difference, especially during the Emergency, where the treatment meted out to ordinary dissenters was gory. Two films bring out some of the shocking realities. Anand Patwardhan's documentary film *Prisoners of Conscience*, or *Zameer Ke Bandi*, was made in 1978, and contains interviews with many ordinary resisters. Among the most famous martyrs to the Emergency was the Kannada actor and activist Snehalata Reddy, whose painful death forms the core of a series of films made by historian and feminist Uma Chakravarti, called *Jail Diaries*. Snehalata Reddy and her filmmaker husband T. P. Reddy became internationally renowned after they adapted U. R. Ananthamurthy's classic novel *Samskara* into a film, which won a National Award as well as a prize at the Locarno Film festival. They were friends with George Fernandes and provided him support when he was on the run. They attended clandestine meeting groups and helped organise resistance against the Emergency. Like thousands of others, they also supported the dissenters through an underground network. The husband and wife were both arrested and sent to Bangalore Central Jail without any formal charges. Snehalata was psychologically tortured by the police in jail. Excerpts from her secret prison diary were later published by Ananthamurthy. Reddy was denied proper medical treatment despite having severe asthma attacks and blackouts almost every day. The superintendent also curtailed her interviews for alleged misbehaviour with him in front of the inspector general. In her diary, Snehalata narrates the inhuman conditions in the jail. Her fellow women inmates were served food which was devoid of proteins, minerals, fruits or vegetables. She resorted to a hunger strike for nine days before her demand for better diet for the fellow prisoners was met. Her diary makes for unbearable reading as she describes her constant breakdowns, collapses and suffering. After her interviews were stopped, and when she had no one to share her anguish with, her diary becomes even more plaintive. The government offered to release her on conditions that she found unacceptable despite her frailty. Given the seriousness of her condition, she was finally let out on parole for a month on medical grounds. However, she passed away within five days of her release. In effect, this beautiful actor was murdered by the state.

The status of political prisoners, hard-earned during the freedom struggle against the British, has now disappeared from the rule books and practice. The Emergency was not the last occasion to see political prisoners in Indian prisons, nor the last time that the state imprisoned people for political reasons. From alleged Maoists, to separatists or secessionists in Kashmir, Assam, North East and other places, to alleged terrorists, to alleged traitors, the state has continued to send people to jail in large numbers, although they are not given the status that was once accorded the political prisoner. After independence successive governments created a halo around freedom fighters, while actively repressing those fighting for freedom and rights of the poor. While political prisoners continue to resist state power, none today are accorded the status of being one.

Reading about these cases was depressing and yet somehow it also put my own situation in some perspective. The library was my lifeline but it was not easy to reach. I had to endure the scrutiny and sometimes contempt of the warders whenever I went for my *dimagh ki dawai* or to the library. I had the requisite permissions, yet I still had to adopt an ingratiating air with no assurances of success. It was humiliating to supplicate *sevadars* and officers for such things, as I had to do when I stood in queue for my medicines or loitered around there while the *sevadars* hollered at us. These everyday acts of humiliation did not count for much in anyone's eyes. It would have sounded ridiculous to all of them if I spoke of human dignity. I didn't know how I would ever live down such degradation, even if I got out of there. I would ask myself, how does one live after this. How else but shamelessly! Insolently!

It was generally observed that those who came to Tihar after deliberately breaking the law had a happier time in prison, than the ambiguous or innocent ones who were likely to suffer much more heartburn. The 'professionals' not only tackle imprisonment better, in what must be the greatest irony of the prison system, often they are even treated better. Those who had accidentally committed murder, those whose crimes were not premediated, those who had made an error of judgement, or had been trapped, were the worst sufferers. Everywhere I turned I found sorrow and anguish and helplessness. Many would approach me to make a film on their life, or their case, while some just wanted to speak to an empathetic listener. The worst sufferers were those without families, or lawyers, often with no visitors, people facing life sentences, who had been there for months, with no joy, no outlet, no release. I had my books, my writing, some respect and some deference; I had a wife, brothers, friends, lawyers and good wishes. Sometimes I felt that given so much deprivation around me, I had no right to mourn my lot or complain against anyone or anything. I found that everybody inside was a victim of misfortune, even if they were perpetrators of acts that are considered illegal.

I would perform little acts of generosity – offering people chai, samosas, *laung*, and other little things – but it had no meaning as kindness had no meaning in that labyrinthine world. It did no good to be generous in jail where we had so little anyway. Should I have given away my clothes, which reached me after an arduous process, or money, which was now not earned by me? I could not. I was generous enough with all the eatables which my family brought from the jail canteen, and with the little money I had, but beyond that I could not make any difference to the sea of misery around me. The poor got along somehow. They would improvise little household objects, mirrors, cutters, and choppers made of sharpened pieces of plastic cut from broken plates or buckets. They also made *achars*, of *neembu* and *mirchi*, with salt, *chaat* masala and mustard oil. And yet they could also surprise you with their *joie de vivre*. Once, as Eid was approaching, some of the boys received new clothes from home. They tried out the new clothes and began to prance around in them, which amazed me.

In India, the prison lifestyle and rules emerge from a reforming ideology, promoted by our religious ethics, which is itself premised on the notion of leading a *satwik* or pure life. Smoking, drinking and eating meat are vices. Vices, it is assumed against all empirical logic, lead to crimes. This logic overlooks the fact that crime is an act, planned or unplanned, but an action in time which more often than not is a spur-of-the-moment decision, as in most cases I had observed there, and not a reflection of one's character. Playing ludo was not considered a vice, but playing cards was (the Urdu word they used there was *aib*), although both games relied on chance, and chance was what had brought most of us there. Chance, I say, not acts. Many professional criminals lead lives remarkably free of vices, and many, or most afflicted with the so-called vices, never commit any crime. Almost 80 per cent of the Delhi Punjabis drink and eat meat and other non-vegetarian food, many smoke, and are lecherous or fond of women, many are passionate gamblers on Diwali, but are they criminals? Anyway, the definition of crime keeps changing; and one person's violation is often another person's profit.

In Tihar none is seen as particularly brutal or reprehensible. There was a young man, Guddu, who looked like a boy because he was only four-feet tall, but was in prison for brutally murdering his wife. He had severed her head and had even showed me the pictures from his chargesheet. He sometimes sang *Baul* songs and fetched our food. Nobody appeared exceptionally brutal because it is a fact that people are not merely what their *crimes* define them to be. Murder, rape, drugs, kidnapping, the heinous crimes which lead to an extended spell in jail are not 'acts' or 'actions' that exhaust the identity of a human being. Murderers come in all shapes and all seasons. Most, as Justice Mullah reminded us, happen by accident. Some are crimes of passion, some are committed because of a dubious sense of honour. Everybody in Tihar is there for doing 'something', after all. But not everybody who does 'something' is in prison; and not everyone inside is a monster. Their violations say nothing about whether a person is petty or generous, mean or dignified, malicious or graceful, rude or polite, stingy or large-hearted. That is why one does not cease to be a moral subject just because one is in jail. Therefore, it is unsurprising that everyone in jail feels violated; or that everybody appears almost human to everybody else.

It is like the Urdu couplet, '*Har aadmi mein hote hain das bees aadmi / Jisko bhi dekhna hai use baar baar dekh*' (There are many beings inside a single one / Look closely, and look again, before judging). After all, when we say someone was 'treated like a criminal' what we mean to say is that the treatment was disgraceful, shameful, atrocious – i.e., the treatment was less than human. In Tihar, when we interacted with one another, we didn't think of each other as a 'rapist' or a 'murderer'. Generally, in most prisons, when inmates interact with one another, they don't discuss guilt or repentance, they simply ask the charge under which a person has been arrested. Even if you are rich or powerful you will be locked up at night; the lowest warder could insult you; you had to show respect and deference to officers; you might well be stripped and body-searched every time you leave the *deorhi*. There are a million other ways in which prisons inflict humiliation and shame upon everyone inside, regardless of background, class or status. Therefore, it equalises and allows inmates to find kindred souls in each other. Also, it is difficult to be terrified of someone when you live in close proximity with them, sometimes for years. Life is more banal than dangerous. People who are regarded as dreaded terrorists, even people convicted of heinous terrorist acts, roam around, sometimes, in the most inconspicuous manner. They may have a guard escorting them, like every inmate who lives in the high-security wards, but otherwise there is nothing to indicate, other than their beards, that they may be among India's most wanted. And indeed, the so called 'terrorists' are sometimes the most innocuous people in jail.

We must remember that almost everyone has, at some point, broken a law – however minor it may have been. Everybody has sinned, by omission, if not commission. Those who are in Tihar, doing time for their misdeeds, are at least expiating, atoning, repenting, paying for whatever they have done. It may be argued that being in jail elevates them morally, ennobles them, because, unlike others, they are paying here and now for their sins. Once you are inside, therefore, you have already paid your dues. Especially if you are someone famous or with a reputation, merely entering jail can be punishment enough, because you lose your reputation and your fame the moment you cross the gates to come inside. The length of your stay doesn't matter; mere sentencing or mere arrival in jail is punishment enough. Everyone who lives in jail knows and understands that everyone else there is also, like them, an accused, but also a victim: a victim of chance, of rashness, of foolishness, of impulsiveness, of an arbitrary legal system which entraps people on a whim, where the process is the punishment. Is there anyone in Tihar who thinks he deserves to be there? Is there anyone in jail who thinks they were justly convicted? I met few who belonged to either of the categories. Everyone feels badly done in by the legal system. This is not the same as admitting whether they have committed the crime they were charged with. They may admit to the crime, but they also feel that the conviction was unjust or illegal. It is the judicial process that tries and convicts them, and therefore, they have a right to a legal defence; and if their defence is not heard or the treatment is unfair, they justly feel violated. After all, they are not on a *moral* trial and nobody is demanding expiation from their conscience. Many would be happy to suffer that punishment. Many would like to pay reparations, to be tried under a law of torts, rather than of punitive incarceration. But the system does not give them a chance to do so. And it's not as if every murderer, every law-breaker, every transgressor, every 'criminal' in the big wide society, is in jail. Most escape, only some are punished.

Angela Davis concludes her remarkable denunciation of the US prison system, *Are Prisons Obsolete?* (2003), with a story about South Africa from 1993, when that country was on the cusp of transition. A foreign student, Amy Biehl, working for the African National Party, was stoned and stabbed to death by a large group of black men. Four of the men accused were convicted of her murder and sentenced to eighteen years in prison. In 1997, Amy's parents decided to support the amnesty petition that the men presented to the Truth and Reconciliation Commission in South Africa. The four apologised to the Biehls and were released in July 1998. Two of them later joined the foundation set up in Amy's memory. In June 2002, they accompanied her mother Linda Biehl to New York, where they all spoke before the American Family Therapy Academy on reconciliation and restorative justice. When asked how she now feels about the men who killed her daughter, Linda said, 'I have a lot of love for them.'

There are many who might repent of their acts, who may want to make amends to their victims or their families, but the present judicial system simply locks up people, putting them away for years. It certainly punishes. But it does not reform. And it does nothing for the victims, for those who have suffered, except giving them a vague sense of satisfaction that their tormentors are suffering. Studies show that when a member is killed, the family wants more than mere incarceration of the culprit; they also want compensation and counselling, and nursing and handholding and emotional and moral support, none of which is forthcoming from the state. It is possible to think of reparations that the culprit/accused can pay to make life more liveable for the families of victims. This reparation can be both emotional and material. A heuristic exploration of an alternative was portrayed in the Rajesh Khanna and Meena Kumari film *Dushman*, in 1970, where a truck driver who accidentally kills a man is tasked with staying with the family of the deceased and helping them out. Give the inmates a chance, some of them might surprise you with their ardour to set things right, even if they have not been as wrong as we make them out to be.

Mahmood Farooqui, known for reviving Dastangoi, has just completed his book on Tihar and on prisons around the world.

13

Anushashan Parva: The Dictatorship of the Acharya

Tridip Suhrud

1

It was his year of silence. Even before the Emergency which had sought to silence the voices of dissent was imposed, he had commenced his silence. Congress Member of Parliament from Nagpur Vasant Sathe visited Vinayak Narhari Bhave (Vinoba, 1885–1982) at Paunar, soon after the declaration of the Emergency. Vinoba, in a written statement, characterised it as '*Anushashan Parva*'. Sathe and the proponents of the Emergency interpreted it as an endorsement of the Emergency as a period of greater discipline, while those who opposed it saw the reference to *Anushashan Parva* as an unambiguous reference to the *Mahabharata* and the counsel of Bhishma to the newly anointed king Yudhisthira to follow Rajdharma.

There is an image from that period of the ageing Sarvodaya leader and the fifty-eight-year-old prime minister. They are both resolutely staring into a void, not just distant emptiness but an ethical void or even a moral precipice. They are looking not at each other, not even in the same direction. His eyes are hidden behind thick, dark glasses. He sits on a platform, resting against a bolster, yet erect, with his left leg folded under the right one, and the right one bending at the knee, his bony hands, their fingers crossed, rest on the knee. She is at the same level, albeit on a chair, her head covered by an exquisite handwoven saree, her spine erect, not resting against the back of the chair, the two fingers of her left hand ever so lightly touching the thumb of the right hand. Neither show even a hint of a smile or even of a conversation that might have taken place or will possibly take place in the next instance. Two figures, in proximity enveloped in their own stillness. A stillness that is not suggestive of equipoise, of *sthtitapragna*, something that the older man has been striving to cultivate all his life.

This stillness does not characterise other images of Vinoba and Indira Gandhi (1917–84). They have known each other intimately, even fondly. The bond is more intimate than most realise. Indira's father (whose political heir she was) Jawaharlal Nehru and Vinoba were contemporaries (Jawahar being by four years the younger of the two) and were 'heirs' or 'successors' to the person who they both acknowledged as their '*Rahbar*', pathfinder, M. K. Gandhi. It was Gandhi who had declared to the delegates of the All-India Congress Committee on 15 January 1942 that, 'I have always said that not Rajaji, nor Sardar Vallabhbhai, but Jawaharlal will be my successor' (Gandhi 1979, 224). A few years before this, on 15 October 1940, writing from Sevagram, Gandhi introduced Vinoba to the country as the 'individual satyagrahi', a struggle he recognised as 'perhaps the last civil disobedience struggle which I shall have conducted' (Gandhi 1978, 103). Gandhi, after consulting with the Congress Working Committee, decided that the civil disobedience will be commenced by Vinoba and will be confined to him only. He answered the questions about his choice: 'Who is Vinoba Bhave and why has he been selected?' In a lengthy introduction, Gandhi described Vinoba as a 'Sanskrit scholar', 'a born teacher', one who believes in 'universal spinning being the central activity which will remove the poverty in the villages and put life in their deadness.' One who has 'abolished every trace of untouchability from his heart. He believes in communal unity with the same passion that I have.' And one who believes that the 'charkha is the most suitable symbol of non-violence which has become an integral part of his life' (ibid. 104–05).

This in part earned Vinoba the title and the responsibility of being a 'spiritual' heir to Gandhi, thereby creating a divide between the realms of the political and the spiritual, a divide that Gandhi considered to be false. He sought to imbue his politics with deep spirituality and his religious quest – even to see God face to face – was never devoid of the sharp awareness of the political. This divide between the political and the spiritual, between the realm of power and the domain of seva (as constructive work), came to the fore sharply after Gandhi's assassination in 1948.

2

Six weeks after Gandhi's assassination, a few men and women gathered at Sevagram – between 11 March and 15 March 1948 – to discuss the future of the country and the role of Gandhi's teaching in the new *fiza* (term used by Nehru). This was attended by many leading men and women of the country – with the exception of the ailing Sardar Patel – that included Rajendra Prasad, Vinoba Bhave and Jawaharlal Nehru. Very curiously – almost unbelievably so – this was the first time that Vinoba and Jawaharlal met face to face. Vinoba acknowledged this: 'Jawaharlalji and I have belonged to the same family for at least twenty-five years, but we have actually never met until now; today we meet face-to-face for the first time' (Gandhi 2007, 65). Vinoba attributed this to the largeness of the 'family', that is the community of Gandhi's associates. The fact that two of Gandhi's closest associates never met during his lifetime cannot just be attributed to the largeness of the community of co-practitioners. The reason is likely to lie in Vinoba's unease with, and even opposition to, any form of institutional structure and the realm of politics.

Vinoba set the tone of the meeting before Nehru came, declaring, 'My personal instinct has always been rather opposed to the fetters of the institutions' (Gandhi 2007, 31). He advocated for 'fraternal bonds' over bonds of institutions. What Vinoba was arguing for was doing away with the Congress as an institution, as a political party, and creation of a brotherhood, guided by nothing but an inner sense of the working of a fraternal group, intended only to serve and relinquish the realm of the political altogether. The brotherhood that he proposed was to have minimal rules, no organisation, no property or even a bank account. What he proposed was a '*mela*',[1] not an organisation, and most certainly not one inhabiting the realm of the political, where each member would be guided by their sense of 'personal integrity'.

[1] This was a term used by Shrikrishnadas Jaju (in Gandhi 2007, 37).

It fell to Nehru to draw the attention of the assembly to the major issues, 'fundamental questions', that confront the country and khadi to him was secondary, 'like branches of a tree, not the root of the matter' (Gandhi 2007, 58). And fundamental to him was 'political work' – political sphere once created cannot be undone, he laboured hard to get this fundamental question conveyed to the assembly. He said, 'The implication was that the Congress should be dissolved and replaced by a new institution that would not be political. Then a new political institution would also need to be created – because political work should still have to be done. . . . Political life cannot simply be brought to an end' (ibid. 61).

Vinoba while arguing for *samaj* or *sangha* would claim that he was following his *Swadharma.* The very purpose of life for him was to remove the delusion that prevents us from recognising our *Swadharma*, our duty. In 1932, while lodged in the Dhule jail for his participation in the civil disobedience movement, Vinoba gave eighteen lectures/talks on the eighteen discourses of the Gita to his fellow inmates. These were later published as the celebrated *Talks on the Gita*, from the notes made by Pandurang Sadashiv Sane (Sane Guruji). Therein, he defines *Swadharma* as that which is equal to one's measure, neither great nor lowly. The purpose of the Gita, in fact of the *Mahabharata*, is for him removal of delusion regarding *Swadharma*. 'The purpose of the Gita is to remove the delusion that prevents us from the performance of our *Swadharma.* Arjuna was confused about his *dharma.* He was gripped by a delusion concerning his *Swadharma*. . . . The Gita's main task is to remove that delusion, that attachment' (Bhave 2005, 24).

Performance of one's duty requires one to be unattached to the care of the body (care only to the extent that the body is the instrument of service, of performance of *Swadharma*), as the body is impermanent, transient; while the Self, the *Atman*, is eternal, imperishable. This lack of care of the body extended to other domains for Vinoba. He came to regard all organisational structures, institutions – one may say including the Ashram to the extent that it had rules of conduct, and of course the Congress – akin to the body, an envelope that was ephemeral, and like the body could be the source of temptation, delusion, leading to the loss of the recognition of both *Swa* and *Swadharma*. Gandhi would also argue that performance of duty is observance of morality. But Gandhi goes beyond the relationship of duty and morality by claiming that performance of duty leads to both self-knowledge and self-rule (Swaraj) (Sharma and Suhrud 2010, 56). Gandhi had, by linking *Swadharma* to Swaraj, laid the ground for the undeniable necessity of the political. It is this necessity of the political, even for the performance of *Swadharma*, that makes Gandhi sensitive to the need for organised structures, institutions and processes. Gandhi, unlike Vinoba, would never argue for an unfettered institution-free existence, even to perform seva.

For Vinoba the ideal is not a Satyagrahi seeking Swaraj (although his commitment to both is second to none) but is a *Karmayogi* as defined by the Gita. *Karmayogi* for him is an 'embodiment of self-restraint' (Bhave 2005, 54). Karma, that is performance of desireless action, is for him *Swadharma*. This capacity for desireless action, Vinoba argues, leads to *Sanyasa*, not in the sense of renunciation of action but as a state of desireless action. He regarded the idea of *Sanyasa* as 'grand and sacred'. He said, 'This idea, one may say, is the highest point reached by human imagination and reason, it is the pinnacle of human thought and experience. There is unprecedented joy in the very contemplation of this idea' (ibid. 71–72). He wanted to be a Karmayogi, a *Sanyasi*, where one is 'inwardly inactive while doing everything, and doing everything while outwardly remaining inactive' (ibid. 72).

Vinoba suggests that this desireless action becomes possible when one acquires the capacity to dedicate the fruits of one's action to God. This dedication is made possible through devotion, *bhakti*. The attainment of this state for him is 'the Sovereign Science of the Service to Humanity' (Bhave 2005, 122).

And yet the question of both recognising and determining *Swadharma* remains. Vinoba makes a two-fold argument, of the immutable, unchanging nature of certain duties, and of contingent and transient duties. He states that *Swadharma*, to be called that, comes naturally – *Swabhavik* – to everyone; the idea of searching for it is strange. '*Swadharma* of a man is born along with him'

(Bhave 2005, 208). From this he makes a case for the desirability of *Chaturvarnya*. 'The *Chaturvarnya* system appeals to me essentially because there are naturalness and *dharma* (duties) in it. Nothing can be gained by evading one's *Swadharma*. . . . It is a distinguishing calling of *Chaturvarnya* that people should continue to follow their ancestral callings, provided they are not unethical' (ibid 209). He laments that a valuable part of one's life is 'wasted' in finding a calling, and 'to avoid this Hinduism has devised the concept of *Varnadharma*'. He further argues that this part of *Swadharma* is immutable; the other is contingent upon *Swadeshidharma*, *Swajateyadharma* (belonging to a community) and *Swakaleendharma* (belonging to a particular time) (ibid 269). All these and *Ashramdharma* (duties contingent on stages of life) provide the changing aspects of duty, '*Varnadharma* does not change, while *Ashramdharma* changes' (ibid 270).

The period of silence that he had adopted is rather telling. It was not a spiritual silence, but more akin to a political one. It was caused by a deep division in the Sarvodaya community, which, under Jayaprakash Narayan's (JP, 1902–79) charismatic leadership, was increasingly becoming 'political'. The Sarva Seva Sangh which came to be established after the 1948 Wardha meeting had, for Vinoba, its basis in 'spirituality with its four elements of truth, nonviolence, fearlessness and non-opposition to any individual person' (Tandon 1992, 144). Having failed in his attempts to persuade either the members of the Sarva Seva Sangh, or Jayaprakash Narayan, Vinoba decided to observe silence for one year, from 25 December 1974. He reportedly broke his silence only once during the Sarvodaya Sammelan which commenced on 15 March 1975. 'On the last day of the Sammelan, Vinoba went to the Guest House where JP was staying, broke his silence for two minutes and pleaded with him to give up the conflict with the government, while continuing his movement. He told him that since he had already displayed his strength, he should like Lord Krishan leave the battlefield' (ibid. 145).

3

What then was Vinoba's *Swadharma*? Did he see it as responding to a particular period or was it that determined by a community?

Vinoba had within one decade of Independence written a tract called *Lokniti*.[2] This tract lays out in detail what he considered to be the ills of politics, *Rajniti*, and an advocacy for *Lokniti*, a state of community life which has no place for either politics, elections or even governance. It also contains a section wherein he outlines what he considered his *Swadharma* in this ideal condition of *Lokniti*. The tract begins with his disenchantment with organisational structures, particularly the two dominant ones: religious institutions (*dharmasanstha*) and institutions of governance (*shashansanstha*). He argues that the purpose of both these institutions has been fulfilled and their continuance can only do harm. 'It has become necessary for the society to be free from both these' (Bhave n.d., 62).

The problem with institutions of governance is that people speak against them when they do ill – have done so since the time of the *Mahabharata* – but never against it when it does what seems to be good; we are crushed under the burden of gratitude and are willingly led like a herd of goats (Bhave n.d., 63). Even if we were to secure good governance, he argues, we are deluded as, 'Good governance (*sushashan*) is an illusion' (ibid. 65). It is an illusion because it cannot lead to the development of virtues. He concludes that government is an unnecessary institution and asserted, 'After 1947 we have become more enslaved' (ibid. 66). He blamed the managerial class – politicians, bureaucracy, police, armed forces, lawyers and judges and the priestly class in case of religious institutions – for the disorder. He stated that the idea that the government, especially a democratic one, is the locus of legitimate power is misplaced. *Satta*, the Sanskrit word for power, means *sat-ta*, the existence of God or truth.

---

[2] *Lokniti* was originally written in Marathi. The year of publication is not given but the textual evidence allows us to place it in the year 1957 or early 1958. He refers to the leaders of the USA (Eisenhower, 1953–61), Soviet Union (Bulganin 1955–58) and United Kingdom (Eden, 1955–57), and there is a reference to an election in Tamil Nadu in 1957. See, *Lokniti* in *Vinoba Sahitya*, General Editor Gautam Bajaj, editors of volume 16, Mira Bhatt and Parag Cholkar, pp. 55–182. All translations from the Hindi done by Tridip Suhrud for this chapter.

Power in the sense of *Satta* can only belong to God and can be wielded by *Satpurush* (men of virtue, the Acharya, the seer, the preceptor). Quoting poet Tulsidas, Vinoba says, 'The punitive power should be wielded by the *Sanyasi*' (Bhave n.d., 72). The ideal should be the absence of government; it can happen when power breaks down and goes to each individual. He called this *Prajya* (*Praja* [people] + *Rajya* [self-rule, state]); the ideal was *Prajya*, not *Rajya* (ibid. 82). A Sarvodaya society was for him a *shashan-mukta*, not in the sense of absence of government, but freed from the need of government. In such a stage, what remains is virtue. 'In the final stage there will be no government; only moral/ethical norms will remain' (ibid. 85). He said that it was the responsibility of all those who claimed to have faith in Gandhi to awaken the people and dissolve the state. Followers of Gandhi were deluded because they believed that it was their responsibility, under all circumstances, to run the state, to provide *sushashan* (good governance); instead, they should work for *swashashan* (rule of the self).

In a section titled *Ganatantra* (Republic) or *Avagunatantra* (Republic of Vice), Vinoba argued against the institution of political parties and elections based on universal adult franchise. He claimed that 'political parties are enemies of the people' (Bhave n.d., 97). If political parties are unnecessary and enemies of the people, voting 'is a farce'. He claimed, 'I have hitherto not voted' (ibid. 103). He composed a verse, '*yatra yatra electionam, tatra karya na vidyate*', which he explained, 'wherever there is an election, there will be no work, but destruction of action itself' (ibid. 106). If the elections were to be discarded, the principle of the rule of the majority would also meet the same fate, he stated: 'Greatest good of the greatest number' is a dangerous phrase.

Through this tract, Vinoba often refers to himself in the third person, as 'Baba'. Vinoba had a capacity to play with words to further his rhetorical purpose: *Ganatantra–Avagunatantra*, democracy–demonocracy, welfare–ill-fare. In one such instance, he said, 'Baba has characterised the present-day democracy as demonocracy' (Bhave n.d., 117).[3] And then declared, 'Sarvodya

[3] The phrases 'demonocracy' and 'ill-fare' are in the original.

does not believe in democracy' (ibid.). In a section that dealt with the role of women in polity, he declared that women should consider themselves 'above' party politics. They are above party or factional politics as they represent the power of the mother who does not take sides when her two sons fight. Their role was to free men of politics. 'My advice to women is that they should make a minute study of politics and take a vow to free men of politics' (ibid. 130).

During the discussion on the role of women in politics, he introduced the idea that had been hitherto latent in his argument – that of a hierarchy of virtues and the special role that men (women having declared themselves above politics) of superior virtue should be accorded in any dispensation. He called them *Sajjan*, men of virtue, and then further classified them as *Sishta Sajjan* (literally, civilised goodmen) and *Visishta Sajjan* (men of special virtues). There was the third class of men, who were uncouth and crass. While *Sishta Sajjan* should participate in politics and work as functionaries of political parties, they should not determine the course of things. The 'controlling power' should be with the *Visishta Sajjan*; they should be like the umpire who does not participate in the game but has the controlling power (Bhave n.d., 131). How is this virtue to be determined; how should the roles be assigned to those who are above party politics and are unelected? – Vinoba does not specify these till this point in the tract. He has hitherto not given any positive attributes of *Lokniti*, but defined it in negation – not this, not this, *neti, neti.* Having established the need for men of virtue, he defines the role of Sarvodaya as seva, service. This characterisation of Sarvodaya as seva is a severely circumscribed version of the original propounded by Gandhi, which was deeply political, transformative, seeking to intervene in the structures of political economy and challenging established social and cultural hierarchies. By identifying Sarvodaya with only seva, to the exclusion of all else, Vinoba made Sarvodaya bereft of its political and transformative imagination. He then identified seva as that force which will lead to the dissolution of power (ibid. 135–36). For him seva had one clear purpose – the purification of the heart. Thus, Sarvodaya had to lead to purification. *Lokniti* is that seva which leads to purification (ibid. 136). Vinoba, though deeply suspicious of power and advocating its dissolution, is aware that virtue and morality is also exercised by some kind of power, however differently constituted, legitimised, communicated and exercised. This power he calls *Shakti* (force). Thus, *Rajniti* has *Satta* while *Lokniti* has *Shakti*, and thus the movement has to be from power politics to politics of strength and force. *Rajniti*, or politics, for him must break down as soon as possible because it was *Shunya Niti* – that it had a moral void, a vacuum (Bhave n.d., 148). He advised therefore to be indifferent to politics, refrained from voting and characterised voting booths as '*bhut*', ghost. This indifference was to be cultivated because Baba did not wish to concede that the political realm could be purified, while insisting that the public life and private lives were capable of reform through a change of heart.

What then is to be done till such time that *Lokniti* is established? He was asked this question by another Acharya, Acharya J. B. Kripalani. Kripalani asked him, "'You have no faith in the present party politics. If the party were to disappear, what will remain? Have you found a solution, a method?" I told him, "No. I have not. But I will respond to you in the language of the Sufis, that I have not found *tarikat* (a method, mode) but I have found *hakikat* (truth, principle).'" The principle, the truth, that he had found was *Acharya Kula*, the collectivity of the Acharya. Who is an Acharya? Not just any teacher, not just a person of special virtue, *Visishta Sajjan*, but one possessing three qualities. Guru Nanak had described the Acharya, Guru, as one who is *Nirbhaya* and *Nirvair* (fearless and without enmity); Baba added one more quality, *Nishpaksha* (neutral, not of any faction). Such men – and the assumption is, albeit unstated, that they will be *ajanma brahmachari* (lifelong celibate) – will form a *Kula*, a community, a *Sangha*, as 'in Kaliyuga the power of *Sangha*, community, is necessary' (Bhave n.d., 170). He defined the *Acharya Kula* thus: '*Acharya Kula* is a spiritual collectivity built on the foundation of *Lokniti*' (Bhave n.d., 171). The foundation of *Lokniti* is Sarvodaya that is seva. What is the role of the *Acharya Kula*? How is it to be characterised? The second question is easier to answer, as Vinoba has a clear view on that. He called it the *Anushashan* of the Acharya (ibid. 170).[4] As one of the finest scholars of Sanskrit of his times, Vinoba was aware of the many meanings of the word *Anushashan*. They are, 'to rule, to govern, to order, to teach, to direct, advise, address, to punish, chastise, correct' (Monier-Williams 1986, 40). The Acharyas were *Anushashaka* – those who govern, direct, instruct and punish. Why do we need the rule of the preceptor? Quoting the Acharya among the Acharyas, Shankara, Vinoba states, 'common folks cannot absorb, comprehend any idea unaided, on their own' (Bhave n.d., 171). The *Anushashan* of the Acharya would place before the people a vision and would have the *shakti* (not *satta*), to rule, to govern and also to punish. '*Acharya Kula* is a spiritual organisation. We have to place before the people well-considered views, that emerge from an unhurried and quiet mind; this is the spiritual vision' (ibid. 173).

The *Acharya Kula* has a twin function – to be what Vinoba calls *Tarak* (which can be translated both as 'saviour' and 'pathfinder') and *Prerak* (the one who inspires). When both these attributes combine they acquire the ultimate power; Vinoba calls it *Shiva Shakti* and *Shubh Shakti*, both the benevolent power and the power to destroy. The world, Vinoba was certain, would attain peace if it were to work under the *Anushashan* of the Acharya. When he presented this idea of *Acharya Kula* and *Lokniti*, Vinoba was asked, '. . . In the true sense what is the alternative to democracy that you have to offer . . . Or does the Baba want a political system in which people have no place?' He gave a clear, unambiguous response. 'There is no alternative to democracy. If it is possible to conceive of one, it is *Acharya Kula*' (Bhave n.d., 173).

4

Here, we have a vision of the order that Vinoba wanted for India. It is a vision that is not apolitical but deeply anti-political. It is anti-political not because he wants for the *Acharya Kula* the power (with the idea itself providing its legitimacy) to govern, to rule, to advice and to chastise. It is anti-political because in his *Lokniti*, *Lok*, that is people, have no place, no role, no agency. It is not just an absence of a role, it is non-recognition of the need for *Lok* in any collective, political or otherwise. Even the 'passive'

---

[4] This section is called, *Acharya Kula: Acharyo ka Anushashan.*

role as electors, or voters, is denied. There is no recognition that we as people, however flawed, moved by *swarth*, self-interest, have aspirations not just for ourselves but for *Kula*, *Gram* and *Sangha*, for collective identities larger than ourselves. This possibility is the very ground from which any consideration of collective life emerges.

It is anti-political because it is fundamentally unethical. Vinoba is unwilling and unable to recognise that there might be more than one idea of virtue, ethics, normative considerations, or visions of the good life, and that such multiplicity is desirable. Any idea of virtue that denies the very possibility of another conception is without virtue and is violent.

Vinoba is anti-political because for him Sarvodaya in the final analysis is not a practice that each one engages in. His Sarvodaya even as seva is subsumed by the *Anushashan* of the *Acharya Kula*.

Vinoba is anti-political because in the *Anushashan* of the *Acharya Kula*, Swaraj – both as self-rule and rule over the self – is not possible as this *Anushashan* does not grant the individual, the *Swa*, the possibility of following *Swadharma*. An order that does not recognise *Swadharma* forecloses Swaraj, is fundamentally a closed system, a totalitarian imagination. Vinoba, who sets out in search of liberation, *mukti*, *moksha*, eventually by negation of the political creates a macabre vision, an idea so staggeringly anti-political that even Mrs Gandhi is stilled.

References

Bhave, Vinoba. 2005. *Talks on the Gita*, translated from the original Marathi by Parag Cholkar. Paunar: Paramdham Prakashan. 16th edition.

———. n.d. *Lokniti*. In *Vinoba Sahitya*, Volume 16, gen. ed. Gautam Bajaj, eds. Mira Bhatt and Parag Cholkar. Paunar: Paramdham Prakashan. 55–182.

Gandhi, Gopalkrishna, ed. 2007. *Gandhi is Gone: Who will Guide Us Now*. Ranikhet: Permanent Black.

Gandhi, M. K. 1978. *The Collected Works of Mahatma Gandhi*. Volume 73. New Delhi: The Publications Division.

———. 1979. *The Collected Works of Mahatma Gandhi*. Volume 75. New Delhi: The Publications Division.

Monier-Williams, Sir Monier. 1986. *A Sanskrit-English Dictionary*. New Delhi: Motilal Banarasidass.

Sharma, Suresh and Tridip Suhrud, ed. 2010. *M. K. Gandhi's Hind Swaraj: A Critical Edition*. New Delhi: Orient BlackSwan.

Tandon, Vishwanath. 1992. *Acharya Vinoba Bhave*. New Delhi: The Publications Division.

14

Debating the Idea of Freedom (In the Context of 25 June 1975)

Gopal Guru

> Mother you used to tell me when I was born your labour was very long. The reason mother, the reason for your long labour: I, still in your womb, was wondering: Do I want to be born, do I want to be born at all in this land?
>
> (Rokade in Dangle 1992, 1)

> Oh mother instead of cutting my umbilical cord why did not you slit my throat with your sharp nails. You are scared of my possible imprisonment or even my death by hanging.
>
> (Dhasal 1975, 72)

> Free—do--m! Free—do--m! Free—do--m! which ass are you really referring to?
>
> (Dhasal 1975, 72)

> I am suffocating, I cannot breathe freely, in contaminated social conditions.
>
> (Dhag 1992, 112)

Let me begin this essay with the question, why debate Freedom? This question invites our attention primarily for two reasons: first, ironically, it is the imposition of Internal Emergency (25 June 1975) that requires interpretative and explanatory ground to be covered to help us gain a precise articulation of the conception of freedom. This precision is demanded in a discursive situation where the idea of freedom carries not one but multiple and at times intersecting meanings depending on who is contemplating the idea of freedom. The other important reason is that the imposition of

Internal Emergency is also a pivotal political development in the life of Indian democracy in that it offers, from the Dalit vantage point, an opportunity to rethink the conception of freedom, give it new dimensions, if not an alternatively new perspective. The Dalit point of view is crucial to problematise the settled understanding of the Emergency which, in the eyes of its opponents, is seen as a dark shadow on Indian democracy. This dark shadow was basically seen in terms of the loss of civil liberties, a loss that was perceived as if it was a general experience and a common concern for every Indian. Well! Was this really the case?

Debating the idea of freedom, arguably, becomes relevant in the context where this idea, as compared to other concepts such as justice and equality (Ganguli 1975; Sen 2009; Datta Gupta 1979; Beteille 2001), has received far less attention from the intellectuals (Sen 1999; Mahajan 2013; Khare 1984). The other core concepts such as equality and, more importantly, justice, have been relatively fortunate to have received greater academic attention by the scholar, since they are visible in the people's struggle, but only as an outcry. In the struggle for rehabilitation by 'displaced' people, the victims of 'development projects', who continue to be displaced by such projects, such outcries did occur, from time to time; and these should be seen as a cry for a second (and even third) freedom. In this context, the Emergency does create the much-required new context for organising a different debate on these key concepts. It does provide an immediate and new context to reflect on the complex structure of the concept of freedom.

Before I dwell at some length on the complex relationship between the idea of freedom and the imposition of the Emergency, it is necessary for me to voice my difficulty, which is to glean out an affirmative meaning that lies underneath the dark shadow, to engage with the dominant meaning which may be politically correct rather than theoretically conscious. Those sections of Dalits who found the Emergency rule not so much an impediment to their freedom, could be accused of having a narrow vision of freedom, and, also, of being incapable of thinking out of the box. They might extend this accusation to Ambedkar and argue that Bhimrao Ambedkar was a statist who sought everything, including freedom, through state intervention. The middle-class conception of freedom would thus suggest that for Dalits the state was the ultimate universe of freedom. This presupposition needs a far more nuanced and detailed deliberation, which, unfortunately, due to the specific focus on debating freedom in the context of the Emergency, cannot be attempted in this chapter.

The aim of the chapter is two-fold: first, it tries to discuss the normative limits that are inherent in the dominant claim which involves the assertion that the fight against the Emergency was everyone's fight for defending freedom against slavery (Sudarshan 1994, 81). The Dalit response to the Emergency has a different story to tell, which is the second point discussed in this chapter. They did not hold the same view as JP, as these Dalits from Maharashtra, Madhya Pradesh and Andhra Pradesh overwhelmingly voted for Indira Gandhi's Congress in the 1977 Lok Sabha election (Joshi 1981, 136). Such Dalit response suggests that the dominant claim suffers from another theoretical limit in that it not only subsumes in its generalist thrust other conceptions of freedom, conceptions that are premised on either civil society or the state, but also ignores the question central for Dalits – which is the universe of freedom: civil society or the state?

Arguments

First, let me rather provocatively argue that the attempts that were made, and the customary arguments that were forwarded, by the opponents of the Emergency, for the collective mobilisation aimed at restoring democracy, howsoever lofty, are essentially flimsy on the following grounds. Firstly, the attempts and arguments for freedom that spring from the imposition of Internal Emergency look at the event rather than looking at unfreedom as the life condition which is socially constituted, morally mutilated (shaped) and historically arrived at. This idea of freedom, as invoked particularly by the middle class during the Emergency, was thus regarded as self-evident, requiring no effort on their part to trace the historical trajectory of the concept under consideration. Without its historiography, I argue, the middle-class concept of freedom or democracy is imprecise and arbitrary in nature. Such response lacked the dept of historical analysis of the structures that underlie and renew the experience of unfreedom, estrangement or entrapment that has unfolded in myriad forms. The historiography of the concepts suggests an ontological inseparability of the human being from the dreaded forms of unfreedom which find their expression not only in the scholarly narratives of the anti-caste thinkers such as Jyotirao Phule and Ambedkar, but also in the poetry of leading Dalit poets such as Rokade and Dhasal. From the deep sense of exasperation that the poets have with their respective mothers, as seen in the epigraphs to this chapter, for them the conception of freedom is in the inception of unfreedom.

Secondly, the imposition of an Internal Emergency brings to bear on the political sensibility of the Dalit, the truth of the state as the premise of freedom, rather than regarding civil society as the universe of freedom. Such conception of freedom does run contrary, if not contradictory, to the conception of freedom as has been supported by the middle class in the particular context of the Emergency. For the middle class, I further argue, it is the socially and closely guarded, rather than open-ended or competitive, sphere of the state that forms the universe of freedom. The state, for such a class, is required to safeguard its interests from the possible aberration that might erupt from the civil society[1], or when a 'mass of people' seeks to stamp out its privacy on certain days, such as 6 December in Mumbai or 14 April. Let me try and present the arguments that I hope would seek to sensitise the debate over the limits of the concept of freedom that keeps getting triggered off depending on whether it has 'political', or 'emancipatory', purposes.

Thirdly, the phenomenon of the Emergency has brought into focus the dynamics of the cognitive space that has a bearing on the definition of freedom. Thus, the longer the distance between the middle class and the state, the truer is the experience of freedom for the former. Members of such a class do not feel comfortable when the state comes too close to them and threatens to control their privileged position, both in the private and public realms. It is the excesses of the state that galvanise members of such a class against

---

[1] Javed Alam said Congress party lumpen were attacking the middle class.

the advances of authority into their individual freedom. Dalits, on the contrary, need access to state support, and hence they want the state to be closer to them in terms of affirmative interventions into their worsening conditions. They find the imposition of the Emergency as an appropriate framework – in fact, an opportunity sphere within which they gain a real experience of freedom that results from the state's initiative to come closer to them. Thus, in the second section, I plan to argue that the imposition of the Emergency gives rise to a variant conception of freedom which in turn becomes discernable through the notion of excess and access – excess for one, access for another.

From the Dalit point of view the following is the best possible scenario that has emerged from the imposition of the Emergency. For the Dalit, being closer to the legal-rational Weberian state means greater guarantee of freedom from the local structures of exploitation and discrimination. The Dalit needs a state that becomes exceptionally active during the Emergency. It is such an emergence that can help the Dalit get some hold of freedom against the local configuration of the oppressive power of brahmanism and capitalism. Brahmanism, I argue, is configurated in caste practice, while capitalism is configurated in the micro forms of exploitation such as money lending and price gouging of essential consumption items.

Finally, I would like to argue that the Emergency gives rise to two conceptions of the state of exception and hence contrary, if not contradictory, ideas of freedom that exit as an uneasy conundrum. At the top end exists the dominant conception of 'negative freedom', and at the bottom end exists the idea of 'positive freedom'. In the final section I will discuss two conceptions of 'positive freedom'. I shall also differentiate the Dalit conception of the state of exception as an opportunity against those who are said to have extended their support to the Emergency.

Conception of Freedom is in the Inception of Unfreedom

The debate on freedom is necessary for it offers an opportunity to fathom its ontological depth. I would argue that the conception of freedom does not emerge from one contingent event such as the

Emergency. It is, on the contrary, ontologically linked to the birth of a person. Unfreedom that coincides with the biological birth is of the experience of being an untouchable that embodies myriad forms of unfreedom. It is in the very 'conception' of being that they – the untouchables in India and the blacks in the US – experience unfreedom. The untouchable's experience of unfreedom thus can lead us to coin the following formulation: 'The conception of freedom is in the inception of unfreedom.' Such formulation can be extended from India's conception as an independent nation to the conception at birth of being an untouchable. Thus, one cannot think of freedom without tracing the roots of unfreedom, right at the very inception of either a person's birth or that of the nation's birth in 1947.

I shall deliberate on this rather important constitutive condition of freedom by taking recourse to the literary work by some of the leading Dalits poets from Maharashtra. Excerpts from the poems that have been cited in the beginning of this chapter, suggest that the natural/biological fact of birth is ontologically linked to the truth of unfreedom. The poetic conversation that both the poets imagine with their respective mothers has one thing in common. In both, the poet expresses a deep sense of anxiety about being free at all.

The apotheosis of the foetus, in Rokade's poem, and the infant, in Dhasal's, does not grow, making the conception of the foetus or the birth of an infant a moment of blessing. In fact, as the excerpts suggest, for both poets, birth is a kind of curse, a blame or an ontological mistake that they attribute to their parents. One could stretch the element of anxiety further by saying that the mothers, as it were, gave birth to twins: a biological entity and an ontological anxiety. Building further on to the essence of the poems, one could say that 'the foetus is untouchable', and hence is already and always unfree. An estranged being. The poets do suggest that the untouchable foetus, unlike the upper-caste male foetus, or infant, is ontologically underprivileged and hence is helplessly condemned to link unfreedom with the misfortune of being born to a mother who knows that her children are likely to be thrown into a hostile world that is surrounded by the dreaded form of unfreedom.

The Foetus is Untouchable

From the imaginary conversation of the poets, one may conclude that they do not see any option between the natural truth of biological birth, and the moral truth that becomes discernable in an untouchable's social death rather than in the natural birth as a happy and socially celebrated moment. The poets' imagination suggests that their mothers do not have the option to hypothetically consider that giving birth to a child is not going to be privileged neutral. In her universe of distress and frustration, there is not even the 'veil of ignorance' as the possibility of estrangement is already always present in the very conception of a foetus. The foetus is untouchable.

Conversely, in the case of the upper-caste, arguably, there is no 'veil of ignorance', and hence the social privilege of the foetus is already, and even always, a priori, decided. Those hierarchically and hence socially privileged castes who do use the 'veil of ignorance' for making their birth 'privileged neutral', use it for hiding their social privilege and thus saving themselves from falling into the 'banality of birth'. Birth without the veil becomes banal, when someone shamelessly, and seamlessly, brandishes his/her socially privileged birth. Wearing one's privileged caste on one's sleeve is as banal as decorating one's body with gold. Such people thank their parents for offering them the spatio-temporal advantage to enjoy freedom across time and space. They use the idea of freedom in order to increase their power of self-worth, but at the expense of others' moral degradation. The estranged – untouchables – carry caste on their back as carapace to legally protect themselves from castiest slurs and onslaughts. They have no relief from this crushing moral burden.

Both the poets are entangled, as it were, in an ineliminable sense of anxiety, whether they would ever be able to gain a stable hold on freedom as they appear in the public sphere. Can they appear without the sense of anxiety? Both the poets suggest that it is unfreedom that overshadows the premise of freedom even in its negative form. Disentangling oneself from the crushing caste code becomes impossible for an individual. But the question is, do they suggest that it is an existential problem which reduces birth to a fate that cannot be transcended? One could decode the hidden meaning that is right there in the texts of the poems. Anxiety, which underlies and renews a frustrating sense of unfreedom, in the ontological sense, right from the poets' being in their physical existence, in the material form as a fetus in their mother's womb, is already, always unfree. 'The fetus is untouchable'.

The fact of the mother's labour (Rokade) and the mother's failure to cut the umbilical cord (Dhasal), both carry the truth of unfreedom. Both these poets, however, do not invite us to admit and acknowledge, as it were, the interior sensory grasp of the agony, anguish and anxiety that both the poets seem to ontologically attach to the moment of their respective births. In fact, they morally compel us (particularly us sentient beings) to acknowledge that it is the caste system which is stuffed with the ideology of purity–pollution. It is the caste of mind that underlies and renews the experience of unfreedom, estrangement, entrapment and social imprisonment. Thus, in the poets' literary expression, the concept of birth, or even death, are causal expressions that make sense on the ground that they are the result of the alienating structures governed by the sensory ideology of purity–pollution. But for those who define freedom in terms of wielding social power to perpetuate the experience of unfreedom, such literary expressions are casual in that such socially dominant groups do not attach any moral credence to such expression (Kateb 1977, 141). The deep sense of anxiety and scepticism expressed by both the poets question the very idea of birth as blessing. In fact, birth, for both of them, is an opportunity to challenge the structures of alienation and unfreedom with which the poets express their anguish of birth.

Both poets, Rokade and Dhasal, however, resist being caught in the logic of fatalism which would then suggest two options: the best thing is not to be born (Rokade) or to die as an infant (Dhasal). Neither their conversation nor their moral quarrel with their mothers suggests a desolate wisdom, because such a quarrel is transcendental in nature.

Rokade's and Dhasal's poetic conversation with their respective mothers complicate the relationship between the moment of birth and the conception of freedom. It is we who are supposed to unpack the complications by looking inward. Thus, the blame as a reactive attitude in principle calls for an accountability to change. This makes it imperative on our part to offer a more reasoned and ethically sensible response to the complaint between the foetus/infant (the poets) and their mother.

Thus, let us not lend credence to the self-serving argument that both poets had a personal grudge with their mothers who gave birth to them only for them to step out and into a sphere of confinement, a kind of cattle pen, *kondwada* in Marathi (Daya Pawar). Let us resist the suggestion that would reduce the question of unfreedom to an innocuous level where it becomes a matter between the poet and his mother. In fact, the poet's conversation is immanently poised to draw our attention to the external understanding of socially produced unfreedom. They make a larger comment about the caste-based, hierarchically driven society. It is interesting to note that the middle-class understanding of freedom, present in most critiques of the Emergency, does not or cannot raise such a question. As the essence of the two poems cited above shows, both poets, Rokade and Dhasal, do not look at the fact of their birth as a moment of freedom that they are in a position to celebrate.

The birth question does not indicate the poets' existential reification into unfreedom. In fact, it is a caustic comment on the caste society that produces a prison-like existence for both poets. For some, both these expressions suggest that the foetus is already imprisoned but not always in confinement. This inner meaning of the poet's painful sarcasm resonates with Baburao Bagul's and Babasaheb Ambedkar's understanding of birth as a radical opportunity. Both suggest that the foetus is already untouchable, but its apotheosis can make it grow into a revolutionary figure. For both of them an untouchable's birth is a challenge for self-determination.

Using self-determination as the plank to define freedom, by taking hold of oneself, can be traced to Ambedkar's thinking on self-determination – that he would not die as an untouchable. He said, 'unfortunately for him he was born a Hindu Untouchable. It was beyond his power to prevent that, but he declared that it was within his power not to die as a Hindu' (Keer 1954, 253). His declaration suggested that he had no capacity to rectify the moral deficiency of unfreedom that is associated with an untouchable

Hindu. What is in his capacity to say no to is unfreedom, humiliation and discrimination. In Ambedkar's determination, 'the foetus is already always untouchable'. Not in my hands to be born as an untouchable Hindu, but it is in my hands not to die as one. Here Ambedkar does not treat birth as the source of a self-curse but as a challenge, if not an opportunity, to set off on the road to freedom, a kind of apotheosis to freedom. He believes in his agential capacity to the accountability to change (Surwade 2002, 145). For Ambedkar, the power of determination defines freedom, and freedom means power-packed action to break and overcome fetters. The destruction of shackles creates a melodious music that is aesthetically much more superior to any form of music (Kusumagraj 1998, 10).

This anxiety is similar to the anxiety that Bhimrao Ambedkar expressed at the time of Independence, which is almost similar to the scepticism he expressed while handing over the Constitution to the Indian Republic: 'On the 26th of January 1950, we are going to enter into a life of contradictions. In politics we will have equality and in social and economic life we will have inequality.' His anxiety was about whether we will be able to separate Max Weber and Manu while governing the country.

The poets' conversation, in the context of the Emergency, brings into dispute the relationship between social consciousness and the nature of social order. The poet in Rokade links his mother's labour at the time of his birth to the conditions of unfreedom that have been historically extended to the present and that are likely to continue even in the future. Thus, the poets suggest, the history of unfreedom and its possible continuation without which the concept of freedom cannot be adequate. In this sense, the conception of unfreedom is present in the very inception of freedom. As the experience of Dalits show, they arrive first not at freedom but at unfreedom. Ambedkar does say, 'the moment the word self-rule is uttered, we are reminded of the history of oppression, suppression and injustice. We are scared that the same history would get repeated in the future and yet we too need self-rule' (Govt of Maharashtra 2002, 239).

Ambedkar's scepticism about the promise of freedom resonates with the scepticism that the Dalits have about the promise of democracy and freedom that the opponents of the Emergency rule gave to the Indian people. The question that one has to raise here is, was this promise inclusive, or was it a promise that was exceptionally and essentially premised on the freedom for some?

Emergency as the State of Exception

As has been documented by several observers and scholars (Frank 1977), during the Emergency period, the government led by Mrs Indira Gandhi, was responsible for committing excesses such as the repression of the press and of civil society activists, suspending civil liberties, rounding up thousands of protesters, demolishing houses of the poor, and retrenching thousands of workers (Frank 1977, 467). The primary thrust of anti-Emergency protests was rather instinctive and hence reactive. The sudden imposition of an Internal Emergency made the middle-class reaction rather instinctive in its political nature. The campaign against the Emergency was led by the middle classes/civil-society activists who, arguably, invented the content of freedom which in its negative thrust meant keeping the repressive power far away from its conception of life without constraints. It experienced a sudden advance of the state towards its civil liberties and it felt ambushed by the former. Hence its feeling was intensely instinctive rather than instructed by the history of unfreedom. The middle class enlarged itself in the civic and political spheres, and naturally acted instinctively rather than consistently against the sluggish performance that normally does not go with a genuinely liberal/welfare state. It lacked consistency in offering responses to the subtle and not-so-subtle forms of state repression. Its rhetoric on the protection of individual liberties prevents its own idea of negative freedom from interweaving it with the idea of others' conception of freedom. The reaction of those who were at the receiving end of the state excesses was instinctive because it, in an actual sense, impacted the emotional sensibility of those who had to face the untoward experience of excesses. Thus, for the minority, the brunt of the violence of the Emergency was reported to be quite brutal, both in terms of material loss and mental trauma.

But for the middle class it was relatively sober in as much as it sought to shrink the discursive space of self-expression. However, the opponents of the Emergency were successful in translating what was an individualist issue into a collective one, meaning it made negative freedom, the hallmark of individual freedom, to masquerade as the freedom of the entire society.

This translation of individual freedom into collective freedom, is arguably absent in normal times where the suppression of the freedom of expression is individual, such as the banning of movies, books, paintings, etc. As I shall show in the last section on Dalits, negative freedom may not form a core concern for some sections of Dalits. In fact, let me state this with equivocation, the assuring nearness of the state that the Dalit experienced during the Emergency was affirmative and positive, creating, thereby, a space for the Dalit to feel free.

The idea of 'negative freedom' exists as an uneasy conundrum. At one end of this conundrum, it seems it is the left and liberal who have been in the forefront to defend negative freedom. At the other end of the conundrum, it is the right-wing parties that have joined the anti-Emergency bandwagon. As the mixed character of the protest against the Emergency shows, the struggle to protect negative freedom has a spiral, rather than a linear, orientation. The spiral mode, in the particular context of the Emergency, as mentioned earlier, accommodates even parties that do not have a bright record of standing for the freedom of the socially oppressed. In fact, such parties, in the name of defending negative freedom, managed to be a part of the bandwagon, although they undermined the social freedom of a large number of people, women and the untouchables. The linear progression of the concept, in contrast, would follow a trajectory that will avoid a hotch-potch combination of the forces opposing the Emergency and galvanise into the action for freedom, those who are transparent in their purpose, in other words, those who stand for freedom which is more or less all-encompassing.

This enabling criterion would consider political parties that are stuffed with a caste of mind and of communal intentions as an aberration to the concept. But, as the congeries of forces opposing the Emergency suggests, a segment of the left, liberals, socialists and rightists were all on the same page: negative freedom or defending democratic rights. Such a jumbled political formation was bound to disrupt the linear progression of the concept from negative freedom to positive freedom by progressively eliminating right-wing politics that does not want to take the blame for supporting social conditions that produce the experience of social unfreedom. Taking the moral initiative in blaming oneself is also to take the responsibility of minimising the scope for unfreedom. The linear progression would treat negative freedom as an initial condition and social freedom as an essential condition of emancipation. Thus, I choose to argue that it is necessary to problematise the very notion of freedom in the particular context of the Emergency.

Jayaprakash Narayan's plea for freedom, thus, was vaguely right and precisely wrong. It was vaguely right because it sought an endorsement for the call for protecting negative freedom which was not the top priority of those for whom the imposition of the Emergency came, as it were, as a blessing in disguise. It is precisely wrong on the count that it excluded those who saw something positive in the imposition of the Emergency. The reaction of the middle class was basically instinctive and hence reactive in the sense that it was devoid of the depth of historical analysis of the structures that underlie and renew the experience of unfreedom, estrangement or entrapment, that for the marginalised sections unfolded in myriad forms on an everyday basis. As stated earlier, the historiography of the concept suggests an ontological inseparability of the estranged human being from the dreaded forms of unfreedom which find their expression not only in the scholarly articulation by anti-caste thinkers such as Jotirao Phule and Ambedkar, but also in the poetry of some leading Dalit poets such as Rokade and Dhasal.

The Emergency as the State of Exception: A Dalit Point of View

Arguably, for the Dalit, the Emergency also came as the state of exception which, in terms of the conundrum, was different from the middle-class conception, that was defined in terms of normal, routine life of a high-profile presence in the active public sphere that was threatened by the state which through the Emergency arrived at their doorsteps. For Dalits, it was a state of exception. This idea of 'a state of exception' must be theorised and documented, for the state went knocking, with sincerity and efficiency, on the doors of money lenders, pawn brokers, fair-price shopkeepers, etc., who were forced to return the pawned articles to the Dalits and also to other poor non-Dalits.

Dalits, in addition, also link the Emergency with the state of exception where the normal state of unfreedom is replaced at least temporarily by the freedom (tangible and material) provided by the state through the twenty-point programme. Thus, for Dalits, it is not surveillance of the state but the support it provides that defines the state of exception. Meaning, the state becomes exceptionally active through its performance in favour of Dalits, at least the Dalits in the states from where the Congress party got the overwhelming support in the 1977 Lok Sabha elections (Joshi 1981).

One could possibly see evidence of a electorally mediated endorsement of the Emergency in the practical experience that the Dalit had of the state and its apparatus. The endorsement was based on the practical experience with the performance of the state and its sincerity to sideline Manu and bring to the central stage of its activism, Max Weber. Although Weber's affirmative reference has been brought in in the specific context of Maharashtra, the particular reference does have normative bearing on the other regions of India. Thus, it was the actual performance rather than routinely given promises that makes the Emergency a state of exception particularly for the Dalits. During the Emergency period, they could observe and experience the state catapulted out of its sluggishness and acting in favour of Dalits, bringing some immediate relief to their acute condition of hunger and helplessness that was aggravated by the drought conditions that the state of Maharashtra had experienced just before the Emergency.

They needed to reclaim their piece of land, metal vessels, and even musical instruments that they had pawned with the local pawnbrokers and moneylenders. They felt driven towards the state for its support which came rather easily without the invocation of the language of rights and mass protests that were already slackening after the influence of the Dalit Panthers was neutralised and the Dalit leadership was coopted into the pacificatory structures. Since this power with its content of defiant energy was weakened by the drought situation, was considerably depleted by the cooption and inactivism of the Dalit leaders, including the Dalit Panthers, the common Dalit had to rely on the state to exist and exist meaningfully without any deflation of dignity.

Most of the Dalits, along with other non-Dalit poor, got their pawned articles and metal vessels back from the local moneylenders, through the courtesy of the state. Dalits also got their musical instruments that they had pawned with the local pawnbroker and moneylenders.[2] Thus, in the perception of the Dalit, it was the state intervention through the Emergency that helped them in conserving their musical skill – a skill that they used not only for earning their livelihood but also for enlivening their life with some aesthetic zest. Thus, for the Dalit the Emergency was also a 'state of exception', but in a different, perhaps affirmative, sense. In this sense, it was for the first time that they observed, and experienced, the strict separation of Max Weber from Manu. During the Emergency, the upper-caste bureaucrats, at least for those Dalits who sided with Indira Congress in the 1977 election, were forced to act in accordance with Weber's legal–rational authority, rather than with Manu's caste codes that were embedded within the bureaucratic person. This normally manifested itself as hard prejudice, cold indifference and unreasonable bias. During the Emergency, the Dalit could walk in the street with their fear of the local lords drastically reduced. Thus, the state, during the Emergency, came to them perhaps in its most punctual mode, if not in its pure and ideal form.

References

Beteille, Andre. 2001. Equality and Universality. *Economic and Political Weekly* 36.38: 3619–25.

[2] My own personal experience, where my parents felt happy when we got our utensils back in the kitchen. I could also observe that the other families had the same rewarding experience of the Emergency.

Dangle, Arjun, ed. 1992. *Poisoned Bread*. Hyderabad: Orient BlackSwan.

Datta Gupta, Sobhanlal. 1979. *Justice and the Political Order in India, 1950–1972*. Calcutta: KP Bagchi & Company.

Dhag, Bhagwan. 1992. *Beimani* (Betryal). *Asmita Darsha* (Marathi). Special Number. Aurangabad.

Dhasal, Namdeo. 1975. *Golpitha* (Marathi). Mumbai: Neelkantha.

Frank, Andre Gunder. 1977. Emergence of Permanent Emergency in India. *Economic and Political Weekly* 12. 11 (12 March).

Ganguli, B. N. 1975. *Concept of Equality*. Shimla: Indian Institute of Advanced Study.

Govt of Maharashtra. 2002. *Writings and Speeches of Babasaheb Ambedkar*. vol. 18, Part I. Mumbai: Dr Babasaheb Ambedkar Source Material Publication Committee.

Joshi, Barbara. 1981. SC voters, New Data and New Questions. *Economic and Political Weekly* 16.33 (15 August).

Kateb, George. 1977. Freedom and Worldliness, in the Thought of Hannah Arendt. *Political Theory* 5.2 (May). JSTOR.

Keer, Dhananjay. 1954. *Dr Ambedkar: Life and Mission*. Mumbai: Popular Prakashan.

Khare, R. S. 1984. *The Untouchable as Himself*. Cambridge: Cambridge UP.

Kusumagraj, Swar. 1988. A Dalit poem printed on back cover page in Marathi. Walva (Sangali): Hutatma Printing Press.

Mahajan, Gurpreet. 2013. *India: Political Ideas and the Making of a Democratic Discourse*. London: Zed Publishers.

Pawar, Daya. 1974. *Kondwada*. Pune: Mehta Publishing House.

Sen, Amartya. 1999. *Development as Freedom*. New York: Alfred A. Knopf.

———. 2009. *The Idea of Justice*. New York: Allen Lane.

Sudarshan, R. 1994. The Political Consequences of Constitutional Discourse. In *State and Nation: In the Context of Social Change*, ed. T. V. Sathyamurthy. New Delhi: Oxford UP. 55–87.

Surwade, Vijay, ed. 2002. *Ambedkars' Speeches in Marathi*. Mumbai: Lokwangmay Graha.

15

Why did She Impose It and Why did She Lift It?: Revisiting the Indian Emergency of 1975

Peter Ronald deSouza

The Emergency of 1975–77 has rightly been characterised as a dark period in India's democratic journey. Perhaps its darkest. Revisiting it now, on its fiftieth anniversary, yields many interesting insights into the challenges faced by a postcolonial democracy as it seeks to manage the many pulls and pressures of its complex and contested politics. In the Introduction, we have identified several questions concerning the fateful legal choices that were made, the institutional infirmities that allowed it to happen, the dark side of human agency that found expression in the atrocities that took place and finally, of course, the huge human costs that were exacted from vulnerable populations. These narratives are necessary to understand how democracies, just with a little push by narcissistic and paranoid leaders, soon become tyrannies. We are at a similar juncture in democracies across the world today. In many democracies, including the USA, symptoms of executive overreach, similar to the ones we experienced in 1975, are appearing.

One line of enquiry that is missing in the many studies of the Emergency, however, is the exploration of the subjective factors that form a part of the decision matrices of the main protagonists, Jayaprakash Narayan, Justices Sinha and Krishna Iyer, Morarji Desai, Sanjay Gandhi, and the many civil servants and judges who played a part in the events that followed. The subjectivity of the most important protagonist, Prime Minister Indira Gandhi, has been significantly understudied. She made the crucial decision to impose the Emergency. She gave her approval to the orders that were put in place to give it bite. And it was she who, going against advice, unexpectedly, decided to lift it.

While these studies detail the excesses of the Emergency, they do not adequately engage with the inner world of the main protagonists. They may recognise the place of human agency in the unfolding of events, but they do so minimally, merely recording the decision made or the action taken but without exploring the subjective universe of the decision makers and of the actors who gave it substantial materiality. This gives us an incomplete picture. Studying subjectivity is important since it enables us to map the key factors of the person's inner world and to give weightage to them in providing an explanation. These factors constitute the decision matrix of the protagonist being studied. In this chapter, I hope to outline the decision matrix of Mrs Gandhi, to examine what led her to impose the Emergency and what prompted her to lift it. Such an exercise, I believe, will give us not just a deeper understanding of why it happened but also a better understanding of the crucial place of leaders in a democracy and of how and why they respond in particular ways to the dynamics of power.

Scholars such as Ranajit Guha dismiss the significance of the individual personality of leaders in their commentaries on the Emergency. Doing so is limiting as it seeks to explain historical events by looking primarily (if not only) at the logic of capital, and fails to engage with the 'inconvenient facts' of the key decision makers that have resulted in fateful historical events. Think of Gandhi, Mandela, Hitler, Thatcher, Castro, Ho Chi Minh, Mao Tse-Tung; and now Erdogan, Duterte, Modi, Xi Jinping and Trump, among others. Their subjective world is important to understand their decisions.

Here is an illustration of Guha's argument:

> Innumerable biographers of Indira Gandhi have suddenly descended on us their wares, and it is impossible to turn the pages of a periodical without a piece of psycho-history being pushed into our faces. . . . Indira Gandhi has no claim to originality in either respect; her conduct of government has been as undemocratic as her father's and her rhetoric as liberal – until a crises closed in and the rhetoric had to stop. The present Emergency therefore

> represents no radical break with a democratic past but an aggregation of a chronic denial of elementary freedoms and justice. (Guha 2002, 578–80)

In contrast to Guha's position, I hope to foreground the subjective (which is more than just the psychological) dimension of the main protagonists. This, I believe, is important and must be added to the analysis that considers the political and economic dimensions of the Emergency. It would give us a fuller explanation.

The Emergency was indeed a 'radical break with a democratic past'. It was a significant rupture. In what follows I shall try and discuss why it happened by adding to my analysis a discussion of Mrs Gandhi's inner world that constituted a big part of her decision matrix.

Two questions must be asked simultaneously to understand the Emergency with regard to Mrs Gandhi's actions. Why did she impose it and why did she lift it? If one asks each one of the questions separately, as is often done, one will get different answers than if one were to ask them simultaneously. When one asks the two questions together, one's analytical gaze is also directed towards an examination of her inner world because one feels it will help to understand the motivations that drove her to the two decisions (Steinberg 2005). I will, in what follows, map the different elements of her decision, and build a decision frame that comprises both the external factors of a polity under stress, that she had to consider, as well as the internal factors that lent significance to her reading of the political situation, which led her to the decisions of imposing the Emergency and lifting it. This acquires a salience because while she may have had reasons to impose the Emergency – and many explanations have been given of why she did it – she had no clear reasons to lift it, especially since she had a pliable parliament, an obliging judiciary, an indulgent press, and a cooperative bureaucracy. Why then did she lift the Emergency is a question that requires a serious answer. In this chapter I shall attempt to provide it.

Mrs Gandhi's Decision Frame

One may legitimately ask at this juncture: why all this fuss about a prime minister's 'decision frame' particularly in a parliamentary democracy where the doctrines of 'collective responsibility' and '*primus inter pares*' are important? Is not this singular focus on the PM a bit excessive? Not so. I go with the observation made by P. N. Dhar (2001), that in the real world it is the PM and the PMO that makes all the crucial decisions in a parliamentary system. The doctrines referred to earlier may be useful normative brakes on the abuse of power but in practice they are quite feeble and unable to constrain a strong prime minister. This was true in the India of the 1970s. It is equally true in India since 2014 (Ganguly 2023; Shankar 2018).

The decision to impose the Emergency was made by Mrs Gandhi alone. Her decision to impose it in fact surprised her cabinet colleagues who were summoned to an early-morning (6 am) Cabinet meeting on 26 June 1975 to ratify what had already been proclaimed around midnight by the president. Like the decision to impose, the decision to lift the Emergency was also hers alone. This latter decision went against the advice of the same trusted advisers on whom she had relied when making the first decision. It may be worthwhile to record here that it was easy for her to impose it because she had already weakened the institutions of the Supreme Court, the Congress party, and the Cabinet, which may have opposed the imposition, and so in the confidence that she would encounter little opposition she went ahead with her intention to impose the Emergency. But this does not explain why she lifted it. Since we are reading both momentous decisions together, we need to go beyond the easy argument of her authoritarian attitude and habit and look for additional causes.

In addition to the weightage that the external factors had within her decision frame, it is the internal factors, her subjective world, that, I hold, gave her assessment of the situation in 1975 a certain distinct colouration. She felt that the nation was under the risk of a growing anarchy and that it was she alone who could stem this descent into chaos. This is a view ridiculed by many but she repeated it in a TV interview with Jonathan Dimbleby.[1] Rather than dismiss such a reading as merely a sign of her paranoia, or

[1] Indira Gandhi Interview, *TV EYE*, 1978. https://www.youtube.com/watch?app=desktop&v=q8aETK5pQR4

her narcissism, which it certainly was for her to believe that she alone stood between stability and anarchy ('*après moi, le dèluge*'), and leave it at that, we must examine its validity and explore why she felt it necessary to impose an Emergency, that, at first glance, was at odds with her father's political philosophy and at variance with the worldview of Gandhiji, both of whom were her political and ethical mentors. The answer lies in an understanding of her inner world and how it influenced her decisions. A good place to begin such an analytical investigation is the few biographies written about her that provide interesting insights into her personality and how she responded to challenges and to fluid events (Malhotra 1991; Mehta 1977 & 1980; Jayakar 1995; Singh 2017; Frank 2002). It may not be out of place here to mention that as a child she often saw herself as Joan of Arc.

Oriana Fallaci's interview with Mrs Gandhi in 1972 sets the tone.

> We were together for more than two hours, and when the interview was over, she left the office to accompany me to the taxi waiting for me in the street. . . . She looked tired that day and all of a sudden I exclaimed, "Deep down I don't envy you, and I shouldn't like to be in your place". And she said, "The problem is not the problems I have, it's in the idiots around me. Democracy, you know . . ." I now wonder what she meant by that unfinished phrase. (Fallaci, reproduced by Sri Kantha 2014)

To understand the Emergency better we need to disaggregate the historical episode into three separate phases. The first is the phase before 25 June 1975. Here we would look at the external conditions that drove Mrs Gandhi to declare an Emergency. With respect to this decision, we need to ask whether it was in fact the only way to save the country from the imminent anarchy that she claimed was going to descend on India (the Dimbleby interview) or was it, instead (as is the dominant view), an attempt to save her own PM chair from the negative consequences of the Allahabad High Court judgment? The second phase is the twenty-one months that followed the imposition. It concerns the violence and brutalities visited on Indian citizens by the Emergency regime. Examining it is important not just to assign responsibility but also to create safeguards against its repetition. The present situation in India, that has been referred to in some circles as India's undeclared Emergency (Ganguly 2023), makes such an analysis urgent. The third phase is the lifting of the Emergency. We need to explain why Mrs Gandhi lifted it and by doing so went against the counsel of those who had advised her to impose it in the first place. This is a puzzle that needs an explanation. Since the second phase has been well documented, I shall, in this brief chapter, limit myself to exploring primarily the first and the third. By expanding the explanatory field, I shall try and respond to the nagging question: why did a postcolonial democracy, seemingly with the throw of a switch, morph into an authoritarian polity for a period of twenty-one months and then, with a similar flip of the switch, return to being a normal, raucous, democracy? This reversal is historically remarkable. Did the experience produce an afterlife that is still being felt today?

External Elements of the Decision Frame

The Emergency took place within twenty-five years of India becoming a Republic. In the life of a polity this is a very short time. In the case of India, it is a particularly brief period especially since the new nation needed years to recover from the trauma of the Partition. In these two and a half decades, from 1950 to 1975, a slow transformative revolution had begun to take shape where millions of persons had, for the first time in history, entered the political domain as citizens, speaking out, making claims and growing their demands on the state. Democracy was transforming India as well as being transformed by India (Sheth 2018; deSouza et al. 2022). As a result of this intensification of politics, particularly in the eight years before June 1975, significant changes had taken place in the landscape of politics. The demand side of politics was growing faster than its supply side. The Congress had lost ten state elections to the opposition parties in 1967 (Kothari 2012). Mrs Gandhi, unwilling to be a puppet of the Congress old guard, the Syndicate, split the party in 1969 and won the ensuing General Elections in March 1971 with a huge majority of 352 seats, in contrast to the 16 seats won by the old guard. The elections were her coming of age. She had connected with the masses and her rhetoric of '*garibi hatao*' had found resonance with them.

This electoral success was soon followed by her victory in the 1971 war with Pakistan, leading to the formation of Bangladesh in December 1971. In the months prior to the war, India had, on humanitarian grounds, hosted 10 million refugees from the erstwhile East Pakistan. While she was clear on the merits of the humanitarian policy of giving them sanctuary it placed a severe strain on the nation's finances, requiring her to visit London, Paris, Berlin and Washington to ask these governments to also share the burden. In the 1971 war India was threatened by the US that had ordered its 7th fleet, led by the nuclear aircraft carrier USS Enterprise and nine other warships, to the Bay of Bengal to browbeat the Indian navy that had blockaded the ports of East Pakistan. The US show of strength was in support of Pakistan. Mrs Gandhi did not blink and ordered her defence forces to continue their military action leading to the liberation of Bangladesh (Raghavan 2016, 677). President Nixon and his Secretary of State Kissinger disliked her and referred to her as a 'bitch' and 'witch' (as revealed in their notes) after they had met her in the months prior to the war.[2] After the liberation of Bangladesh she was feted as a hero. To either Khushwant Singh or Atal Bihari Vajpayee is attributed the description of Mrs Gandhi, after 1971, as Durga. This was the public image that she had acquired of being a fearless leader. Further, in the 1972 Assembly elections in West Bengal, that followed the war, the Congress (R) won 216 out of 280 seats polling 49 per cent of the vote. Siddhartha Shankar Ray, her close friend and advisor, was installed as chief minister. Mrs Gandhi was at her zenith giving her the feeling that her agenda was the correct one and that her position as prime minister was indispensable for national success.

[2] 'Nixon returned the Prime Minister's slight on November 5 by keeping her waiting for 45 minutes for a meeting at the Oval office. Gandhi kept cool in the brief talks that followed. She was, however, not one to take any slight from anyone. When Nixon called on her at the Blair House, she kept him waiting for 45 minutes to emerge from her room. Nixon got the message.' https://www.news18.com/news/opinion/when-nixon-made-vulgar-remarks-about-indira-gandhi-but-got-outwitted-over-indo-pak-war-2875105.html (accessed 7 August 2024)

The political decline began within a few months in 1973. The Navnirman student movement in Gujarat, which was launched at the end of 1973, shifted the location of politics from the Assembly to the streets and compelled Mrs Gandhi to ask an elected Congress chief minister, Chimanbhai Patel, to step down because of charges of corruption against him. The senior leader of Congress (O) Morarji Desai then went on an indefinite hunger strike in April 1975, demanding elections to the Assembly which had been under the President's Rule for a year. She thought it better to buy peace and conceded the demand. In the elections that followed Mrs Gandhi's Cong (R) lost several seats; and although it was the largest party after the elections, the results produced a hung assembly. Democratic theorists of this period have ignored the 'inconvenient fact' of a duly elected government being asked to resign because of a politics of protest. Paradoxically the protesters who had lost the election, in effect, won the post-election politics of the state.

Seeing the victory of protest politics in Gujarat, Jayaprakash Narayan launched a similar anti-corruption movement in Bihar with plans to make it a nationwide movement. He gave it a Gandhian ideological character when he called it the *Sampoorna Kranti Andolan* (or movement for total revolution) which was not just for a change of government but for a change in the nature of politics itself. (See the chapter by Anand Kumar.) Political groups which had lost the General Elections in 1971 were energised by this new political turn as protests erupted across India. As the movement spread, chief ministers of Congress states reported to the Centre that they would not be able to manage the law-and-order crises that was developing (Dhar 2001). In parallel with this was the railway strike launched by the socialist leader George Fernandes which went on for twenty days from 8 May to 27 May 1974. He boasted to his comrades that the strike would bring the economy to its knees (Jaffrelot and Anil 2021b). Mrs Gandhi broke the strike using repressive measures including physical assaults on the striking workers, dismissal from work and the use of the armed forces to man the railways. This was her second major challenge.

Soon after the breaking of the strike, Railway Minister L. N. Mishra was assassinated on 3 January 1975 by a bomb that exploded under the dais from where he was addressing a crowd at the Samastipur railway station in Bihar. Mrs Gandhi was shaken by the assassination and blamed it on a 'foreign hand'. The 'foreign hand', she believed, stoked unrest in India. (See the chapter by Sahni.) There were reports that the US consulate in Bombay (Mumbai) had been meeting with the protesters in Gujarat (Dhar 2001). The earlier 1973 assassination of Salvador Allende in Chile (*The Wilson Quarterly* 2003) was also blamed on the 'foreign hand'. Fidel Castro, based on reports from his intelligence agencies, personally warned her that she was next on the hit list (Baru 2024). RAW told her that their sources gave them to believe that an assassination plot was being hatched by the Bangladesh army against Sheikh Mujibur Rahman (Sharada Prasad 2020 & 2021). She asked RAW to alert Mujib who dismissed the reports as baseless since he did not believe his own people would assassinate him. He and his whole family were murdered by some army officers on 15 August 1975.

To add to this anxiety about the 'foreign hand' attempting to destabilise the nation, as had happened elsewhere, and which was not a fantasy or paranoia since it had already happened in Chile (1973) and the Democratic Republic of the Congo (1961) (see the interview given to Piers Morgan by Jeffrey Sachs who mentions 90 attempts at regime change by the CIA),[3] was the growing chaos that resulted from the two calls given by JP and Morarji respectively. JP, on the night of 24 June 1975, at a huge meeting at the Ramlila Maidan in Delhi, gave a call for 'total revolution'. He reportedly appealed to the police and armed forces to disobey orders from the government that was (post the Allahabad judgment) considered illegitimate. There is considerable confusion about the exact phrasing of JP's call. Was it to disobey orders of an 'illegitimate government' or was it to disobey 'illegitimate orders' of the government? This both angered and shook Mrs Gandhi for, in her and her advisors' view, it amounted to sedition. Coming from JP it carried considerable political weight because of his national status.

[3] Sachs refers to over 100 regime change attempts by the CIA. 'The CIA's Dark History Regime Change' https://www.youtube.com/watch?v=2PuRX1k1lWU (accessed 20 June 2025)

She saw it as a threat to India's stability. Coupled with this was Morarji's call to the people to gherao the PM's residence and the parliament, not allowing her to emerge till she resigned. Morarji's call raised the political temperature which was already very high. Both calls produced an adversarial politics that made dialogue and accommodation nearly impossible. To compound matters, Mrs Gandhi got reports of dissidents, such as Chandrashekar, Mohan Dharia and other 'young Turks' of her party, being in conversation with JP (Jaffrelot and Anil 2021b). This also upset her. It suggested that there was not just dissension in her party but also treachery. Her confidence that her party would stand by her in this growing crisis began to wane. While these two calls, just discussed, are chronologically after the Allahabad High court judgment, which I shall discuss shortly, her sense of uncertainty and her feeling that she was surrounded by risk (if not enemies) led her to believe that decisive action was required. Her biographers discuss the many times in her life when faced with similar situations of uncertainty she acted decisively and forcefully.[4] The psychologist Steinberg saw this as an attribute of 'dominance' in her.

To this growing political anxiety was added the discomforting news of the state of the economy. (See the chapter by Errol D'Souza.)

> . . . by 1974, India was once again in economic difficulties. The war for Bangladesh in 1971 had ended in victory – but it pushed ten million refugees onto the Indian economy and produced a substantial budget deficit. In 1972 and again in 1973 the monsoon failed, producing not only drought but a shortage of food and an increase in its price. Power generation declined, as did agricultural production and the demand for manufactured goods. Unemployment followed. Finally, the decision of the Arab oil producers to raise prices in 1973 drained India's foreign reserves and deepened what was now a serious recession. Once again, as in the mid-1960s, the siren voices of the world market were heard – the World Bank

---

[4] A profile of her personality prepared by an academic psychologist has found her to be ambitious, dominant, contentious and reticent (Steinberg 2005).

> and the IMF – serenading India with promises of aid, but simultaneously demanding changes in Indian economic policy. (Lockwood 2015, 867)

For an economy that is monsoon-dependent, and where large sections of the population are reliant on agriculture, this meant a growing livelihood distress and increasing political discontent (Frankel 1978). It was this discontent that the opposition groups tapped into leading to an increased instability of the political order. India's foreign exchange situation was also fragile. It got exacerbated by the huge hike in oil prices by the OPEC countries in 1973, placing considerable pressure on the economy. On economic policy Mrs Gandhi was at a crossroads. Should she make a leftward course correction, as suggested by P. N. Haksar, the deputy chairman of the Planning Commission, or should she shift the policy frame to the right as was being recommended by her chief economic advisor, P. N. Dhar? Strong decisions on economic policy were urgent. Her penchant was to move to the left (Dhar 2001). This was the fifth key element in her decision frame that needed urgent attention.

So when Justice Sinha of the Allahabad High Court gave his judgment on the ten charges of electoral malpractice in Raj Narain's petition, of which he dismissed eight major ones but found her guilty of two minor charges, thereby declaring her election void, it added one more dimension of uncertainty to her decision frame. S. S. Ray, her legal advisor, suggested an appeal to the Supreme Court. This was done. Justice Krishna Iyer, the vacation judge, heard the appeal and granted a stay on her dismissal but with conditions that were humiliating. She could continue as PM but not vote in parliament or be paid the attendance allowance. Reports suggest 'Indira Gandhi's immediate reaction was to resign, and her private secretary RK Dhawan typed out her resignation' (Sharada Prasad 2021). It is unclear whether this initial reaction to resign was because she felt humiliated by the decision and offended by the conditions, or whether she had bought into the norms and conventions of the constitutional order that her father had bequeathed to the nation and that she did not want to undermine. The court orders left her in a state of deep psychological distress. The biographies and some of the memoirs record this indecision. It may not be out of order to mention that she got the news of her dear friend D. P. Dhar's death on the day of the Allahabad High Court judgment. Indira Gandhi was deeply troubled by the collapsing world around her.

It is unfortunate that not much attention has been given to scrutinising Mrs Gandhi's inner turmoil. What should she do? The nation was in crises. Her personal world was in upheaval. The external environment was hostile. How should she respond, especially since she saw herself as the only person capable of steering the state through these turbulent waters? Reading of her angst one is reminded of Agamemnon in Euripides' play *Iphigenia at Aulis* where he is faced with the hard choice of either sacrificing his daughter to please the gods and let the winds blow so that the army could sail, as advised by the priests, or desisting from the sacrifice and taking the risk that the winds would not blow and the restless army would mutiny and kill them both. Mrs Gandhi's inner world was being churned as, simultaneously, her decision frame was growing in complexity.

Examining this period of uncertainty is important because it provides clues to why she imposed the Emergency. To sum up, the six major external factors that constituted her decision frame are (1) the growing politics of protest leading to the fear that the state would be unable to deal with the growing anarchy, (2) the twenty-day railway strike that threatened to bring an economy already in crises to its knees, (3) the conspiracies within her own party to unseat her, (4) the fear of the foreign hand in a hostile world of Machiavellian geopolitics where regimes unfriendly to the dominant superpower were being destabilised and their leaders assassinated, (5) an economy that was under severe stress from two failed monsoons and the five-fold increase in oil prices and, (6) the unfavourable court judgments that humiliated her reducing her authority as prime minister. We must not forget that these challenges came together just twenty-eight years after Independence. In 1975, we were still a very young postcolonial democratic state surviving in an increasingly hostile global environment.

When we add to these external factors, the internal factors that comprised her decision frame, we get a more complete picture of why Mrs Gandhi imposed the Emergency. To say that it was her authoritarian personality is just too simple. In the absence of access to her private papers we will have to construct an argument from fragments in the press, from copies of her correspondence with others, from memoirs, from commentaries, and most of all from the biographies (Dhar 2001; Jaffrelot and Anil 2021a & 2021b; Frank 2002; Fallaci; Jayakar 1995; Kapoor 2015; Kaviraj 1986; Malhotra 1991; Mehta 1977 & 1980; Prakash 2019; Sahgal 2012; Sharada Prasad 2020 & 2021; Singh 2017).

Internal Elements of the Decision Frame

If we accept the significance of the subjective dimension, of social agents making decisions based on their cognitive ordering of the world, especially in the case of important political leaders, then we must explore the nature of the inner conflict that enveloped Indira Gandhi after she heard the court Judgment (Jayakar 1995, 270, 274). This was a conflict she alone had to resolve. It is important to give it focused attention since she was a key actor in this period of Indian history. If she resigned, she would be true to the morality of the constitutional order her father had built for postcolonial India. If she did not resign, then she would be disparaging his legacy. She had spent too many years with him, and his intellectual friends in India, England and the world, to know how important the moral order, and the moral life in politics, was to Nehru. She could not belittle it. He was her moral and political guru and even though she was an adult, and her own person, the foundations of her worldview had been laid by Nehru and Gandhiji. The right thing to do, therefore, was to resign.

But Mrs Gandhi also learnt from her father's letters, and from his life of political struggle (nine years of which were spent in prison), that fighting for a free India was also very dear to him. It was so important that the politics of the freedom struggle always gained precedence over the demands of his family. Nehru's wife Kamala, who was suffering from tuberculosis and had to be admitted to sanitoriums across the country and abroad, had to bear her illness alone with support mainly from Prabha (JP's wife) and the young Indira. Nehru, faced with this domestic responsibility, chose instead to go to jail for his politics rather than abandon it and stay with Kamala. This could not have been an easy decision for him. If she resigned, Mrs Gandhi believed, India would descend into anarchy. Nehru's India was at risk. JP who was leading the agitation against her, a protest that gained many decibels after the court judgments, was an important public figure in politics who enjoyed the appellation of being regarded as the Lok Nayak (people's leader). But Mrs Gandhi believed he was also one who shied away from the responsibilities of the office. Nehru had offered to prepare JP to take over from him, when he demitted the office, but JP declined the offer (Sharada Prasad 2020 & 2021). Mrs Gandhi had been told this 'inconvenient fact' about JP that he was unwilling to bear the responsibility of the office. Resignation by her would therefore hand over a nation in turmoil to a person who was both unwilling and unable to discharge the duties of the office – especially now. Which of Nehru's legacies should she, therefore, honour?

S. S. Ray offered Mrs Gandhi a way out. This was supported by her son Sanjay Gandhi, his street-level political allies, and the Congress President Dev Kant Barooah. Sanjay was insistent that she not resign and assured her that he would handle the political fallout that followed. He had no patience for Nehruvian niceties. Ray told her that there was a provision in the Constitution that allowed her to remain in office and attend to the political crises. She could impose an Internal Emergency, under Article 352, alongside the External Emergency which had been proclaimed during the 1971 war and which was still in place. A written resolution from the Cabinet to the president calling for an Emergency was what was required for the presidential proclamation to be issued. This she did although she got the proclamation issued before the written Cabinet resolution. The proclamation was subsequently to be endorsed by parliament. This too she managed to do, which was easy, because of her party's majority in parliament. On the face of it, she had met the constitutional requirements through which she became a 'constitutional dictator' and not an authoritarian tyrant (Lijphart 1978).

From her biographies, we can draw out five aspects of Mrs Gandhi's personality that shed light on the grounds for these two momentous decisions. The first is her lonely childhood. Her education was regularly disrupted as she was shifted from school to school across India and abroad. She therefore had no long-standing friends who she could trust and who she could go to for advice. When she was a teenager, she got very upset by a remark by Vijaya Lakshmi Pandit, that she was ugly. This meant that she was not even close to her father's sister who was in politics. Her teenage years were consumed by her caring for her mother who, because of her illness, made her grow up ahead of her years. The story of her life gives a reader a sense of her loneliness and the fact that she had few people to whom she could confide. This trust deficit, together with subsequent events of loss and betrayal, explains why she was so dependent on her son Sanjay Gandhi. Her friends from London, Romesh Thapar and P. N. Haksar, had also begun to distance themselves from her.

The second aspect that we must note is the intellectual and moral influences on Mrs Gandhi of three of the greatest Indians who fought for India's freedom. Nehru through his letters to her (Nehru 2004a), and his reliance on her as the hostess in the prime minister's residence, exposed her to world history, important ideas of science such as those of Einstein and Darwin (Nehru 2004b), and world leaders such as Tito, Nasser and Nyerere who were also working to build a postcolonial and just world. Gandhi was very fond of her and took a personal interest in her affairs. The biographies reveal a close relationship between them. He queried her about her studies and her personal life like a favourite *chacha*. She carried out his instructions of helping in the refugee camps during the upheaval of the Partition. It is important to note her commitment to work in the refugee camps after the Partition where she went regularly (sometimes daily) following Gandhiji's directives. Tagore too was her mentor when she went to Shantiniketan to study. She was exposed to his imagination of a different India and also learnt from him about the rich civilisational heritage of India. The philosophies of these three humanists, I believe, Indira Gandhi carried within her. They were integral to her own worldview. There is no way we can read her indecision by ignoring these influences and seeing her actions as if they emerged from an empty space. If historical context and an individual's political socialisation is important to explain events, decisions, and personalities, then the central place of these three mentors in Indira Gandhi's worldview cannot be diminished.

The third aspect of her personality, that we must add to the list, is her courage. There are several episodes mentioned in the biographies affirming this. Let me mention one. Once when she was travelling by car in Delhi, in the aftermath of the Partition, she saw a Muslim man being harassed by a mob. She stopped the car, got out, confronted the mob that was threatening physical violence, put the vulnerable man in the car, and took him to safety (Frank 2002). Through her untiring work in the refugee camps she had experienced, first-hand, the trauma of communal conflict and the risk of anarchy. It perhaps frightened her and was an outcome she wished to avoid.

The fourth aspect is her obstinacy. Three stories reveal this aspect of her personality. Her decision to marry Feroze Gandhi, against the wishes of both Nehru and Gandhiji, confirms this obstinacy. They thought Feroze was not suitable for her on many counts, but she went ahead anyway compelling them to accept her decision. Another story relates to the advice from her doctors not to have children because they felt she was too weak and too frail to carry a foetus (Jayakar 1995). She rebelled against this advice as well, and was reputed to have stated that since she had married to have children nothing was going to stop her. The third is her resistance to the Congress old guard who wanted her to be only a '*goongi gudiya*' that they could control. She did not comply and instead split the party. These episodes show her streak of stubbornness to do what she believed needed to be done even in the face of many cautions and opposition.

The fifth aspect, similar to the fourth, is her independent mind and her decisiveness. We saw an expression of it when she went to war to liberate Bangladesh against the warnings of the USA. We saw it again when she gave the go ahead to test the nuclear device in 1974 even though her economic advisors warned her that the economy would face difficulties as a consequence of the sanctions that were going to be imposed. They were. This independence was evident again in her nationalisation of banks and in the abolition of privy purses – two policies that she thought were necessary to move India in a more socialist direction.

Here again we see five factors that were part of Mrs Gandhi's decision frame. These internal factors are loneliness, obstinacy, decisiveness, courage and the intellectual-moral influences that shaped her worldview. Her subjectivity was shaped not only by these psychological aspects of her personality but also by societal expectations and her resistance to the patriarchal attitude of the Congress Syndicate. She was called Indiramma in many parts of India. Indira Gandhi resisted these structures of control through her choices; whether it was in her marriage to Feroze, her determination to have children, or her refusal to be a '*goongi gudiya*'.

Relations, Influences and the Decision Frame: Nehru's Daughter, Sanjay's Mother

From this set of external and internal factors I can reconstruct the tensions within her decision frame that she had to reconcile when she made a decision. I recognise that often such reconciling does not take place since in real life people are not *fully* rational agents and also that the eleven factors I have listed may in fact not be rationally reconcilable. The real world is often different from the world of abstract theory. Social agents act inconsistently. They live their lives with incompatible values. Rationalisation and rationality have an uneasy coexistence in an agent's life. They act on impulse, prejudice, anxiety and even obstinacy, especially in a fluid context. They always make decisions in a context of information deficiency. These factors have to be taken into account when we examine her tyrannical decisions along with the fact that she was a lonely person, obstinate, firm-willed, courageous, decisive and suspicious, who had to respond to a court decision that humiliated her and sought to remove her from office, at a time when the nation was faced with multiple crises. Street politics, encouraged by senior politicians who had fought for Indian independence, and importantly, who had lost elections, were threatening to overpower the institutions of the state. She believed (perhaps rightly, perhaps wrongly) that she stood between them and anarchy. As India's first woman prime minister in a patriarchal political set up, Mrs Gandhi did not have the luxury of deferring her decision since things had come to a head. Not having the *aparigrahic* philosophy of Gandhi of non-attachment, or the complex philosophical vision of Nehru, or even the deep humanistic worldview of Tagore, she imposed the Emergency to defuse the crises, as an immediate response, similar to Karna throwing the divine spear at Ghatotkacha. Karna had received it as a boon from Indra and had reserved it for use in his anticipated duel with Arjuna. But in the heat of the battle, needing to urgently diffuse the rampage being caused by Ghatotkacha on the Kauravas, he used it. It could be used only once. It was not available for future use. Was Mrs Gandhis's imposition of the Emergency her Karna moment?

In the days following the Allahabad High Court verdict, Mrs Gandhi was in the throes of an inner struggle between the two important political characters that relationally had influence on her emotional and subjective being. She was the daughter of Nehru, the nationalist and liberal democrat. This required her to uphold the norms and conventions of a constitutional democracy and resign after the Allahabad High Court judgment. She was also the mother of Sanjay, the street-level politician who had no time for constitutional refinements. She felt the need to protect him from the political criticism that was growing against his business activities. Sanjay believed that political and muscle power alone was important. Once acquired, power should not be given up because of some court order, especially if there were constitutional ways to bypass the court's decision. If she could impose an Emergency, and still be consistent with the Constitution, then she must do so.

S. S. Ray gave her a solution to reconcile her two personas, of daughter and mother. Mrs Gandhi could become a constitutional autocrat. She need not discard the Constitution. She had 'power', which was declining, but before the court decisions, she also had 'authority'. The court took 'authority' away from her (in a Weberian sense) or at least it diminished it considerably. It had to be restored. This she did by imposing the Emergency, by acting according to the letter of Article 352 except for the small lapse in the sequencing of the proclamation. Nehru's daughter, in this narrow zone, was not in conflict with Sanjay's mother. But the conflict grew as she came to know of the Emergency's excesses, especially the sterilisation excesses. These were conveyed to her by

P. N. Dhar. The tension between her two key personas now began to grow into a conflict. They could not be aligned or contained. She had to choose between being Nehru's daughter or being Sanjay's mother. Sanjay wanted her to prolong the state of Emergency. She was troubled by his arrogance and his arbitrariness (Frank 2002). Against the advice of Sanjay and his coterie, she chose to be Nehru's daughter. She lifted the Emergency and went a step further: she lifted all curbs on political parties even to the surprise of all those who had been imprisoned (Jaffrelot and Anil 2021b). Her critics formed the Janata Party, campaigned against the Emergency's excesses, and trounced her in the 1977 General Elections that were called. The Janata Party got 295 seats to her 154, and got 41 per cent of the vote to her 34 per cent. In 1977 she was duly punished by the Indian voter for the authoritarian excesses of the Emergency. But she was forgiven in 1980, three years later, when she came back with 353 seats and nearly 43 per cent of the vote, more than the Janata Party had got when they defeated her after the Emergency was lifted in 1977.[5]

Shifting the Gaze from Mrs Gandhi's Subjectivity to the Working of the Emergency State

The above narrative may seem as if it is diminishing the Emergency's excesses. It is not my intention to dilute their gravity as clearly stated in the introduction to this book and to this chapter, and across the book. I have a limited objective here which is to broaden the analysis by seeing the Emergency in three phases so that we get a better understanding of it. I have limited myself primarily to the first and the third because the second, the Emergency's atrocities of torture, encounter killings, arrests under MISA, media censorship, demolition of homes and sterilisation, have been widely documented.

---

[5] A brief note needs to be recorded here that these two personas of mother/daughter that I have used is not a gendered reading of her behaviour and decisions. It is a biographical reading. I would make the same argument if the person was a father/son. To me this argument suggests itself from the details of her biography. We can here separate the painter from her painting.

There is one analytical theme, however, that is missing in the many studies mentioned here. It concerns the state 'as a social organisation' that has its own dynamics of power which produces a logic of behaviour that is only partly regime-dependent. In many senses it is regime-independent. Because it is the custodian of rules and regulations, has coercive authority, and enjoys a legitimacy that is promoted by state institutions, it often becomes oppressive. In postcolonial societies which are seeking to establish a social and political order and attempting to fuse disparate social geographies into a national imaginary, this is mostly the case. There is no other path available in history for postcolonial societies but to create and rely on such a state structure. (See the discussion in the Introduction on the Huntington thesis.)

Such an oppressive state structure manifests itself under conditions of Emergency when the state of exception become the normal. We see the expression of such tyranny in particular instances of state violence (see Kannabiran's chapter), or its arbitrariness (see Sanan's chapter), or the many cases of score settling (Navin Chawla's lists), or acts of resistance (see Anand's chapter), or the delegation of authority to layers of the state that should not have got it. We need to explain why a democratic state that was proceeding along rather well, suddenly, on 25 June 1975, transformed into an authoritarian one. What happened to the constitutional superstructure that had been so carefully built and grown? This is the same question that must be asked in many Western democracies today, in 2025.

As a result, one is compelled to ask, whether, in addition to Mrs Gandhi's involvement, officials such as Chawla, Bhinder, Bansilal, Dhawan, Kapoor, Sanjay, Tamta, Bhagat, etc., who were active implementers of the tyranny that had descended on the polity, and judges such as Chandrachud, Bhagwati, Beg, etc., who could have struck it down (see the chapter by Sudarshan) should also not carry some of the blame for the excesses. The state personnel, especially the higher bureaucracy, police officers and judges, and the media owners were also complicit through their acts of commission and sometimes through acts of omission. (See the chapter on media by Philipose.) They gave Mrs Gandhi's authoritarian decision a material existence. Why did they collude?

State personnel in such contexts are complicit, both morally and legally, when they enable the initial authoritarian decision, and the authoritarian proclivity of the head of government, to transform a liberal state into a tyrannical one.[6] This is the juncture at which the 'rule of law' becomes the 'rule by law'. This shift from 'rule of law' to 'rule by law', and the normalising of the state of exception, enabling thereby the entrenchment of an executive state, remains an enduring legacy of the Emergency. This is a lesson that all post-Emergency regimes have learnt, none more so than the one currently in power in Delhi and Washington in 2025.

The blame for the tyranny must therefore be shared by the leader, the regime, the bureaucrats who manage oversight institutions, and the police and judges who are complicit. It is here where tyranny lies, where an Emergency-like situation can be created and experienced even in normal times. Complicity and collusion by the officials of a liberal state is what enables a democratic state to become, overnight, as in 1975, an authoritarian one, and, over many nights, an oppressive one.

When looking at the functioning of the state during authoritarian periods we find the tendency of officials to over-read the intentions of the autocrat, to imagine what would please them, and then to act based on this over-reading. In the USA this is referred to as 'anticipatory obedience'. Officials may do so out of fear, loyalty, ambition, greed, or just small-mindedness. But they act on their reading of the regime's expectations. Looking at such behaviour involves an investigation of the subjectivity of the key personnel. Think of Justice Khanna and then compare his decision in the *ADM Jabalpur* case with that of Justice Bhagwati, and one will appreciate the importance of delving into subjective explanations. (See Sudarshan's chapter.) The authoritarian Indian state that emerged during the Emergency was guilty of such anticipatory obedience. It used its enormous coercive power to terrorise dissent and dissenters. The Emergency proclamation converted authority into power and this was then used, even by

[6] We see this tragically as Netanyahu's Israel produces a genocide in Gaza in 2024/25 while the Western world, complicit and colluding, does nothing.

lower officials, without the regular constitutional constraints, particularly since the writ jurisprudence had been suspended by the *ADM Jabalpur* verdict.

The authoritarian state that rose during the Emergency was partly driven by Sanjay Gandhi and his cronies. He caused power to shift from the PMO, headed by P. N. Dhar, to the PMH, the prime minister's house, where an alternative office was in operation headed by R. K. Dhawan. Mrs Gandhi's indulgence of her son, the cowardice of her party colleagues to question her decisions, the timidity of the courts to challenge the unconstitutional actions of her officials who framed and implemented the government orders, and, of course, the police who were overzealous in their execution, all contributed to the violence of the Emergency. The extent of such collusion, and the excesses that ensued, has been documented by the Shah Commission.[7] We perhaps need another

[7] In a personal note to me in response to an earlier draft, Errol D'Souza offers this analysis of why this happens. I am quoting it at some length. 'Dictators who run authoritarian regimes usually suffer from the delusion that they are popular and have the adoration of the people and their popularity must not be allowed to be dislodged by the actions of those misguided elements seeking to bring them down. Those who are seeking to remove the leader are deemed to be plotting against the country itself. A dictator takes the position that his/her interests and those of the country are one and the same. They cannot entertain the possibility that the challenge is against them personally. . . . Any persons taking part in a demonstration or uprising against the leader are then deemed to be a threat to the country from within. It could follow – and there is a persuasive argument to be made here – that the method followed to contain such threats are thought to be befitting the circumstances and, in the extreme, may result in atrocities. The delusion of the leader may then propagate to others who serve the leader as they too believe they are locked in a struggle with traitors, and they may deceive themselves that any punishment they belt out or atrocity they commit is necessary for the cause of the country. It is also good to create imagined enemies especially when the times are those of uncertainty as choosing stability promised by a dictator may be a preferred alternative to a desperate population going through economic upheaval and troubling times over anarchy.'

Shah Commission 2.0 in India today if we are to understand the collusion and complicity in the cases of Fr Stan Swamy and Professor G. N. Saibaba.

This brings the discussion to the second question: Why did Mrs Gandhi lift the Emergency? If she was a constitutional dictator, which she was, then why did she lift the Emergency, announce elections and withdraw all the restrictions on free campaigning. Was she being cunning or was she being sincere? Some say that she was being strategic since the intelligence agencies had assured her that she would win an election if it was held (Tully 2018). But then did she, as an autocrat, have to permit free electioneering, a situation that autocrats do not normally do? There are next to no examples across the democratic world where suspension of civil liberties and democratic rights has been reversed by the autocrat who wants to revert to democracy – not Erdogan, not Orbán, not Netanyahu, not Rajapaksa. They have had to yield to public protests and political movements of opposition. In January 1977, Mrs Gandhi was not facing such public protests when she lifted the Emergency.

I think her decision to lift the Emergency and end the excesses by restoring the democratic process was sincere. She realised that her decision to impose the Emergency was erroneous, producing outcomes that would have horrified and saddened her father. As her father's daughter she could not live with such a situation. It amounted to betrayal. The reports of the atrocities, of what was being produced by the state's overzealousness, horrified and mortified her. She had to make a bold decision once again to reverse her earlier decision. She had to rectify her error. So, against the advice of her son Sanjay and his coterie, she not only lifted the Emergency but also its tyrannical furniture. Nehru's daughter overruled Sanjay's mother.[8] I use these two terms,

[8] Ehud Olmert, the former prime minister of Israel, reflecting on the genocide in Gaza in an interview with Ezra Klein in the *New York Times* said this in response to the line of questioning on what needs to be done:

> As a retiree of being almost 50 years in the center of the national arena of such a volatile and exciting country, I'm asked every now and then: What do I have to say about what makes a person a great

daughter/mother, much to the dissatisfaction of many readers, who see it as too simplistic, as short forms to indicate complex universes of motivation. By invoking the idea of a daughter, I am invoking the layered processes of socialisation by which the worldview of a subject is produced. In Mrs Gandhi's case it would range from the debates during the freedom struggle, to the human horrors of the Partition, to the probing discussions on decolonisation that took place in her father's drawing room, to the aspirations and resistances among political leaders to build a state structure, to ideological initiatives such as the nationalisation of banks, and so on – a long list of factors. Likewise, in the case of the mother. Daughter/mother are two subjective universes that need deconstruction. By introducing them to explain Mrs Gandhi's decisions on the Emergency, I thereby invite readers to enter the two universes and reflect on their own biographies, and see how it influences their choices, an exercise which I expect will add to the explanatory framework. It is of public significance in Mrs Gandhi's case because she was prime minister. The framework also works in the case of the ordinary citizen.

Mrs Gandhi's opponents were released from jail and were given complete freedom to campaign. She lost the election. The Janata government that came to power punished her for the

---

> leader? What makes a person a man of history rather than just a passing political phenomenon? I used to say that, in my mind, one of the things that characterise a great leader is the ability, when the time comes, to make a decision that is 180 degrees opposite to everything that he has preached for and believed for and fought for and defended for all his life. There comes a moment when you have to take a decision and the only reasonable, rational, logical, healthy decision is the opposite of everything that you stood for.

One wonders if Mrs Gandhi's assessment of the 'historical moment of lifting the Emergency' can be read through this lens of Ehud Olmert. She may not be the great leader of history but it cannot be denied that the moment of lifting the Emergency was such a moment of realisation. *The Ezra Klein Show,* 11 June 2025. 'Ehud Olmert on Israel's Catastrophic War in Gaza'.

https://www.nytimes.com/2025/06/11/opinion/ezra-klein-podcast-ehud-olmert.html (accessed 20 June 2025)

Emergency's atrocities by putting her in jail. Ironically, they made her a martyr. In three years, she returned to power in the election held in 1980 when the Janata experiment collapsed through its internal contradictions. Mrs Gandhi won about 43 per cent of the vote as against 34 per cent in 1977. Indian democracy was back.

Conclusion

While there are many issues that have been raised by scholars in the articles on the Emergency, and also in this edited volume, I would like to conclude my chapter by reflecting mainly on four. Two of them are methodological in character and two are concerned with substantive issues. The first methodological issue, quite naturally, is on my argument that we must look at the subjective dimension of Mrs Gandhi's decision frame. Some have responded suggesting that this argument is too reductively psychological and gives inadequate attention to structural and other contextual issues. This is a misreading. I have laboured to succinctly present the six external elements in her decision frame. Others have responded to my seeing Indira Gandhi as Nehru's daughter as being carried away by a Shakespearean flourish. Nehru cannot be likened to Hamlet's father's ghost. Since the last word on the comparison is yet to be said, let me park it here and proceed.

I find this scoffing at the subjective dimension of decision making – part personal psychology and part meaning-making by the social actor – quite extraordinary. Intellectuals who are critical of bringing the subjective back, I am sure, are happy to read and appreciate Foucault's lectures, delivered at the University of California at Berkeley, on parrhesia where he dwells on the motivations of the key characters in Euripides' and Sophocles' plays. These critics are prepared to see Raskolnikov's murder of an old woman in Dostoevsky's *Crime and Punishment* as an act to be regarded in 'act utilitarian' terms, thereby going beyond literary theory into social theory. Further, they are prepared to endorse the concept of the 'banality of evil' that Hannah Arendt formulated when she commented on Eichmann's trial in Jerusalem, but are, paradoxically, unwilling to extend this same methodological space, of exploring motivation, to Mrs Gandhi's decision to impose the Emergency. This is a methodological inconsistency.

Mrs Gandhi is no less a social agent than any of those discussed in literature and the humanities. Since she occupies the position of prime minister, in one of the most complex polities in the world, her decisions and motivations are significant and have a real-world impact. They cannot be ignored. We need to bring them out for analytical scrutiny from the nether world of suppression by ideology. This I have tried to do. By discussing them I am not giving her a free pass on the atrocities of the Emergency. She remains responsible, as do other important members of the state, for the huge cost that ordinary citizens had to pay for that period of tyranny. This must not be forgotten or diminished. But that should not convert us from being researchers searching for scientific explanations into ideological warriors seeking to exclude and deny.

Which brings me to my second methodological point. In the case of momentous events such as the Emergency, social scientists, it seems to me, pursue the facts which corroborate their theory (in this case a theory of tyranny) up to a point; but when 'inconvenient facts' which their theory cannot accommodate begin to appear, they shift their narration from scientific explanation to ideological posturing, which allows them to ignore these 'inconvenient facts'. The theory thus remains unchallenged. By ignoring Mrs Gandhi's decision matrix, this is what has happened in the studies of the Emergency. Such a surreptitious shift from scientific explanation to ideology has to be called out. It will benefit the study of Indian democracy.

The first substantive issue is the complicity of the officials of the state, particularly those who occupy the checks-and-balances institutions. Tyranny cannot acquire a material existence without such complicity and collusion. When the 'rule of law' becomes 'rule by law' (a transformation that must be studied both theoretically, in terms of its implications, and empirically, in terms of its effects), democracy gets considerably diminished, and much effort has to be expended later to get it back on track. In the last few years, we see this across democracies such as Turkey, Hungary, Poland, the United States, Bangladesh, India and most paradoxically Israel. As political scientists studying the Emergency, we need to investigate the causes and reasons for such complicity. Tyranny is not only driven by the tyrant at the top but also by the officials who adopt a behaviour of 'anticipatory obedience'. Sophocles' play *Antigone* illustrates this attitude of complicity when the Theban elders submit to Creon's tyrannical orders to permit the burial of only one of Antigone's brothers and leave the other's body in the battlefield for the animals and vultures to devour. The Theban elders fell in line with this tyrannical order. Creon presented himself as the state. Hence the orders of the state could not be disobeyed. Only Antigone resisted, by invoking the higher law of Zeus.

The second substantive issue I wish to draw from this study of the Emergency is the place of narcissistic leaders in politics. This is not a stealthy attempt to bring back the role of the great leader in history but is instead an attempt to reoccupy the place, vacated under pressure from structuralists and institutionalists, of the powerful leader in politics whose decisions have implications for the future of a democracy. We see such powerful leaders everywhere, who are not constrained by political institutions (in fact they become quite feeble in the face of the leader's aggression) or by core principles such as 'separation of powers' and 'checks and balances'. Sitting in 2025, one sees such executive overreach everywhere. We need therefore to ask: what are the necessary and sufficient conditions that will make the rule of law, not rule by law, effective? India's Emergency is one place to go to for an answer.

References

Baru, Sanjaya. 2024. The Return of the Foreign Hand. *The Wire*, 14 August. https://thewire.in/government/return-of-the-foreign-hand (accessed 13 July 2025)

Dayal, John and Ajoy Bose. 2018. *For Reasons of State: Delhi Under Emergency*. New Delhi: Penguin, 2018.

deSouza, Peter Ronald, Mohd Sanjeer Alam, Hilal Ahmed. 2022. *Companion to Indian Democracy: Resilience, Fragility, Ambivalence*. New Delhi: Routledge.

Dhar, P. N. 2001. *Indira Gandhi, the 'Emergency' and Indian Democracy*. New Delhi: Oxford UP.

Dimbleby, Jonathan. 1978. Interview with Mrs Gandhi. *TV Eye*. https://www.youtube.com/watch?app=desktop&v=q8aETK5pQR4 (accessed 20 June 2025)

Frank, Katherine. 2002. *Indira: The Life of Indira Nehru Gandhi*. Boston: Houghton Mifflin Harcourt.

Frankel, Francine. 1978. *India's Political Economy 1947–1977: The Gradual Revolution*. Princeton: Princeton UP.

Ganguly, S. 2023. Modi's Undeclared Emergency. *Journal of Democracy* 34.3 (July): 144–55.

Guha, Ranajit. 2002. Indian Democracy: Long Dead, Now Buried. In *The Small Voice of History*. Ranikhet: Permanent Black. 578–80.

Jaffrelot, Christophe and Pratinav Anil. 2021a. Interpreting the Emergency. *Heidelberg Papers in South Asian and Comparative Politics* 79 (New Series) (January).

———. 2021b. *India's First Dictatorship: The Emergency, 1976–1977*. New Delhi: HarperCollins Publishers.

Jayakar, Pupul. 1995. *Indira Gandhi: An Intimate Biography*. New Delhi: Penguin.

Kapoor, Coomi. 2015. *The Emergency: A Personal History*. New Delhi. Penguin Books.

Kaviraj, S. 1986. Indira Gandhi and Indian Politics. *Economic and Political Weekly* 21.38/39: 1697–708.

Kothari, Rajni. 2012. *Politics in India*. Hyderabad: Orient BlackSwan.

Lockwood, D. 2015. The Indian Emergency in Economic Context. *Proceedings of the Indian History Congress* 76: 865–74.

Lijphart, A. 1978. Emergency Powers and Emergency Regimes: A Commentary. *Asian Survey* 18.4: 401–07.

Malhotra, Inder. 1991. *Indira Gandhi: A Personal and Political Biography*. Boston: Northeastern UP.

Mehta, Ved. 1977. The New India of Indira Gandhi. *The New Yorker*, 14 Feb: 56–101.

———. 1980. Indian Politics: A Family Affair. *The New Yorker*, 17 March: 98–157.

Nehru, J. 2004a. *Letters from a Father to His Daughter*. New Delhi: Viking.

———. 2004b. *Glimpses of World History*. New Delhi: Penguin.

Prakash, G. 2019. *Emergency Chronicles: Indira Gandhi and Democracy's Turning Point*. Princeton: Princeton UP.

Raghavan, Srinath. 2016. Decoding the Emergency. *Seminar* 677.

Sahgal, Nayantara, 2012. *Indira Gandhi: Tryst with Power*. New Delhi, Penguin Books.

Sharada Prasad, R. V. 2020. Was Emergency Inevitable?. *Open*, 19 June. https://openthemagazine.com/essay/was-emergency-inevitable/ (accessed 13 July 2025)

———. 2021. 14 Days to the Darkest Phase of Indian Democracy. *Open,* 15 June. https://openthemagazine.com/columns/14-days-darkest-phase-indian-democracy/ (accessed 13 July 2025)

Shankar, Shylashri. 2018. The State of Emergency in India: Böckenförde's Model in a Sub-National Context. *German Law Journal* 19.2: 197–218.

Sheth, D. L. 2018. *At Home with Democracy: A Theory of Indian Politics,* with an Introduction by Peter Ronald deSouza. New Delhi: Palgrave Macmillan.

Singh, Khushwant. 2017. *Extraordinary Indians: A Book of Profiles,* ed. Mala Dayal. New Delhi: Aleph Book Company.

Sri Kantha, Sachi. 2014. Indira Gandhi: Interviewed by Oriana Fallaci – Parts 1 and 2, *Ilnkai Tamil Sangam,* 24 Dec 24. https://sangam.org/indira-gandhi-interviewed-oriana-fallaci-part-2/ (accessed 13 July 2025)

Steinberg, B. S. 2005. Indira Gandhi: The Relationship between Personality Profile and Leadership Style. *Political Psychology* 26.5: 755–89.

The Wilson Quarterly. 2004. The Allende Affair. https://www.wilsonquarterly.com/quarterly/undefined/allende-affair (accessed 13 July 2025)

Tully, Mark. 2018. Foreword. In *For Reasons of State: Delhi Under Emergency* by John Dayal and Ajoy Bose. New Delhi: Penguin.

Editors and Contributors

Anand Kumar is the Dayanand Bandodkar Chair Professor at Goa University. He taught sociology at Jawaharlal Nehru University (1990–2014) and Banaras Hindu University (1979–89). He earned his degrees from BHU (MA), JNU (MPhil), and the University of Chicago (PhD). He is a recipient of the Lifetime Achievement Award from the Indian Sociological Society and has held fellowships at the Indian Institute of Advanced Study (IIAS), Shimla, and the Nehru Memorial Museum and Library (NMML), New Delhi. The author and editor of twenty books in Hindi and English, he has also served as a visiting professor at eight Indian and six international universities.

Anupama Roy is a professor at the Centre for Political Studies at Jawaharlal Nehru University, New Delhi. Her research and publications are in the fields of citizenship studies, political anthropology of public institutions, constitutionalism, law and democracy, and gender studies. She is the author of the books *Citizenship Regimes, Law and Belonging: The CAA and NRC in India* (Oxford University Press, 2022), *Mapping Citizenship in India* (Oxford University Press, 2010), and *Gendered Citizenship: Historical and Conceptual Explorations* (Orient BlackSwan, 2005). She has co-authored the book *Election Commission of India: Institutionalising Democratic Uncertainties* (Oxford University Press, 2019), and co-edited *Dimensions of Constitutional Democracy* (Springer, 2020) and *Poverty, Gender and Migration in South Asia* (Sage, 2008). Her research articles have appeared in various national and international journals.

Deepak Sanan served in the Himachal Pradesh cadre of the Indian Administrative Service for thirty-five years. He has written on diverse issues of public policy including public finance, fiscal federalism, sanitation, the power sector, delivery of basic services and development in Himachal Pradesh, both while in service and later. His recent focus has been on land governance and state capacity, and a concern about the second coming of fascism in contemporary times. His deeply held views on constitutional values has led to his being an active member of the Constitutional Conduct Group of former civil servants since his retirement in 2017.

Errol D'Souza is Vice Chancellor of GITAM (Deemed-to-be) University, and former Director of IIM Ahmedabad. He has held appointments such as the IFCI Chair Professor at the University of Mumbai, India Chair Professor at Sciences Po, Paris, Senior Fellow of the National University of Singapore, Visiting Scholar at Columbia University, New York, and Visiting Professor at the Turin School of Development of the ILO. He was Director of the National Housing Bank, and is currently Member of the CMC Vellore Governing Council and on the Board of Directors at Shram Sarathi, Udaipur. He has been associated in various capacities with the UGC, ICSSR, and the RBI, including as Member, Technical Advisory Committee on Monetary Policy.

Gopal Guru is former Professor at the Centre for Political Studies, Jawaharlal Nehru University, New Delhi, and former Editor of the *Economic and Political Weekly* (EPW). He has published the following edited volumes: *Humiliation: Claims and Context* (Oxford University Press, 2009), *The Cracked Mirror: An Indian Debate on Experience and Theory* (with Sundar Sarukkai; Oxford University Press, 2012), *Experience, Caste, and the Everyday Social* (with Sundar Sarukkai; Oxford University Press, 2019), and *Spheres of Injustice* (with Albeena Shakil; Routledge, 2023).

Gyan Prakash is the Dayton-Stockton Professor of History at Princeton University where he directed the Shelby Cullom Davis Center for Historical Studies from 2003 to 2008. He was a member of the influential Subaltern Studies Collective until its dissolution in 2006, and has been a recipient of Guggenheim and the National Endowment of Humanities fellowships. He is the author of several books, including the widely acclaimed *Mumbai Fables* (2010), which was adapted for the film *Bombay Velvet* (2015), for which he wrote the story and co-wrote the screenplay. His latest book is *Emergency Chronicles: Indira Gandhi and Democracy's Turning Point* (2019). He is currently working on a book tentatively titled, *After Empire: Culture in Postcolonial India.*

Harsh Sethi worked as Consulting Editor of the monthly *Seminar* for two decades. Earlier he was with Sage Publications as Acquisitions Editor. He also held positions of Fellow at the Centre for the Study of Developing Societies, and Deputy Director at the Indian Council of Social Science Research. He has co-edited several books including *Foul Play: Chronicles of Corruption*, and contributed chapters and written both research and popular articles. His major areas of interest are the political economy of development, social movements and human rights and civil society organisations.

Kalpana Kannabiran is a sociologist and legal scholar whose work has focused on the intersections of sociology, law, literature, gender studies and social movements. Among her books are *Tools of Justice: Non-Discrimination and the Indian Constitution* (2012), and *Law, Justice and Human Rights in India: Short Reflections* (2021). She has edited two volumes of *Routledge Readings on Law* (2022), edited and translated *The Speaking Constitution: A Sisyphean Life in Law* by K. G. Kannabiran (2022) and edited *Law, Justice, Society: The Selected Works of Upendra Baxi, Vol 3: Law and Society* (2025). She is currently Distinguished Professor, Council for Social Development, New Delhi.

Mahmood Farooqui is an acclaimed writer and performer, distinguished for his achievements in reviving *Dastangoi*, the lost Urdu storytelling artform. He has written, directed and performed more than twenty-five *Dastans* across more than a thousand shows. In addition, he has been preparing the next generation of *Dastangos* and has trained dozens of them. He has also authored two books on the subject in Hindi and Urdu. He has written five books, translated one, and is a frequent essayist. He writes on history, politics, literature, culture and films. His most recent publication is *A Requiem for Pakistan: The World of Intizar Husain* (Yoda Press). Farooqui received the Ramnath Goenka

Award for non-fiction for his book on the Indian Uprising of 1857 titled *Besieged: Voices from Delhi*. He has been honoured with the Ustad Bismillah Khan Award by the Sangeet Natak Akademi, the Mirza Ghalib award for Drama by Ghalib Institute, and has been a Visiting Fellow at the universities of Michigan and Berkeley, California. He studied at Doon School, St Stephen's College, New Delhi, and the universities of Oxford and Cambridge as a Rhodes Scholar. He is married to filmmaker Anusha Rizvi and lives in New Delhi.

Pamela Philipose, presently the Ombudsperson of the New Delhi-based news portal, *The Wire.in,* has also served as editor-in-chief of Women's Feature Service, an organisation mandated to highlight gender concerns in the mainstream media. Earlier, she was a senior associate editor, *The Indian Express*, with independent charge of the opinion pages. A recipient of prestigious awards for her journalism, her book, *Media's Shifting Terrain: Five Years that Transformed the Way India Communicates*, was published by Orient BlackSwan in 2019. Her latest book is *Framing the Media: Government Policies, Law, and Freedom of the Press in India* (Orient BlackSwan, 2025).

Peter Ronald deSouza was the Director, Indian Institute of Advanced Study (IIAS), Shimla, for two terms (2007–13). Prior to that he was Senior Fellow and Co-Director of the Lokniti Programme of Comparative Democracy, at the Centre for the Study of Developing Societies (CSDS), New Delhi (2003–07 and 2013–20), and Professor and Head, Department of Political Science at Goa University (1996–2003). He is currently Senior Research Associate, African Centre for Epistemology and Philosophy of Science (ACEPS), University of Johannesburg, and Trustee of the Institute of Social Studies Trust. He has served as a consultant to UNESCO, International IDEA, UNDP, The World Bank, Inter Parliamentary Union (IPU), Ford Foundation and Social Science Research Council (SSRC). His recent publications are *Companion to Indian Democracy: Resilience Fragility, Ambivalence* (with Mohd. Sanjeer Alam and Hilal Ahmed; Routledge, 2022) and *Keywords for India: A Conceptual Lexicon for the 21st Century* (with Rukmini Bhaya Nair; Bloomsbury, 2020). He writes for *The India Forum*, *The Indian Express* and *Frontline*.

Ramaswamy Sudarshan has been the founding Dean and Professor at the Jindal School of Government and Public Policy, O. P. Jindal Global University, Sonipat, in the National Capital Region of Delhi, since 2012. He obtained an MA in economics from the School of Economics in Delhi in 1974. He was elected to a Rhodes scholarship and joined Balliol College, Oxford, where he obtained an MPhil in politics. He secured a research fellowship at St. John's College, Cambridge, where he studied the judicial review of economic legislation, specialising in the interface between law and economics. From January 1984 to June 1991, he served in the Ford Foundation's South Asia Office in New Delhi as Assistant Representative and Program Officer for Human Rights and Social Justice. In 1991, he joined the United Nations Development Programme (UNDP) in India as Senior Economist and Assistant Representative for Governance and Public Policy. In 2000, he joined the UNDP in Jakarta as Senior Governance Advisor. In 2002, he was appointed Policy Advisor for Justice and Governance at the UNDP Oslo Governance Centre. In 2005, he relocated to the UNDP Asia-Pacific Centre in Bangkok, where he served as the Regional Policy Advisor for Governance, Human Rights, Rule of Law, Justice, and Legal Reforms. His publications comprise edited books, articles and UN policy reports, reflecting his interdisciplinary research, teaching and policy experience in human development, law, governance, institutions and public policy.

Ravi Arvind Palat, Emeritus Professor of Sociology at the State University of New York at Binghamton, and Faculty Affiliate at the College of Wooster, Wooster, OH, is an historical sociologist and political economist. His books include *Capitalist Restructuring and the Pacific Rim* and *The Making of an Indian Ocean World-Economy, 1250–1650: Princes, Paddy Fields, and Bazaars.* He is currently working on two books: one on the construction of national cuisines and the other on the impact of the Americas on early modern Asia. He had previously taught Asian Studies at the

University of Hawai'i at Mānoa and sociology at the University of Auckland.

Rukmini Bhaya Nair is Honorary Professor of Linguistics and Literature at the India Institute of Technology Delhi (IITD) and Global Professorial Fellow at Queen Mary University of London (QMUL). She received her PhD from the University of Cambridge and was awarded an honorary doctorate by the University of Antwerp for her contributions to narrative theory. Author of ten books and around 200 articles, her academic works include *Lying on the Postcolonial Couch; Narrative Gravity: Conversation, Cognition, Culture* and *Poetry in a Time of Terror* (Oxford University Press, 2002, 2003, 2009). Most recently, she coedited the reference volume *Keywords for India: A Conceptual Lexicon for the 21st Century,* with Peter R deSouza (Bloomsbury Academic, UK, 2020). An award-winning poet, Nair has published three volumes of poetry with Penguin. The *Oxford Companion to Modern Poetry* writes that her work is 'widely admired . . . for its postmodern approach to lyrical meaning and feminine identity'. Her writings, creative and critical, have been included on the syllabi of Chicago, Delhi, Harvard, Kent, Toronto and other universities.

Tridip Suhrud is a writer and translator working on the intellectual tradition of Gandhi and the intellectual and literary history of modern Gujarat. He has published forty-one books in three languages. He is currently working on a possible nine-volume archival history of the testimonies of the peasants of Champaran titled *Thumb Printed* (three volumes published). He is Professor and Provost, CEPT University, Director of Lalbhai Dalpatbhai Institute of Indology, and President of the Governing Council of MICA.

Ujjwal Kumar Singh is a professor at the Department of Political Science, University of Delhi. His research and publications are in the areas of law and politics, constitutionalism and democracy, social movements and rights, political institutions and state theory. He is the co-author of the book *The Election Commission of India: Institutionalising Democratic Uncertainties* (Oxford University

Press, 2019), and the author of *Political Prisoners in India* (Oxford University Press, 1998) and *The State, Democracy and Anti-Terror Laws in India* (Sage, 2007). His articles have appeared in several national and international journals. He has been a visiting fellow in universities in India and abroad.

Varun Sahni is Professor of International Relations at Ashoka University, Sonipat. Earlier, he spent three decades (1995–2025) at Jawaharlal Nehru University, New Delhi, teaching international politics and writing on nuclear deterrence, regional security, emerging balances in the Indo-Pacific, evolving security concepts, emerging powers, Latin American issues, foreign policy, maritime geopolitics and river waters. He wrote his doctoral thesis at Oxford University (1991) on the political role of the Argentine navy. For his 'outstanding contribution to research and teaching', he was conferred the V. K. R. V. Rao Prize in Social Sciences for 2006. He has also served as the 10th Vice Chancellor of the University of Jammu (2008–12) and the 8th Vice Chancellor of Goa University (2016–21).